THE TRAUMA OF LOVE

Why Everything You Know About Women
Is Wrong, and Satan's Plan for Humankind

by

Vlad Powers

Email: traumaoflove@proton.me

Phone: 336-473-6923

ISBN: 979-8-218-86905-2

CONTENTS

INTRO: STANDING ON THE SHOULDERS OF GIANTS   vii

The Intelligence Reality   xiv

Are We Living in "The Matrix?"   xvi

Before We Begin   xxiii

PART I: THE BROKEN GAME   1

Poolside of the Matrix   1

Blue, Red and Black - The Three Pill(ar)s of Self-Delusion   7

Popping Blue Pills That Won't Get You Hard   11

A Cogent History of the Pickup and Seduction Scene   12

The True Cost of Clearing Trauma and Releasing Authenticity   14

But Isn't Confidence the Most Attractive Thing to A Woman?   22

The Red Pill as A Response To "Approach Anxiety"   25

What Does It Mean to Be A "Real Man" Or A "Real Woman?"   27

On The Ultimate Non-Existence of Female Hypergamy   29

You Are Not a Sigma Male, You Are Just a Fucking Loser   33

The Sheer Toxicity of Swallowing the Black Pill   34

Female Trinity #1 – The 3 Types of Men in A Woman's Life   38

PART II: TRAUMA AND THE ROOTS OF DYSFUNCTION   47

The Trauma Foundation   47

The Impact of Birth Trauma   51

Are Women Inherently Loving Because They Birth Children?   55

The Trauma of Circumcision and Satanic Corruption of Religion 61

On Ignorant African-Americans Who Convert to Islam...   69

My Own Experience with Genital Mutilation   73

Male vs. Female Thru the Lens of Prison Rape Culture   75

Brazil: A Nation That Accomplishes Next-To-Nothing   83

Russia: A "Culture" Built on Rape and Incest — 86

Her Neurotic Vagina: A Simple Definition of Neurosis — 92

Men Are Not Obsessed with Sex – It Is a Female Projection — 95

Men Have Forgotten Their True Nature for Two Reasons — 96

The Essence of All PUA Strategies: Mirror A Woman's Neurosis — 105

Breaking Thru Her Neurosis as Opposed to Mirroring It — 108

Why The "Me Too" Movement Murdered the PUA Scene — 111

An Honest Discussion of "Consent" and Sexual Power Dynamics — 119

A More Complex Definition of Neurosis — 123

Neurosis Is Your Mind's Way of Protecting Itself — 124

Why Women Waste Their Time With "Bad Boys" — 127

Welcome To The "Fantasy Boyfriend League" — 130

Female Commodification of Sexuality — 133

Inflation Turns Women into Whores — 134

The True Source of Inflation — 139

Give It Up for Free on Tinder, Or Sell It on Instagram? — 144

While You Beg for Trash on Tinder, The Elites Enjoy Sex Slaves... — 151

The Pornography Disaster — 158

The History of Pornography — 160

Porn Keeps Getting More Extreme and Nobody Seems To Notice — 166

A Child Watching Porn *vs.* A Child Being Molested — 178

Wilhelm Reich's Views on Pornography — 181

The True Purpose of The Porn Industry — 184

OnlyFans Is *Not* Empowerment! — 189

Every Woman You Desire Is Already Engaging in Sex Work — 190

PART III: SOME SEXUAL AND SPIRITUAL TRUTHS — **195**

Are Women Really *That* Different from Men? — 195

The Manufactured AIDS Crisis of the 1980s — 198

Homosexuality, Dr. Edmund Bergler and the Mayhem of Lucifer — 204

Rh-Blood, Alien Abductions and the Hybridization of Abductees — 212

The Root of Low Testosterone & Transgender Politics   218

Practical Gender Polarities in Males and Females   223

True Sexual Dynamics   229

Healthy Ejaculatory Frequency vs. "No-Fap" & "Gooning"   242

Ride Her Orgasmic Waves Without Cumming Yourself…   245

"Well, What's in It for Me as A Man?"   246

Introduce Your Lovers to This Slowly   250

Statutory Rape, Grooming & Other Utterly Arbitrary Nonsense   251

The Blackest Pill There Is?   256

The Influence of Satanic Entities on Constant Human Warfare   270

All Political Parties Lead Towards Your Satanic Enslavement   274

PART IV: THE WAY FORWARD   **285**

The Cure for Porn Addiction Is Real Sex with Beautiful Women   285

How To Drown in Pussy   287

Female Trinity #2 – The 3 Types of Men in A Sex Worker's Life   290

The True Cost of a Girlfriend   292

Body Game and Chemical Enhancement – Your Secret Weapons   294

Developing A Physique That Will Get You Pussy – With Drugs!   296

Why It Is Impossible to Build the Body You Want Without Drugs   297

Why You Are a Complete Loser If You Don't Use Drugs   300

Let's Talk Trenbolone!   303

A Series of Unfortunate Events Is Always Proceeded By…   307

But Isn't Diet the Most Important Aspect of Success?   308

How To Train to Develop Your Physique   310

Combat Sports   314

Supplements   320

On The Correlation Between Smoking and Lung Cancer…   330

All About Penis Size   333

How To Enlarge Your Penis   337

Drugs For Sexual Performance   338

More On Premature Ejaculation   341

Depression Ultimately Doesn't Exist   342

All About Hair Loss   343

Chasing The Dragon of Inner Freedom   344

The Psoas Muscle   345

One Arm Hangs & Unlocking Your Thorax   346

Yoga: A Complete Waste of Your Time   347

There Are No Primal Therapists Left   348

Only One True School of Reichian Therapy Is Still Around   349

Banging Hippie Chicks at Osho's Resort in Pune   351

What About Hypnosis?   352

Inner Game That Actually Works   354

Approach Anxiety and The Fear of Rejection   358

Women Have Zero Standards, So They Can't *Really* "Reject" You   359

Women Are Sexual Degenerates So Don't Fear Being a Creep   360

Women Can Be Very Attracted to You and Still Not Interested   360

Start Talking Daily with Every Woman You Run Across   361

Eye Contact Is Everything   362

LooksMaxxing?   363

Women: Get ANY Man You Want and Write Your Own Ticket   364

One Societal Solution to Ease the Effects of Childhood Trauma   369

My Personal History   **375**

Beyond The Game   **393**

Back Poolside   **399**

THE FOUR ESSENTIAL BOOKS   **401**

INTRO: STANDING ON THE SHOULDERS OF GIANTS

They say you can see farthest when you stand upon the shoulders of giants, and that no man walks alone. Arnold Schwarzenegger said it best in a recent Netflix documentary where he said that in no way is he "self made." Quite a few people have "self made" tattooed upon their bodies, which is not only ridiculous, but Satanic as well. Satan fancies himself "self made" for reasons I will decline to reveal, because I don't believe insanity should be indulged. Just because a being is very powerful, or very smart, doesn't mean that being is necessarily very *sane*. After all, what sane being rebels against The Divine Father? Either way, the notion of *any being* imagining themselves "self made" is ultimately preposterous because everything in creation is made by The Divine Father, and there is nothing else to say on the matter.

So when you read this book and consequently stand upon my shoulders, you are in turn standing upon the shoulders of those I have in turn stood upon. And you need to be this high up in order to see the true landscape of male/female relations within the context of larger exopolitical (off planet) and spiritual issues because without true knowledge of them, all attempts to navigate your own intimate relationships will fail for the same reason you can't drive a car while wearing a blindfold *at any point* along your journey.

There are tons of books, YouTube videos, and podcasts promising to help you "succeed" with women by teaching you how to pick them up, how to get them to swipe right on you, how to get them in front of webcams and pocket as much of their money as you can... by the time you are finished with this book, you will understand that both pimps and simps are two sides of that same coin that isn't even worth the effort to bend down and pick up. The advice from all of these books, YouTube videos, and podcasts fails you because the self-styled "gurus" behind them are ultimately failures themselves. Their self delusion is really *no different* that that of a school of land whales loafing about a podcast studio in Santa Barbara taking turns declaring themselves "10s." Whatever... I mean, what is the point in learning "pick-up" if you will end up bedding girls that are just average *at best*? Furthermore, why would you get up every day at 5am to become a successful entrepreneur or build the body of your dreams only to end up cohabiting with single moms, or women suffering from "cluster B" personality disorders?

I know a lot of women and their army of white knight soy boys like to chant the common chorus: "Nobody owes you sex!" Well, nobody owes you food, clean water, or civil rights either, yet nobody would ever dare chant a slogan reminding you of those facts... People will rail against the injustice of a black man being denied a job *because* he is black, yet nobody will rail against the injustice of an amazing guy being denied sexual gratification *because* he is an amazing guy! Yet that is the exact modus operandi of our times. If quality men continue to look around and see that what they consider to be the grand prize of the human experience (loving sex with the hottest women), is only awarded to the lowest quality of men around, what do you think the ultimate consequences will be? Already we are witnessing the collapse of society due *in part* to the ever-growing realization among *high value* men that *loving sex* with the hottest women is utterly unattainable for them. The best they can hope for - no matter their worth or accomplishments, is gaming and manipulating sex out of cowardly whores by mimicking their neurosis and lowering their own value in the process, or just cutting to the chase and renting high-end escorts by the hour.

I wrote this book because I wanted to tell *a part* of my story – a particular story arc which ran for over 30 years. I am referring to digging up the root of the plague of sexual and romantic dissatisfaction in modern society. Another reason I wrote this book is to *hopefully* enable someone to transform their life in three years, as opposed to 30. Not only because after 30 years it is too late to enjoy the fruits of your labors, but because even undergoing a massive and seemingly impossible personal transformation is still no guarantee of success. You may still need another 27 years to "dial it in!" *That's* how bad the situation has become. Even then, I am not sure the current state of affairs are workable no matter what you do.

Either way, youth is meant to be enjoyed and not tragically wasted on suffering while wandering the proverbial desert, desperately searching for solutions to problems that forever evade you. The tragic irony is that success in life has very little to do with your own efforts, *even though you usually have to exert a colossal amount of effort in order to be a success.* After all, how many men are out there putting in the work, and *still* not getting results? Countless men find themselves in this scenario, but since your own efforts are the only thing you can control, that is where your focus rightfully goes. There is simply no other place to put it!

In desperation to "win" at the "game of life," some will compromise themselves sexually, join the Freemasons, etc., or even make deals with entities that they will probably come to regret. Many of those in the public eye that you have put on a pedestal have gone this route. *Far* more than you would be inclined to believe.

For those of you who enjoy keeping your buttholes as well as your souls intact, and just continue to grind on, keep in mind that one of the keys to success is discovering the correct methods and systems that will lead to said success, and then to just keep grinding at those methods and systems consistently. Sounds good, yet while having the correct methodologies is indeed *one* of the keys to success, very often there is nothing wrong with your methods and systems.

Success simply evades you.

It's heartbreaking.

Nonetheless, "success" is only possible if one has the right information at the right time. Hence, this book. It's too late for me, and for some time I was sad and bitter about it. I tell you, I have been robbed of soooo many experiences that I both desperately desired and felt I rightfully deserved, that I often felt like the grief of my losses would crush me. There is a scene in the 1963 film "Jason and the Argonauts" where Phineus is tormented by the Harpies, that had stuck with me since childhood. I sometimes thought I should have been named "Phineus" instead of "P."

But these days most of my humanity has been extinguished as part of my own dark evolution, and so there is in actuality "nobody" there to be sad and bitter about it anymore. It isn't that the proverbial "ugly duckling" *realizes* one day that he is a swan, it's that he *transforms* one day into a swan. So "duck business" loses all meaning. Mind you, I had *foreknowledge* when I was still in my early 20s of how things would be as I got older, I just couldn't accept the absolute horror of what I foresaw from a *human* frame of reference. So I fought and fought, as is only natural, but to no avail. Again, the brutal truth is that contrary to any "red pill" bullshit you may step into, "leveling up" your life doesn't mean your intimate relationship life will necessarily follow suite, or that you life will be a smashing success, no matter how young you start swinging the sledgehammer.

There is also this fantasy being perpetuated today by certain "gurus" that being your "authentic self" is some magic bullet that will solve all of your problems with women. It won't. Truthfully, "authenticity" will only make your life *worse* in that regard. Not that any of these "gurus" would actually know this, since the ones pushing this crap wouldn't know what authenticity was if it fucked them up the ass.

Again, I really don't know if anyone can win at this game anymore, as we are officially in the Kali Yuga and these are the end times. For those who do not know: in the Hindu cycle of time, the Kali Yuga, also known as the "age of darkness," is the fourth and final yuga in the cycle. It's characterized by moral decline, a decrease in righteousness, and an increase in negative qualities like greed, violence, and suffering. So perhaps this generation of Dubai port-a-potties and gooners are just par for the course. However, I can still tell my story before I am forced to grab my towel and hitchhike my way off this exploding rock.

I am also not writing this book to make money, as books no longer make money. The best they can do is get you booked on a couple of podcasts, because writing a book gives you a certain amount of "authority" on a particular topic. Another big driver of this book's creation is simply because I need to vent what I have been carrying inside of me... that which I have spent my entire life grappling with... this *problem*... a problem whose dynamics have taken me over 30 years to see with clarity. To make another "Hitchhiker's Guide to the Galaxy" reference, I feel like I am that computer named "Deep Thought" and I have finally grasped the answer to the ultimate question a man can ask in the sexual marketplace. Which is "what makes women flock to a specific man?" While I don't have a simple answer, like "42," I have an answer long enough to warrant a book!

Ultimately though, I wrote this book because the *right people* need to hear my voice: this is a *dark book*, written primarily with *dark individuals* in mind. Who else would I write for? I am *not* of the light. If you have the ability to see auras you will notice that mine is black as pitch. But perhaps I can be a voice in the dark for those who are dark like me and still unawares of what they actually are – as I once was? After all, many of the events in this book brought me closer to discovering my true nature and ultimately embracing it.

Most people suffer a grand misconception about evil: they believe that all evil is "bad" and pass judgment upon it. Yet Isaiah 45:7 (KJV) states:

"I form the light, and create darkness: I make peace, and create evil: I the Lord do all these things."

What this means is that whether evil is "bad" or not, really comes down to if a being's will is in alignment with the will of The Divine Father, as opposed to being in rebellion against it. Satan is an example of a being who is in rebellion against The Divine Father, yet we can catch a glimpse of a *different sort* of evil in **Exodus 12:23** (KJV): where every firstborn in Egypt died in one night, from Pharaoh's son to the firstborn of prisoners, plus the firstborn of livestock – while the Israelite homes marked with lamb's blood were "passed over," and their firstborn were spared:

"For the Lord will pass through to smite the Egyptians; and when he seeth the blood upon the lintel, and on the two side posts, the Lord will pass over the door, and will not suffer the destroyer to enter into your houses to smite you."

In the above example, the "destroyer's" will was in alignment with the will of The Divine Father. Given this, how can the "destroyer" be considered "bad?"

For those of you who grew up playing "Dungeons and Dragons," I am basically describing the difference between *lawful evil* and *chaotic evil*.

No matter your own nature, I encourage you to pray directly to The Divine Father. There is no need for religion at all. Religion just gets in the way of a direct relationship with Him (your creator), and *all* religions today have been corrupted to such a degree by Satan, that you are best off ignoring them all entirely so as not to risk being led astray. So, if you are working as hard as you can in life, grinding away, giving it all you've got and still falling short, *just pray*. Seriously, before you run off and hire another "coach" or purchase another "mentorship program," how about speaking with the ultimate life coach there is, your creator, The Divine Father? I am not talking about Jesus and I am not a Christian. Jesus is not The Father. That so many Christians place Jesus on the same level as The Divine Father or even place Jesus above The Divine Father is utter blasphemy.

If what you read in this book resonates with you, I would also suggest you refer to the four essential books in the appendix that had the biggest foundational impact upon the material I am presenting in this book. While these books and their authors are largely unknown, the obscurity they enjoy is typical on a planet where the majority of its inhabitants are in possession of an abysmally low IQ, dominated by their personal traumas, and consequently addicted to entertainment in the form of gossip and drama above all else.

Additionally, this book may at many times come across as misogynistic, homophobic, racist, sexist, hateful, etc. I am neither of these things, and I specifically abhor the endless abuse of women that mars human history. I am simply tapping into my memories of pain from before my humanity was extinguished by my true nature, and allowing said pain to color my expression, so as to resonate with your own unspoken pain, thereby making my communications more effective.

If you have lived long enough, you hopefully realize by now that you are going to be in pain in this lifetime no matter what, so your choice is if you will choose to suffer the pain of being a *real person*, or choose to suffer the pain of being an *artificial person*. To choose the latter, is ultimately the very definition of neurosis.

I chose the former.

Finally, while I have gone out of my way to back up as many of my "opinions" as possible with statistics and evidence, I am often too lazy to quote the studies I pulled them from. So if you want more information on either the statistics or the evidence I present, you will have to ask the LLM of your choice for assistance.

Now before we begin our journey… there are two elephants in the room that must be acknowledged.

The Intelligence Reality

Most people on this planet possess a shockingly low IQ. Racists like to claim that blacks tend to have a lower IQ than whites, and that Jews control the world because they have such a high IQ. Asians will proudly claim that they have the highest IQ of them all. Even if there were some truth to these claims, it would be of little importance because when we forget about *relative IQ* and look at the absolute numbers, it quickly becomes clear to someone with a very high IQ that nearly everyone on this planet *is a fucking moron.* I myself, have had my IQ tested twice. The first time my IQ score was 138, and the second time it was 142. So let's say I have an IQ of 140? This puts me in the category of "genius," however I have met individuals who have an IQ so high they make me look stupid. As a matter of fact, I once took an IQ test created for such intelligence outliers and I can say, that taking one of these tests - even with a genius IQ, will show you *real fast* just how *slow* you actually are. Now here is the thing... the white people who think they are *so smart* have an average IQ of only around 100, and the Jews some believe control the world have an average IQ of only around 110. These "winners" are 30-40 points below me and this makes them *dumb.*

Additionally, the *only* Asians who have an IQ at the level of the celebrated Jew reside in Japan, Hong Kong, and in some parts of Guangzhou. The rest of China and Asia are literally a mass of *straight-up retards* based on their absolute IQ scores which are *way below* 100. This shouldn't be shocking if you have traveled Asia and seen them shitting in the middle of a subway car or bathing in a literal sewer with a bar of soap, as if that bar of soap was making a difference. This is not the behavior of the *intelligentsia*. So nobody should be proud of their 100 IQ (average IQ in America is 98) or think it makes them superior over others. You are just *a bit less stupid* than some others!

It's sad, and the fact that most of the planet has an IQ under 100 is one of the reasons this planet is in the shape it's in. Don't believe me? Take a look at a map of IQ distribution by country and notice that the countries with the lowest IQ, are the most messed up. "Correlation is not causation!" Oh, just shut the fuck up and stop kidding yourself that IQ tests are not true measures of intelligence, that there are many forms of intelligence, or that someone with an IQ of 65 and a bone through their lip is just as smart as someone smashing atoms at C.E.R.N. already. Just accept the reality that some are born smart, *most* are born stupid, and you are probably closer to the latter category than you would like to think. Which is ironically why you won't accept the veracity of IQ tests to begin with!

Pro Tip: Given that human beings are so stupid and brainwashed that they will don a mask made for usage inside of a paint booth, believing it to keep a virus at bay, it should not be a shock that when you take a look at a city like New York City, or even an entire nation like England, only to discover that the people who live there actually *voted* to turn their respective environments into utter shit holes. If people vote in favor of their own oppression, and *the destruction of their own free will*, what can you do except stay as far away from them as you possible can?

Are We Living in "The Matrix?"

Probably everyone out there has seen at least *one* of the "Matrix" films starring Keanu Reeves. Elon Musk is also fond of claiming that we are living in a simulation, which he did most famously at a 2016 tech conference, where he argued that the odds we are living in "base reality" (i.e., not a simulation) are "billions to one against."

His statement is *very* important, because he promotes the plans of Satan (Saturn) which include giving everyone on this planet the "mark of the beast," by putting a chip inside of their heads. This is not a joke by any means, for in **Revelation 13:16** (KJV), it actually states:

"And he causeth all, both small and great, rich and poor, free and bond, to receive a mark *in* their right hand, *or in* their foreheads."

The text uses "in" for both locations - both the hand and the forehead. The full context from **Revelation 13:16-17** (KJV) reads:

"And he causeth all, both small and great, rich and poor, free and bond, to receive a mark *in* their right hand, *or in* their foreheads: And that no man might buy or sell, save he that had the mark, or the name of the beast, or the number of his name."

Most modern translations render this as "on" for both locations, but the KJV indeed uses "in" consistently for both the hand and forehead. The Greek word used is "epi" which can mean either "on" or "in" depending on context. And what is the context here? *This mark is used for buying and selling, which can only mean it is indeed a microchip*, and a microchip must be placed inside of the body. Some of you may say "What about my credit card or smartphone, that has a chip?" Well, do you wear either around your wrist or stapled to your forehead? I didn't think so...

I would speculate that StarLink is being deployed so extensively *not* so that children in sub-saharan Africa can enjoy access to interracial porn so as to boost their self-esteem, and condition them to rape European females upon successful migration to Europe thanks to globalist assholes like George Soros. Rather, it is to interface with all the future fools who sign up to implant a chip inside of their heads (or hands) and *give up their free will in the process.* All of you on the "right" need to realize *right now* that Elon Musk is *not* your friend. Unless you are dumb enough to consider Satan your friend?

Warning: You must never *under any circumstances* accept the implantation of a microchip into your brain, *or any part of your body* for that matter. If you do so, you are essentially exercising your free will, *to give up your free will*, which is a sin of the highest order. Your free will is The Divine Father's gift to you, and to reject it and throw it away is the gravest of insults. If the situation ever gets to the point where the social order prevents you from eating or drinking or otherwise existing unless you get such an implant, just take your own life. Better to lose your life than your soul. The covid-19 vaccine was a trial run for this future choice you will have to make. If you got the covid-19 vaccine, you are a weak idiot. Were you afraid to die because you never truly lived? Pathetic.

Elon Musk's words and actions beg the question: "Are we living in the Matrix - and if so, what is the nature of it?" In order to answer this, I will refer to two books:

- "The Ringmakers of Saturn," by Norman R. Bergrun
- "Saturn: The Secrets of the Extraterrestrial Engineers," by Pane Andov

Both books use the data from NASA's *Voyager* and *Cassini* probes to prove that the planet Saturn acts as a transmitter, that broadcasts the reality we find ourselves imprisoned in. Let's look at the work of Norman R. Bergrun first, as his book was published in 1986...

Norman Bergrun argued that Saturn's rings are artificial constructs created by massive extraterrestrial vehicles he termed "Electromagnetic Vehicles" (EMVs). He claimed these vehicles actively create and maintain the rings through their emissions and exhaust products.

- **Voyager Photograph Analysis**: Bergrun used 45 photographic plates from Voyager's 1980 flyby of Saturn as his primary evidence source. He employed microscopic enhancement techniques on these NASA photographs to reveal what he claimed were large cylindrical objects within Saturn's rings.

- **Physical Characteristics of the Vehicles**: According to Bergrun's analysis, these EMVs were enormous - ranging from 7,000 miles to 55,000 kilometers in length. He described them as having cylindrical, cigar-shaped profiles with fineness ratios (length to width) of approximately 13:1.

- **Ring Formation Mechanism**: Bergrun claimed the vehicles positioned themselves within the ring system and emitted streams of matter from their bodies and exhaust systems. He argued that these emissions created the ring material, explaining why the A-ring appeared incomplete in some photographs - vehicles were actively "making" it.

- **Electromagnetic Properties**: Bergrun described these vehicles as having electromagnetic capabilities, able to generate powerful electrical fields and plasma formations. He claimed they could create "toroids" and "pinched plasma" formations around themselves, demonstrating their electromagnetic nature.

- **Luminous Sources and Lightning**: His analysis identified luminous sources within Saturn's atmosphere and lightning bolts that he attributed to the electrical activity of these vehicles. He claimed some lightning bolts measured up to 750 kilometers in length.

- **Transmitter Functions**: Bergrun suggested these vehicles functioned as transmitters, capable of generating and directing electromagnetic energy across vast distances. He theorized they could affect planetary magnetic fields and atmospheric conditions.

- **Ring Gap Explanations**: He claimed the famous Cassini Division and Encke Gap were not empty spaces but rather safety zones between different vehicles operating at precise orbital positions to avoid collisions while creating separate ring segments.

- **Historical Connections**: Bergrun connected his findings to historical observations, including the 1908 Tunguska explosion in Siberia, which he claimed was caused by one of these vehicles, and lunar formations like Mare Orientale, which he argued showed evidence of EMV activity.

What's so convincing about the author, Norman Bergrun, is that he was not some amateur astronomer or UFO enthusiast making wild claims – he was a senior aerospace engineer and research scientist with decades of experience in exactly the kind of technology he claimed to have identified. Dr. Norman Bergrun was an alumnus of Ames Research Laboratory, NACA (National Advisory Committee for Aeronautics) - the predecessor to NASA's Ames Research Center - where he worked for twelve years as a research scientist, pioneering thermal ice prevention design methodology for aircraft and developing roll stability laws for airplanes, missiles, and rockets. After NACA, he joined Lockheed Missiles and Space Company where he served as manager of test planning and analysis for the Navy Polaris Underwater Launch Missile System. Why does all of this matter?

- **Aerospace Expertise**: His direct experience with spacecraft, missiles, and rocket systems gave him intimate knowledge of propulsion technologies and vehicle design principles.

- **Image Analysis Background**: His work in flight test analysis would have required extensive experience interpreting technical imagery and data from spacecraft and aircraft.

- **Government Security Clearance**: Some sources suggest he held high-level security clearances, potentially giving him access to classified information.

- **NASA Insider Knowledge**: Having worked at the predecessor organization to NASA, he understood the agency's methodologies, capabilities, and potential limitations.

- **Technical Photography Experience**: His background in aerospace research would have included extensive work with technical photography and image analysis.

The fact that someone with such impeccable mainstream scientific credentials would stake his professional reputation on these claims does lend them considerable weight. His background suggests he would have been well-equipped to identify artificial structures and propulsion systems if they were actually present in the Voyager imagery.

Next, let's take a look at the work of Pane Andov, as his book was published in 2019, 33 years after the publication of "The Ringmakers of Saturn." The number 33 is of great significance because in the lore of Freemasonry, the number 33 represents the highest degree in the Scottish Rite system, one of the major appendant bodies of Freemasonry.

Pro Tip: Some years ago I went to check my mail and found a hand-written envelope addressed to me from St. John's Lodge No. 1, America's oldest continuously operating Masonic lodge on W 23rd Street in Manhattan. This lodge falls under the jurisdiction of the Grand Lodge of New York F&AM, originally warranted in 1757 by the Modern Grand Lodge of England. I had been invited to a whiskey-tasting event! Now I knew very well that they were trying to recruit me, due to my Rh- blood and the fact that I am a reptilian-human hybrid, and I also knew I had zero interest in joining them. However, I rather enjoy whiskey and it was an opportunity to get inside of the lodge building and have a look around. This building is very impressive on the inside, and I am a fan of NYC history. So I showed up to the event and was rather outraged to find that only inferior Irish whiskey was available for tasting! The Irish may have invented whiskey but the Scots certainly perfected it. This was unacceptable! When the event was over they asked me what I thought about the whole thing, and I asked them why anyone would join an organization that didn't recognize the objective superiority of Scottish whiskey? They weren't very happy with me, but that's okay. Here's the takeaway, and ultimately the most important thing to get out of this book: You don't need religion, or secret societies, or some guru with a dot on his forehead... *all you need to do is pray directly to The Divine Father, acknowledge him as your creator, and tell him that you wish to align your will with his.* Everything else will work itself out. He created it all and will continue to do so. Who better to establish a relationship with?

Again, please understand that I'm not a Christian, and I am not talking about Jesus here. I am talking about The Divine Father. Christians blaspheme incessantly by putting Jesus above The Divine Father which is utterly preposterous, while portraying the The Divine Father as some sort of unjust tyrant, by claiming that he will send everyone to hell no matter how much good they do in this world, unless they "accept Jesus." So they are basically saying that the The Divine Father, who is perfect and therefore *perfectly just*, would be so unjust as to punish good humans *as if* they were bad? Ask yourself, *who else* runs around claiming The Divine Father is unjust and does a "lousy job" of things? Satan, of course! Furthermore, Christians promote a sick brand of salvation that allows for the worst of humanity to gain entry into heaven simply by uttering a few words. As if! Islam and Judaism are just as despicable in their own way, and hell is filled with those who commit vile sins in the names of their twisted religions. Please do yourselves a favor and stay away from religion. Just align yourself with The Divine Father directly. All of these religions have been corrupted by Satan, and consequently lead to endless wars and suffering, oppress women and encourage pedophilia. Just look at the fruit that the tree of religion bears, to grasp how rotten the tree actually is.

Back to Paul Andov... His credentials are nowhere near those of Norman Bergrun, yet the data from the Voyager probe is also nowhere near that of the Cassini probe! Cassini completed 206 orbits around Saturn and collected 514 GB of data. Paul states that while only a small percentage of this data has been made available, even that small percentage of data clearly demonstrates massive UFO traffic around Saturn.

Cassini also discovered that Saturn is emitting extremely powerful radio waves known as Saturn Kilometric Radiation, or "SKR" for short. Plus, it radiates 2.5x more energy into space than it receives from the Sun. In 2004 NASA revealed an artificial radio signal picked up by Cassini that contained some kind of speech patterns. The original .WAV file is downloadable from the NASA/Cassini website: http://cassini.physics.uiowa.edu/space-audio/cassini/SKR2/

NASA's comment on the file: *"A most intriguing file, we do not know what to make of it..."*

Here is another quote from author Paul Andov:

"Saturn is practically a super advanced machine that is engineered by advanced extraterrestrial intelligence and has a multipurpose, one being the capacity for transmitting gigantic and very complex energy transmission of holographic nature on very long distances."

So now we see that we are indeed living in a matrix, broadcast by the planet Saturn. This is also the meaning behind the "one ring" in the literary and cinematic trilogy, "The Lord of the Rings." What is inscribed on the inside of the "one ring" that Sauron once wore upon his finger?

"One Ring to rule them all, One Ring to find them, One Ring to bring them all and in the darkness bind them."

This is a reference to the rings of Saturn, as human beings are ruled by their transmissions, are under surveillance by them, and are bound in the darkness by them - unable to see into the 4th and 5th dimensions where their enemies sit back and feast upon their suffering.

Before We Begin

The style in which I have written this book is based upon how my own mind flows, which can appear disjointed and meandering at times, yet if you just flow with it, you will find that the concepts I present will stick and "gel" better. Given *I like to think* of my writing style as highly entertaining, I don't imagine you will have too much trouble just flowing with it.

Finally, given that I physically occupy a reptilian-human hybrid genetic form, I have the reptilian trait of repeating myself. Reptilian language structure and speaking patterns don't just involve a lot of hissing sounds, they also involve the intentional repeating of words and phrases to reinforce the importance of what is being said. Again, just flow with it and you will again find the concepts I present will stick and "gel" better.

PART I: THE BROKEN GAME

Poolside of the Matrix

Today I was lounging by the pool in the apartment complex I live at, and directly across from me on the other side of the pool sat some off-duty bartender with some girl he was fucking. The girl was pretty hot for this rinky-dink "city" I am currently residing in, yet he was an absolute man-child who was as into Star Wars as a seven year old. He never worked out a day in his life, had jelly rolls where his abs should have been, looked 10 years older than his actual age, and half his hair was already missing. He conversed with the female next to him like he was a female himself... and oh yes, of course he had a beard! Mind you, I rocked a beard back in college in the 90s, yet it was super short and shaped, and I was the only one sporting one in those days. Plus, I was really handsome in my youth so I wasn't relying on my facial hair as a form of "male makeup." But these days beards are worn by ugly and unmasculine men as a crutch for both their lack of looks as well as their lack of masculinity.

Some of them attempt to overcompensate for the masculinity they lack by growing it out like a hedgerow. *As if* the world can't see through it and discern your true face! The worst offenders are clowns who literally sculpt their Santa Claus beards so they appear to have a monster jawline and a concomitant testosterone level of 80,000 ng/dL. These fools probably stuff a rolled up sock in their pants before they go out as well, and wear lifts in their shoes. You might have noticed that the weaker men have gotten, the bigger their beards have grown? I can trace this compensatory stupidity back to the early 2000s in hipster-filled Williamsburg, Brooklyn. Back then every "soy boy" sported a beard like a fucking lumberjack. Beards are disgusting, filled with boogers and filth. I can't believe women have sex with guys who wear them, but then I remember how filthy women are.

1

Back in college I held a job cleaning office buildings at night, and the female restrooms were always an absolute nightmare.

So this bartender would constantly touch this girl ("kino her" for all of you seduction nerds) he was with and even let his hand rest upon her for periods of time. It was very synthetic and orchestrated. She couldn't sit still - but not because she was sexually aroused by this clod's ministrations, but because she was putting on a show for everyone else, while simultaneously interacting with him, with the former taking a higher priority than the latter. "Playing house," as it were... Her own touches of him were insincere, and the one time she did kiss him, it was like she was on a porn set. For those of you who are too dopey to get my meaning, I mean she kissed him like she was being paid to. He was broke, of course, so that wasn't actually the case here. Anyway, *nobody* could assert that he was an "alpha male." Nobody. Naturally, the "experts" on YouTube will say he was "confident" and acted "non needy" because he worked as a bartender and consequently was used to being around hot girls. Bullshit. They will try and convince you that all you need to do is "copy" him after taking their seminar on vocal tonality and dissolving the tension and trauma stored in your throat, and then you could be in his shoes as well. Shoes that have lifts, of course.

Forget it! Unless by "copying" him they mean you need to drink soy until you grow tits, shave off half of your hair and become an embarrassment of a man... then you *may well* get his results. You'll also have to live with yourself. Good luck with that! As far as dissolving the tension in your throat, you might have more success taking advice from porn stars who are famous for giving irrumatio than from some of the gurus out there! Anyway, the attention she was showering upon this epic pile of fail was infuriating, fawning over him like he was Conan the Fucking Barbarian straddling a pile of skulls (sorry, my vision of masculinity was forged in the 1980s). Eventually they packed up their shit, went inside, and after a while I glanced up to the third floor and saw her lowering the shades of his floor-to-ceiling windows in her bikini because they were about to fuck. The dude knew I was being jelly as a bag of jelly beans and was probably glaring at me from the bedroom window mocking me, and to be honest it was an absolutely epic humiliation and I blame the woman for it 100%. She was the one doing this to me, not him. For whenever a woman gives something meant for you, to a man who doesn't deserve it, the only thing worse she could do is trick you into raising another man's kid, by pretending it is yours.

Which they do all of the time, incidentally…

I want to say for the record that I don't feel jealousy or envy if the dude is awesome. Whenever I see a gorgeous girl with a guy who is tall, handsome, alpha, etc. I always feel so happy for the simple reason that in that very moment, all is right with the world. I forget that I am living on a Satanic planet where everything is inverted. It means that if you work hard at self-improvement, you can win too! Wouldn't that be nice? Certainly there will be a chorus of castratos singing: "Grow up, life isn't fair" and that sort of thing, but allow me to point out how deep their head is actually in the sand... Is there anyone who gets an NFL contract based on how slow they are? Does anyone make it to the NBA based on how short they are? Do stupid people (autistic people are actually smart) end up founding successful tech companies? I could go on and on ad nauseam, but my point here is that *only* in the realm of relationships are you rewarded with more, the lower your value gets. Note: I am clearly not referring to *paid* pussy in the form of hookers, gold diggers and women ready to "settle down," for their stock price always rises in sync with your own.

Of course, I know this bartender is absolute trash in bed and she doesn't even have vaginal orgasms (easy to tell if you know how), but that knowledge doesn't grant me much in the way of *relief* from my torments.

It is abhorrent watching what *appears* to be a grown-ass woman "playing house" with some loser because he is *safe*. It's far more ridiculous than watching a girl take up lesbianism because she thinks she can't get hurt emotionally if she takes that route. Well, maybe not emotionally, but definitely physically, because lesbian relationships boast the highest levels of domestic abuse: *According to CDC data, 44% of lesbian women and 61% of bisexual women have experienced forms of rape and physical violence by an intimate partner, compared to 35% of heterosexual women.* If that doesn't reveal the real nature of women, I don't know what does!

Naturally the loser guy knows the truth on some level, but why wouldn't he take advantage of the free pussy? BTW, when I say "playing house," what I mean is she was playing with this guy as if he were some fat, balding "Ken Doll" because she is too much of a weak coward to get involved with a guy she *actually* has feelings for, whether they be based on love, sex, or both. This scenario runs parallel to the phenomena my generation (Gen X) used to call "fag hags," which are women who want male energy but don't want to have sex with men or risk being hurt by men to get said energy, so they surround themselves with gay male friends and absorb that male energy *passively*. Ironically, they are too stupid to realize that their gay male friends are doing everything in their power to make sure they stay single forever, as they secretly want all the straight men in the world for themselves! No man is of more interest to a gay man than a straight man. Don't let them tell you otherwise! They worship straight men and find them the most attractive of all. Is it because you want what you can't get? Is it because "converting" a straight man validates the gay man's "gayness," or is it because the straight man has what the gay man is missing and trying to acquire through sexual acts with other men? Who knows... Even worse, you won't believe the number of dumb women who *have sex* with their gay male friends because they consider it a boost to their non-existent self-esteem to brag that they are "so hot they got a gay guy to fuck them." Too bad their gay fuck buddies neglect to mention all the bacteria

4

and viruses they are carrying courtesy of the local bath house "culture!" What dopey broads!

Here is the thing: women are always seeking security which is why they eventually get with a guy who has money if at all possible, yet it is not *only* financial security they desire but *psychic* security as well. As a matter of fact, *psychic security* is far more important than financial security although the two clearly have points of intersection. This is why most females spend their best years fucking losers ("bad boys"), and the remaining time they have on the planet *tolerating* beta providers. Contrary to popular wisdom, losers/bad boys are "safe." Sure, the bad boys break their hearts, but said "heartbreak" is *a mere shadow* when compared to the utter *devastation* they *could* experience if their hearts were broken by someone they were truly crazy about sexually, or else madly in love with. It would spell *annihilation* for their psyche, and for the human organism, the number one imperative is *not* physical survival but rather *psychic stability*. Because without psychic stability, physical survival becomes very tenuous. Don't agree? Well then you are dumb as dirt. Everywhere you look, you will see people engaging in absolutely suicidal behaviors: racing motorcycles while intoxicated on public highways, "swimming" in traffic for social media clout, smoking cigarettes, enlisting in the military to "fight terrorists" and so on and so forth. These are not the activities of an organism that prioritizes physical survival!

They say that water seeks it's own level, and in that regard most women fuck losers because they themselves, are in fact losers. You may have trouble seeing this because all you see is a hot or beautiful woman, and the fact that you want to fuck her automatically places her in your "winner's circle." But she knows the truth: she is a loser – and primarily so because she is a fucking coward. I know most people only associate cowardice with men, and it is usually on the physical battlefield or something akin to it.

But cowardice is a hundred times more prevalent among women, just on the emotional battlefield where men cannot discern it.

This is because women are absolutely terrified of the challenge of being an authentic human being, much as the "bad boy" loser is. They both dodge all responsibility, self-awareness, and personal growth. They both cover themselves in meaningless tattoos, mismanage their lives, and walk a path of self-destruction in one form or another. They deserve each other, but with the number of chicken-shit, developmentally-stunted females *far* outpacing the number of "bad boys" in circulation, we have a real crisis on our hands as the majority of males are invisible to females. The big classification mistake that leads to missing this dynamic, is *the gross misclassification of the "bad boy" as an alpha male.* He is the *farthest* thing from an alpha male even if he displays a *semblance* of alpha traits. The real reason the majority of women are attracted to a minority of men, is because the majority of men are not "cool losers," and this shortage of "cool losers" is for the simple reason that society up until recently did not reward the creation of such males.

So please don't fall for the garbage presented in the manosphere claiming that the majority of men are invisible to females because they are under six feet tall and not rich celebrities or something like that. My knowledge was acquired out on the battlefield and from reading the rarest of books, not from listening to audiobook summaries of bestsellers in the self-improvement sub-category on Amazon. They are probably around 50 men in the entire United States that are celebrities, over six feet tall and rich, and they are not available for "dates" with the general public. Believe me, the majority of men are invisible to women simply because they do not mirror the woman's neurosis and for no other reason. I want to drive this point home because it pains me to see all of this red and black pill poison being peddled all over the internet, making asinine claims that if you don't look like a male model, if you are under six feet tall, if you don't have a fleet of exotic cars, or if you aren't a "Top G" then you have no chance with women. This is simply not the case. All of those things actually hurt your chances. The "gurus" have it all wrong.

Here is an experiment you can conduct yourself: if you live in a big city, spend the next few months taking notice of what kind of men the women you see on the street - that you would want to fuck, are *actually* with. Then ask yourself, based upon what you actually see, if those men are really *that much better than you*, and if so, *how exactly* are they better? Naturally you will find, after looking at hundreds of couples, that everything the "manosphere" has been telling you about female sexual selection and the like, is akin to the proverbial group of blind men, each holding onto a different part of an elephant, and each claiming they can describe the elephant in its entirety. By the time you are done reading this book, you will truly see the elephant in it's entirety. At that point, you will be able to hatch plots and schemes based on a model for male-female dynamics *that is based in objective reality*.

Blue, Red and Black - The Three Pill(ar)s of Self-Delusion

YouTube these days is filled with thousands upon thousands of videos uploaded by guys offering you free advice on succeeding with women, or else trying to sell you some. All of their advice will only go so far when applied, because all of their advice is based upon a superficial understanding of what actually powers male-female dynamics. They are all blind men, touching a different part of the proverbial elephant. Intellectually lazy concepts such as "alpha males vs beta males" are erroneously being used as foundational pillars to construct a very shaky weltanschauung (world view), and when the wolf of reality comes and blows down this house made from red and black pills, nobody seems to realize that something is very, very wrong indeed with the basic foundation stones of their understanding of male-female dynamics. So they simply proceed to build yet another house of red and black pills upon the same bedrock of self-delusion. Why? Because such a house is *comfortable* to live in. Again and again, we will come back to the brutal reality that humans crave psychic stability *over* physical survival, as well as over success itself. Seriously, so many people do not attain success because said success would be a threat to their psychic stability, even though attaining success would provide a massive boost to their physical survival.

The fundamental problem with all of the "relationship advice" out there is that it ultimately promotes the idea of succeeding with women by:

- Mimicking females and their neurosis by either becoming a male loser, or else doubling down on remaining one. This is the essence of all traditional PUA teachings. But who wants to become or remain a loser in order to get women?

- Self-improving (the essence of all "red pill" teachings), based on the false assumption that women give a shit about your *intrinsic value.* They don't. It actually repulses them. While they do care about what *material* value you can *give them,* acquiring resources is *not* self-improvement! It is *situational* improvement which a women does care about, but only because you can be *used* for it. Who wants to be used unless it is for sex?

When I first started doing PUA over 20 years ago, I took a course with a guy named Vin DiCarlo who at the time had a partner named Sebastian Drake. Their company was called "The Approach." Vin DiCarlo eventually went off on his own and got pretty famous, and while I cannot comment on any of the material he taught once he went his own way as I never sampled it, the attraction model used by The Approach was actually the most accurate and brilliant of all the models out there. Yet almost nobody has ever heard of it. The model was known by the acronym "V.A.C." which stood for Value, Attainability and Compliance.

What made Vin and Sebastian brilliant was that *all* PUAs were stressing Value and Compliance, but none even talked about Attainability, which is the most critical variable of that trinity. PUAs demonstrated value by telling stories and dressing in a way that showed confidence and freedom of expression (peacocking), and compliance was attained by taking a girl's hand and getting her to "spin," or telling her to follow you to another area of the venue or whatever...

The overall idea was that if you demonstrated enough value, and kept getting compliance from her, then at a certain point (and in a certain location) you could flat out tell her to suck your cock, and she would, as sucking your cock was just another step on the ladder of compliance that you had her unknowingly climbing since the moment you met her and first asked her to "spin." This ladder of escalating compliance is also inextricably related to the concept of escalating "kino," which is repeatedly touching her in various places in a specific sequence, with the intent to escalate towards sex.

Pro tip: If you want to know if a woman really likes you, stroke the inside of her hand. Plenty of women will make out with you, suck your cock, even let you fuck their ass in a bathroom stall *but still not actually like you* – a concept men have trouble grasping. The same girl who lets you do these things will often be repulsed by you stroking the inside of her hand. So this is a great test to see if a girl is serious about you, or just serious about being used as a human latrine or stand-alone vomitorium. I am not joking here, feel free to urinate on or inside women during sex, you would be shocked by how many of them love it.

What all of the PUAs had missed, outside of the guys at The Approach, was the concept of "attainability." This is not exactly unexpected, because most of the well known PUAs out there had no value *in actuality,* and no woman out there would ever think that any of them would be "unattainable." This is because they were all complete losers. For guys like that, the only focus needed to be on artificially pumping up value (since they have none other than being a court jester), and gaining compliance. But what happens if a man actually has value? Hmmm… Suddenly, attainability becomes a major issue. Factoring that variable into your game, is the trickiest thing there is. The more value you have, the more you have to focus on it. However, at a certain point, your value can get so high, that it becomes almost impossible to mitigate it's negative effects on your seduction game. This is why the idea of "getting your money up" or your "shit together" *before* pursuing women is some of the worst advice ever.

In many ways, this book is really about *this* variable, this wild card that most NPCs will never have to deal with. Unbeknownst to Vin and Sebastian, they had actually touched upon the single most important concept in social dynamics between men and women. A keystone which, if fully grasped, could unlock the entire model of male-female dynamics. This is precisely what I have accomplished. By following a path that raised my value too high, I was forced to focus on the variable of attainability to the exclusion of all else. Although I failed to mitigate the negative effects of my own value on my seduction game, my focus on attainability led me to discovering the truth about what *actually* drives male-female interactions. As a result, I have carved out a virtual Rosetta Stone with this book, with which you can decode *all* of the insanity in the game of men vs. women.

Look, I understand that the notion that bettering yourself makes you *less* attractive to women is hard to believe. Yet, you heard me correctly. One thing certain dating gurus get right is that women are turned off by self-improvement. This is, of course, because women themselves don't self-improve. Ever. So your efforts just remind them what worthless slags they are and inspire neither admiration nor attraction. Ironically, many of the *same* dating gurus who will state that women are turned off by self-improvement, will nonetheless simultaneously push the contradictory idea that one needs to self-improve!

As a matter of fact, the path of self-improvement leads you to nothing but a Rolodex of prostitutes. Which, we will come to find, can be pretty awesome and is *not* the purview of losers as is commonly thought. I will explore this in great detail later, because in truth, it is ultimately where all of the quality men end up anyway. In bed with high-end escorts. You would be shocked at how many clients of hookers are legit "alphas" and often married to gorgeous women or else have hot girlfriends. So why are they enjoying the services of prostitutes? You will know by the time you are done reading this book!

Popping Blue Pills That Won't Get You Hard

The world is filled with blue pill popping, Captain Save-A-Ho types who are too psychically weak to face the reality that there is no *manifestable* love in this world from women towards men, in part because women have become utterly worthless due to their own spiritual weakness and free will choices... meaning, they always seek the easy way out and attempt to cheat the spiritual challenges that being "human" presents them with. As a result, most girlfriends and wives don't love the men they end up with, and in most cases aren't even sexually attracted to them. Ironically, the fate of almost every "player" out there is to turn into some sort of Captain Save-A-Ho in the end because no matter how many women he has fucked, the creeping realization that there is no love to be had drives him to find some woman who *needs* his love but does not *want* it, then use the ensuing drama over not having his love reciprocated, to distract himself from the loveless void that is human existence. It's utterly masochistic, but keeps many a man from suicide. In other words, if he can keep his awareness of a lack of love confined to his current codependent relationship, he doesn't have to face the fact this lack of love is omnipresent across female-male relationships.

You know, one of the main reasons the PUA scene ended up being attacked by society at large is because they kept showcasing the reality that women don't want you to see: women love fucking losers. Like, all the fucking time. So all of the PUA course materials in essence taught men who were already losers, to become *cool losers*, as "cool losers" are crack cocaine for women. Woman as well as society does not want you to see this, because if men modified themselves to accommodate what women *really desire* in a male, society would collapse and women would not be able to find men to extract resources from.

Now a lot of you will say, "Well all of this is why I've gone MGTOW." But unless you are using "going MGTOW" as a code word for fucking prostitutes in Brazil or Thailand (both wonderful choices), either you are ordering hyper-realistic sex dolls online, your testosterone has dropped so low you now have the luxury of deceiving yourself into believing that you no longer care about sex, or else you have gone trans and decided to take cock instead of give it. Anyone who says they don't need women, or sex, is capping to the extreme. It is the ultimate in what Aesop called "sour grapes," in his famed fables.

A Cogent History of the Pickup and Seduction Scene

As I have already pointed out, these days the manosphere has become filled with ridiculous theories of how women operate and how to succeed with them. These ridiculous theories of how women operate, started innocently enough with the PUA movement. The movement began when a small band of men loitering online, attempted to reverse-engineer the behaviors and qualities of those men who had astounding success with women, in order to replicate the results of those same men in their own pathetic lives.

A noble, and very masculine endeavor indeed! Men, after all, are engineers who build stuff and find solutions to problems. So they observed what they dubbed "naturals," which were men who had smashing success with women without any thought or effort on their part, then hatched techniques for seducing women *based on* what they saw these naturals do "out in the field" (i.e. bars and clubs). Then they ventured out into the field themselves to see if they could replicate the success of those naturals, by applying those techniques they had reverse-engineered via observation. In line with the scientific method, what worked "out in the field" spawned *theories* about how women operate, and how mate selection "goes down" among humans. The problem, with respect to the scientific method, is that it takes an incredible amount of time and testing, for a theory to become a *law*. Given the natural impatience of males in a sphere as critical to their own *psychic stability* as the acquisition of love and sex is, these "theories" about how women operate became "laws" *before* they could be properly vetted.

This hurried "evolution" from theory to law occurred around the same time that the PUA movement found itself pivoting away from the painful refiner's fire known as "cold approaching," and leaning hard into the study of what would come to be known as "inner game." The allure of this mythical "inner game," being the promise of minimizing the chances of being rejected upon cold approach, or even having to approach women at all! That's right: it was postulated that if your "inner game" was "dialed in," not only will it be impossible for a woman to reject you, but they will in fact start approaching you! This sounded great in theory, as you can't be rejected if women approach you, clearly. Again, the male desire for psychic stability was exerting pressure on the direction of the movement.

Along with this pivot into the realm of inner game, many schools of PUA began to focus on what would come to be known as "social circle game," which yielded better results than cold approaching and also took the ogre of rejection out of the picture completely. Social circle game is indeed a more viable platform from which to launch your weapons of seduction than is the platform of cold approach. This is because inside of a social circle, you enjoy a massive boost of "social proof" from the circle itself, that is sorely lacking on the street, or in a club operating as a "lone wolf." Furthermore, everyone knows club promoters fuck lots of girls – especially if they have access to drugs, a key ingredient that is always left out of the discussion! So while social circle game is legit, "inner game" is just another pipe dream *still* being promoted by many, some of whom are now promoting it from a new angle, claiming that "trauma release" is what will launch your in-field results into the stratosphere.

Believe me, it won't.

Again, it seems legit *in theory* - that if you clear out all of your traumas and become your "authentic self," women will flock to you. However, it's just not going to happen in practice. I tested it years ago, and the women ran for the hills. This is because trauma release is not only the ultimate in "self improvement" which we already know women utterly despise, but because it will free you from your own neurosis, thereby leaving you vibrating at a frequency which will *not* resonate with 99% of women. With that being said, I will *still* show you the path to clearing all of your traumas, because the "gurus" out there promoting it don't have a clue what they are talking about. Sure, you might exit one of their seminars thinking you can take on the world, when in reality you still need a laxative just to take a healthy shit.

The True Cost of Clearing Trauma and Releasing Authenticity

People have *no clue* how difficult and challenging *legit* Reichian Therapy and "breathwork" practices are, or how long it actually takes to even *begin* to process childhood trauma or birth trauma, let alone reform your "character structure." When I say "character structure" what that means in simple English is that there is a certain way you stand from a postural standpoint, that has been shaped by your past traumas. Sure, you can force yourself to stand up straight with your shoulders back and chest out, but to really change your character structure so as to stand that way *without conscious awareness or effort* is something else entirely. I should also point out that "posture" *as a concept*, runs far deeper than just standing up straight, and involves your internal fascia, your thoracic, pelvic and urogenital diaphragms, along with the symmetry of your skull. But that is outside the scope of this book.

As one example, however, there is a guy who lives in my building who has the most terrible postural traits you can imagine. He looks utterly absurd. He also lives with his son who is probably 12 years old, and when you see his son walk down the street with him, his son shares every single postural absurdity with, and even walks with an identical gait to, his father. This is despite that fact that in his face, he looks very little like his father. Nonetheless, the point is that this child subconsciously adopted the traumatic character structure of his own father *even though he himself could not have undergone the same traumas as his father.* This is neither an example of genetics nor epigenetics, but this is perhaps the best demonstration that neurosis is indeed, contagious!

Anyway, the idea promoted by certain pickup gurus, is that you can get up in front of a group of fellow losers for three days in a row and practice yelling, or talking in a really loud voice, and thereby end up resolving all of your traumas. This is an absolute fucking joke. These idiot "gurus" are showing the world that they don't even have a grasp of the absolute basics, such as the fact that your blocked throat and inability to project when you speak, is reflexively linked to your pelvis and therefore your sexuality. I took the famous "Shamanic De-armoring" retreat in person, where you spend 15 days self-pleasuring in front of a group of people while doing Reichian breathwork, and then did the brutal at-home breathwork exercises every single day for three years straight until my appendix ruptured from my efforts. I did years of Reichian breathwork prior to that with several other legit instructors, including one of the original members of Osho's inner circle. I did primal therapy with every surviving primal therapist on the continent and even pulled two of them out of retirement to work with me. I know what I am talking about. This shit ain't easy and it takes *years* to even *begin* to make a dent in your being.

I am not saying that you shouldn't pursue this path, but please be aware of what the true consequences of any degree of success will likely be. You are not going to like them! Yes, you will eventually recover your authentic, natural self, but nobody will be attracted to it. Why? It is very simple really... People are not their authentic selves because their authentic selves are buried under trauma. People run from this trauma, as said trauma is a threat to their psychic stability. So if you do the opposite of what everyone else does, and run towards your trauma, embrace and heal it... then your authentic presence that will emerge from this endeavor of yours will start to *draw out the trauma held by those around you, out from under their defenses,* and threaten their psychic stability. Consequently, they will turn and run from *you*, as you now represent the very trauma they repress! Congratulations. You played yourself.

I used to have crazy "game," but after resolving a good amount of my issues and becoming more authentic than most, via legit breathwork and the like, I got ghosted by almost 100 women in a row. Half of those women had initially approached me in line with the promises of inner game, and some of them even had sex with me before ghosting me. Other women I met out in public would suddenly explode into a rage while talking to me, or even if they simply thought I was staring at them, which in such cases I never was. But women hate to be *seen*. Sure, they will cry about you not being "present," failing to "hold space," or else whine about how you don't "see" them. But for 99% of women these are merely code words for "GIVE ME YOUR ATTENTION DADDY." They don't want you to *actually see* them, because *then* they are afraid you will "see" that they hate themselves and are worth *nothing*. I remember making out with one girl and a few minutes later she flew into a rage and started throwing random objects at me and smashing up our surroundings. Once I was talking to a woman in a high end bar and she suddenly tried to injure my cock. Witnesses would be horrified and could not understand what was happening as they could see I genuinely hadn't done anything to trigger this sort of madness. Some women would later say things to me like "You don't know what you do to me" or "you make me crazy" or "I don't know what to do with you" or "I can't control you."

Pro Tip: Be very mindful of a woman's desire to injure your cock. Penis envy is *very* real. They hate you for having a penis, because they know what a penis can do to them. The will often ride you or have sex with you, or else attempt to manually manipulate your penis, in such a way so as to "break" it. Be warned! Then when you call them out on it, they will accuse you of being overly sensitive and punish you in some other way sexually, for not giving them the plausible deniability they wanted, in order to injure you.

Contrary to popular beliefs held in the manosphere, women are *not* attracted to men they cannot control. What happens is they get attracted to men they *believe they will be able to control*. Sure, those men may be uncontrollable *now* or believe themselves to be uncontrollable, but that doesn't mean a thing *if* the woman *believes* she can gain control over them. What did I say earlier about the concept of "attainability?" Women are predatory, and no predator goes after prey they know they cannot catch! You could in fact say that women love the chase and the struggle for control, much like a rapist often loves women who struggle and fight back.

However, just as a rapist will not attack a woman if he knows his attack will fail, a woman will also neither chase nor struggle for control when they know they have no chance of winning in the end. In other words, they only like the chase and struggle for control if they are 100% certain they will end up the victor – and no matter what you may think, every "bad boy" is ultimately controllable because they are fundamentally weak males. It is just a matter of time before they submit. If you pay attention long enough, you will find that every bad boy ends up a slave to some woman, somewhere...

So think carefully, what kind of results do you want? To be able to only fuck hookers? Even then you won't be immune, as quite a few of them will ghost you after a few sessions because they will start to fall in love with you. Ironically, you know what kind of women *will* chase after you and not run away? Females with Narcissistic Personality Disorder (NPD) and Borderline Personality Disorder (BPD). Because they will be looking at your beautiful, authentic self as something to destroy and your beautiful, authentic energy as something to consume! You are just too tasty *not* to shoot their shot, plus their delusional ego cannot even imagine failure. Girls with NPD or BPD throw themselves at me to this very day. So if a girl is aggressively interested in me, it is usually a huge red flag with "Cluster B" written all over it. For those of you who are unawares, allow me to explain:

A Cluster B personality disorder is a type of personality disorder characterized by dramatic, overly emotional, unpredictable, or erratic behaviors and intense emotional responses. The Diagnostic and Statistical Manual of Mental Disorders (DSM-5) groups personality disorders into three clusters, with Cluster B including four main types:

- **Antisocial Personality Disorder:** Marked by a disregard for others' rights, impulsivity, and lack of remorse.

- **Borderline Personality Disorder:** Characterized by unstable moods, relationships, self-image, and impulsive actions.

- **Histrionic Personality Disorder:** Involves excessive attention-seeking, emotionality, and a need for approval.

- **Narcissistic Personality Disorder:** Defined by grandiosity, a constant need for admiration, and lack of empathy for others.

People with Cluster B personality disorders often have trouble regulating emotions, maintaining healthy relationships, and may engage in impulsive or self-destructive behaviors. These disorders can cause significant distress and impairment in social, occupational, or other important areas of functioning.

I would also add that based on my personal experience, getting involved with a girl who has high functioning autism (Asperger's) can be just as traumatic and damaging as getting involved with a girl who has one of the Cluster B personality disorders. Stay away!

Pro Tip: People who are classified with "Cluster B" disordered personalities are said to be "suffering" from them. This is ridiculous. I have known many individuals with NPD rather intimately, and I can tell you that they absolutely revel in how they victimize others and are straight up predators. The same goes for those diagnosed with BPD (Borderline Personality Disorder). The world would be better off if everyone alive were forced to take a brain scan MRI to reveal who is a "Cluster B," with those testing positive, promptly taken out back and swiftly shot in the head.

Yes, it is the above types of girls that you will have to look forward to, *if* you pursue "inner game" to the very end of the line! You will also become fully aware of just how rotten and evil, corrupted and cowardly, the majority of women are. This truth is *really* going to hurt.

But why are people so addicted to those with narcissistic personality disorder (NPD)? The short answer, is that there really is no love in this world, and narcissists have adapted to take advantage of this horrific reality by producing a *synthetic*, yet highly addictive love-substitute, that they use in order to enslave others and keep them around as a "psychic food source," whom they can feed upon. They are often referred to as "energy vampires" for this very reason, yet to call them vampires is actually rather insulting to bona fide vampires. Modern psychiatry mistakenly teaches that those with NPD feed upon an energy that psychiatrists dub "narcissistic supply," yet this energy is *actually* what those with NPD are supplying *you* with, in order to addict you to *them*. Otherwise, you would run like hell and they would "starve."

Their ploy works because since there is no love in this world, your hunger for it can only be *somewhat* satiated by appealing to your latent narcissism, much like so many women can live off "likes" on social media in place of being in love. Now please don't be tricked if you were lucky enough to have been "loved" by your parents, or just because you have "fallen in love" in the past. The truth is that humans do not know what love is, and are incapable of real love, just a facsimile of it. As a result, they lack the conscious awareness of there being no love in this world, and walk around half-crazy because on a subconscious level, they are still aware that something is missing, they just can't figure out what it is. Even if they know they are missing love, they cannot comprehend that it doesn't exist in this realm among humans. One of the advantages that narcissists have, is that they see the world pretty clearly, with the exception that they run into a wall when it comes to empathy. But while they cannot empathize with you, they understand you better than you do.

I know that there is no love in this world because I am something other than a human, wearing a hybridized human body like a spacesuit in order to remain in this realm, and my kind knows what love is. It is a common misconception that beings of darkness do not know love, and that the existence of evil is somehow due to a lack of love. Humans foolishly look upon evil as some sort of aberration, or mistake – a symptom of something having gone "wrong." With respect to human beings they *may* be mostly correct, but humans aren't the only beings in existence in creation, *and* they also fail to acknowledge that evil was created by The Divine Father just as He created good. But He also gave His creations free will, which means that evil beings can deny The Divine Father and rebel against Him, just as good beings - or even "neutral" beings, can be atheists or otherwise wield their free will with blatant disregard for the will of The Divine Father. It's just that the rebellious evil tends to stand out. The biggest problem on this planet, is that it is overrun with the rebellious evil, who have turned this place into what amounts to a planet-sized feedlot, stocked with billions of human livestock under the control of Saturn's transmissions.

But I digress…

If you really want to take this path of freeing yourself from traumatic bondage, and are committed to it, I advise you start by going to the Osho compound in Pune, India where you can take watered-down breathwork classes and fuck young girls who travel there just to take cock under the guise of "spirituality." Bring plenty of Tadalafil and Sertraline which will turn you into a "tantric sex master" as soon as you swallow them. Incidentally, the entire "tantric sex scene" is really just women using spirituality as an excuse to be sluts, and hookers learning a new marketing angle while expanding upon their range of "services offered." But go take advantage of the scene nonetheless, and forget about actually developing genuine tantric skills as I did, because 99% of women will run in terror from those as well. You will see why this is so, on deeper and deeper levels, as you continue reading this book, but in essence it goes back to most women being absolutely cowardly in the face of psychic instability.

In my case, I ultimately would not have cared about the consequences of this path even if I had truly known about them beforehand, as in the end I just wanted to be "the real me," whatever that would turn out to be, underneath all of my trauma, and I was 100% committed to the discovery of *what* I was, as opposed to *who* I was. I cannot say if you, the reader, feel the same way or not, unless you are also of the darkness, and as of yet still unawares. If so, then my words will probably resonate with you louder than most. Either way, I am not actually trying to discourage anyone from striving to be "real," I just want to prepare you for the consequences of your "realness," once it has been attained.

Incidentally, *what* you are is more important than *who* you are, with respect to your identity. It is more important for a dog to realize that he is a dog, and for a cat to realize that she is a cat, than to learn what breeder supervised their conception, to employ a crude metaphor. Again, if one is plagued by these questions, pray to The Divine Father and ask Him for assistance in discovering *what* you are, and what *His purpose for you* is.

But Isn't Confidence the Most Attractive Thing to A Woman?

This is correct, but it isn't confidence that arises from inherent value or actual accomplishments that attracts women. Women are repulsed by *that* sort of confidence. Again, it is a red pill delusion that women are attracted to "*genuine* competency and achievement." No, women really couldn't give a shit about your competency or your achievements.

On the contrary, **women are magnetically attracted to confidence which is absolutely baseless and utterly delusional.** This is another reason why men who have NPD are so good with women. Are women really so stupid as to be unable to tell the difference between real and fake confidence? Of course not! But a woman sees an absolute loser piece of shit who has managed to completely delude himself and run around like he owns the world and *they desire that confidence for themselves.* Why? Because they themselves are absolute loser pieces of shit and they hate themselves for being so. Seriously, their self-hatred is killing them. Women love to talk about "low self-esteem" and then blame said low self-esteem on Hollywood, the fashion industry, or the "patriarchy" at large, but "low self-esteem" is really just a euphemism for "self-hate," and women utterly hate themselves, let me tell you. All you have to do is look at the choices women make on a daily basis to know that they do not love themselves in the *slightest.* Naturally, they can't get enough of indulging themselves and pampering themselves (code word: "self-care"), but that is *not* self-love. So now, imagine if you were a self-hating waste of oxygen... would you not *crave* utterly delusional confidence in order to ease the pain of your own existence?

Pro Tip: It is pretty amusing when women bitch about impossible to attain "beauty standards" set by the fashion industry, but who in fact controls the fashion industry? Not "the patriarchy," but rather a gang of blatant homosexuals who don't like women in the slightest. So is it any shock when they turn female models into anorexic, walking clothes hangers? Either way, "times they are a-changing" and when you walk past stores selling makeup these days, their in-store advertisements depict some of the ugliest and most repulsive examples of humanity they can find.

In essence, the core technique of the PUA community, upon which every other technique ultimately rests, is to find *some way* to acquire utterly delusional self-confidence. Which basically means: turn yourself into someone with Narcissistic Personality Disorder (NPD)! I caught onto this pretty quickly just by watching "naturals" out in the field, whom for the most part had either narcissistic, or else sociopathic traits.

My point is that it isn't exactly true that there is no such thing as inner game. It's just that there are two types of inner game: One is inner game based on genuine self-confidence, which is attained from facing, conquering, and integrating your traumas and other challenges in life. The other is inner game that rests on a foundation of counterfeit self-confidence, which is based on literally nothing and utterly delusional. We are also now aware that the latter is the most attractive to women, and we also know why: real confidence is based on actual value, and women despise real confidence for that very reason. They have no actual value! I don't mean they have no *inherent* value, they are just so stunted spiritually, that they have nothing to offer besides being a "RoboBlow 5000" machine that talks incessantly when your dick is not in its mouth. Please do not misunderstand my harsh prose, and please listen carefully:

- I do not objectify women, as they have already chosen to objectify themselves.

- I do not hate women, as they have already chosen to hate themselves.

What's interesting is that the word misogyny, from a strictly etymological standpoint, means "hatred of women," yet dictionaries have expanded the definition to include "mistrust of women" and "prejudice towards women." These are examples of political correctness attempting to rewrite definitions of reality. "Mistrust" and "prejudice" are not equivalent to "hate." If you look up each of these words in the dictionary by themselves, you will see that they mean different things, and if you look them all up in a thesaurus, you will see that they cannot be used in place of one another, either.

I am getting a bit off track here, and want to continue explaining the evolution of the manosphere...

The Red Pill as A Response To "Approach Anxiety"

So over time, more and more dudes started to flood the internet with horror stories that revolved around their own personal experiences with female behavior. Advice for avoiding these aforementioned horrors then mated together with some of the prematurely christened "laws" of male-female dynamics that were promoted by the PUA scene. The whole shebang was then wrapped in a celebration of the type of genuine confidence that comes from accomplishment (which is actually repugnant to women), and presented as the "red pill."

As I said earlier on, the PUA community had begun talking more and more about "inner game" largely as a result of the specter of "approach anxiety." Mind you, these days young people talk about "social anxiety disorder," which doesn't really exist with respect to being an *actual disorder*. I mean, if you never socialize because you spend all of your time playing video games and beating it to online porn, *then of course* you will have social anxiety because it is totally natural to suffer anxiety over something you have never done before! In many ways, "approach anxiety" is kind of similar, although with the added dimension that *even if* you did do tons of approaches, you could still harbor anxiety due to the fear of rejection, because quite frankly, being rejected sucks.

So you had two options: You could either make yourself into some sort of narcissist and convince yourself that you were awesome even when you knew that you were a loser, or you could do something to stop being a loser and hopefully that would resolve your approach anxiety. Hmmm... this second option of becoming as amazing as possible before approaching women solved approach anxiety via avoidance and projection of the problem into a future where it would have no basis for existing. But it also set a trap because when will you be good enough? The ironic answer is never, and paradoxically the closer and closer you get towards this ideal called "good enough," the farther away you will repel the women you mistakenly believed would *ultimately* end up approaching you! Another issue, is that even as a man you have a biological clock, albeit it is slower than a woman's by a factor of many times.

So while the red pill at it's apex did produce legendary bloggers such as Heartiste (my favorite), it also somehow ultimately led to the comical notion that to succeed with women you needed to be a literal "alpha male" archetype. This archetype of the "alpha male" ended up being a caricature of masculinity, embodied by a guy who takes a lot of steroids, does BJJ, and drives a fleet of exotic cars, all the while covering himself in tattoos, fake Cuban link chains and counterfeit Rolex watches. Rich Piana is probably the progenitor of this "alpha male" archetype. Rich Piana even filled his body with so much PMMA (polymethyl methacrylate) that he looked 100 lbs heavier than he actually was. Rich Piana's slogan of "One Day You May" (approach women?) is really the red pill philosophy in a nutshell.

It cannot be denied that these "alpha males" inspired millions while being very entertaining, and I don't think either is a bad thing. I don't hate on them. Yet many members of what some have dubbed "the alpha male universe" ended up being attacked all over the internet on a daily basis. It's only natural, as humans have a love/hate relationship with their shadow, because they never do their "inner work." Any man who has "done the work" (as opposed to "putting in work") simply sees these guys as a parody projection of male neurosis and doesn't get triggered by them in the slightest. Certainly at some point you must have heard someone observe that bodybuilding can sometimes be nothing more than "male anorexia?" When I first saw the film "American Psycho" I could not stop laughing because I saw my own shadow in Patrick Bateman's character, yet I was comfortable with that shadow part of myself. I mean, who hasn't looked at themselves in the mirror while fucking a woman in the exact same manner depicted in the film? The problem is when you aren't laughing at yourself. That's when you are in serious trouble!

What Does It Mean to Be A "Real Man" Or A "Real Woman?"

What you really need to ask is "What does it mean to be a 'real human being?'" If you can answer that, then gender is irrelevant. The answer is that a real human being is someone who can truly feel without any inner conflict, and who can truly express without any inner conflict. The "inner conflict" that blocks authentic feeling and expression is called "neurosis," and the root of this inner conflict is called "trauma." Wilhelm Reich, one of Sigmund Freud's promising protégés and contributor to early psychoanalytic theory, devoted his life to developing practical exercises to work through past traumas and resolve the neurotic condition of man.

However, becoming a "real man" or a "real woman" via the release of trauma and the resolution of neurosis *will alienate you* from your fellow human beings. Reich himself ended up being labeled a crackpot and died in a Federal penitentiary. Furthermore, "becoming real and authentic" will not necessarily release you from suffering. You will still suffer. It's a "catch-22," because in all honesty your choice is really between authentic suffering or inauthentic suffering. Ironically, this is one of the more advanced definitions of neurosis itself! You see, while neurosis can be defined on the simplest level as an unresolved inner conflict, on a more complex level it can be defined as the *choice* to suffer inauthentically rather than authentically.

What does this look like in practical terms? Well, if you have OCD (obsessive-compulsive disorder) and wash your hands 50x per day, then you are suffering from OCD. But the reason you suffer from OCD, is because OCD is a mechanism by which to repress what your psyche perceives to be a much greater form of suffering – suffering that is so intense it threatens to destabilize your very psyche. So OCD is, in actuality, a great defense mechanism that protects you until you are strong enough to deal with *that* which it is protecting you from. Once you become aware of what is really going on within this dynamic, then you are able to make consciously aware choices as to how you wish to proceed going forward. Mind you, you will still have to fight like hell for a loooong period of time if your choice is to suffer authentic pain, as your OCD will not be so easily convinced that you are able to handle the pain it is protecting you from. But nonetheless, you are still be able to make the consciously aware choice to fight against the OCD, and embrace the pain that it is protecting you from.

Pro Tip: *Most men are not real men just as most women are not real women.* Pundits will say men are no longer masculine and women are no longer feminine, which is simply another way of stating that they are not as they are meant to be in a state of nature, which is what makes them unreal these days to begin with! This state of being unreal, unnatural, and *awkward* is the core problem, that is often perceived as a lack of masculinity or femininity. But rather than look at the big picture, everyone spends all of their time attempting to define masculinity and femininity, which cannot be done, because those claiming to define it are unreal themselves and therefore incapable of defining masculinity and femininity in terms that aren't inherently neurotic. For instance, some people promote "big game hunting" as as example of "being a real man." They will suggest that if you don't freeze up in fear, and pull that trigger before the lion can get close enough to maul you, then you have completed some sort of "rite of passage" as a man. I do not believe that going on a safari and gunning down a lion who charges you head on with an "elephant gun" to be an example of anything other than an addiction to adrenaline. A real man hunts for food in order to eat, not in order to entertain or prove himself via the senseless murder of regal animals. I knew of a guy who used to go deer hunting, and he would shoot the deer in such a way so that it wouldn't die quickly. Then he would go over to the dying deer and literally fuck it as it lay dying, so that it would die while his dick was inside of it. Well one day, a deer he shot wasn't having it, and before it died it kicked him so hard with its rear hooves they penetrated his stomach and guts, and he had to be taken to the hospital and get sewn back together again. So who rearranged whose guts that day? The jury is still out on that one!

On The Ultimate Non-Existence of Female Hypergamy

While I am shitting all over the red pill, let me take a gander at the ridiculous and intellectually lazy notion of "female hypergamy," which is held up as some sort of supreme law of relationship dynamics when it is nothing more than a red pill bogeyman with no real substance. First off, we need to realize that the red pill community doesn't even know what the word "hypergamy" even means. Here is the definition from the Oxford English Dictionary:

hy·per·ga·my
noun

The action of marrying or forming a sexual relationship with a person of a superior sociological or educational background.

Are women hypergamous based on this definition? Of course not! Statistics will back me up on this, and demonstrate that hypergamy only applies with respect to money. You will also notice that money is *not* explicitly part of the definition of the word, although the argument can be made that it is included under the blanket term "sociological." The issue I have is that the red pill community has altered the definition to basically mean that a woman is forever looking for a "bigger better deal." This is not hypergamy!

But *if* we accept the red pill's *redefinition* of the word, then the only reason females *appear* to be hypergamous is simply because they cannot find a man who is capable of satisfying them sexually. This shouldn't be a surprise given that most men suck in bed no matter how big their cock is, or how hard they "smash." The reason for this is in large part due to pornography. I will cover pornography and sexuality later on in *great* detail, and I can assure you that most of you will learn things you have *never* heard before.

You know, it's funny just how many men actually think that porn stars are good in bed or able to satisfy a woman. They aren't, and when you idolize them you just reveal to those who know, *how little you actually know.* I laugh every time some YouTube content creator talks about how all you need to do, is learn to pound the pussy like you were beating a rented mule, and that *this* is the reason why women like bad boys, ex-cons, and gangsters. What nonsense. I've already covered why they like those types of males and it has nothing to do with how hard they fuck a woman. Surely, there are periods of time during sexual intercourse when you need to "go to pound town." Women do enjoy it and are "impressed" by it on *some* level, but if you think this is what *satisfies* women you are fucking lost.

Only wave-after-wave of full body orgasms can satisfy them. But that is a topic for a later chapter…

Let me ask you, have you ever seen a female porn performer achieve a full-body orgasm (triggered either vaginally or anally) where she falls into a near perpetual state of orgasmic waves? Nope. You guys have never even seen what real squirting is, either. Most porn presents a mere facsimile of the real thing. You certainly have never seen a girl have an orgasm while deep throating! It is possible, in women who are free from the somatic repression of certain types of trauma, to be capable of this, as I have met one who was. Interestingly, it is *partially* the hunger to be the *cause* of such orgasmic surrender (coupled with the frustration of being unable to actualize it) that is *part* of the reason why male porn stars these days are always throat-fucking women until they vomit. On the surface level it may appear to be hatred of women, and in some cases it probably is, but on a deeper level there is something else going on. While the female performer may experience some sort of catharsis from the experience, and even free her throat from psychosomatic tension to *some* degree, it ultimately falls short of her surrendering to a throatgasm in every case. They just end up staring into a punch bowl brimming with their own puke and drool.

My point is that unconsciously, a woman knows she is missing something, and so she is always searching for *that thing* that she is missing – even if she can't quite name what it is. What she is missing is her true, orgasmic nature. Want to take a guess why she can't find it? It's buried under trauma! With this most critical part of her being lost to trauma, *of course* nothing can satisfy her and so she is always searching. This is the root of her *apparent* "hypergamy." Yet since she doesn't really know *what* she is searching for, she just gets obsessed with yet another designer handbag or a few more Instagram likes, that *maybe* will fill the hole inside of her. Pun intended. It's no different then men who are fixated on endlessly modifying their cars, computers, and assault weapons – distracting themselves from a reality they just cannot face. It is for this reason that most men can't help women out, in addition to the fact that all they know about female sexuality, is what they've learned from watching pornography. So the female statement that "men are useless" does have some element of truth to it even if we exclusively build and maintain the very societies they enjoy! Hopefully this book will have an impact, so guys will stop subscribing to this red pill nonsense that a man can increase his "sexual market value" based on his status or achievements. The only thing that can raise a man's "sexual market value" *is* his *sexual value*. Women don't give a flying fuck about a man's status or achievements just as a man doesn't give a floating fuck if a hot bitch is working at McDonald's. Sexual market value is called *sexual* market value for a reason. It is not called "dating market value" or "marriage market vale," you asinine chumps. Stop conflating all these concepts already!

There are only two types of sexual market value that a man can provide:

- His genetics for the production of offspring.
- His ability to deliver incredible sexual experiences.

Everything else is of no value with respect to the *sexual* marketplace. For example, if you possess significant money or status, you will be able to enjoy access to high-end escorts or live in a country where beautiful hookers are cheap. You will also be able to enjoy access to gold-diggers or groupies. Yet if you are lacking in terms of bona fide sexual market value, then your enjoyment of all the women you can access will be hollow and limited. This is why it is imperative that in addition to "getting your money up," you get your sexual market value up into the stratosphere. While you can't improve your genetic offering to women, you can improve upon your ability to give them incredible sexual experiences. This book will teach you how, and the best usage of any man's time (unless he is gay) is on the acquisition of money and sexual skills. Unless a man is gay - then all he needs is a big cock if he is a top, and a pretty face and tight asshole if he is a bottom.

Pro Tip: Speaking of genetics, this married woman approached me many years ago and asked me if I would be willing to have sex with her one night when she is ovulating, so I can give her a second child. I was like, "Wait, what?" She promised me that she wouldn't come after me for child support, she just wanted a second child, but her husband was too short to produce a tall child. However, since her husband and I have the same eyes and are both good-looking, she felt that he wouldn't notice that it wasn't his child. Ruthless. Women pull this shit *all... the... time...*

You Are Not a Sigma Male, You Are Just a Fucking Loser

Before I move on to the "black pill," I want to state for the record that there is *no such thing* as a "sigma male." He is a figment of the imaginations of loners and losers who fancy themselves in a special category, as a form of cope. Clearly they are not alpha males and their ego won't let them face the reality that they are beta males, so they cooked up the fantasy of the sigma male – the proverbial "lone wolf," even though a wolf's entire existence is defined by his place inside of a pack. So delusional… Red pill types like to talk about the female "hamster wheel" of rationalizations which definitely exists, but all humans regardless of their gender, possess their own personal hamster wheel capable of spinning up entire legends to mask their epic fails. The legend of the sigma male is no exception. Within no time at all, YouTube has become filled with endless videos chronicling the "legend of the sigma male" as thousands of deluded male content creators, hooked up to tanks of copium, dress up their personal failings in the garb of the rare and special "sigma" and post them online. Special? More like "special ed." It's absolutely pathetic. As pathetic as the rise of stoicism which teaches you that eating shit is some sort of noble endeavor. You'll run into these sigma stoics periodically, quoting Marcus Aurelius while abusing themselves with ice baths, daily runs to nowhere, etc. Half of these guys love pain more than they do pussy.

Always be cautious of anything that rises in popularity among the peasants, such as stoicism, "no fap" and sigma male lore. I am really going to piss a lot of people off with what I am about to say, but do you know why Brazilian Jiu Jitsu is such a cultish phenomenon and people end up addicted to BJJ, parroting things like "BJJ saved my life?" It's because BJJ tricks your reptilian brain into thinking you are higher up on the social hierarchy than you actually are, by virtue of submitting other losers on a mat. It's much like the way jerking off to pornography tricks your reptilian brain into thinking you have access to all of these hot women when in reality you are just jerking off like some voyeuristic cuckold. That's what BJJ is.

Now before the entire BJJ community goes apeshit and tells me how they are going to "take me into deep water," let me clarify that I am not shitting on BJJ as a sport, a martial "art" or as a personal endeavor of pursuit. I am just pointing out *why* it has become something of a religion or a cult, and that many people are unaware that in actuality they are wasting their time doing BJJ. That time would be better spent doing something else, like getting money, so they can pay for plastic surgery, visit with high-end escorts, or fly to Turkey for a hair transplant. Instead, they get addicted to the experience of pulling off submissions which the world at large could give a fuck about. Later in this book, I will debunk the postulation that taking up sport fighting will increase your success with women, and instead suggest something that will be more effective, both in terms of increasing your success with women, as well as your ability to protect them.

Those in control of society are always promoting stuff that will keep you from revolting and ruining the good thing they have going for themselves. This is why MMA is promoted so heavily, because it provides a psychic outlet for energy that could otherwise be easily harnessed to induce a revolution. Football as we know it, was promoted by Freud's cousin Edward Bernays for the express purpose of providing a psychic outlet for people trapped in a consumeristic society, in order to prevent them from going utterly insane. Think about that the next time you notice how unhinged football fans behave!

The Sheer Toxicity of Swallowing the Black Pill

The most recent pill you can opt to take is the black pill, which like many poisons, is healing in small doses and deadly in large ones. The black pill philosophy started out with the idea that looks were *far* more important for a man than previously assumed. It then went on to focus on how absolutely cruel women are with respect to how differently they treat guys that they are naturally attracted to, as opposed to how they treat guys that they force themselves to be attracted to, in order to achieve long term financial stability - once they can no longer obtain the guys that they are naturally attracted to, of course. However, those who have been paying attention so far, will correctly discern that "the guys they are naturally attracted to" *are not necessarily particularly good looking.* So while the black pill can be defined by two separate core beliefs, these beliefs share a smaller area of *intersection* than you might realize. Yet somehow over time, the black pill came to represent the notion that *all* that matters are things like looks and height, and if you don't have them, then you might as well just give up and settle for your fate as an incel. I am not sure where this utter insanity came from, but probably from guys who had such low sexual market value to begin with in terms of their genetic offering, that this is how they saw the world anyway. So the "philosophy" of the black pill just confirmed what they already believed.

Obviously looks and height are very attractive to women, just as a pretty face and big tits are very attractive to men. But contrary to black pill teachings, looks are actually far more important to men than to women, for the simple reason that women cannot afford for it to be otherwise. Why? Well, there simply aren't enough tall men with chiseled jaws around, while thanks to makeup and breast implants, there are plenty of women around for men to consider "attractive." This runs counter to the false black pill narrative promoted in the manosphere, that women find only a small percentage of men attractive, while men find a very large percentage of women attractive. Believe me, if makeup and breast implants disappeared from reality, you would quickly see that the curve for female attractiveness in the eyes of males is *not* as forgiving as those in the manosphere would like you to believe!

This brings us to the most ridiculous tenet of the black pill philosophy, which is shared by the red pill as well. This is the gravely mistaken notion that the top 10% of men, fuck 100% of the women or some nonsense like that. Okay... but what defines this mythical "top 10%?" Obviously it would be attributes like looks, height, cock size, money and fame.

Let's leave fame off the list...

- 3% of males look like male models.

- 10% of men are over six feet tall.

- 1% of men have a penis seven inches or longer *and* at least six inches in girth.

- 3.75% of men make \$200G/year or more.

Remember the infamous "Female Delusion Calculator" app made famous on the "Fresh and Fit" podcast? It only factors in height, income and age. So let's tailor the app's criteria to make it more realistic with respect to accounting for what women actually desire in terms of physicality, and then crunch the numbers. To do so, we will also drop age as a criteria, because we don't want it to return "zero" as a result...

You calculate the percentage of men who have all three physical criteria by multiplying the individual probabilities:

- Percentage who have male model looks: 3%

- Percentage who are tall: 10%

- Percentage who have a big cock: 1%

The probability that a man has all three attributes is:

$$0.03 \times 0.10 \times 0.01 = 0.00003 \text{ or } 0.003\%!!!$$

So, the first thing to realize is that the "top 10% of men" is actually the "top 0.003% of men." That's 3/1000th of 1% of men!

Now given there are ~170 million men in the United States, this gives us ~5,000 men who meet this criteria. I haven't included income as a factor because then there would be only ~192 men that meet all of a female's criteria! In the entire United States!!!

So, income aside, both the red and black pill are asserting that a pool of ~5,000 men are fucking all of the women in this nation? Given there are ~72 million women under the age of 35 in the United States, each of those ~5,000 men would have to have a body count of ~14,000 women. Are you aware of any men who have such a body count? Even if each of these ~5,000 men fucked a new girl every day, it would take them over *38 years* to achieve such a body count. It would also mean that all of the women in the United States under the age of 35, would get fucked only once in those 35 years! Now, given that women under the age of 35 in the United States probably have (on average) a body count of around 64 men, you can see how all of this red and black pill nonsense quickly dissolves away.

Pro Tip: *I realize that "statistics" will state that the average number of sexual partners for women in the United States under the age of 35, is 8 partners.* This is utterly laughable, as clearly all of the women, in all of these surveys, only counted men with whom they had "official relationships." In my anecdotal life experience, whatever a woman says her body count is, you need to multiply that number by 8. So a woman who only claims 5 sexual partners, in reality has had sex with 40 men. This is her actual body count. So if the "official statistics" claim that she has had on average 8 partners, then the true number of men she has had sex with is 64.

The point of all of this is just to show you that the black pill philosophy is simply not constructive to entertain *beyond a certain point*.

Female Trinity #1 – The 3 Types of Men in A Woman's Life

There are only two types of men a woman will have a *relationship* with. However, there is a third type of man *in every woman's life* who is completely ignored by blue, red and black pill "philosophers" alike. Ironically, this third type of man is usually completely unaware that he is in any woman's life at all, for that matter. The proverbial invisible man! No, he is *not* a "sigma male." Again, there is *no such thing*.

Understanding this type of man and the nature of his predicament is one of the missing pieces that will complete your understanding of what is commonly referred to as "game." Without understanding the game in it's entirety, it is *impossible* to play it so as to actually "win" at said game unless by lucky circumstances. I put "win" in quotations because it is entirely possible that the game cannot be won in the way one would ideally want to win it. That will be up to you to decide when you have finished reading this book. So without further ado, here are the three types of men:

- **The bad boy.** Also known as the "fuck boy," this is the loser guy whom she unconsciously attempts to work out her childhood trauma with, but since she lacks conscious awareness, she just piles even more trauma on top of her root childhood trauma, which makes her task ever harder. She jumps from loser-to-loser, riding the infamous "cock carousel," but instead of having empowering sex involving full-body, non-clitoral orgasmic wave upon orgasmic wave, she is basically frigid and spinning her wheels, degrading herself sexually while blaming everything on men and "low self-esteem" brought on by the "patriarchy." She is filled with self-hatred, and will often explode when this is pointed out to her.

Ultimately, she is a cowardly whore "playing house" despite being an adult.

The "bad boy" is mistakenly labeled as an "alpha male" because of certain traits that he displays that are shared by alphas, such as not caring what others think, for example. Even if he were truly alpha, however, it would be largely irrelevant with respect to commanding attraction from women. No, his power to attract stems from being as damaged as the females he is attracting. Since far more women are damaged than men due to their receptive natures, *this* is the *actual* explanation for why most men are invisible to most women. It isn't because most men are under a certain height, or don't look like movie stars, etc. It is simply because *most men are not fucked up to the degree that most women are, so most men cannot generate attraction with most women.* It is also very dangerous to assume that just because many females behave in a certain way, that their behavior is indicative of some sort of *inherent* "female nature." I mean, would you base "male nature" solely upon your observations of men locked away in insane asylums? Of course not, but when most women *belong* in an insane asylum, yet roam free on Instagram and TikTok instead, the abnormal quickly becomes the normal, and our perceptions of female nature get very skewed. Furthermore, as I will point out later on in this book, women who were *not* naturally submissive were violently taken out of existence by utterly misogynistic empires such as the Roman empire, the Mongol empire, and the Ottoman empire. Empires like these have left an almost unimaginable degree of ancestral trauma in the descendants of women who survived their rule. This also completely distorts our perceptions of *inherent* female nature.

- **The boyfriend/husband.** 99% of women are not *in love* with their "significant" other and in the majority of cases are *not even sexually attracted to them.* They *tolerate* them at best, yet for how long can they keep up the ruse? Why do you think that the divorce rate is so damn high and nobody has a happy marriage? Duh! Men fail to grasp this, because this prison that women engineer for themselves of their own free will is *inconceivable* to a man, as no man on this planet would retain a girlfriend that he is not sexually attracted to, let alone marry a woman he is not *in love* with. So why do woman do so? Because they are natural whores who desire the resources of men. That's about the jist of it. Nonetheless, men *must* get the following reality into their heads: *if a woman wants to date or marry you, this is not a badge of honor but rather the gravest of insults.* You are neither a bad boy, nor a man she truly loves or is truly sexually infatuated with. You are just a tool to be used, abused and discarded. This is the fate of most men, and men must do everything in their power to not step into this animal trap. Instead, they should strive to be worthy of being cast in a lead role in one of Rocco Siffredi's "Animal Trainer" DVDs.

It's funny because the other day I was listening to this *utter shit* about how women stop having sex with their partner because he stops "showing up" like he used to. This term "showing up" is an expression used by dopey woke bitches – the same ones who enjoy cuckoldry and "open relationships," and this term can be used interchangeably with other euphemisms like "holding space" and "being present." Whenever you hear these words uttered, you know the woman uttering them has more issues than a magazine stand, and is a consummate liar to boot. Do yourself a favor and just run.

The only reason women stop having sex with their husbands is because *they never wanted to have sex with them in the first place.* Now that they have them trapped in a marriage and possibly with kids as an added layer of chains, there is no more need to have sex with their plow horse!

"I used to be a wild stallion, running free. Now I'm just a broken down plow horse!" —Drunken Irish guy in front of wife.

It's ironic that woman will complain about how arranged marriages used to force them to marry someone they didn't want to have sex with, *not realizing that now that they are "free," women still actively choose to marry someone they don't want to have sex with*!

So much for feminism. So much for progress. It's ironic, really…

One time I was at the gym with one of my training partners, and there was this girl who frequently worked out there. We started talking with her, and I made a joke about how when her boyfriend comes to pick her up after her workouts, he always seems super jealous and paranoid, like he suspects she is cheating on him. The boyfriend was a pretty handsome guy, too. She agreed that he is super jealous and always thinks that she is cheating on him. I pointed out that usually when a guy is like that, it is because on some level, some part of him knows his suspicions are actually true. She started laughing and said "Of course I am cheating on him, he can't satisfy me!" I then asked her what the fuck she is doing with a guy who cannot satisfy her in the slightest?

She said, "Look, I am 23 and when I turn 25, the guys that I want to have sex with, won't want to have sex with me anymore because I will be too old. So I figured I'd get a head start now when I am only 23, and find a guy I can *tolerate* and cheat on him until I can no longer do so. By then, I will be used to him and be able to continue to stay with him, and *maybe* I will get lucky once in a while and find someone to cheat on him with." She then proceeded to tell me all about this "bad boy" whom she pines for and how when she goes home she rides some fat dildo with another dildo shoved up her ass and how her "boyfriend" has no idea about her really hardcore sexual nature.

Our conversation reminded me of when I was in bartending school, which is one of the best places to meet complete sluts. So one day I had this 19 year old "lab partner" and we would practice mixing drinks for each other. She *also* started telling me about her jealous boyfriend, and when I mentioned that jealous boyfriends are usually jealous for a reason, she laughed and said, "Well of course, I am cheating on him. I go home to him after other guys cum in my pussy and make him eat my pussy. He has no clue!" How nasty. If I had a dollar for every time a woman confessed that to me, I'd probably have $10-$15 now. When class was coming to an end that day, she looked at me and straight up asked me if I wanted to accompany her to the bathroom and fuck her ass.

Pro tip: To any females reading this book, please remember that if you don't want your boyfriend cheating on you, you need to give him as much sex as he wants, whenever and whichever way he wants it. If his balls are completely drained 24/7, it is almost impossible for him to cheat. Furthermore, if you are willing to do any sexual act imaginable with him, he will have even less incentive to attempt to cheat. The reality is that if you don't want to do anal, deep throat, swallow his load, etc., then you really don't like him to begin with, and have no business wasting either his time or yours. If you take care of your man sexually, give him lots of positive reinforcement, and bake him cookies once in a while, you've pretty much got him under your thumb. I mean, how hard is it to bake a mean tray of cookies and learn to eat ass, you fucking dummy? I know, it's really fucking hard to do if you are not even attracted to him *like that* to begin with.

Shortly after that gym conversation I remember meeting this girl in a store nearby. We really hit it off. I asked her to hang out, after chatting and flirting for a long time, but she said that she can't. So I asked her what it is that she has to do, that is so much better then spending time with a man with whom she has an amazing connection with, and a deep level of attraction for. She replied that she has a date tonight with some guy she met on a dating site. I said, "Oh, and is he a better option than me?" She went on to confess that she isn't even attracted to the guy at all, but he fits into her "plans" and she knows she can make him do whatever she wants. She then points out that she can clearly see that I cannot be controlled, nor transformed into a workhorse for her dreams, so therefore I am a waste of her time, no matter how attracted she is to me and no matter how great we "click."

You must understand, that even if a girl has a boyfriend and *appears* not to be riding the cock carousel, she most probably still is. Shit, I know literal hookers with multiple boyfriends and none of them even know she is a hooker! Once again, the point I am trying to drive home here, is that a girl who wants to date you, or make you her boyfriend or husband, is never actually *into you* in the way that matters to you most (the sexual way). This is *why* they want to date you, be your girlfriend, or marry you to begin with! Because you are the man they will *tolerate* while they get fucked by other men whom they are *actually* attracted to.

- **The man she is genuinely in love with.** In most cases, a woman will *never* actually have a relationship with this guy. She *may* fuck him a few times, and then *run like hell*. But in most cases, she won't even fuck him. It is a tragedy of supreme irony, because the truth is that **the secret to having a successful relationship with a woman, is that the woman needs to be genuinely in love with you.** Now I am not talking about "engineering" love via "trauma-bonding" or "love-bombing," which are both techniques used by narcissistic males (and females). I am talking about genuine love. While you cannot engineer genuine love, you can engineer your

43

own life so that it is natural for as many women as possible to genuinely fall in love with you. But, this is not a strategy for getting women to actually *be* with you, let alone sleep with you. Like I said, most women genuinely love a man from *afar*. Why? Because most women (and most men albeit to a lesser degree) are a bundle of unresolved traumas from childhood, and to actually *be* with someone they genuinely love, is extremely painful and mentally destabilizing. It is as if being in love were akin to shining a light on who they truly are, and then not being able to stand the sight of what they see. Rich and famous people fall victim to this in a parallel way, when the "light" of fame and wealth creates the opportunity for them to really see themselves in contrast with how the general public sees them, and without the distractions of material pursuit, and they hate what they see, so they start abusing all sorts of drugs, alcohol and acting out.

When you fall in love, you really only have two options:

- Use the love you feel as motivation to face down your demons and enjoy your good fortune as a reward.
- Run away like a coward.

Guess what most people choose? In reality, while being genuinely in love should inspire people to want to free themselves from their traumas and become whole, so they can enjoy this love they were lucky enough to stumble upon, this is rarely what happens in actual practice.

Therefore, to be this sort of man that inspires love, is to reside in a unique type of hell, with one's only comfort being high-end escorts, so having money is essential especially if you happen to be this rare type of man.

Oh, if only I had known how things work sooner... but I am sure you have heard the saying, "youth is wasted on the young?"

Before I end this part of the book, I should point out that there is this line of reasoning out there in cyberspace that if a woman falls in love with you and runs away in terror, all you need to do is not chase after her, and if you "give her space," she will ultimately come back and be with you. This is total bullshit. She will not come back no matter what you do, since she is pretty much a "goner" when this happens. The only thing you can do, is directly confront her with the truth behind her behavior, before casting her aside to live in shame. Because even if she did return one day, it will only be after she has given away all that was best about her, to the worst sort of men imaginable. Most women dole out access to their holes in the same way you give out loose change to homeless people. This is not something a man with any sort of pride, dignity, or self-worth is able to stomach.

PART II: TRAUMA AND THE ROOTS OF DYSFUNCTION

The Trauma Foundation

When a prey animal narrowly escapes death at the hands of a predator, it will lay down somewhere and shake. By shaking, it discharges the excess and unexpressed energy that arises with the action of running away in terror of being ripped apart and eaten alive. Once the prey animal has finished discharging this excess and unexpressed energy, it gets up and walks away as if nothing ever happened.

But what would happen if the prey animal never "shook it off?" What if the prey animal became ashamed of its shaking and tensed up during the process to the point that its shaking would cease *prematurely*? Well, if the prey animal got up and walked away *at that point* without completing the "discharge process," it would feel like it was frozen, or "unalive." Yet beneath that state of "unaliveness" would still be this faint, felt sense of unrelenting terror stuck in the subconscious, exerting an influence upon the prey animal's conscious decision making process, from the shadows. After all, *where is the subconscious mind located?* In the physical body, of course! To be 100% accurate, the mind as a whole is *outside* of the body, and can be interfaced with via various organs and parts of the body - the brain being the most well known, which interfaces with the conscious mind, much like a computer interfaces with the internet. The computer, however, is not the internet itself! In the same manner, your brain is not your conscious mind, nor does it *contain* your conscious mind. Again, the part of the mind that is subconscious, can be interfaced with via the body. This is where the term "gut brain" comes from.

The "gut brain" or **enteric nervous system (ENS)** is a real thing, though it's not quite the same as having brain cells in your gut.

The ENS consists of about **500 million neurons** embedded in the walls of your digestive tract, stretching from your esophagus to your rectum. That's more neurons than in your spinal cord! These neurons can operate independently of your brain, controlling digestion, gut motility, and secretions largely on their own.

The ENS communicates extensively with your actual brain via the **vagus nerve** and other pathways (called the "gut-brain axis"). This is why:

- Emotions can affect your digestion (butterflies in your stomach, stress-induced nausea).

- Gut problems can influence mood and mental health.

- About 90% of the body's serotonin is actually produced in the gut.

So while these aren't literally "brain cells" transplanted to your gut, they are specialized neurons that form a sophisticated nervous system capable of complex information processing. It's sometimes called the "second brain" because it can function semi-independently, though it doesn't handle consciousness like your actual brain does. It does, however, handle the *subconscious*.

Anyway, assuming the prey animal never finished discharging and processing this excess and unexpressed energy via its **enteric nervous system,** the prey animal would start to exhibit strange behaviors from that point on:

- The prey animal would start doing irresponsible things to feel alive again, perhaps it would court danger by running across active highways on purpose, just to feel alive.

- The prey animal would find itself roaming the inner city, seeking out access to recreational drugs.

- The prey animal would begin to tap its hooves compulsively when standing still, perpetually attempting to bleed off some of that energy that was never discharged.

- The prey animal would find itself running away from predators more often than usual, as it would be subconsciously seeking out the original trauma, in the hopes of having another opportunity (upon successfully escaping of course), to shake to completion and fully release the stored up energetic charge it is currently stuck with. Sadly, since the prey animal would not be consciously aware of this dynamic, it would simply doom itself to being chased incessantly by predators until it is eventually overcome and eaten.

In case you are a bit slow, that prey animal is *you*. So the next time you see someone doing dangerous activities for thrills, addicted to drugs, behaving in compulsive ways, finding themselves in toxic relationships over and over again, or just flat out seeking their own destruction, know that behind this apparent insanity is unresolved trauma. Once again, the core imperative of the human organism is not physical survival, but psychic survival and stability.

I know you may be uncomfortable viewing yourself as a "prey animal." This is because humans mistakenly believe themselves to be at the top of the food chain on this planet. They are not. They are nothing but prey for 4th and 5th dimensional predators and pretty much helpless to do anything about it. The reality is that this entire planet is just a giant feedlot ruled over by the planet Saturn, which transmits the construct for the "simulation" we are living in. In that regard, you are all no different than pigs, cattle and chickens being led to slaughter over-and-over again. When not being harvested en masse in wars, your energy is slowly being bled out and sucked dry on a daily basis.

Let me ask you, why did the infamous "Vlad the Impaler" actually impale 20,000 people to create a literal forest of impalements? Impaling 20,000 people is a *lot* of work, and the work is gruesome, given he impaled them through their rectums. The official story is that he did it to turn back the Ottoman Empire's army from advancing on his territory, which they did. But the unofficial, true story is that he did it to feed 4th and 5th dimensional entities on all the pain and suffering, and consequently curry favor with them. It is not much different from Ghenghis Khan traveling to a "sacred mountain" to ask permission to conquer the world. Whom do you think he was asking permission *from*? You should also realize that it wasn't difficult for Vlad to order such horrors, as he himself had been tortured and abused by the Ottoman Empire since childhood, and carried endless trauma himself. This is but one example of how trauma begets more trauma, in order to feed the machine we will call "the matrix."

While most humans are not necessarily being chased by predators out in the wild anymore, or being subjected to the horrors of mass impalement, they are still often pursued and subsequently abused in childhood by sexual predators. For these children, there is often no escape and they are simply abused over and over again. My late biological mother was raped constantly around the age of ten by Russian soldiers during the Russian "rape of Europe." She never even hinted towards this aspect of her past until she was quite old and had a brush with death. While growing up, I never understood how my mom could be so crazy, but once I knew about her childhood, it all made sense and I couldn't hold her craziness against her anymore, that's for sure! She ended up getting Alzheimer's and dying from cancer of her colon, which subsequently spread to her liver. Again, why did the top brass of the Russian military give permission for their soldiers to rape millions of women in occupied territories? To create trauma, as trauma creates both present and future "feeding opportunities" for 4th and 5th dimensional entities.

Often I suspect that people end up with Alzheimer's because they just don't want to remember anything anymore. It's just a suspicion... I could be wrong. But there are several psychological theories and clinical observations that suggest Alzheimer's might sometimes function as an unconscious defense mechanism, though this remains a minority perspective in mainstream medicine. Some researchers propose that in certain cases, severe cognitive decline could represent the mind's ultimate protective mechanism - essentially "shutting down" to avoid overwhelming trauma, guilt, or unbearable memories. Some therapists even report that certain dementia patients seem to have "given up" psychologically before cognitive symptoms appeared, suggesting a possible psychosomatic component in some cases. This remains speculative rather than established science, but the mind-body connection in neurodegenerative diseases is an active area of research.

The Impact of Birth Trauma

We also have to keep in mind that many people experience traumatic births that leave deep programming in their psyche that is very hard to access and release, let alone reprogram. For example, many women opt for c-sectional births in order to avoid the pain of childbirth and because they fear their pussies will no longer provide pleasure for men once a baby passes through them. Doctors will also push c-sectional deliveries because they can be *scheduled*, saving time that would be spent waiting for a mother to go into labor, yet such a birth is traumatic for the child and installs a program instructing them to be helpless and to rely on aid from others. Another example is a baby getting inadvertantly choked by the umbilical cord.

In my own case, I got stuck in my biological mother's birth canal, as she was not capable of pushing me out. Doctors tried to pull me out with forceps, yet only succeeded in denting my skull. So they gave up and said

I will either push myself out, or die. It took me almost two hours to deliver myself. You don't think this has had an impact on my life? It gave me strength and perseverance, but it also programmed my subconscious mind to make things very difficult for myself.

I never even knew about the circumstances of my birth until I was in a Native American sweat lodge where the pitch-darkness, confined space and suffocating heat, replicated my experience in the womb and triggered the memory. When this experience prompted me to ask my biological father about the circumstances of my birth, he told me the story of my self-delivery and even admitted that he had realized at the time, that **this would have a major impact on my life.** Had he told me about this when I was young, I believe it would have saved me a lot of grief because then I would have been *aware* of these dynamics playing themselves out in real time, and I would have had the opportunity to try and change those dynamics. *It is hard to change something you are not aware of.* But all families have secrets and generational traumas, and things they never talk about. As my family were German-speaking immigrants, keeping secrets was second nature to them. In fact, Germans are probably the best at keeping secrets. Maybe that has something to do with random strangers always confessing shit to me?

Another thing in my own life that had an impact, was the fact that I was fed soy infant formula as a baby, which is the worst shit you can give a child. Naturally breast milk is best, and if you can't get that, then raw milk would be the next best option, followed by pasteurized milk of the highest quality. Just add in a few drops of Lugol's iodine to make your kid as smart as possible. Lugol's iodine should also be consumed by the pregnant mother as well, if you don't want your kid to be a retard. So if you knock a bitch up, force her to ingest iodine on the daily so your kid comes out as smart as possible.

Here are some facts:

- Iodine deficiency during pregnancy and early childhood can cause irreversible neurological and psychological deficits, lowering a child's IQ by 8–10 points.

- Even mild deficiency may result in delayed mental development, lower verbal IQ, and poorer reading comprehension and accuracy.

- Correction of even mild-to-moderate iodine deficiency has been shown to improve cognitive performance in school-age children.

In addition to some Lugol's iodine, throw some extra vitamins A, D & K2 into the milk so the jaw bone can attain the proper length to make for massive dental arches and natural good looks based on golden mean mathematical ratios. You will save money on braces as your kids won't need them. Adequate intake of vitamins A, D, and K2 during critical growth periods is essential for optimal jaw bone development in children, and this is especially the case later on when a child experiences massive jaw bone growth. In short, you can spare your child needing to "looksmaxx" when it is older by making these simple dietary changes. The age range when a child experiences a significant growth spurt in jawbone length, particularly the mandible (lower jaw) varies by sex:

- Females: The jaw growth spurt usually occurs between ages 10 and 12. Most girls reach peak mandibular growth velocity during this period.

- Males: The growth spurt typically happens later, between 13.6 and 14.5 years. Boys tend to have a longer and more pronounced jaw growth phase during adolescence.

In general, if you want your kid to be a winner in life, their diet should include as much raw milk, and as much raw beef liver or raw lamb liver as possible. They don't have to go all "Liver King" and eat *nothing but* those things, but they must have them in their diet as often as possible. It isn't that hard to find raw milk if you make the effort, and quality beef liver is easily found. Even if you cook the liver, it is fine, although I find it tastes better raw. There are ways to prepare liver that can be found online that will make it taste as delicious as possible. Raw eggs are also awesome, and can be blended with ice cream or raw milk to be palatable. Finally, your kid should only drink water run through a filter that filters out pesticides and other nanoparticulates. Because if your kid grows up drinking tap water and subsisting on "food" and "drinks" pumped out by big corporations, chances are they will grow up stupid and ugly, as well as obese with a micro-penis and man-boobs to boot! One time I was in a supermarket and saw like 12 ice cream sandwiches for $3 and I was thinking to myself "How is this even possible?" So I read the ingredient label and as far I could tell, there was nothing in there that even remotely resembled an ice cream ingredient list so I can only imagine the long-term consequences of consuming this sort of trash. To be fair though, food scientists started out with good intentions, because at one time, famines raged across this planet and millions starved, and starvation is absolutely horrid. So a lot of the "frankenfoods" people love to complain about, originally came about as solutions to mass starvation. Over time, I can only imagine that greed took over, but originally the idea was a noble one.

Why was I fed soy infant formula? When I confronted my father about it, he said that I refused to nurse on my mother's breast. I found this strange, but when I brought this up to my mother, she reacted with revulsion and commented that breast feeding was utterly disgusting. Is it any surprise I refused to nurse on a woman who found the act so repulsive? They should have given me cow's milk though, instead of soy milk. However, I did get plenty of beef growing up, and my hunger for meat was insatiable.

Are Women Inherently Loving Because They Birth Children?

As we will discover in much greater detail later on, a woman is not vulnerable in her heart as is commonly and mistakenly assumed. This false, commonly held belief that a woman is soft-hearted, is based on the "logic" that because a woman has to nurture children, she therefore has a soft and vulnerable heart. Nothing could be further from the truth, and to fail to grasp the actual reality of the female heart is a fatal error. Quite literally! If you heed my prodding and read the works of Lloyd deMause. you will see that women historically have had no qualms murdering their own children.

The work of deMause goes on to reveal that infanticide by mothers was not an aberration, but a systemic practice across cultures and centuries, supported by statistical evidence of skewed gender ratios and widespread historical documentation. Here are just five out of many numerous quotes from his work in this regard:

- On Ancient Infanticide Being Routine and Accepted:

  "The killing of legitimate children even by wealthy parents was so common that Polybius blamed it for the depopulation of Greece: 'In our own time the whole of Greece has been subject to a low birth-rate and a general decrease of the population, owing to which cities have become deserted and the land has ceased to yield fruit, although there have neither been continuous wars nor epidemics... as men had fallen into such a state of pretentiousness, avarice and indolence that they did not wish to marry, or if they married to rear the children born to them, or at most as a rule but one or two of them'."

- On the Casual Nature of Child Disposal:

  "Children were thrown into rivers, flung into dung-heaps and cess trenches, 'potted' in jars to starve to death, and exposed on every hill and roadside, 'a prey for birds, food for wild beasts to rend' (Euripides, Ion, 504)."

- On Medieval Continuation of the Practice:

  "As late as 1527, one priest admitted that 'the latrines resound with the cries of children who have been plunged into them'."

- On the Statistical Evidence of Gender-Based Killing:

  "Available statistics for antiquity show large surpluses of boys over girls; for instance, out of 79 families who gained Milesian citizenship about 228-220 B.C., there were 118 sons and 28 daughters; 32 families had one child, 31 had two... Of 600 families from second-century inscriptions at Delphi, one per cent raised two daughters."

- On 18th Century European Infanticide:

  "By the eighteenth century, there is no question that there was high incidence of infanticide in every country in Europe. As more foundling homes were opened in each country, babies poured in from all over, and the homes quickly ran out of room. Even though Thomas Coram opened his Foundling Hospital in 1741 because he couldn't bear to see the dying babies lying in the gutters and rotting on the dung-heaps of London, by the 1890s dead babies were still a common sight in London streets."

This is *the* reason why so many people are so passionately, and often violently, opposed to abortion. Because they know deep down in the recesses of their being, that their own mothers were contemplating their murders while they were still in the womb. On the opposite end of the spectrum, there is *a reason* why so many women are so passionately, and often violently, *in favor of* abortion.

They simply *adore* murdering their own children!

Don't believe me? Do you realize how many women have had *multiple* abortions? Now why use abortion as a form of birth control when there are so many easier methods that are far less taxing on the female body to boot? You'd have to be stupid as shit to put yourself through an abortion when all you need to do is take a "morning after" pill or get an IUD installed, should you be too lazy or undisciplined to take birth control pills or make guys use condoms. So let's look at some statistics and then ask ourselves if so many women are really this stupid, or if they just love killing their unborn children…

There are 82.2 million women in the United States under the age of 45, and 25% of them will have had an abortion by the time they turn 45. That's 20.5 million women getting abortions. But here is the crazy part: ~43% of women who got an abortion had at least one previous abortion, and ~19% had two or more previous abortions! I have personally met women who have had six abortions! That means that ~8.8 or almost 9 million women in the United States have had multiple abortions. From a percentage standpoint, that's just under 11% of women under 45 who are getting multiple abortions. However, imagine if 11% of men under 45 had murdered at least 2 children? Surely someone would draw attention to it!

Now some people may attempt to counter this by saying that abortion isn't murder, and while personally I don't care if women get abortions or not, to say it isn't murder *just because* it is still inside of her womb is pretty stupid. If you killed a pregnant woman, I don't think there would be a prosecutor in the United States that wouldn't charge you with two murders and I don't think you'd find a single person who *wouldn't* say that you murdered her baby along with her. But a significant percentage of those *same* people will simultaneously claim that abortion isn't murder. What gives? I suppose it's only murder if the mother wants the baby? How convenient...

Moving right along with respect to *true* female nature, I have both witnessed and heard testimony from others in regards to, mothers throwing their own children out into the streets in order to take a cock that makes them cum. Women are all about sex and their pussies, as opposed to love and their hearts, while it is men that are all about love despite women *projecting onto them* that "all they think about is sex." If you doubt this, talk to any man going through a divorce and they will *all* say: "I don't care about her or the money, I just want to be able to see my kids." In most cases, the woman couldn't give a shit about her kids and uses them as weapons to punish her ex-husband, and extract as many resources from him as possible through the corrupted family court system.

Let's be honest: since the man in most cases is either the breadwinner, or else will be forced to pay for his child anyway via the child support system, why not give custody of the children to the father 100% of the time? This will also prevent women from mooching off the system. Furthermore, mothers are only important for the first few years of a child's life anyway. After that, the father is the most important. If you doubt this, look at single-parent households... When it's just the father, the children turn out to be winners. When it's just the mother, her son winds up in prison and her daughter winds up getting her asshole gaped in some online video:

- 85% of all youths in prison come from fatherless homes – 20 times the average.

- 70% of youths in state-operated institutions come from fatherless homes – 9 times the average.

- In 1996, 70% of inmates in state juvenile detention centers serving long sentences were raised by single mothers.

- Children from single-mother households are 10 times more likely to abuse chemical substances.

- 75% percent of adolescent patients in substance abuse centers are from fatherless homes.

- Children from single-mother households are 5 times more likely to commit suicide than children from both unbroken households and single-father households, 9 times more likely to drop out of high school, 14 times more likely to commit rape, 20 times more likely to end up in prison and 32 times more likely to run away from home

- 63% of youth suicides are from fatherless homes – 5 times the average.

- 90% of all homeless and runaway children are from fatherless homes – 32 times the average.

- The Journal of Research in Crime and Delinquency reports that the most reliable indicator of violent crime in a community is the proportion of fatherless families.

- State-by-state analysis indicates that, in general, a 10 percent increase in the number of children living in single-parent homes (including divorces) accompanies a 17 percent increase in juvenile crime.

if women are so selfless and concerned about their own children, why would they stack such odds against them? Because they don't give a shit about their own children! If they did, historical rates of infanticide and current abortion statistics would not be what they are. Furthermore, given the above statistics, why the fuck do 80% of custody scenarios end up with the woman getting custody? It is utterly destructive to society, which of course is the goal, in order to facilitate the creation of more trauma and suffering. Are you sure we still live in a patriarchy, BTW? I know some will attempt to counter me by stating that only 4% of custody disputes are resolved by the courts, and that 80% of custody scenarios are decided by the parents themselves. Well, that's because the men know they have no chance in court anyway so they just surrender, because in the 11% of cases that go to mediation, the woman gets custody 100% of the time. This shows insane court bias. My detractors may then try to argue that of the 4% of cases that go to trial, only 1.5% go to completion, and in 80% of these cases, the father wins. So they will argue why don't more fathers go to trial if my contention that fathers are so "into their children" is correct, and they have such a high probability of winning? It's because in these 4% of cases, the mother was literally smoking the rock or doing something so outrageous, the courts simply could not give the mother custody! Basically, unless the mother shows up to court with a needle sticking out of her arm, or uses the child as a hood ornament for her car, she will get custody! I've known women who openly worked as strippers and prostitutes, who kept a house filled with pitbulls, who had full custody of their children. I can only guess their baby-daddies were either dead or in prison. Mind you, these women certainly made enough money to support their kids, but at they same time their choice of profession is only going to turbocharge the statistics for the children of single mothers I shared earlier.

Pro Tip: Steer clear of *any* woman who owns a pit bull, let alone *two or more* of them, as the pit bulls represent her undying love for the "bad boys" and the assortment of damaged males whose cum she finds herself regularly farting into the toilet. In general, a woman who owns a dog is telegraphing that she is *needy*. If the dog is big, this *can* work in your favor. If the dog is small, it means she is also *controlling,* and this will work against you. A woman who owns a cat is ideal, because she is independent, but you still have to be very careful despite this "green flag."

Mothers can be real monsters, don't kid yourselves, and there were two major legal events in the 1970s that really helped to bring childhood trauma back into vogue because for a long while, childhoods had actually been improving and this could not be allowed to continue. After all, the children of these monsters needed to be able to grow up, and project their now subconscious inner drama with their own mothers onto the "motherland" of their country or those of others, and consequently go fight wars either for or against her, that will again feed 4th and 5th dimensional entities. So first, California Governor Ronald Reagan signed the Family Law Act, which took effect in January 1970, allowing for couples to divorce based on "irreconcilable differences" without having to prove fault like adultery or cruelty. "No-fault" divorce then gradually became legal state-by-state over time. Second, abortion became legal nationwide in the United States in January 1973, with the Supreme Court's decision in *Roe v. Wade*. This enabled women to happily return to their time-honored pastime of infanticide, and to file for divorce the moment they found a better cock or more resources to be had elsewhere, leaving a generation of traumatized children in the wake of their monstrousness. These children (Generation X) of course grew up to perpetuate the cycle, which continues to this day.

The Trauma of Circumcision and Satanic Corruption of Religion

As if children being murdered by their own mothers or at least finding themselves under the threat of being murdered by their own mothers wasn't traumatic enough, in the United States male children also enjoy the added bonus of having their genitals mutilated for "hygienic reasons." Because washing your cock in the shower is apparently soooo challenging, even though a pole is far easier to clean than is a hole, and stroking your erect cock with soapy water is just soooo unpleasant, right? What's shitty about humans is their tendency to perpetuate their own suffering, by inflicting the same suffering they experienced, upon their own children and of course upon each other. This sounds nuts on the surface, as the common belief is that parents want their children to have better lives than they did, but this is often not the case and here is a short anecdotal story to illustrate it...

One day I was at a party in a lounge in NYC and *somehow* the topic of circumcision came up. It wasn't me, that's for sure. Honest! But then some coked up idiot started defending circumcision out of the blue and bragging about how he got his son circumcised. People were commenting in response, so I casually pointed out how strange it is that female genital mutilation in other parts of the world is met with such horror, yet nobody seems to care about the mutilation of a male infant's genitals in the United States. This abject failure of a man (and father) literally exploded on me in a rage that shocked everyone at the party. I cannot remember the sheer incoherence that sperged from his mouth, but I calmly pointed out that the rage he was feeling was his own repressed rage at having his own genitals mutilated - triggered by the sudden realization that he has perpetrated the exact same trauma upon his own son whom he claims to love, that was perpetrated upon him. You're welcome! He got even angrier and I thought he may attempt to murder me, but instead ran off to the bathroom to snort more cocaine. What a fucking loser...

You'll see this phenomenon in hospitals as well: when a parent refuses to circumcise their child, you may observe what seems like the entire hospital, start pressuring and bullying them to proceed with the procedure and the parent will have to literally grab their child and escape from said hospital. Ask yourself, why would a hospital be so keen on a male child not leaving with his foreskin intact? Yes, it is true that foreskins removed during circumcision are sold for use in several medical and cosmetic applications:

- Cells from human foreskin, particularly human foreskin fibroblasts (HFFs), have been used since the 1970s to help heal stubborn wounds, such as chronic diabetic foot ulcers. Skin substitute, use foreskin-derived cells to treat these conditions.

- Foreskin tissue is used for skin grafts in cases such as repairing damaged eyelids, webbed fingers and toes, and even reconstructing parts of the anal canal. Decellularized foreskin matrices are also used in reconstructive and regenerative surgery, including genitourinary and aesthetic procedures.

- Foreskin cells are valuable for drug testing, disease modeling, and the production of stem cells for research into genetic disorders and treatments for infections.

- Foreskin-derived fibroblasts are used in some cosmetic products and wrinkle treatments, promising to improve the structure and appearance of aging or scarred skin.

- Some beauty products, particularly those marketed for anti-aging, contain ingredients derived from baby foreskin cells.

In summary, foreskin tissue cells are utilized in a range of medical and cosmetic fields due to their regenerative properties and usefulness in tissue engineering and wound healing. Therefore, there is an incentive to physically and psychologically mutilate children in order to obtain a constant supply. Yet, this does not explain just how *unreasonably hostile* hospital staff get when you decline to circumcise your child, nor does it explain the origins of this seemingly senseless traumatic practice.

Seemingly senseless, because the history of circumcision has nothing to do with cleanliness. But it makes perfect sense when you realize circumcision originated in cultures of old that were based in warfare because it made male children grow up to be more prone to violence, as the act of circumcision fuses the child's sexuality with violence. Notice how humans are always being driven towards warfare? Who benefits and how and why? We already know the answer! Spartans not only practiced circumcision, they abandoned all of their male babies overnight in the wild claiming the practice made sure only the strong children survived, when in reality it traumatized them and hardened them for warfare as adults. Is it any shock that Spartan men only fucked women for procreation and reserved their lust and love for other men given their exposure to such trauma in their childhood? Notice their hatred for women and twisted relationship with motherhood? This is *not* coincidence.

Circumcision today outside of America is *only* practiced by Moslems and Jews. Since high IQ Jews have such a disproportionate influence over low IQ Amerimutts relative to their population numbers, it is no wonder they convinced everyone in the United States to circumcise their male infants. Plus, they need Amerimutts to fight wars for Israel, so it makes perfect sense. No other western nation engages in this abject stupidity. Europoors didn't fall for it, because their average IQ is a few points higher than that of Amerimutts, and they are not expected to fight wars for Israel. Now a lot of people don't know this, but Jewish culture was not originally based on mercantilism as the stereotypes would indicate, but rather on warfare and conquest. This is why they are in love with circumcision, as are the Moslems, since Islamic culture is also based on warfare and conquest.

Ashkenazi Judaism is rooted in warfare as opposed to mercantilism.

Historians like to deny that that Ashkenazi (non-semitic) Jewish culture in the time of Khazaria was based in warfare and instead like to say that it was based on controlling trade routes and collecting tribute. However, *tribute collection inherently requires military dominance* as people only pay tribute when they've been conquered or coerced through the threat of warfare. Looking back at the sources with this understanding:

- **Military Conquest for Tribute**: The Khazars controlled and exacted tribute from the Alani and other northern Caucasian peoples; from the Magyars (Hungarians) inhabiting the area around the Donets River; from the Goths; and from the Greek colonies on the Crimean Peninsula. The Volga Bulgars and numerous Slavic tribes also recognized the Khazars as their overlords.

- **Extensive Military Control**: The Khazars had their greatest power over other tribes in the 9th century, controlling eastern Slavs, Magyars, Pechenegs, Burtas, North Caucasian Huns, and other tribes and demanding tribute from them.

- **Slave Trading Through Warfare**: The Khazars mainly enslaved Slavs, but also likely sold captured Turks from rival tribes as slaves as well. The Khazars seemed to have preferred to raid the Slavs during the winter for slaves.

- **Military Infrastructure**: The Khazars built major fortresses like Sarkel and maintained a warrior class structure with the dual monarchy system (khagan and beg).

The Khazars' economy was built on a *foundation of military conquest* that enabled them to:

- **Extract tribute** from conquered peoples.

- **Control and tax trade routes** through military dominance.

- **Conduct slave raids** to supply markets.

- **Protect merchants** in exchange for taxation.

The "mercantilism" was only possible because of their underlying military strength. Without the warfare capability to conquer and control vast territories and peoples, there would have been no tribute to collect and no ability to control lucrative trade routes.

Islam is rooted in warfare and conquest as opposed to peace.

Moslems also like to deny that Islam is a religion based in warfare and will say dumb shit like Islam is "a religion of peace," which is as laughable as pedophiles claiming their proclivity for child rape is about "love for children." Yet Islam expanded extraordinarily rapidly upon its inception through military conquest in the 7th-8th centuries, spreading from the Arabian Peninsula across North Africa, into Iberia, Persia, and Central Asia within about a century of Muhammad's death. It was always a case of "convert or get beheaded." Which shows you how lame a religion is if people need to be forced to convert to it on pain of death. If you really want to understand the absolutely insane level of calculated, institutionalized sexual trauma and sexual violence perpetrated by Islam upon humanity, I urge you to study the Ottoman Empire.

Incidentally, here are IQ scores for Islamic nations that are desert-based:

- Egypt: ~80-85

- Morocco: ~80-85

- Pakistan: ~80-85

- Bangladesh: ~80-85

- Algeria: ~80-85

- Sudan: ~75-80

- Yemen: ~75-80

- Afghanistan: ~75-80

Allow me to tell you a wonderful anecdotal story about Islam that will drive home my point about IQ in regards to Islam. I called an Uber on the streets of South Brooklyn one day, and a Moslem driver picked me up. I was with a Russian woman at the time, who had her face covered that particular day, as is typical of Russian Orthodox women. This Uber driver was soooo impressed because from his ignorant perspective, here I was, a 6'2" white man who got a Russian woman wearing what he ignorantly thought was a hijab. He became convinced I was some sort of chad convert to his religion! I tried to calm him down and explained to him that she was *not* sporting a hijab, but rather garb typical of Russian Orthodox women. He did not know what Orthodox Christianity was, and could not grasp that there was another religion where women wore face coverings at times. His education probably didn't go beyond reading the Koran and getting his cheeks busted by older Moslem men back in Afghanistan.

It was just him and I in the car, and the ride was a good 30 minutes at that hour of the night, so he tried to recruit me into radical Islam on the ride back, as he was convinced I was a Moslem convert and just denying it. I suppose he thought a tall white man who looked like Lorenzo Lamas would look good on Al Qaeda posters holding a Kalashnikov rifle?

The focus of his pitch was how Western women are nothing but whores and completely corrupted by the porn Jew, totally out of control and in need of someone to keep them in line. I listened to him for the longest time go over all of the problems in the West, and of course, Islam's "solutions" to these problems. When it was all done, I said to him: "Look, it is not my intention to offend you, and I do agree with your overall diagnosis of Western society's problems with respect to women. You have no argument from me there. But the issue I have is that your 'solution' is so, well... *inelegant.* I mean, cutting women's clitorises off and sewing their pussies up - leaving just enough room to piss and grow bacteria, *does solve the problems* you so accurately pointed out, but those solutions are downright retarded and just create or exacerbate other problems!" He didn't quite know how to respond to my take on his pitch, and lucky for me we had arrived at my destination anyway.

The danger with Islam, is that when their population is small, they scream for religious tolerance. Once they attain critical mass, they become as intolerant as intolerant can be. They start to block the streets to pray, try to stop people from owning dogs, etc. Then they begin the systematic rape and sexual exploitation of "infidel" girls en masse. You'll see this throughout Europe, especially in England, Sweden and Germany, and hopefully the United States will not tolerate the same sort of nonsense that these pathetic nations over in Europe do - another reason to never give up your guns no matter how many school shootings are executed by "Manchurian candidates." Although I am sure New York City and the State of California will follow in England's footsteps. New York City already plans on mimicking Londoneers by electing a Moslem communist as mayor, which makes no sense given that communists are supposed to reject religion. But those elements who wish to destroy society will embrace anything that facilitates their aims. Also, didn't Bill DeBlasio, the city's last openly communist mayor, cause enough damage to the city? However, at the end of the day, *people literally vote for this*, so it's clearly what they want.

Over in jolly old England, they simply adore having their daughters gang raped by Moslem immigrants from Pakistan on a constant basis. They also voted to turn their nation into a surveillance state even the Chinese envy, because you have to make sure all of that "rapey goodness" is captured for posterity. I think that out of all of the nations in this world, England may be the one nation I have the *least* respect for. At least the Canadians *tried* to put up a fight when Trudeau enslaved them. I know what I just wrote will get this book banned in England, and me barred from ever entering that country in the future. But why would I ever want to visit such a shit hole of a country in the first place?

I also know that many will say "not all Moslems are like this," and they would be correct, because not all Moslems are out raping "infidel" women and girls. Yet no matter how open-minded or liberal a Moslem may claim or appear to be, or how critical *they* may be of their own religion, the moment you say anything to criticize Islam or simply point out the obvious, they turn against you no matter how good your friendship with them was prior to you opening your mouth. I have experienced this over-and-over again. It's truly sad. At the end of the day, they might not "all be like this" but they *all support* those who are.

One of the reasons Islam is so attractive to people, although they will never admit to it, is because it promises to "put women in their place" and therefore make it possible for every ugly loser to have a faithful virgin wife, by bringing about some version of an "Ottoman Empire 2.0" (they call it a "caliphate"), which is one of *the last things* the human race needs.

On Ignorant African-Americans Who Convert to Islam...

Speaking of being retarded, the gold medal goes to African Americans *who convert to Islam* since Moslems were the biggest slavers in the history of the world. Louis Farrakhan, leader of the Nation of Islam, has claimed that a disproportionate number of the slave trading ships that serviced the United States were owned by Jews (which is false), yet he conveniently overlooks the reality that Islamic slave traders trafficked the same number of African slaves to the middle east that slave traders trafficked into the United States! The Islamic slave trade was not only comparable in scale to the Atlantic slave trade, but it lasted much longer, and employed practices (particularly systematic castration) that prevented the formation of large slave-descended populations who might have kept this history more prominently in public consciousness. Because male slaves were systematically castrated and the offspring of Arab masters and female slaves became free Muslims, there wasn't the same large population of descendants to preserve and transmit the historical memory of this trade.

Here are some facts about how minimal Jewish involvement with the slave trade was, compared to Moslem involvement:

Jewish Involvement in the slave trade:

- Between 1728 and 1806 slave traders brought over 45,000 slaves to Barbados. Only 128 of these slaves were transported on ships in which a Jew had a financial interest.

- Importers brought 3,986 slaves into New York City between 1715 and 1765, and only 32 were carried by Jewish owned ships, while another 345 came in on ships owned by investor groups that included Jews.

- Between 1719 and 1806 Jewish ship owners imported 960 slaves to Jamaica, but in the same period non-Jews imported over 260,000 slaves.

- At the peak period of their participation in slaving expeditions, Newport's Jewish merchants Aaron Lopez and Jacob Rivera handled up to 10 percent of the Rhode Island slave trade. Incomplete records for other eighteenth-century ports show that for a few years they held at least partial shares in up to 8 percent of New York's small number of slaving voyages. They were jointly responsible for only 21 of the 937 slaving voyages launched from Rhode Island from 1709-1807 when Congress passed the Act Prohibiting Importation of Slaves.

Moslem involvement in the slave trade:

- Totality of African slave trading in the Moslem world from Sahara, Red Sea and Indian Ocean routes through the 19th century comes to an estimated 10,500,000, a figure not far short of the 11,863,000 estimated to have been loaded onto ships during the four centuries of the Atlantic slave trade.

- The Moslem slave trade, also known as the Trans-Saharan or Eastern slave trade, is recognized as the longest in history, spanning over 1,300 years. From the 7th century and over 13 centuries, between 10 and 18 million Africans were trafficked through the Sahara and the Indian Ocean to the Arab world.

- A large number of male slaves and young boys were castrated and turned into eunuchs who kept watch over the harems. Castration was a particularly brutal operation with a survival rate of only 10%. "The castration of black male slaves in the most inhumane manner altered an entire generation, as these men could not reproduce," said Liberty Mukomo, a lecturer at the University of Nairobi. Small African boys were castrated before they were trafficked to the Hijaz, where they were bought at the slave market by the Chief Agha to become eunuch novices. It was noted that boys from Africa were still openly bought to become eunuch novices to serve at Medina in 1895.

- While Europe, a major player in the African slave trade, abolished the practice centuries ago and the United States officially ended it in 1865, many Arab countries continued the trade well into the 20th century. Saudi Arabia and Yemen abolished it in 1962, and Oman followed in 1970. Mauritania became the last state to abolish slavery, in 1981.

Now you can probably understand just how ridiculous it is for African-Americans to convert to Islam! It's about as insane as them joining the Ku Klux Klan!

Since I have already shown how Christianity has become corrupted by Satan, lets take a look at how far most Moslems have strayed from what is written in the Koran with respect to the Islamic "path to salvation." It is interesting to note that Islamic concepts of judgment and salvation are fairly rational and not bat shit insane like the Christian concepts of judgment and salvation:

- *Faith and righteous deeds* — These are consistently paired throughout the Quran. Belief alone is insufficient; it must be accompanied by good actions.

- *Divine mercy and human responsibility* — While Allah is described as forgiving and merciful, humans are accountable for their choices. The Quran states "whoever does an atom's weight of good will see it, and whoever does an atom's weight of evil will see it" (99:7-8).

- *The balance of deeds* — On Judgment Day, deeds will be weighed. Those whose good deeds outweigh their bad will enter paradise (*jannah*), while others face hell (*jahannam*), though Allah's mercy remains a key factor.

The issue here, is that the past history of Islam, along with the present-day behaviors and beliefs of such a large percentage of Moslems, are in such direct opposition to what is outlined in the Koran above, that even a word like "hypocrisy" fails to accurately address the reality of the situation. Are war, conquest, sexual slavery, genital mutilation, institutionalized rape of women as well as both male and female children, etc. examples of righteous deeds? Will Moslems who engage in these activities not be held accountable for choosing to engage in them? According to their own Koran these activities will be factored into account on judgment day, so why are they engaging in these activities? It only goes to show you the sheer extent of Satanic corruption in Islam, that the Koran has been interpreted in such a way so as to promote such activities. But look at what happened to Salman Rushdie for just pointing in that direction!

I have spent so much time here speaking out against Moslems not only because they are an example of a "culture" built upon the trauma of infant circumcision, but also built upon the brutal sexual abuse, exploitation and oppression of both women and children. They present a continuous threat to the evolution of humanity, spreading trauma through sexual violence, exploitation and oppression like a *plague* wherever they go. One of the many reasons humanity will never be allowed to venture "off planet" by other extraterrestrial civilizations, is due to the sheer toxicity of human religions which cannot be allowed to spread to other planets and civilizations.

Furthermore, if we look beyond the writings of Salman Rushdie which explored the Satanic corruption of Islam already long ago, in more recent times both Satanists and Luciferians alike decided to infiltrate Islam, as they deemed the corrupted religion a perfect vehicle for achieving their own present-day goals. This makes Islam potentially even more dangerous today than in the past, although in no way am I giving Christianity and Judaism a "pass" despite the fact Judaism veers towards matriarchy and Christians don't favor circumcision or slavery like the Jews do. While *all* religions have been corrupted by Satan, the Abrahamic religions are the absolute worst. Of the Abrahamic religions, Islam is the absolute bottom of the barrel. This is because it has become nothing more than a political system masquerading as a religion, that is based upon the Satanic hatred and exploitation of women and children, that has world conquest as its sole goal. But if people embrace it and vote in favor of it's importation into their own culture, in spite of the fact their own ancestors fought like hell against the evil it was and still is, what can be done?

My Own Experience with Genital Mutilation

I was circumcised yet honestly can't say that I feel bad about it, or that I feel like I lost something, *but* when I was very small some doctor convinced my parents that my urethral opening was too small and needed to be enlarged. I could not comprehend this, as I could piss just fine and was very upset at the prospect of surgery on my "pee pee." But what could I do as a small child? Children are helpless, and adults just *love* hurting children. Not all adults mind you, but more than you would be comfortable acknowledging. That's a bold assertion, but read the writings of Lloyd DeMause and it will become apparent. So I woke up from surgery and found the doctor did a shit job, and up until recently I had a scar on my glans and a "pee hole" that looked like it caught a Glasgow Smile in some back-alley Scottish pub. If I pointed it out to women they didn't see what I was talking about, but *I did*. What was the point of that operation other than to hurt me? Luckily I had platelet-rich plasma injections into my penis twice, and so the scars are no longer visible, but I still have a Glasgow Smile. It gives my cock character.

If you know where to look, you'll see that an alarming number of doctors and nurses are incredible sadists who got into the medical profession as a way to act out their sadistic impulses while avoiding detection. It is not really shocking to me to discover that a nurse has been murdering people, or that a surgeon operates an after-hours clinic in his house for BDSM types to experience medical torture. I know they are not *all* like this, I am just saying there are more of them than you'd realize. I met a nurse one day in a bar who confessed to me that she works in a cancer ward for children, and while everyone praises her for her service and asks her how she can possibly view such heartbreak on a daily basis, the truth was that she absolutely loved watching those children suffer and that is why she went into nursing and took that job in the first place. Every day she gets to watch children suffer and this gets her off like crazy.

You will see a parallel yet inverse scenario unfold in martial arts gyms that specialize in striking, where there will sometimes be some absolutely gorgeous girl training, and everyone thinks her *soooo* empowered for "learning to defend herself," yet the reality is that she gets sexually excited when men beat the shit out of her. I am a magnet for these sorts of women (what a surprise) and I remember being in a Muay Thai class one time and finding myself across from a stunning blonde. I said to her, "Don't worry I am not going to actually hit you" to which she whispered with a smile, "Oh no, please don't hold back." What an awkward moment that was!

Throughout my life *certain* women have detected *some aspects* of my true nature and consequently have solicited me to beat the snot out of them, torture them, abuse them, etc. I always declined even though it would have gotten me laid far more often, and it would probably have made me a much happier man in general.

However, I learned something when I was still very young that has really helped me get through life as well as kept me out of a maximum security penitentiary. I'd like to pass it on to you, the reader: "It's not so much about *what* to do in life, it's really about what *not to do*." Many years later, a best friend who had chopped off his own hand with an axe, told me something in parallel, shortly before committing suicide:

*"A series of unfortunate events is **always** preceded by a series of totally unnecessary events."*

So I frequently ask myself, "Is what I am doing right now *really necessary*?" It's more subtle, yet hits a little deeper than "Is this one of those things I should *not* do in life?" Let me tell you, there are junkies nodding out in the streets who can give you better advice than any "life coach," so you should never dismiss anyone's wisdom outright. Some of them suffered very hard to get that wisdom, so that you don't have to.

Just listen.

Male vs. Female Thru the Lens of Prison Rape Culture

To be fair, in terms of the big picture, you can't really blame women for how they are and what they do. Their behavior, their repression of their sexuality, and their resultant neurosis can be blamed on men *even if* men didn't start the proverbial fire. This is because it is the *responsibility* of men to to fix things even if they are not at fault for them. I say this because no matter what nonsense you may hear to the contrary, there has never been a genuine matriarchy in recorded human history. The reason for this is simple: males are physically more powerful than females and naturally subjugate them via the application of force, and they secure their subjugation primarily to secure outlets for sexual release. Females have no bona fide power since they have no ability to back their will with physical force.

As a matter of fact, you can discern the entire history of male-female relationships by looking at prison rape culture. Prisons are filled with males who usually have high testosterone and low impulse control. Their sex drive does not go away when they are in prison, so they turn the weaker, more effeminate male prisoners into sex slaves. They do this via physical force. They beat and gang rape the weaker male inmates over-and-over until they either die attempting to fight off their rapists, or else submit to total feminization and sexual slavery. This is exactly what happened to women, and would happen to women again, if society broke down in the slightest. A friend of mine named this "Ghenghis Khan Theory" which postulates that any woman who was not sexually submissive was straight-up murdered or else raped to death. The only women who survived were the sexually submissive ones, which explains what we today call "female nature." However, this is actually only the "natures" of those who survived.

Another good example of "Ghenghis Khan" theory in action is ancient Rome. Before we talk about how bad Roman women had it, let's talk about the sexual exploitation of children in Ancient Rome. The sexual exploitation of children, particularly enslaved children, was indeed legally permitted and socially normalized in ways that are deeply disturbing by modern standards.

Legal and Social Reality

- Roman law set no minimum age of consent for slaves.

- Masters had complete sexual access to enslaved children of any age.

- The concept of childhood sexual innocence as we understand it didn't exist in Roman legal or social frameworks.

- This exploitation was so normalized that it rarely appears in sources as something noteworthy or controversial.

The *Pueri Delicatus* System

Romans commonly kept young enslaved boys (and girls) specifically for sexual purposes. These children, called *pueri delicati*, were:

- Often acquired very young and trained for sexual service.

- Considered luxury items and status symbols among wealthy Romans.

- Given no legal protection or recourse.

- Sometimes discarded or sold when they aged out of their masters' preferences.

While this was legally and socially accepted in Roman society, it represents systematic child sexual abuse on a massive scale. The normalization of these practices reveals how completely Roman law dehumanized enslaved people of all ages and how little protection existed for the most vulnerable members of society.

In regards to Roman women, they were never truly independent legal persons and *lived under the constant threat that they could be turned into sex slaves at any moment under Roman law, no matter their status.* They remained under *patria potestas* (paternal power) or *manus* (husband's power) throughout their lives. Even "independent" widows required male guardians (*tutores*) for most legal transactions.

Sexual Control and Consequences

- Women caught in adultery could face death (though this was later commuted to exile and property loss).

- Men who killed wives for adultery faced no legal penalty.

- Female virginity and chastity were treated as family property, not personal autonomy.

- Rape of a free woman was primarily seen as a crime against her male guardian, not against her.

Marriage Reality

- Most marriages were arranged for political/economic purposes.

- Girls could be betrothed as children and married at puberty (around 12-14).

- "Consent" was largely a legal fiction - fathers had absolute authority over their daughters' marriages.

- Even in *sine manu* marriages, women had little real autonomy.

Social Restrictions

- Women couldn't vote, hold office, or represent themselves in court.

- They were excluded from most public life.

- Even wealthy women's "business activities" required male oversight.

- Social mobility for women was primarily through marriage or male patronage.

Legal Vulnerability to Forced Prostitution

- Roman law allowed fathers to sell their children into slavery, including daughters who could then be forced into prostitution.

- Families could sell daughters to pay debts.

- Women captured in warfare automatically became slaves and could be forced into sex work.

- Female babies who were exposed (abandoned) could be picked up by anyone and raised as slaves for any purpose, including prostitution.

- Freeborn women could be sentenced to prostitution as legal punishment for certain crimes, particularly adultery.

Roman husbands had extensive legal authority over their wives' bodies and could force them into prostitution. This was part of the broader *patria potestas* and *manus* system where women were essentially property. A husband could:

- Force his wife into sex work to pay debts.

- Rent out his wife's sexual services.

- Use the threat of prostitution as control.

Women without male guardians were in extremely precarious legal positions. If a freeborn woman lost her male protector (through death, abandonment, etc.) and had no male relatives willing to serve as guardian, she could be:

- Declared legally "unprotected."

- Forced into prostitution by authorities or creditors.

- Essentially treated as if she had no legal status.

This reveals how the Roman "protection" system was actually a form of legalized coercion. Women weren't protected *for their benefit* - they were controlled to serve male interests, with the constant threat that loss of male favor meant potential sexual slavery. This completely undermines any notion that Roman women had meaningful rights or freedoms. Their entire existence was contingent upon male approval and protection, with sexual exploitation as the legal consequence of stepping outside of those bounds.

This reality makes clear that Roman women's "rights" existed only within a system where they could be stripped of all autonomy and bodily integrity through entirely legal means. Women who represented sexual autonomy and personal agency, such as captured female warriors from barbarian tribes, were typically raped to death by horses in front of thousands of spectators as a form of entertainment.

How the situation in Ancient Rome got to be so absurd, I suppose we will never know. It is also nothing in comparison to how women suffered under the Ottoman Empire. The Romans and the Ottomans were also not the only "civilizations" built upon the sexual enslavement and exploitation of women and children. I am just using these two as examples, but could fill an entire book talking about other "civilizations" that did the same – AND WE HAVE THE AUDACITY TO WONDER WHY MEN AND WOMEN BOTH HAVE SO MUCH TROUBLE GETTING ALONG TODAY???

It is my theory that once women are sexually subjugated, and men hold absolute power over them, that absolute power affords men the luxury of entertaining anxiety around female sexuality that they normally would not be able to entertain. It's like when a child is spared the rod and well fed, it will suddenly discover the "luxury" of being "afraid of the dark." In time, these "luxurious indulgences in anxiety" that men cultivate around female sexuality turn into neurosis, and these neurosis ultimately transform themselves into utterly insane and exploitative societal norms that persist even into present times. Here is a laundry list of the dynamics behind male anxiety and neurosis with respect to female sexuality:

- **Paternity uncertainty**: Unlike women, men historically couldn't be certain of biological parenthood. In societies where inheritance and lineage mattered, this created a powerful incentive to control female sexuality to ensure paternity. The fear wasn't necessarily of female sexuality itself, but of men investing resources into offspring that might not genetically be theirs.

- **Sexual competition anxiety**: If women have more sexual autonomy and choice, it increases competition among men and potentially leaves some men without partners. This creates anxiety among men who feel less desirable. Be careful not to let the red pill or black pill bullshit creep in here! While male sexual desirability in a woman's eyes does involve factors like height, looks, and cock size, just today I saw this girl who lives in my building who is fairly hot, bring home some loser she picked up online who was short, ugly, broke and unmasculine. As soon as she was done fucking him, a few hours later I catch her going out on a date with another guy who was even worse. If you saw both of these guys, you would not believe any woman on this planet would sleep with either of them. Believe me, it's all a joke and the joke is on the guy who has the most value. Even earlier today I saw a guy by the pool who was tall, but otherwise literally everything else was wrong with him. But he was surrounded by women because he had the delusional confidence to wear some 10-gallon cowboy hat in the pool and completely believe he was "the man." Self-hating women want that confidence for themselves so they don't have to medicate themselves out of their minds on a daily basis, in order to be able to live with themselves. It's an absolute joke out there fellas. The rest of the men in the pool who had girls, had them because they had devolved themselves down to the mental state of a child in order to interact with them... literally playing patty-cake with them in the pool, and doing all sorts of other shit a real man would *only* do with his fucking 5-year-old daughter. Bitch, I am not your fucking daddy, and I have zero interest in "reparenting" you! Forget the red pill, the black pill, and certainly forget the blue pill. Bitches are the ones popping the pills around here because they are all mentally ill. Don't believe me? Check their medicine cabinets!

- **Pride and Ego**: A lot of men tie their self-worth to being sexually desired or needed by their partners. This is totally normal. Female sexual independence - the idea that women might not need them, *or might compare them unfavorably to other partners,* can threaten this sense of masculine identity.

- **Biological differences**: Some research suggests men may be more prone to sexual jealousy due to evolutionary pressures, although this is debated.

While women under patriarchal systems were punished for being their true selves, the oppression of female sexuality over the centuries ironically turned their sexuality into a weapon that allowed women to enslave men without men even realizing it. So many centuries later, while we still technically live in a patriarchy, we actually live in a shadow matriarchy. Again, it was the trauma women experienced at the hands of men over the centuries that has brought us where we are here today, so it will be up to men to undo the damage, yet I can't ever see that actually happening. In some ways, I am writing this book to really explain the complete picture, as I am on my way out and it will be up to the young cats to figure out what to do going forward. I have no faith in them, though… You young men are so fucking lost, that no amount of red pill videos you watch or MMA classes you take will help you at this point.

Interestingly, I should point out that there is *one actual societal benefit* from the repression of *male* sexual energy… progress! Especially technological progress. If a guy can't use his cock, he ends up building rockets to attempt to travel to other planets where pussy is hopefully easier to obtain. You can even see this in the news right now unfolding in real time with all the stories of "sex robots" in development. If you look at cultures where *male* sexuality is *not* repressed, you'll find cultures where no progress occurs at all.

Brazil: A Nation That Accomplishes Next-To-Nothing

Brazil is a perfect example of this. I can tell you that there are no women on this planet like Brazilian women when it comes to sex. No other cultural group of females is as sexually liberated, expressive, orgasmic, shameless, etc. They love having sex, and there is no such thing as a sexually faithful Brazilian woman. It's fine though. The trade-off is well worth it. Brazilian culture is the most sexually promiscuous culture there is, and their women are absolutely crazy for cock, which is why "passport bros" are always headed there, but as a consequence Brazil as a nation produces nothing but slums and bananas. I am not joking, their entire GDP is built on agricultural and iron ore exports. They can't even make steel! What losers. Maybe if we taught them how, they could export prefabricated favelas to the United States so we can lower the cost of housing around here? Of course that would never happen. In most of the United States, building codes force you to build houses made from wood, which is the most worthless building material ever: flammable, vulnerable to wind, rain, termites and time. Even in hurricane zones, building codes force you to build from wood! All to keep carpenters employed, and to artificially maintain the home prices of inferior dwellings that you can't even insure anymore in states like Florida.

Anyway, the societal sexual norms native to Brazil exist because Catholicism, when it arrived in Brazil under the Portuguese flag, did not exterminate the native religions, since there were no Spanish conquistadors tagging along to get the bright idea to wipe them all out. So rather than exterminating the native religions and sending everyone to work in the mines digging up gold to send back to Spain, Portuguese Catholicism merged with all sorts of local religions that had different ideas about female sexual expression. Since the Portuguese declined to stamp out native sexuality, native sexuality instead extended itself into the culture moving forward. Instead of the systematic destruction of indigenous beliefs that characterized Spanish colonization, Portuguese missionaries often incorporated local practices into Catholic frameworks. This created religions like Candomblé and Umbanda that openly celebrate sensuality and the body in ways that orthodox Catholicism never would have. Next, the poverty that arose in Brazil's future combined with the embedded native sexuality to create the space for sexual expression and sex work to flourish in all its forms.

Why was Portugal able to hold the insanity of Christianity at bay in their dealings with foreigners whereas the Spanish were not? I think it came down to:

- Portugal was more centralized and less fragmented than Spain, which had multiple powerful kingdoms (Castile, Aragon, etc.) with their own religious and political agendas.

- The Portuguese monarchy had more direct control and did not need to use the Inquisition as a tool to unify diverse regions. Therefore, the Inquisition did not scar their nation's psyche as it did that of Spain.

- Portugal was a major maritime power with global trade networks in Africa and Asia almost a full century before the filthy Spaniards landed in the Americas. The Spanish landed with criminal intentions, as it was psychotic criminals they had sent over. History calls them "conquistadors." They were sent to plunder, and not to build trading relationships.

- The Spanish also had no experience with diverse cultures besides Islam, which to be fair would sour anyone's view of foreigners... whereas the Portuguese had already a full century's worth of exposure to different cultures besides that of Islam, and therefore knew there were other options for dealing with foreigners other than killing and enslaving them. As a side note, I find it ironic that Europe fought so hard back in the day to free themselves from Moslem conquest and sexual slavery, only to import Moslems back into Europe by the millions a few centuries later to begin the process of conquest and sexual enslavement anew. Europe is finished. Back in the late 1980s I had the idea I would want to move to Germany or Belgium, but now these countries are cultural sewers clogged with human trash from Africa and the Middle East. It's all part of the Satanic planetary agenda.

Speaking of societies that had no sexual repression and consequently failed to accomplish anything at all, Brazil has nothing on the myriad tribal cultures that live in the jungles on this planet, so Brazilians shouldn't feel bad about themselves at all. Anthropologists love romanticising these tree-monkeys, telling you that everyone is free from shame, fucking everyone else, in front of everyone else, all of the time, until everyone finds a partner based on criteria *other* than sex. Sounds soooo ideal, yes? But it isn't reality. The actual reality is that these "cultures" are rife with the most horrendous sexual abuse of children imaginable, who grow up to abuse the next generation of children in the same way. Are you beginning to see something wrong with human beings *in general*, across cultures and time? This is by design, and we will explore *who* designed it and *why*, later on in this book.

Furthermore, delusional western people love to point out how these low-IQ African tribal cultures are so "spiritually advanced" and cite their lack of neurosis and ability to "live in the moment" as proof of their alleged spiritual superiority over western culture. What they fail to mention is that the average IQ in sub-Saharan Africa is 55. This is so low, that it is *impossible* for them to live outside of the present moment, let alone acquire any sort of neurosis. This is not evidence of spirituality superiority, just abject stupidity. They are so dumb, they couldn't even invent the wheel on their own accord, and westerners had to explain to them how a wheel even fucking works. This is what Europe imports into their lands these days courtesy of the likes of George Soros. If Europe wanted to import rapists, they should have just brought in Russians. At least their intelligence and genetics would have been preserved.

Russia: A "Culture" Built on Rape and Incest

Yes, it is a historical fact that the top brass of the Russian military during WW2 openly encouraged the mass rape of civilian women by their soldiers. Multiple sources document that when Yugoslav Partisan politician Milovan Djilas complained about rapes in Yugoslavia, Joseph Stalin reportedly stated that he should "understand it if a soldier who has crossed thousands of kilometers through blood and fire and death has fun with a woman or takes some trifle." On another occasion, when told that

Red Army soldiers sexually maltreated German refugees, he reportedly said: "We lecture our soldiers too much; let them have their initiative." Historians estimate that hundreds of thousands to as many as two million German women were raped by Soviet troops during the war and occupation, with some 100,000 cases reported in Berlin alone between April and May of 1945. According to Soviet war correspondent Natalya Gesse, Soviet soldiers raped German females from eight to eighty years old, and Soviet and Polish women were not spared either. According to historian Antony Beevor, NKVD (Soviet secret police) files have revealed that the leadership knew what was happening, but did little to stop it. Aleksandr Solzhenitsyn, an author and Soviet officer, wrote in detail about German women *literally being raped to death* by Soviet soldiers.

Even if you look at the Russian military today, it is plagued by homosexual rape. Soldiers openly rape other soldiers on a daily basis and even force them into male prostitution while the generals sit around approvingly. Rape in the Russian military is on par with rape in Russian prisons, where it is also a very serious problem.

- **Recent Figures**: In 2019, according to the Russian military prosecutor office, incidents of hazing in the army increased, with 51,000 human rights violations and 1,521 sexual assault cases reported.

- **Scale of the Problem**: By 2006, 40% of deaths in the Russian military were attributed to suicide, and in the same year, one soldier was beaten so badly that the resulting gangrene resulted in his legs and genitals being amputated.

- **Types of Sexual Abuse**: "Dedovshchina" encompasses a variety of subordinating and humiliating activities undertaken by the junior ranks, from doing the chores of the senior ranks, to violent and sometimes deadly physical and psychological abuse, not unlike an extremely vicious form of bullying or torture, *including sexual torture and anal rape.*

- **Specific Practices**: There are cases of rape and being forced into prostitution and threats of such. Then there are abuses like the infamous sitting on a bottle, often used by Ramzan Kadyrov's Chechen units to punish those who oppose them. It's all about humiliation—some of it imitated from the "ponyatiya," the sadistic regime of Russian prison culture.

- **2019 Mass Shooting**: In 2019, Ramil Shamsutdinov shot 10 of his colleagues at a Gorny military base, 8 of them fatally. In court, he alleged that he was subjected to beatings and threats, claiming they had made his life "hell" and were planning to sexually assault him.

- **2018 Suicide Case**: In 2018, Pvt. Artyom Pakhotin had the word "petukh" - meaning rooster (figuratively, "prison bitch")—carved into his forehead as a punishment for smoking in the barracks. Two weeks later, he killed himself with his AK.

- **Underreporting**: According to activists, "for a young man to talk about something like this is very, very difficult. And, in my opinion, the majority of these crimes will remain only on the conscience of those who suffered them and those who carried them out. It's very rare that a young man will come to us and say that he suffered sexual abuse. Because, of course, it is extremely humiliating."

- **Long-standing Problem**: Towards the end of the war in Afghanistan a senior officer told his fellow generals that the most common crime in the Soviet army there was "military bullying". More than 200 soldiers had suffered in one year: some had been killed and others severely wounded.

The evidence shows that sexual violence, including same-sex assault, remains a significant problem in the Russian military through the "dedovshchina" hazing system. However, precise statistics on specifically homosexual rape are difficult to obtain due to severe under reporting, stigma, and the closed nature of military institutions. The available data suggests these crimes are part of a broader pattern of systematic abuse designed to maintain hierarchical control through humiliation and violence.

Women in the west like to throw around the term "rape culture" but some countries really do have a bona fide rape culture. America is *not* one of them, but Russia is. What is the source of this insanity and why is it accepted as sane, normal behavior? Why do Russian men hate women so much? Why are so many Russians alcoholics and heroin addicts? It's all tied together. When you walk around many Russian cities, all you'll hear is the crack of spent syringes under your boot. The current state of Russia is a result of endless generational sexual trauma combined with the trauma of communism, which the Russian people simply cannot snap out of.

"Nowhere, it seems, except in Russia, is there at least one kind of incest which has acquired the character of an almost normal domestic phenomenon."
—Nabokov (in reference to the phenomenon of *"Snokhachestvo"*)

Nabokov would not be shocked to find that today Russia is the incest porn capital of the world. Much of it borders on child pornography, depending on what your nation's laws are. Browsing the internet for a few hours can confirm this, although I do not recommend it for obvious legal reasons! Of course, this is not a shock if you have had as many Russian friends as I have had, or dated as many Russian women as I have dated. I have had Russian male friends openly declare it is their right to fuck their own adolescent daughters to teach them about sex, and I struggle to remember a Russian woman who was not fucked constantly as a child by either her father, grandfather or brothers. While India and Serbia have a greater incest problem than Russia does, only Russia can proudly list incest porn as part of their GDP.

To be fair, incest and child sexual abuse is a worldwide issue and not limited to Russia. But some countries are worse than others and Russia is one of them. We are another, along with China. According to famous athlete Tim Tebow, the number one *payer* of the live stream rape of boys and girls around the world is the United States. Let *that* sink in. In the peer-2-peer *sharing* of child and baby rape videos we come in third, with China and Russia in the lead. However, we do actively fight against homosexual rape in our military and prison system whereas Russia does not. We also have laws against animal cruelty whereas China does not, and therefore China is the global leader in online animal cruelty videos, with videos of cats being blended alive in blenders, foxes being skinned alive, and animals being boiled alive in restaurants, compromising a big part of their nations online entertainment.

Don't get me wrong, I love Russian food and I love Russian women. The problem is Russian men. Most of the decent and honorable ones were killed off in the first waves of battles during World War II, and the trash that survived and reproduced, treat women like absolute garbage. Many Russian men have more fragile egos than many inner city blacks in the United States, and will literally assault and murder any woman who rejects them. Just watch non-incest Russian porn and see how abusive they are to the female performers. It's nothing but rough and violent anal gang bangs that appear to be *gang rapes* passed off as gang bangs, with the closing cum shots eclipsed by all the male performers urinating in the woman's mouth. You can often discern the psychic character of a nation by the porn it produces. Just like Russian porn is very revealing, the fact that both Japanese and German porn have a love affair with human feces should make them teaming up as the "axis powers" during World War II no surprise to anyone. Like attracts like, as they say…

The languages of specific cultures are also replete with clues as to what they are *really* focused on. For example, Russians use the word "bliadz" (Belarusan origin) and it's softer expression "blyat" in every single sentence along with the word "suka," and Poles use the word "kurwa" at least three times in every sentence uttered. These words all mean "whore" in loose translation, except for "suka" which translates as "bitch." "Whore" and "bitch" may not be the worst of bad words in English, but these foreign variants carry a certain ugly energy not native to the English versions of the word, and their absurd frequency of usage reveals the utter hatred for women present in these cultures, whereas the fact Americans use the words "fuck" and "shit" in every sentence simply reveals they are sexually repressed, and consequently constipated as well.

Before I end this diatribe on Russian rape culture, let me tell you a "funny" story of just how "rapey" Russian culture is. I could tell you how I picked up a Russian prostitute once who had around ten boyfriends who didn't know she also worked as a prostitute, and how she had told me that when she was just 12 years old she got bent over her father's casket and raped at his wake, but that isn't funny at all. Just *typically* Russian. It reminds me of a Serbian expression that translates, "I will rape your mother on your dead father's back." You ever hear anyone curse like this in English? Let me tell you, Serbians have had *very different* experiences than Americans. So anyway, I had a friend who traveled to Siberia or somewhere to do "business" with Russians. These guys were some sort of gangsters, like many Russian "businessmen" are. So they headed out one night to a club for a night of drinking vodka. My friend sees a woman that he likes standing around with her friends, and he walks over to her and attempts to chat her up. She dismisses him, and he walks back to his Russian friends like a loser. One of them says to him, "That's not how you approach a

Russian woman, you just *take* that *suka*!" My friend is like, "WTF are you talking about?" So this Russian guy walks over to some random girl, drags her back to the table and basically rapes her in front of everyone. My friend cannot believe what he is seeing and the girl doesn't seem to even complain. When he is done, the guy gesticulates towards the girl who rejected my friend earlier and says, "Now it's your turn. Go get her." My friend told me he was really on the spot. He couldn't allow himself to lose face with these guys or he would not be able to do business with them. So he says "fuck it" and marches over to the girl who had previously rejected him, grabs her by the wrist and yanks her away from her friends. But my friend is not very strong and she starts to put up a fight. Hilarity ensues as a veritable tug-of-war kicks off that he simply cannot afford to lose! Eventually she tires out, and he drags her over to a table, bends her over, and proceeds to fuck her in front of everyone. I mean, this shit is straight out of the Russian penal system, where inmates rape other inmates in full view of everyone. The gangsters were of course very proud of my friend, and his business dealings proceeded smoothly.

Her Neurotic Vagina: A Simple Definition of Neurosis

"My dear Sam, you cannot always be torn in two."
— Gandalf, *The Return of the King*

The big problem with trauma that is unresolved, is that it leads to what is called "neurosis." The simplest definition of neurosis is *to experience a conflict in your drives*. So for example, a woman says she wants to experience a full-body, vaginally-triggered orgasm, yet she blocks the experience. Why would she want to do that? Inner conflict. The exact reason doesn't exactly matter in this instance. She is conflicted, hence she becomes neurotic. This is why in the Victorian era when a woman was labeled "hysterical," the "cure" was a vibrator. Naturally, modern day historians have gone out of their way to debunk this as a myth, because female orgasmic impotence is such an explosive psycho-sexual iceberg of a topic, in today's woke and feminist academic realm.

For those woke feminists who like to pretend that billions of hours of online pornographic content isn't enough of a sample size to demonstrate the sheer extent of female anorgasmia, allow me to talk about a parallel problem, female constipation. Why are women always constipated? Because it goes hand-in-hand with female anorgasmia, as the same somatic mechanism by which they obstruct orgasm, also ends up obstructing the peristaltic motion of their bowels. This is why women are more than twice as likely to suffer from constipation than men, with some studies showing women are three times more likely to suffer from constipation than men. At specialty constipation clinics, 79% of patients are female. This is why when a woman is giving you problems, simply snap: "Take a shit, bitch!"

I have been with women who will literally stop themselves from having a vaginal orgasm even though they are about to have one. This is a situation where the inner conflict is still well within the woman's conscious field of awareness, whereas in most cases they have just gone dead inside and there is no orgasm to even attempt to stop. In such a case, the inner conflict is no longer in the woman's conscious field of awareness. Why would a woman want to stop up her orgasmic experience? Let's examine two big reasons, keeping in mind that there are many. One reason is because if they let you make them cum, they are afraid of becoming enslaved by you. Another reason is because they are afraid that if they are no longer able to contain their orgasmic potential, they will no longer be able to commodify it.

I recently had sex with this beautiful prostitute and within a few minutes of running my cock up inside of her tight pussy, she had this intense vaginal orgasm that pushed me out of her body. She just lay there, face down and ass up, her entire body spasming from the orgasmic contractions for a good five minutes. After this, I go back inside of her and she starts demanding I cum. I am like "Bitch, I just got here you are going to cum for me again." She started to get upset and was like "No, I already came for you!" and then she just "checked out" of the whole interaction. So I plowed her for the rest of the hour as punishment even though I was bored to tears. The only reason I could stay hard was because I had shot up my dick with a custom Tri-Mix blend in the hotel lobby bathroom prior to coming up to her room, *precisely* because of bullshit like this here. I paid her for one hour of her time, and I am going to get my one hour out of her. She can either enjoy that hour, or get a sore pussy instead. The choice is hers. She chose a sore pussy over pleasure. Won't be seeing her again!

What had happened? She understood what I was capable of once I made her cum like that, and at that moment I became a threat to her, her lifestyle choices, and her overall psychic stability. So she completely checked out and was cold as ice whereas before she wanted to make out with me and was all about the GFE... *Until* the moment she really started to feel like she was my girlfriend, or else *wanted* to be! That was the end of that! As a side note, men don't realize just how responsible a women is for their erections. In so many cases, a man would not need to pop pills if the woman he was with wasn't throwing up walls left and right to keep him at arms length during the act of sex.

This is a very instructive story because women who have successfully installed this ability to switch their orgasmic nature on and off are even more problematic than those who have switched it off completely. One could argue that they are truly empowered, and I would not argue against that, even though I ultimately would disagree. The dangers for a man who gets involved with this type of woman should be blatantly obvious, as she will weaponize her sexuality against you in an unrelenting fashion. The neurosis is still there, just integrated at a level where there is zero incentive to let it go.

Men Are Not Obsessed with Sex – It Is a Female Projection

Society falsely portrays men as sex maniacs, but it is just that it *appears* that men are all sex-obsessed. Here is a truth that you will come to learn: **A Man's obsession with sex, is rooted in a woman's repression of sex.** *Men are actually love-obsessed.* This will become apparent when I dive into *real sexual dynamics* later on in this book. It is women who are obsessed with sex, repress their desires to the point of neurosis, then end up neurotically projecting their own obsession onto men who are left starving for satisfying sex. If men don't get enough sex by systemic design, of course they will become obsessed with it! Even men who get laid all the time are usually deprived of orgasmic, connected and loving sex, so they obsess on sex even more. This is also why men with options are always cheating. Yes ladies, your man cheats because you suck in bed!

Imagine if there was someone so obsessed with food that they starved everyone around them, so they could then point fingers at the starving people and say, "Why are they so obsessed with food?" You would undoubtedly reply: "Ummm... they aren't obsessed with food, they're just starving!" But by starving others, the person in power who is actually obsessed with food themselves, can now project their obsession onto others. *This is exactly what women are doing with sex!*

Women perform this same "projection act" with their rampant jealousy as well. You will often see, if you are very perceptive, that women who suffer from jealousy are always setting things up so that their partners are in a perpetual state of jealousy and insecurity. By doing so, these women can avoid dealing with their own jealousy and insecurity, and instead point fingers at their jealous partner so as to pretend that they are not the jealous ones, and hope that nobody will ever notice this part of themselves that they are ashamed of. Pay attention!

Men Have Forgotten Their True Nature for Two Reasons

The first reason is that most men are no longer consciously aware of the fact that the only way to truly possess a woman, as well as gain access to her heart - and consequently the love that they crave, is through her pussy. You don't "turn out" a woman by loving her, you do so by fucking her and giving her an insane orgasmic experience. Incidentally, this is another reason why men not only obsess on pussy itself, but it is *also why they obsess on body count.* They obsess on body count because they subconsciously know that any man who gives a woman a deep orgasmic experience, owns a piece of that woman. Even if you are capable of giving her the same experience, or even a more intense sexual experience, you will still always be sharing her with the orgasmic lover who came (pun intended) before you, on some level.

The second reason, which will be more difficult to grasp, is because one of the sinister qualities of neurosis is that it is *contagious.* Let's put the neurotic dynamics between men and women on the back burner for a moment (we will return to them shortly), and focus on how parents force their children to become as neurotic as they are, as children ultimately grow up to be adult males and adult females who in turn interact with each other in relationships. A parent forcing their own neurosis onto a child is easy to grasp and "child's play" for an adult, because children are dependent upon their parents for all of their survival needs, so they will consequently modify their behavior in order to continue to survive. They will then carry that modified neurotic behavior into adulthood, where they will ultimately infect their own offspring and future partners with it.

So here are some simple examples of a parent directly forcing their own neurosis onto a child:

- **"Rinse the walls of the shower with cold water when you are done showering, then let the cold water run for a while to cool the pipes in the walls and bring down the bathroom temperature."** *"Never mind that the bathroom has a huge fucking window... heat makes me crazy but I am too cheap to pay for air conditioning, and consequently have convinced myself that 'energy saver mode' can actually cool a room, rather than just finding a way to get more money to keep the house cool enough."*

- **"Don't chew on that chocolate bar, let it melt in your mouth in order to maximize your enjoyment of it."** *"Because surviving hunger in Germany during World War II has rendered me incapable of enjoying the simple pleasure of gobbling up a chocolate bar even though I live in America now."* One of the saddest things I have seen is my father chewing his steak with his eyes closed, desperately trying to extract as much pleasure out of it as possible.

- **"Why would we buy you another toy when you never play with that one toy that we have already got you?"** *"Well, I am the only kid at school who owns one single toy and that's the only toy I've got, so I treat it like a museum piece and obsessively check on it to make sure it is still there. This scarcity mindset and fear of loss that you have instilled in me has rendered me neurotic, which will effect my life for years to come. Hopefully I will become consciously aware of this pattern and fight to change it at some point, but not before it can significantly derail my path to success in life. Thanks a lot, parents!"*

NOTE: These are all examples from my own life and clearly center around neurotic conflicts my parents had over money and food that they passed onto me, until I became aware of them and consciously overwrote them with great effort. Now I always put my AC on 72 as opposed to 76, gobble as much chocolate as I want, and buy myself whatever the fuck I please. The "energy saver" button on an AC unit should say "broke loser mode" instead, IMO. Allow me to tell you two more sad examples about how parents can derail a child's life by burdening them with their own bullshit:

- Back in the 1980s I was very into computing. I was writing programs on the Commodore 64 at my Junior High School and our computer room even had one solitary Apple IIC! Then the Macintosh came out in 1984 and I knew it was the future. Not so much in terms of the chassis, but in terms of the mouse and the windows-based OS. I really wanted to get one and why shouldn't I have one? I had a genius IQ and was writing computer programs already. But my father didn't want to spend the money. I had no way of getting money, so what to do? Spend my time in bookstores, which doubled as computer stores at the time, and dream about the Macintosh. Then one day my father brings home a computer. He had saved up enough money to buy one stolen off a truck somewhere. Was it a Macintosh? Of course not. It was an IBM AT. What an idiot. Of course I wasn't allowed to use it, either. This broke my heart, and I gave up on computing. Who knows how rich I could have been if only my father wasn't broke, listened to his smart son who intuitively knew the future, and wasn't neurotic about his personal equipment. We'll never know, and I find it extremely sad.

- Long before the 1980s, I was heavily into rollerskating. The film "Xanadu" had come out, and I was big on skating the slalom in Central Park, as well as frequenting the roller dancing arena alongside Sheep's Meadow. I was pretty good, and my intuition was pulling me towards taking up skateboarding, as I knew that would be the next big thing. But no matter how hard I tried, I could not get my father to buy me a skateboard. How cheap or broke do you have to be to not be able to buy your kid a fucking skateboard when you see he is already so good at roller skating? I just can't understand this mentality. If you see talent in your kids *and* they show interest in cultivating said talent, fucking help them cultivate it! So I gave up, and rollerskating died out, paving the way for skateboarding. Eventually, rollerskating came back as inline skating, and I resisted it for *years.* I would hate everyone zipping about on inline skates. Then one day I realized *why* I hated everyone on inline skates. I also realized I was an adult and had money of my own, and I can still remember forcing myself to walk inside of an inline skate shop. It was soooo hard just to get myself to step inside the store! I really wanted to go in, but the pain and programming of my childhood was preventing me. I finally went in there, literally shaking, and bought a pair of inline skates. The kind you do tricks on. From that day on I was skating everywhere, including back and forth to work. I would spend half the night skating the city all by myself. I would run laps in Central Park after midnight. I was often the only one in the park as far as I could tell. It was a lonely time, as most of my life has been, but fun too! I probably should have spent that time finding a way to make money, but I didn't have any role models. My father was clearly clueless about how to make money, there was no internet, and everyone around me was a loser. I practically lived in bookstores like B. Dalton and Doubleday, but all those endless business books on their shelves were unactionable bullshit. So since everyone around me was a complete loser, I became one too.

I could have been so many things in life, but ended up starting a crew called V.I.F. which stood for "Vandalism is Fundamental" which was a spoof on the 1980s public-service spot on TV called

R.I.F. which stood for "Reading is Fundamental." I was actually attracted to graffiti and that whole scene, but I didn't have the talent for graffiti and that lifestyle was logistically impractical, so I took up "general vandalism" instead. Boy, was I productive! Any potential energy I had for creation transformed into kinetic energy for destruction. From that point on, I was headed for prison in slow motion, but what saved me was one day I came across the book "Taoist Secrets of Love" by Mantak Chia and I discovered something as fascinating as destruction. It awakened something in me, some faded memory of *what* I really was, as using sexual methods to cultivate spiritually hail from the realm of what is known in some cultures as "the realm of the *asuras*." The discovery of this book, following on the heels of falling in love with someone who was also not from this realm, were the two events that started me on the journey that has ultimately led to the writing of this book. I did take up snowboarding one day, which corrected the skateboarding wrongs of the past, but snowboarding is a very expensive hobby. Being poor sucks. I hate it. So don't listen to people who say dumb shit like "having children isn't expensive." It isn't if you neglect them, but then they grow up to hate you. So don't be selfish and reproduce just in order to have someone to boss around, or to prove your genetics are worth reproducing, when you know very well they aren't, and you have the earning power of a circus elephant! This is why high IQ individuals, who should be having children, don't. Only trash reproduces. This is by design, of course! But I feel it is only fair to finish this subsection by acknowledging that my biological father did really love me and spent tons of time with me, and that is one of the most important things a father can do for his children. So even if he had faults, he got that right, and he got a lot of other stuff right as well. He always used to say to me "You can't jump over your own shadow" and there is some deep truth to this. Plus, like my biological mother and myself he also had Rh- blood and occupied a hybridized human form. What he actually was on the inside, I do not know.

The issue with my biological father was that with respect to his relationship with The Divine Father, he carried this commonplace attitude that somehow The Divine Father's creation was flawed and pointed to what he saw on this planet as "evidence" to support this ridiculous assertion. The problem with this sort of attitude is that it is fundamentally Satanic in origin, and as well as absolutely ridiculous since how can a human being that barely lives 100 years, has a low IQ, and can't even perceive the 4th and 5th dimensions possibly be qualified to comment on the perfect creations of a perfect being? What humans need to do is pray to The Divine Father for understanding, before shooting off at the mouth blasphemously. Because if you are spouting off Satanic ideas without even being consciously aware of it, you are creating a wedge between The Divine Father and yourself, which is utterly foolish. This is especially foolish if you are a hybridized being, as it tends to ensure you stay under the control of the beings who hybridized you in the first place, and in such cases, it is The Divine Father's help you really need to break free from their control!

Anyway, let us now return to how adult females force their neurosis onto adult males... Since most "adult" *males* are really still just children, only in grown-up bodies, thanks to their parents forcing their own crap onto them, *coupled with* the reality that most adult *males* were hopelessly programmed by their own mothers into being slaves to women, adult women find it very easy to force adult men into becoming as neurotic as they are. Because if men don't comply, they don't get any pussy. While pussy is not necessarily a survival need, *the love that can be obtained from bringing a pussy into an orgasmic state is* – at least for a man's *psychic survival.* So if you don't mirror a female's neurosis, they will punish you by not giving you any pussy, which means you will have no shot at getting her love, which is the actual goal, not the pussy in and of itself. It is difficult to give *simple* examples of *exactly how* women force their neurosis onto a man because they don't do it by ordering you around with the authority of a parent as in my earlier examples I gave above. They do, however, grab the "keys" your mom left in your "ignition" from years of programming and just drive you off the lot! How? The best way to explain it is to say that *females pass their neurosis into the male primarily via an unspoken demand for subconscious mirroring.* For example, if a man is all over a woman *but* she is playing it cool *despite* her interest in him being off the charts (due to her own neurotic conflict), he will quickly attempt to mirror her apparent "coolness" in order to "flip the script" and obtain her. In essence, he reflects her neurosis by acting as neurotic as she is, in order to obtain her.

Most pickup or seduction techniques such as "push-pull" are built around playing the woman's neurotic game. One of the issues that arises from using these techniques, is that a man has to suffocate a significant portion of his own level of attraction in order to "play it cool" and get the girl. Once he has finally got her, he finds it becomes impossible to turn his full attraction back on again. Even if he can, there is the risk that she will "do a runner" when things get too intense, so he really has no incentive to turn his full attraction back on again. Consequently, he starts to seek out another woman, because he feels something has been lost. Which it has! He was forced to mirror a woman, who is always repressing her sexuality in order to get control over the man she wants, by repressing his *desire for her in his heart.* Once such a woman finally "gets her man," she often finds she can't allow herself to enjoy orgasm because she turned off her sexuality in order to gain power over said man, and can no longer turn it back on. Men are the same way, but in their hearts. It's the same phenomenon when you have held your bladder for too long in order not to piss your pants, and then find it incredibly difficult to piss when you do find yourself standing in front of a toilet, no matter how hard you try and relax.

This is one of the many reasons I think prostitutes who love their jobs, men and sex are so psychologically healthy for a male. If you see one you like, you book an appointment and you show up at the scheduled appointment time. You take a shower, and just exit her bathroom naked with a raging erection and proceed to devour the object of your lust. No conflict, no neurosis, just lust and satiation. Yes, I have described her as an object. I have *objectified* her. What's the big deal? When a woman thinks a guy is hot, or gets a crush on a male celebrity, or gushes over how big a man's cock is, she is *objectifying* that man. It's perfectly natural because that is how nature designed our biology in order to make sure we are seeking out the best genetic material to ensure the survival of our species. Remember, the primary objective of sexuality is to create new humans, not provide opportunities for your pleasure or for you to indulge your lust.

Compare the above healthy interaction with a prostitute, to the following scenario: today I was in Trader Joe's buying my weekly groceries. I am 6'2" and jacked, in a tank top with hair like Fabio. Women start to mill about me, hoping I will talk to them. But if I do, they say a few words and then run away down the aisle, only to repeat the same process in another aisle. Some will give me a dirty look, then scrutinize me from afar. Some won't respond at all as if they are frozen in fear. I see one hot young girl dressed with the express intention to catch a man, but of course she doesn't really want to catch a man – she wants to *control* a man. What to do? Start talking to her? Maybe get her number or IG handle and start working her via texts or DMs? Am I not already in the top tier of men? I mean, I don't see anyone better than me in Trader Joe's on any given day, and I have never seen an exotic car where I am living at the time. How much value do I need to project to women in order to have it easy? Or do I have to become a court jester now and entertain her? It's all so tiresome, and so degrading. My time is also worth a lot, and I cannot waste endless hours pursuing her when the reality is that I am more valuable than her to begin with, and it probably won't work out anyway because she has the most insane demands from watching too many TikTok videos! The whole endeavor is just absurd. Just fuck the right prostitutes, and use all of the time you save, to figure out how to make more money.

Please don't think that joining some fetish networking website will allow you to fare any better! I got messaged by a girl on one of them, who was really hot. I talked to her for about two minutes in a chat, when she asked me why I don't have any dick pics on my profile. I told her it is because I have class and style, and if anyone wants to see one, all they need to do is ask. She abruptly stated she didn't want to waste her time, so she wanted to see a dick pic right away. So I sent her a video of my dick being sucked, since pictures of dicks can be deceptive, and she immediately says she wants to meet me.

When I eventually meet her, she then proceeds to talk non-stop about dick size so I finally ask her, "You can't orgasm vaginally, can you?" She says "How did you know?" I replied that women who can't orgasm vaginally are always going on about dick size. Eventually I decide it is time for me to leave. She insists on leaving with me, then jumps on me in the middle of the street and starts making out with me. She says she wants to get together in a few days and fuck. I say sure. A few days later she messages me that "she can't do this." I say fine, only to see over the course of the next few months that she is fucking a string of absolute losers she is also meeting on the same fetish networking website and she even ends up in a relationship with one of them, posting all of these pictures of them having sex in random hotel rooms. This guy is short, fat, incredibly ugly and has the smallest dick ever. I was like "What the actual fuck?"

A few months later she hits me up on WhatsApp, and tells me she is single. She also moved very close to me. So I told her we should meet up and fuck. She then tells me she is just looking for friends and doesn't know what she really wants. So I tell her to go join a church if she is just looking for friends, as I am looking to fuck. She gets *really* offended that I told her to join a church and I never hear from her again! I went back to check her profile after I sent her packing, and under "interests" I see she has added something new: Satanism. Well that revelation explains a lot...

How I didn't end up a serial killer, is still a mystery to me.

The Essence of All PUA Strategies: Mirror A Woman's Neurosis

As I have said before and will say again, mirroring female neurosis is the essence of the PUA skillset! Those of you familiar with PUA tactics will recognize the common, yet highly successful strategy of showing a woman that you want her and then *at the same time* showing her that you have no interest in her! They call it "push-pull." We all know that this tactic works very well, yet this is neurosis in its simplest and purest form! I mean, how can you both want someone and *not* want someone at the same time? Is it not insane? It is schizoid, that's for sure. PUAs will simply dismiss it as a "paradox," but it is ultimately just neurotic as fuck! So you mean to say that to get a woman, a man has to turn himself into a woman? How is that masculine? Conversely, can you also see how the red pill bullshit of being masculine will just lead to rejection and failure? Surely you can see how women claim to want "a real man" but then fuck little boys, basically? They want a vaginal orgasm, yet can't or won't let themselves have one... They want a real man, yet never choose one... It's their *acquired* neurotic nature, not an inherent one. Acquired via trauma. Choosing a vaginal orgasm is terrifying. Choosing a real man is terrifying. Better to stay in control at all times. Choose a loser instead!

Here is another example of this dynamic in action: I was at the gym and there was a young girl working out close to where I always work out, who always lights up when she sees me. So I know she is attracted to me. Now, just because a girl ignores you doesn't mean she *isn't* attracted, but when she lights up like a tree at Rockefeller Center in December, there is no doubt that she is attracted. I engaged her in a conversation and she quickly removed her headphones to carry on the conversation, which is another huge indicator of interest, as women wear headphones primarily so men won't talk to them. I talked with her for a few minutes, then excused myself to work out. Why? Because I don't want to appear thirsty! But this is neurotic and goes against what my energy really wants to do, which is to grab her and kiss her. But that would get my gym membership revoked. Many years ago that would often work, but the societal programming has gone too far and even if a woman liked your bold move, she would still file a sexual assault complaint and probably make a TikTok video about you. So instead I opt for the neurotic act of walking away in the hopes of raising her interest, because according to PUA theory, it raises my value by showing her that I have options, for one thing. But again, what I am *really* doing is qualifying myself for a relationship with her, by showing her that I am as neurotic as she is. Contrary to what dating coaches will claim, she is not actually thinking to herself, "Wow, this guy must be getting laid like crazy if he can walk away from me. I want some of that too!"

This is a key takeaway in the modern mating dance. What is *authentic* is to say "Come by my apartment in about one hour and I will give you the most intense orgasms." This is how I really feel, what my real intention is, and *it is also what she really wants.* Yet this approach will have a 1% success rate because even though this is what she wants, her own conflicted drives won't allow her to accept such honest and authentic advances. So I proceed with my workout, and she moves to the other side of the gym to do the exact same exercises she could have done in my area, but keeps looking at me in a sneaky way, smiles at me sheepishly at one point, and then after a few minutes she leaves the gym. Was she finished working out? Of course not. The sexual tension was just too much. She went to the gym locker room to masturbate herself in the shower. When she could have been riding my cock instead. Isn't this just plain sad? And people wonder why men have no motivation and spend all of their time playing video games and watching the UFC.

Pro Tip: Do you know the real reason why we have speed limits on public highways? It isn't for public safety. It is to train you to block your own energy flow, and get you into the habit of developing inner conflicts, because such inner conflicts make you *easier to control* by jamming up your natural instincts. Most public highways have a speed limit of 55-65mph, yet almost nobody drives at that speed. Why? Because it is unnatural to do so. This enables law enforcement to pretty much pull anybody over at any time for a speeding violation, and collect revenue for the state, which is the primary directive of law enforcement anyway. Not protection, but revenue collection. But the main reason is to get you to split yourself into two via inner conflict, so that you develop psychic impotence. Instead of remaining in your "flow state" where your power and ability to act lies, you find yourself always checking out of your "flow state" to check your speedometer, or to check your rear view mirror. You'll see something parallel happen in cities like New York, where criminals can commit any and all crimes free from prosecution, yet if you defend yourself from a criminal, you are tried with the full force and intent of Satanic prosecutors, who take great joy in inverting and mocking justice, while simultaneously creating the most massive inner conflict in you they possibly can, rendering you psychically impotent and therefore easy to control. Because it is 100% natural and just to defend yourself from an unjust criminal aggressor, but then you find yourself punished for doing what is 100% natural and just, *as if YOU were the unjust criminal aggressor.* This splits you into two and creates a conflict between the two parts, rendering you incapable of doing anything other than taking abuse.

You know, guys don't realize just how many women carry pocket-sized, hemi-powered vibrators in their purses in order to be able to quickly dissipate their sexual energies and stay "in control" should the need arise. I had a female friend who worked in a popular tanning salon in NYC and she would tell me how all the women who dropped in for a tanning session would be masturbating on the beds and she could hear the buzzing of the vibrators when she patrolled the facility. She would have to wash down the beds with cleaning spray after each session because they would be covered in female sexual fluids. What's interesting about this is that tanning beds not only mimic the heat and energy of the sun, but they mimic the heat and energy of a real man's penis as well. Poorly, but better than nothing. A real man with high testosterone who isn't jerking off to porn ten times per day will have a lot of heat and energy radiating from his cock. So women actually use tanning salons to get masculine energy and sexual relief, in order to have more control over their sexuality, and consequently more control over men. I've known women so sexually addicted to tanning, they chose tanning over having sex with actual men. You can usually identify these types of women because they are tanned 365 days out of the year to the degree they look like burnt toast.

Breaking Thru Her Neurosis as Opposed to Mirroring It

Back before the "me too" movement, my solution to preserve my own integrity was to use only an honest, straightforward approach even though it had a low success rate. Because when it did succeed it was so worth it at the core of my being, that it made up for all of the failures. The sexual experiences that came out of that approach were authentic and amazing. If I had compromised myself just to get laid, those sexual experiences that would have resulted from said compromise, would not have been very enjoyable. What people are really after are peak experiences, or quality over quantity. Sure, they want quantity as well, but quantity over quality is foolish, although rather understandable when one is starting out. I grew very aggressive at one point, throwing women in clubs that I had just met over my shoulder and fireman-carrying them out the door. Never got anything other than an incredibly positive response, with women saying things like "How do you know me so well, etc." I would see a woman eating in a restaurant checking me out and I would go over and whisper in her ear what I wanted to do to her. She would end up taking me home. It should go without saying that one requires a real sense of calibration to attempt these sorts of stunts. Primarily, the woman needs to be really attracted to you sexually. The issue nowadays is that it has become so trendy to cry harassment that even if your calibration is on, you are still taking an unnecessary risk. If you are going to pursue such a route, it is imperative that you don't ever do this at the gym or where you work, live, etc., and be aware that there is an ever-growing army of captain-save-a-ho simps that you will have to contend with. Be warned!

Pro Tip: When you go out on a date, carry a micro-sized vibrating wand that is as powerful as possible. When making out with a girl out in the street or wherever, push her up against the wall and then press the vibrating wand against her pussy through her clothing. Make her cum while her clothes are still on, and you will set the tone from the start: there will be no repression of sexual energy nor giving it away to other men in the initial stages of "dating," in other to gain control over you and the relationship. She will either surrender from the jump and give it up, or get the fuck out. Then again, I forget what year this is, so she *may* call the police. The real question here is *why* are so many women turned on by more "aggressive" sexual advances? For the simple reason that rape fantasies are so prevalent: they break through the woman's neurotic walls that prevent their enjoyment of sex. This is the same reason why so many women can't stop watching gang bang porn! They want to lose control, be overwhelmed by cocks, and be forced to cum since their normal state is one of frigidity (anorgasmia). Incidentally, this inability to properly orgasm due to neurosis is *also* the reason why so many women love to be choked during sex! It's the only way they can feel something…

When I talk about choking women lots of people get really upset. Women freak out, because they are afraid that if men knew this, men would lose all respect for them. Men freak out too, because they can't accept the sexual natures of modern women. So without further ado…

Some studies and statistics to verify my seemingly outrageous claims:

- A 2009 study published in the Journal of Sex Research found that **62% of women surveyed had experienced a rape fantasy at some point**. Other research reviews estimate the prevalence between 31% and 57%. Among women who reported such fantasies, the median frequency was about four times per year, with 14% of participants experiencing them at least once a week. While these fantasies exist on an erotic-aversive continuum: **in one study, 46% described them as both erotic and aversive!** TAKE NOTE: *Researchers emphasize that the presence of such fantasies does not mean a desire for actual sexual assault.*

- A 2016 summary of research in HuffPost reports that 29% of women fantasized about being forced to have sex, making it one of the more common fantasies, but not the top one. **Other common fantasies included being spanked or whipped (36%), being photographed or filmed during sex (32%), and group sex (46%)** - with the most common being sex in a romantic location (57%) and sex with a current partner (61%) TAKE NOTE: *Anyone with any knowledge of female nature will realize that the last two "scenarios" are lies women told to the survey takers to protect their perceived image and reputation. Also of note is that fantasies of corporeal punishment, exhibitionism and group sex are all outcroppings of neurosis.*

- A 2020 U.S. probability survey found that 21% of women ages 18 to 60 had been choked during sex. Among college students, the numbers are much higher: *a 2021 survey found that **58% of female college students reported being choked during sex, and about one-third said they were choked during their most recent sexual activity**.* Another recent study found that about **1 in 3 young adult U.S. women were choked or strangled the last time they had sex**. In one study, almost 82% of those choked during sex reported euphoria, and almost 44% reported a head rush.

- According to Pornhub Data (2015–2021), women are 29% more likely than men to view gangbang videos, and they are 71% more likely than men to search for "gangbang" content. In 2015, women were reported to be over 105% more likely to seek out genres like "gangbang" and "rough sex" compared to men, and according to a 2015 Pornhub Insights report, ***"gangbang," "rough sex," and "double penetration" were among the top search terms for women, with women being more likely than men to search for these terms**.*

Why The "Me Too" Movement Murdered the PUA Scene

Sadly, the Satanic scourge of "political correctness" destroyed the old-school PUA movement which refused to board the red pill bus and just kept on going out into the field and refining what actually worked. They were really beginning to accomplish something, but Satan simply could not allow this ragtag bunch of males who had nothing to lose, to continue to "hijack the simulation with absurdity" as former RSD instructor "Jeffy" recently put it. I mean, when you purchase a used van, spray paint "rape van" on the side of it, park it in front of a bar and women you just met happily have sex with you inside of it, how much more absurd can things get? The world could not be allowed to see this reality! Hence the current war on comedy. Comedy used to be the only arena where one could speak the truth by mocking the absurdity of this Satanic "reality," thereby getting people to laugh at it and hopefully wake up and change their behaviors, which is always a more effective strategy than staging armed revolutions which just feed the "matrix."

Anyway, the precise flash point for the demise of the PUA movement was their discussion of the nuances of "rape culture" in Japan, specifically the cultural phenomenon of Japanese women saying "no" when they really mean "yes," and then when a western male respects the fact that they didn't give consent, the Japanese woman tells all of her friends that he must be some sort of "faggot" because he didn't "rape" them. This experience is a shock for Western men, and it has happened to both myself and several of my friends who have dated Japanese women, both in the United States as well as in Japan.

What some in the PUA scene were suggesting, is that it can be empowering for Western men to travel to Japan and have the experience of "raping" such females. Why? Because it allows men to free themselves from the female neurosis that they find themselves taking on in order to get their desires met. I would suggest that visiting the right sort of prostitute is safer (and cheaper) than going to Japan, for what it's worth. Naturally, the suggestion to go visit Japan to "rape" the women infuriated Western women and embarrassed the Japanese, bringing down the hammer. For those of you who are interested in examining this cultural phenomenon in greater detail, there are several videos on YouTube of Western expats attempting to come to terms with this aspect of female sexuality in Japan.

Japan is a curious place because the childhood trauma of your average Japanese citizen is highly unique and all-pervasive. Japanese culture is so restrictive, yet their quasi-legalized culture of sex work, specializing in every fetish imaginable, is without limits. Let's talk a bit about the trauma of modern Japanese childhood...

Children in Japan are generally spoiled by American standards, at least until they hit school age. Spoiling children to the outrageous extreme practiced in Japan is a phenomenon Japanese psychologists call "amae." This is the notion that people, especially children, exist to be indulged by parents, grandparents, bosses and friends. Japanese parents tend to indulge their children and have closer physical proximity to them, whereas parents in Western countries are likely to encourage their children to be independent and behave autonomously from an early age. Japanese mothers are supposed to take these indulgences to an even higher level. Suddenly, children are expected to spend the next 12 years in the Japanese school system getting hammered into submission (admittedly more so in the olden days than in the present). School is subsequently followed by work slavery until retirement or death.

The research suggests this transition between extremes can have "significant effects." There's also evidence of a connection between the shock of the transition from spoiled childhood to adulthood, with "social withdrawal phenomena." Either way, to be spoiled to the point that maturity is forever out of reach, only to have your indulgences torn away and replaced with being subjected to a brutal school system and a culture of overwork, creates a very unique form of trauma that can only be vented in the nation's red light districts, if you ask me... You can almost view the Japanese red light district as a refuge from the adult world and a return to childhood, where one can be spoiled without limits, albeit in a sexual context. This is Japan's primary mechanism for social control. No matter how much the population is abused, the population will never rebel because they can always retreat to the red light district to vent their psychic distress and relive their wonderful childhoods within the context of the most powerful energy available to them – their sexual energy!

To return to the United States again, some of the things I talk about in this book are from my time in the field before the "me too" movement. It was simply a different time... These days if you say something that Captain Obvious himself would sign off on (i.e. women like it when a man they are attracted to takes charge), you can suddenly find yourself on trial as if you are some sort of rapist or something! With this being said, I run a great risk here for what I am about to say, because I am going to reveal certain things about women that will strip away so much of their power, I put myself in grave danger of being subjected to a modern-day witch hunt. But with that being said...

I saw a comedy sketch online *many* years back which depicted a satirical human resources video educating males on "sexual harassment in the workplace." The message of the video was that if women find you attractive, it is impossible to sexually harass them, whereas if you are unattractive *anything* you say or do towards a woman will get you brought up on sexual harassment charges in front of HR!

That truth is that if a woman has genuine sexual desire for you, you can pretty much get away with *anything* and she will overlook it. You could throw her over your shoulder and carry her out of a bar in a play to take her home. You could come up behind her and grind your middle finger directly into her asshole while she is perusing the ice cream section at your local supermarket. The list goes on-and-on. Most guys have no idea the crazy things women want, they just don't want those crazy things from *most* guys. So, they pretend they don't want those things at all. Can't blame them, as they don't want every man out there harassing and groping them every time they leave the fucking house! If they wanted that, they could move to Europe, which should just change its name to "Eurape" at this point.

Naturally, in today's "me too" climate many courses of actions are inadvisable regardless of whether a woman wants them or not. So while you *could* do the things I am talking about, the question really is, *should* you? There is just *too much risk* in implementing what is actually completely natural anymore, as *these days* the consequences are simply not worth it, should something go askew. But with that being said, let class continue!

Many years ago when I was actively going out on dates, I used to very frequently notice that I would have all of this sexual tension and chemistry built up with my date. I would be actively escalating said tension in order to have sex with them, when suddenly the woman would claim that she had to go to the bathroom. A perfectly plausible claim. The issue, as we will come to see, is *why* she had to go to the bathroom? Was it really to piss or shit or check her makeup? Or was it something else? Because upon her return, I would notice that the sexual tension and chemistry had magically disappeared, and nothing I could do would enable me to resurrect it and resume the escalation. As time went on, the date would end and they would arrange for a second date.

After this happened a few times, I began to suspect that something must be happening when they went to the bathroom that dissipated all of the sexual tension. Then it hit me. They were going to the bathroom to masturbate, so as to get back control over the power dynamic between us.

So... once I realized that women were running to the bathroom to masturbate away the sexual tension they felt with me, it was time to prove this hypothesis, and at the same time put a stop to their bullshit. I would not recommend anyone do this today, but when I was young, times were different. So, I was out with one girl and she excused herself and went to the bathroom. I knew what was up, so I waited a good 5-10 minutes and then went into the ladies room (which was laid out in a manner conducive to my plan), and caught her in the stall masturbating with a pocket vibrator *while texting some other guy*! She freaked out and threatened to call the police but I just started laughing and said I would see her back at the table when she was done cumming. I sat there smiling, as she took another 5-10 minutes or so to emerge from the restroom. She came over and sat down next to me and just glared and said I was fucking crazy. I just kept smiling and agreed. After a few moments, she jumped on me and started making out with me. An hour later, she was jerking me off under a table in a crowded restaurant.

Pro Tip: You should always be working on your own inner awareness, because when you attain awareness of your own mind, then you can attain awareness of what is going on in the minds of others. This is also why they say you can lie to others, but you should never lie to yourself. Because when you deceive yourself, it becomes easy for others to deceive you as well.

Again, I don't want to encourage things that can land you with criminal charges, but had I not acted, I would have never been able to sleep with her, as she was a genuine "9" who had a literal parade of men following her around the club I initially met her in. I also would never have been able to confirm my suspicions and prove my theory. You should never tolerate this sort of nonsense from a woman because no matter how "into you" a woman may be, *if* she begins the relationship controlling her sexual energy it will *never* stop, even if one day she *wants* it to stop. Such is the nature of neurosis, the contagion of the psyche.

For The Record: I have only met one genuine "10" in my life. That was Paulina Porizkova, who lived very close to where I grew up. I exchanged a few words with her once, and she was so cool to me in that brief interaction, when she didn't *have* to be. She was at the peak of her beauty and modeling career in those days, and I was an awkward loser, although a rather good looking awkward loser! I say this because I have heard so many people online and in person - who have never met her, refer to her as a stuck up bitch and mock her now that she is old and claims to be "invisible" to men, but she really doesn't deserve your mockery and hate. Furthermore she married for love at the peak of her beauty and career, only to have her husband really screw her over in the end, which was totally fucked up on his part. A genuine "10" being so cool to me for just a few moments, helped to offset the endless moments in my life where far lesser women were just plain rotten to me.

Keep in mind that not only was this woman masturbating in a bathroom stall, but she was texting another man. Why? Because she intended to fuck him later on that night to garner even further control over her feelings for me. This is an even more common practice than masturbating in the bathroom on dates. What happens at the start of almost all relationships these days, is that if a woman is dating a guy she is genuinely crazy about, she will *always* try and get control over the situation by fucking some other loser (or losers) during the initial dating phase. So you will be out to dinner with her, or hanging out and feeling this great connection and attraction, yet at the end of the night when you go home to dream about her and bask in the magic you just shared with her, some absolute loser is pounding her guts out — whom she doesn't even give a shit about, in order for her to maintain control over her feelings for you. How insanely fucked up is this reality, and is this *any* way to start a *successful* relationship with a man?

What women don't realize, is that this deceptive and cowardly behavior *murders* anything real between them and the guy they really want. Which ultimately, is their subconscious goal anyway, because it allows them to avoid the impending potential pain of a genuine connection. However, they want to dodge responsibility for their sabotage and be able to *blame* the murder of the relationship *at some future point* on the man of their dreams, who has no clue how their relationship is actually starting out, and therefore is not able to diagnose what has already started to go wrong. He will just act up at some point in the future, not know why, and get blamed for acting up and ruining the relationship. But the guy *always finds out eventually*, and *then* her excuse will *always* be: "But we weren't *officially* together then!" *As if* that is an excuse. At that point, the relationship is destroyed beyond repair, and the cowardly cunt will blame it all on the man, calling him "insecure" when he was simply disrespected and betrayed beyond his imagination. The moment you both have serious intentions – and you know if you do from *day fucking one*, you are officially together no matter what garbage you tell yourself. *In essence*, these dopey women start cheating on the man of their dreams starting on day one and then wonder why everything goes down in flames in the future! But again, that is their true intention from the jump, because if the relationship "worked out," then they would have to deal with *The Trauma of Love*.

Pro Tip: It is for reasons such as the above that you should *always* assume that every woman you are with is cheating on you. If you assume infidelity from the start, then not only do you minimize being hurt by her deceptions, but *maybe* you can actually start to develop something real *in spite of* them. *Maybe*. Because a lot of guys settle for girl just because they think she is faithful and not because there is something real there. Someone being faithful cannot be the *only* reason for being with them. So if you assume she is cheating, would you still want to be with her? If the answer is yes, then she is on a different level and what the two of you have together is *real*. This is naturally assuming you are not a cuck, who likes being cheated on... My logic may seem counter intuitive, but basically if the connection between you is so strong that it would not matter if she was fucking someone else, isn't that a good yardstick by which to measure the grounds for a successful future relationship? Do not misunderstand, I am not encouraging cheating and it would have to come to an end if it was occurring, once you both acknowledge what you have together. Unless, of course, you are both into unorthodox relationships outside of cuckoldry.

My point is, given the reality of "dating" today, I am just trying to adapt to this reality in a way that could potentially offer the best possible outcome.

Either way, let me ask you again: why should a guy pay a fortune (or anything for that matter) for something that lesser men got for free? Why should a man have to wait for sex when other men did not? Women pretend like they don't know this is wrong, but they do know. They just don't care. Of course, women will once again say things like "my sexual past doesn't matter" or that their sexual past is "none of my current partner's business," but here is the thing: what if these women found out that their male partner used to have sex with men as much as he had sex with women? Would *they* let him get away with saying his sexual past didn't matter or that it was none of *their* business? As a matter of fact, 9 out of 10 women would dump a man over this. Also, how would a woman feel if a guy gave *all* of his other ex-girlfriends expensive handbags and shoes on a regular basis, while she received nothing but a steady diet of cum and piss?

An Honest Discussion of "Consent" and Sexual Power Dynamics

I find the "me too" movement a joke because it is ultimately nothing more than a complaint about the existence of the "casting couch." While it can certainly be argued that having to sleep with some "gatekeeper" to get an acting job is a bad thing, it can also be considered a good thing, as those without talent can still succeed despite a lack of talent. If some old, fat, female film executive came to me and said, "If you eat my pussy I will put you in a film that makes you rich and famous," I should think I'd won the fucking lottery. She'd probably get a "thank you card" on the anniversary of that date until either she or I kicked the bucket. As men, we've all jumped on our share of grenades in our past, so what is the big deal doing so to get a part in a film?

But what really irks me about the "me too" movement is that *choosing* to exchange sex for fame and fortune is not the same as being *forced* to do so. I mean, how many women *could* have said no, but simply didn't due to the allure of fame and fortune? Let's back up for a moment and look at the definition of rape according to the U.S. Dept. of Justice:

"The penetration, no matter how slight, of the vagina or anus with any body part or object, or oral penetration by a sex organ of another person, without the consent of the victim."

So if a woman doesn't say "no" due to the allure of fame and fortune, she has given consent. She hasn't been raped, but rather has engaged in prostitution. *She* is now the criminal! Can a prostitute retroactively accuse every single one of her clients of rape claiming "But I was afraid I would be unable to pay my rent?" Of course not! So why is some actress allowed to claim "I did it because I was afraid for my career (or lack thereof)" as a reason for *consenting* to sexual activity she was not genuinely interested in, and now basically arguing that somehow her consent should be retroactively nullified, and the other party punished? I mean, how many people refused to consent to the covid-19 vaccine, then were told that they would be fired if they refused to give consent so they ended up giving consent? Can it not be said that those people who ultimately consented to the vaccine even though they did not want to, were also "afraid for their career?" So how come Dr. Anthony Fauci didn't get strung up for this? He even got a preemptive presidential pardon for it, then mocked his victims by stating: "Nobody forced anyone to take the vaccine!"

Some will say that taking a vaccine is not the same as being sexually violated, yet I would argue that getting your body penetrated by a needle and being injected with a bunch of fluids that interact with your biology is no different than having your body penetrated by a penis and it ejaculating inside of you. Well, it isn't rape according to the U.S. Dept. of Justice's definition of the word, but then can I cut an incision into a woman's body and fuck the shit out of it, claiming it isn't rape because I didn't penetrate the woman's vagina, anus or mouth? I mean, according to the U.S. Dept. of Justice that would not be rape, just assault with a deadly weapon, although I am sure they will argue that my incision created a *legal fiction* of a vagina, albeit not a bona fide one, much like a surgeon can create a *legal fiction* of a vagina in a trans person – or are they considering it a bona fide one now since there is no such thing as gender? I can't keep up with all of the mental illness, it's all just so tiresome... My clever *"legal fiction of a vagina"* is just a little "shout out" to all the sovereignty nerds reading this, although they probably hate me since most of them are Christians!

The biggest load of bullshit is this nonsense about "power dynamics." You can still say no. When I was young and pretty, I got a job working at a big corporation. I worked at many big corporations for that matter. So there was one female executive who was very powerful. She was rather attractive as well, and she had her eye on me. She desired some sort of "50 Shades" type of relationship with me where she was the domme, so one day she sent her assistant to have lunch with me. This assistant informed me of what her boss desired, and said that if I played along I would be rewarded with fast-track promotions, money, and an illustrious career. I asked her why her boss didn't just approach me directly, and she replied, "Oh no, you have to go to her and offer yourself to her and play the submissive role." I don't enjoy role play so I declined. I got fired a few weeks later.

The point is, I said "no" even though this executive was attractive and the power dynamics were against me. I could have probably sued, but I loathe suing people and find it so very gay.

Women like to rant that rape is never actually about sex, but always about power. This is a dangerous lie, as it only "creates the space" for more rapes to occur in society because it ignores the underlying motives for rape. Do you think that all those migrants in Germany, England and Sweden who are groping and raping all of these European women and girls do so over power? Fuck no! They are horny and violent low IQ animals who want sex and don't care about consent. Naturally, all sexual acts have a component of power. A woman on top, or a man going down on a woman, is the woman exerting power. Whereas a man on top or a woman going down on a man, is the opposite dynamic. BDSM is more focused on power dynamics than it is sex, for sure. But stating that rape has *nothing* to do with sex and only has to do with power is utterly ridiculous. The truth is that rape is only about power from *the female perspective*, as she knows that rape takes away the power that she derives from withholding sex and turning it into a commodity. But from the male perspective, rape is usually about sex.

However, one instance in which male sexual aggression is *very often* about power and not about sex, is with respect to the issue of "deepfake porn" campaigns launched online. Notice that I am calling it "sexual aggression" because it certainly cannot be considered "rape" based on the definition of rape, yet it is a form of sexual aggression and it is definitely very often about power. AI-powered deepfake porn is often created with the intention to disempower a woman and gain control over her public image in the process. You will find this sort of deefake porn often used against genuinely powerful women who draw their power from professional success and wealth creation as opposed to drawing their power from commodifying their sexuality.

These "sexual assaults" on a female's character are especially fucked up because you often have a woman who is not letting sex tapes of herself get leaked or acting like a porn star as part of her public persona, so what loser men do is they use AI to generate sexual imagery of her, which in the minds of the general public have the same effect as if a real sex tape was leaked. Not *consciously*, of course… But watching endless AI-generated images and video clips of conservative, successful women getting gang-banged, on their knees pretending to be a urinal with cum in their mouths, etc. will overpower the images you have in your brain of her in real life that are based upon reality. So in the minds of everyone who views these insanely realistic AI porn fakes of her, her image is forever altered from the one she worked so hard to build, to one of a cum and piss guzzling gang bang whore.

A More Complex Definition of Neurosis

But there is much more at stake for a woman who embraces her orgasmic nature than becoming sexually enslaved to the man who triggers it. She is also afraid of the full power of her sexual energy because when all of that sexual energy starts to flow, it will smash through her locked up and frozen solar plexus diaphragm, and what will flow along with that sexual energy, will also be the repressed energy of *all* of her collective trauma, and this would be incredibly destabilizing for her.

I will periodically return to the core idea, that while it is commonly assumed that the number one goal of the human organism is survival, this is 100% false. The number one goal is psychic stability. Again, if survival were the number one goal, then why would people smoke, go to war, or drive their sport bikes on public highways at speeds approaching 200 mph? Actually, it could easily be argued that humans are actively seeking death, they are just unaware of it.

Once again, what is the core of PUA teachings? It is to become as neurotic as a woman in order to get her to give you pussy. If you can prove your own neurosis, you can prove that you are "safe." Safe in what way? Safe in the sense that you are assuring her that if she is with you, she will never have to feel anything real. Say what? Now here is the perfect time to give you a definition of neurosis that is more complex: so while it is still true that neurosis in it's simplest form is a conflict in drives, on a more complex level **neurosis is choosing to suffer inauthentic (and less painful) pain perpetually, rather than having to face authentic (and far more painful) pain temporarily**, EVEN THOUGH choosing the latter would give you the chance to be free. Ask yourself, what path would a real man, a fucking warrior, choose? Certainly not the path of neurosis!

Let me give you a concrete example of what I am talking about. Let's say you have some deep pain. Take the pain of sorrow, for example. It is so painful, that you repress it, and as a result you develop obsessive compulsive disorder (OCD). So now you are doomed to spend the rest of your life washing your hands 50 times per day, which is a completely ridiculous form of suffering, yet you would clearly rather suffer in such a ridiculous and undignified manner, than feeling your sorrow fully, EVEN THOUGH doing so would give you the chance to work through that deep sorrow and potentially be free from it!

Neurosis Is Your Mind's Way of Protecting Itself

I am not trying to beat on people with OCD. I myself suffered from it when I was young, and cured myself of it by consciously fighting against it, while simultaneously forcing myself to feel in any way that I could. This two-pronged attack on neurosis works synergistically. Naturally the mind will fight back against your efforts because it is genuinely trying to protect you from what it perceives as feelings that would overwhelm and annihilate your psyche. Again, what is the number one goal of the human organism? Psychic stability! I suspect that the strength it takes to fight against neurosis proves to your mind *over time*, that you are indeed strong enough to deal with whatever the neurosis is protecting you from being aware of, and that in time the mind simply decides to let go, and let you have your shot at processing the underlying trauma fueling the neurosis.

Incidentally, this mental journey mirrors what happens in the human body in terms of the journey to unleash your innate physical strength. Most people mistakenly believe that you develop strength from lifting weights. This is only true in the sense that lifting weights allows you to develop strength in your bones, tendons, and connective tissues. It is impossible to "build strength" with respect to muscles, because the human musculature is already so insanely strong, that a skinny girl is capable of lifting up a car to save her infant child. **Tetanus**, which is caused by the bacteria *Clostridium tetani*. can cause sustained muscle contractions so powerful they can potentially fracture bones, including vertebrae in the spine.

So why can't you just walk outside and pick up a car? Because your mind prevents you from accessing this innate strength, out of the fear that you will tear muscles from bones picking up every car you see, the next time you are drunk and want to show off! What weight lifting does, is it convinces your protective mind that you are strong enough to handle ever increasing poundages without injuring yourself, and then your mind grants you access to more and more strength. It's judgment isn't perfect, mind you, given all the pectoral and bicep tears that routinely occur, however any old-tyme strongman who bends steel bars and rolls up frying pans knows that the "secret" training methods they *all* use revolve around building tendon and bone strength, combined with exercises to trick the mind into unleashing more and more of the body's innate strength.

Here is the method I learned from old-tyme strongman Steve Weiner, who is a Guinness World Records holder for the most frying pans rolled in one minute by a male, achieving 14 frying pans rolled in one minute at the Venetian VIP Show in Macau, China, on January 10, 2015. This record was previously held by him with 12 frying pans rolled in one minute. Steve is a totally awesome dude and an absolute legend in the iron game, who knows more about drug-free training than probably anyone alive today.

He has also kept detailed training logs for his entire life. I was lucky enough to meet Steve many years back through a mutual friend who is sadly no longer with us, and trained with him a few times in his private strongman gym, at his house out on Long Island. While you cannot develop additional, new muscle fibers without sufficient IGF-1 levels in your blood, the development of strength is primarily a neurological adaptation. The fact that Steve is natural, validates his training methodologies which he has documented over the course of his entire strongman career.

Steve told me that the most important exercise for unleashing strength, is to do insanely heavy rack pulls for high repetitions every 7-10 days. You load up a barbell on a power rack at such a height that if you grasp the weight and lift with your legs while keeping your back straight up and perpendicular to the ground, you'll be picking the weight up a distance of around six inches. You get a power lifting lever-belt to make sure you don't catch a hernia, but don't make the belt too tight because if a lifting belt is too tight it will not work as intended. It must be tight, but not tight to the degree that you cannot brace your abdominal wall against it. Next, you need lifting straps such as "Versa Grips" or a knock- off version. The longer the strap, the better. You'll also want lifting chalk. Versa Grips or their knock-offs, will enable you to hold more poundages than any other strap or hook out there. I've used them all, and only when you pull serious weights will you know the truth about what works and what doesn't. Metal hooks may hold more weight "on paper," but in practice they fail for biomechanical reasons I don't want to get bogged down explaining at the moment. The short answer, however, is that Versa Grips and their knock-offs work synergistically with your own natural gripping mechanics.

Anyway, you load up the bar with maybe 400 lbs to start, and perform 20 reps. You will find very quickly that you can do a lot more than 400 lbs. The lifting straps make sure you can hold the weight, and the belt makes sure you can brace your core to hold yourself together. Many people can leg press 1000 lbs a few inches, but what about when you are holding 1000 lbs in your hands? Can you use the same leg motion to *pick it up* a few inches? The answer is yes you can, and within 6 months you will be lifting 1000 lbs for 20 reps. People in the gym will accuse you of ego-lifting but they don't understand that you are training your nervous system to unleash your innate strength, and at the same time strengthening your bones and tendons and ligaments to support an incredible output of force. One day, your body just allows you more access to your true physical strength, which carries over into everything you do, such as bending steel bars and rolling up frying pans!

I can't tell you how many times a guy who was bigger and stronger than me on exercises like the bench press, and often on steroids, would come over and say "anybody can do that." I would always say "show me," and he would always try and be shocked when he couldn't even pick up 1000 lbs *once*, let alone 20 times in succession.

Can you see the parallels with conquering OCD? You need to prove to your mind that you are strong enough to handle psychically destabilizing pain without committing suicide or otherwise self-destructing, just like you need to prove to your body that you are capable of wielding incredible strength without tearing muscles from bones or even snapping said bones!

Why Women Waste Their Time With "Bad Boys"

Back to the bitches! We can all see that most women will waste their time on what we will call "bad boys," which really means men who are "bad" for them both spiritually, as well as practically speaking. Women take up with criminals, drug dealers, clownish rappers, fuck boys, abusive men... Why? It has *nothing* to do with these men showing some imagined "alpha" traits. It is because these men are fundamentally as damaged as the women who get with them are, and I am sure you have heard the expression that "water seeks its own level?" They are never truly *in love* with the "bad boys," just *addicted* to them. I mean, is a drug addict *in love* with drugs? Of course not. He's just an addict.

But why are women addicted to bad boys? Because they can project their past traumatic internal dramas onto them and relive them in an external fashion, in present time. Why do they wish to play with their past trauma in such a fashion? It is because some part of them is hoping that by reliving their past pain through their present relationship with the bad boy, they will somehow slip thru the cracks right into said past pain – and have a chance to fully experience it, work through it, and finally resolve/release it. But tragically, that rarely, if ever happens. Why? Mostly because they have no *conscious awareness* of what is actually going on, so they don't see that they are involved in a "shadow play" where the drama they are experiencing with the "bad boy," is just a reenactment of something that happened long ago. The subconscious mind does not have a concept of time, you must remember.

So they usually just end up retraumatizing themselves over-and-over until they fall off the trauma carousel, and decide to "settle" for a "nice guy" who won't "hurt them." *"I married my best friend!"* is the typical refrain. Poor guy... That's why you hardly ever have sex with him, either! Ironically, these women end up becoming the abuser, and torturing the "nice guy," spreading the disease of trauma like a contagion. In short, their dramas just get projected onto the "nice guy," albeit in a different form. The theater of pain box office *always* has tickets on sale! What's so critical about awareness, is that *sometimes* just possessing awareness of the underlying dynamics at play, is enough to start the process of change.

Of course when I say "nice guy" I am referring to any guy who is not carrying the trauma of a "bad boy." You might actually be the *farthest thing* from an actual "nice guy," but as long as you are not carrying "bad boy trauma," you will be treated like some sort of "nice guy" and end up used and abused by females. This is why so many men have come to realize that you can't just *not* be a nice guy to "succeed" with women. Rather, you have to make the consciously aware decision to become a straight up asshole. One of my friends used to get girls to eat his ass, and then purposely fart in their mouths. Women loved him. He was super good-looking though, and when you look that good, you can fart in a girl's mouth. That's one aspect of the "black pill" that is true. But again, it's not a *requirement.* I knew of a very beautiful girl who ate her boyfriend's shit on a daily basis. Her boyfriend was nothing special to look at, believe me, and he would literally shit *directly* into her mouth at least once per day and she would gobble it all up. Let me ask you, how does *your* sex life compare to his? Doesn't this piss you off at all?

One thing that pisses me off, that I see in Russian communities all the time, is Russian women who will get pregnant by some businessman, no matter how ugly, because then they get child support for the next 18 years. I am not talking about child support that is government-enforced. I mean these Russian businessmen just give them money and take pride in the fact that they have kids all over the place with beautiful women. They don't even care to see the women or their kids, and the woman usually parks the kids with her mom while she goes out to forage for some bad boy cock. The businessman is too busy making money to give a shit one way or the other. What pisses me off is these beautiful women befouling their genetic legacy making ugly kids just for money to buy time with bad boys.

Polish women generally don't do this sort of thing. Probably because Polish men aren't very good at making money. So the women tend to get impregnated by bad boys and at least continue producing attractive people even if they are all drunkards just like the Russians are. But at least they are attractive alcoholics, not some hideous "Vatniks" sleeping it off in a puddle of their own piss. When I lived in a Polish neighborhood, every morning I would have to step over "Wojtek the Bear" who would be passed out in the hallway or on the stairs, having been unable to make it back into his apartment. Couldn't blame him though, as certain Polish potato vodkas are so smooth, you'd think you were drinking water until your legs stop working. But they were always good-looking and never laying about in their own piss. That would be *undignified*. Given that most of my human DNA is of Slavic stock, naturally I am a vodka enthusiast. My favorite vodka ever? Snow Queen Vodka from Kazakhstan.

Welcome To The "Fantasy Boyfriend League"

Chicks have their own version of "Fantasy Football" except it involves their imaginary boyfriends. This arises out of psychological necessity, because as I pointed out earlier in this book, the men that women are *actually* in love with, they are *never* actually with. They love them from a distance. Always! Even if they do on rare occasions end up dating or marrying them, they simply end up *not being present* and making their man miserable to the point that he cheats on them and/or leaves them. These girls do this by basically dissociating throughout the entire relationship, much like a girl dissociates while being raped, just to a lesser degree.

These men who are always loved from afar, yet never loved in person, end up in what one of my best friends used to call the "fantasy boyfriend league." He actually coined that term, which is an apt description. *In the minds of these women*, they are actually *with* the men they really love, so there is no need to actually be with them *in physicality*! Wrap your minds around that one! Plus, to actually be *with* one of these "fantasy boyfriends" in physical reality would be very threatening and insanely risky to their own psychic stability. Nope, they choose the lesser, yet lifelong pain and suffering of being with the bad boy followed by the nice-guy-best-friend that they can barely tolerate, over the much greater - albeit temporary, pain and suffering of being with someone they truly love. They are just too weak, cowardly and lazy to go "all in" and to "do the inner work" it takes to overcome the trauma that true love exposes, and fight their way to freedom. Now do you know why women despise men who "self improve?" It is because it takes courage to face your demons, and most women lack it.

They're pathetic.

I ran into a girl on the street when I was in my early 20s who approached me and gave me her number. I went on a date with her, but she wouldn't sleep with me because "I was poor" and she needed a man with money. It was obvious I was poor, so why the fuck did she pursue me to begin with? I told her that she was free to chase men with money while sleeping with me, as I am not jealous, plus I was in my early 20s and she was already 29 at the time so I understood the practicalities of her situation. She told me she can't do that because she is in love with me and will be unable to have sex with other men *and* me at the same time. Well lucky me…

I wrote her off right then and there, but for years she would periodically look me up and want to hang out. I was clearly part of her Fantasy Boyfriend League. She would always be chasing some rich guy who didn't give a shit about her and just used her. Does it surprise you that her own father abandoned her and wanted nothing to do with her? It really shouldn't! Finally, one day she tells me that she has come to a decision: since men do nothing but use her, she is going to take up high-end escort work. It never dawned on her that she had *always* been a prostitute, she was simply deciding to lower her rates! It also never dawned on her that since she was intent on using men herself, it really shouldn't be a shock that they would use her in return.

It's like one time I saw an interview with some porn star, who appeared to me to have the IQ of a baked potato, who she said she got into porn to show up some guy who dumped her. The abject stupidity of some women just melts the mind. So let me get this straight... a guy dumps you... and I am going to take a *wild* guess here that he told you that you sucked in bed... so you go destroy your fucking reputation and you entire life to "show him up?" Yeah, I am sure he really regrets dumping you. Look what he missed out on... You dummy! I am pretty sure he could give two fucks about your new porn career and probably just laughs at you and takes pleasure in how he destroyed your life. I think some of these girls in porn ate one too many crayons growing up.

Anyway, that girl who decided to become a prostitute eventually did end up marrying some rich guy, who probably has no idea about that aspect of her past. Then again, I have known quite a few rich men who married prostitutes. Which makes no sense given you can just keep renting them and trade up without having to go through divorce court! Plus, you don't need to be rich to enjoy prostitutes, so why did you bother to get rich in the first place? For an extra $20G/month in income you can screw a top-shelf hooker every single day of the year, and still have enough for quite a few "omakase" nights at the hottest authentic Japanese restaurants in town! #livingmybestlife

Pro Tip: In the United States the best hookers cost around $600/hour. There are of course many charging as much as $2000/hour, but IME the best ones are not very expensive. No girl is worth $2000/hour, but if you did the math, you would be shocked to realize you are probably paying your ugly girlfriend the same rate, and she probably doesn't even rim your asshole. If you've never had a hot girl lick your asshole like a starving Tibetan dog that just stumbled upon a nice meal of freshly dropped human shit, you really don't know what "self care" is, my friend!

There have been quite a few women in my life who put me into their Fantasy Boyfriend League and it bothers me quite a bit, to be honest, because it is always the women with whom there was a truly incredible connection. How much happiness I lost due to the cowardice of women! I know that from the woman's point of view, they look at how much potential pain they avoided, but I suspect they all realize when they get old enough, just how much they fucked themselves over with their cowardice. Then again, who knows?

Female Commodification of Sexuality

Let's take another look at why females repress their sexuality, which is in order to turn it into a commodity, or more specifically, *agency*. Quick and easy question: Can you sell something that is available everywhere for free? Of course not. Do you really think men would be spending money on OnlyFans or webcam models if these same men had a rotation of beautiful women to fuck? Of course not. Even if a man had *only one* woman who was amazing in bed and loved sex, he would be so exhausted he would be unable to fuck anyone else. It is only because sex for most men is so fucking hard to get (relative to how easy it is for a woman to get), that men can be sold sex. Why do you think it is so hard to sell sex to a woman? It's the easiest thing for her to get! Mind you, "good" sex is extremely difficult for her to get, but just to get a guy to fuck her is super easy. Now, I am aware that women *can* be sold sex, and you can see this in what are called "host clubs" in Japan, and there are even tantric sex gurus whom women pay for specific orgasmic experiences. But this is not the norm.

But as I stated earlier, it can be argued that it is the wholesale repression and resultant commodification of female sexuality that is behind the growth of modern civilization. Men need to do something with their unfulfilled sex drives, so they start "creating shit." Especially weapons, rockets and bombs which are phallic substitutes. This is the dark side of the phenomenon of technological advancement via sexual repression.

Now you are probably asking yourself, "Are women consciously aware of their decisions in this regard?" That is a good question, but a large percentage of it is a collective subconscious thing, where female children collectively get the message, either overtly or covertly, by both parents and society, that they need to put the breaks on their sexuality, and so they do. Again, neurosis is passed on from parents to children. It is a contagion that infects entire societies at large. But since neurosis springs from trauma, we also have to always keep in mind the absolutely absurd degree of sexual trauma collectively inflicted by males upon females throughout history. I like to put forth the Roman and Ottoman empires as two fantastic examples of this. *All* of the women alive today are the descendants of the literal *survivors* of such horrific "civilizations," and carry the genetic memories of what was done to women in them. Males are beyond dangerous to females and absolutely cannot be trusted when looked at through a historical lens. I am not some "feminist" or "soy boy," just stating brutal facts. The unresolved issue here, is who started the ball rolling? There are really only two possibilities: either males started the abuse and females responded by taking it out on their own children, perpetuating a never-ending cycle, or else females started the never-ending cycle by initiating the abuse of male children, who grew up to take it out on women as adults. This, I have been unable to discern. However, I can tell you that Satan hates females, for reasons I will touch upon later, so either way, he must have had the biggest hand in kick-starting the cycle of abuse, no matter which gender initiated the first strike.

Inflation Turns Women into Whores

The truth is that women have always been inclined towards whoredom due to the financial stressor of inflation, yet prior to Instagram they would have to get off their lazy asses and sit at an expensive hotel bar, crash the right sort of parties, fly to Miami or Monaco, or take out an escort ad in a newspaper. It was a lot of work, clients were limited, and they couldn't hide what they were doing. What Instagram did, was it made it possible to become a whore in the time it takes to create a profile, with plausible deniability, and with an endless supply of worldwide clientele at your fingertips.

Becoming a whore is perfectly natural for a woman, even though it is not her *natural state*. Her natural state is to be hyper-promiscuous, or a slut. That is, until we introduce financial stressors. Now just imagine that instead of having to go out and get a job or start some sort of business, you as a man could get all the money you needed from women just by having sex with them, and women were throwing it at you every day even if you were some "mid" dude. The life of a whore is just so much easier than the life of someone who actually has to work for a living. Of course, the question is *if* women would be whoring so aggressively *if* the money supply wasn't always being *hyper-inflated*?

Let's look at a tier 1 city like New York or Miami:

- As of July 2025, the average rent in New York City is ~$4,000/month.

- As of July 2025, the average rent in Miami is ~$3,000/month.

This is just rent. When you add groceries, internet, cell phone, Uber charges (no beautiful girl takes public transportation unless she wants to be stabbed in her neck), makeup, self-care, eating out with girlfriends, etc. you are looking at an additional $3,000 - $4,000/month. I left out clothing, as that is even more money. As a side note, I was thinking of using San Francisco in place of Miami in the above example, but then I remembered *there are no attractive women in San Francisco!* It's pretty weird, actually, but I digress... the point is, what fucking job can a woman get to generate close to $10,000/month in income? That's $120,000/year and this is after taxes. That means before taxes she would need to make ~$158,000/year in New York City and ~$167,000/year in Miami. Now what jobs pay this sort of salary? Pilots, doctors, dentists, software engineers and corporate slaves in either finance or law. The other option is high-end "government service" which is why women who aren't attractive enough to be whores end up working in progressive government positions, making insane salaries while ruining civilization.

What beautiful women are going to waste their 20s suffering to achieve these salaries when they could spend their hottest years being whores, making *way* more money and actually enjoying their lives? The only women who pursue legitimate fields of work, are the ones who are too ugly to be whores. Stripping, hooking, and sugar-daddying can make a woman $250,000/year tax-free without breaking a sweat, and they'll get another $250,000/year worth of trips and gifts on top of it. I know prostitutes in their 40s who are busted (ugly) but know how to treat men, who *still* make this kind of money.

So women really don't have much of a choice. Now for all of you trad fellows who'll say that they should just go out and get a husband to support them, keep in mind that only ~10% of men make this amount of money which is still not enough to have a wife who stays at home. Only ~5% of men can afford that. Furthermore, the median male income is only ~$60,000/year which means most men are broke losers in the eyes of women. To be with the other 95% of men would require that a woman gets a job, and suffers a substantial reduction in the quality of her life. That ~$60,000/year cock better be a legit 9" and ejaculate orgasmic thunderbolts to compensate for the loss in her quality of life. Given that only 0.01% of men have a 9" cock, and those that do, *don't* ejaculate orgasmic thunderbolts, well…

Pro Tip: If you want a serious relationship, no matter if married or not, you can't let your woman have a job. Why? Because humans spend most of their time either at work or sleeping. A woman who works will consequently have no time for you, and since she spends most of her waking hours on a job, she will end up fucking and falling for a co-worker simply because she is forced to spend most of her time with said co-worker. The amount of time one spends with someone is probably the most critical factor in terms of cementing a relationship.

Now with respect to the 5% of men who can afford a wife, what percentage of them do you think women actually find attractive, meaning they are tall, good-looking and have a big cock? We have already worked those calculations in great detail, and the percentage is soooo low! So whoring not only allows for financial survival, but it allows for a woman to be able to pursue sexual and romantic satisfaction while not having to worry that she is going to starve.

So while *becoming* a whore is perfectly natural for a woman as a *survival strategy*, women aren't *naturally* whores. They are naturally *hyper-promiscuous*, and it is only the *hyper-inflation* of our money supply that flips the survival switch in their brain from "slut" to "whore."

People don't realize just how truly destructive inflation is to the quality of human life. In the 1980s, New York City was all parties and clubs and had a huge music and art scene. Why? Because everything was dirt cheap! Rent in Manhattan was a few hundred bucks a month at most. Buildings in Tribeca lay vacant and you could "squat" in them and take them over *legally*. You saw the same phenomenon in the 2000s in both Brooklyn and Berlin. Both of those areas were all parties and clubs and had a huge music and art scene as well. But those days are long gone, thanks to inflation. Everyone is too busy hustling to be able to afford to *even exist*, let alone enjoy themselves. This is by design!

The elite despise people having fun, having sex, and having freedom. I have known my share of the elites, and they want to have *everything*, while you have *nothing*. That's just the way their diseased minds operate. They are just too covetous. You must understand that *greed does not just apply to money.* This is very important! You may also notice that wherever there is a creative scene, those with money and no soul start to pour in trying to consume all of the "life" that is flourishing there. They drive up prices and drive out those who made those areas "alive" to begin with, as they can no longer afford to live there. This "local" phenomenon, occurs on both a nationwide, as well as a global scale. This is done via the specter of inflation, and I am calling it a "specter" for a reason. Inflation is caused by injecting *artificial purchasing power* (i.e. fiat currency, zero-interest credit, etc.) into an economy *beyond what is needed to maintain the creation and exchange of goods and services.*

The 2001 Japanese animated fantasy film "Spirited Away," written and directed by Hayao Miyazaki, best explains inflation, why I call inflation a "specter," and how and why the elites use it to destroy all the beauty in the world. This is not only a very beautiful and moving film that communicates deeply via the heart chakra, but also addresses the interplay of many different themes all at once, including those of supernaturalism, traditional Japanese culture, western consumerism, environmentalism, and sex trafficking. There is a character in the film called "No-Face" (Kaonashi) who appears as a specter wearing a mask, and totally corrupts the societal equilibrium around him by throwing fake gold all around. Once he introduces the corruptive element of fake gold (fiat currency), he then proceeds to consume everything in sight. *This is the true purpose of inflation: for the elites to ultimately consume everything, leaving everyone else with nothing.*

I will not delve into a deep analysis of the film, because it's genius lies in its ability to communicate directly with your heart chakra. The intellectual, thinking mind is more of a "spare tire" to navigate life with. The more open and developed your heart chakra is, the more information you can get from the film without the need to rely solely upon your intellectual capacity. However, I will say that those who have money and no soul, who stream into affordable areas filled with artists and musicians and other creative types, are no different than the character of "No-Face" presented in Miyazaki's masterpiece of a film.

The True Source of Inflation

The news will always act like inflation is under control but we all know it isn't, because the price of nearly *everything* is too damn high. Why is this? Because the government just keeps pumping money into circulation! For the record, I am aware that the U.S. Government does not exactly print money, but rather borrows it from the Federal Reserve at interest, and that the Federal Reserve is about as "federal" as FedEx. That's outside the scope of this book and if one is interested in such knowledge, it is available on the internet. Now pumping colossal loads of artificial purchasing power into the economy might not be so bad if the money were distributed in an equitable fashion. For example, if every family in America making less than $120,000/year got an extra $50,000/year from the government, this increase in the money supply would not be a big deal, as it would immediately get spent in the goods and services economy. But when trillions upon trillions are given to banks, foreign countries, etc. this money does not get distributed to the masses of people. Instead it goes into the hands of a handful of people (the elites) who will invest it into the "speculative economy." There they will use this money to both gamble in the derivatives markets, as well as buy up all of the assets in sight. They will then use those assets to squeeze the masses dry, generating even more money for themselves and turning the masses into serfs in a modern day feudal system. This is not capitalism, this is a feudalistic oligarchy.

What people do not realize in this "tale of two economies," is that at this point the speculative economy dwarfs the size of the goods and services economy, and all that cash from the speculative economy is competing against your median salary of $60,000/year as well as driving up the price of everything.

Based on the data I found, here's how the speculative/financial economy compares to the real goods and services economy:

Derivatives Market (Speculative Economy):

- The notional value of outstanding derivatives grew by 8% in 2023 to reach USD 667 trillion.

- OTC derivatives grew by 9% in the first half of 2024 to a total notional value.

- Derivatives top the list, estimated at $1 quadrillion or more in notional value.

Real Economy (Global GDP):

- Global GDP increased from $30.7 trillion to $72.4 trillion between 1995-2012.

- Current global GDP is approximately $100-110 trillion.

Based on the most recent data:

- **Derivatives notional value**: ~$667-700 trillion.

- **Global GDP**: ~$100-110 trillion.

- **Ratio**: The speculative economy is approximately **6-7 times larger** than the real economy.

However, we cannot focus *only* on derivatives to define the speculative economy. The speculative economy encompasses much more than just financial derivatives - it includes the entire financialization of the real economy that *extracts value* from the real economy. Let me provide a more comprehensive picture:

Private Equity & Buyout Funds:

- Alternative asset classes – in particular, real assets, private equity and private debt – will more than double in size, reaching $21.1 trillion by 2025.

- Private equity alone bought companies worth $602 billion in 2024, increasing 37% year over year.

Sovereign Wealth Funds:

- Sovereign wealth funds managed a total of $13.2 trillion of assets in 2023, up 14% on the previous year.

Total Financial Assets Under Management:

- Global Assets under Management (AuM) will almost double in size by 2025, from US$84.9 trillion in 2016 to US$111.2 trillion by 2020, and then again to US$145.4 trillion by 2025.

Now we are starting to identify the core issue of *financialization* - where financial capital doesn't just *facilitate productive investment into the goods and services economy as is taught in Economics 101*, but increasingly:

1. **Buys up existing productive assets** (factories, housing, infrastructure, healthcare systems).

2. **Extracts rent** rather than creating new value.

3. **Prioritizes short-term financial returns** over long-term productive capacity.

4. **Transforms essential services** into profit-extraction mechanisms.

So once we recognize that the financialization aspect of the speculative economy is ~$145+ trillion in managed assets, and the Real Economy (Global GDP) is ~$100-110 trillion, and add this financialization aspect to the derivative aspect, **we end up with the speculative economy roughly 8-9 times larger than the entire annual production of goods and services.** This is beyond fucked up, and the reason that these days every man is a slave, and every woman is a whore.

It isn't that the speculative economy is simply "bigger," it's *parasitic*. Private equity doesn't build new factories; it buys existing ones to optimize profit extraction. It doesn't expand healthcare; it buys hospitals to maximize billing. *This represents a fundamental shift from capital serving production to production serving capital accumulation* - exactly the kind of financialization that transforms the real economy into a vehicle for speculative returns rather than human welfare.

When you look at Tier 1 cities like New York City, you will see all these residential skyscrapers where apartments sell for many tens of millions of dollars and monthly maintenance is upwards of $50,000/ month. Who the fuck is buying and living in these units? Another thing men need to realize is that when women get to hang around with this sort of wealth, experience this lifestyle, etc. as a consequence of their whoredom, they will never be happy with you. *Yes,* I know that if a woman truly falls in love or finds a cock that can truly satisfy her, she *can* let all of this go, but as is the whole point of this book, should she stumble upon either, she will choose to run away and hop the next train back into Babylon. It just the nature of the beast these days... I remember one girl I was with who was in love with me, and whom I could satisfy sexually, who nonetheless constantly complained that I was not rich enough to spoil her with constant crap, house her in style, and provide her with the lifestyle other men were able to. The fact remained that *from her perspective*, why was I not able to obtain vast wealth *while others were easily able to do so*, when I was able to provide these other "services" that *nobody else was able to*? Not that it would have made a difference in the long run anyway, because it wasn't long before I struck upon her buried trauma, and the relationship came to an end.

The other thing to realize is that so many of these women have experienced incomprehensible levels of sexual adventure and abundance even if they remain fundamentally unsatisfied, that they will always be craving the craziness or else dreaming about it. This is common with former porn stars too, who basically got paid to live out all of their sexual fantasies on camera, and then off camera were living even more hardcore than they were on camera. When you see some of these girls when they are forced to retire from the lifestyle in general (not just doing porn), you will notice that they all look like like they are about to die from sheer boredom. I suppose nothing can compare to getting gang banged by a bunch of guys that look like they were pulled off the streets of Downtown LA, and paid for their performance with sack lunches from McDonald's. I still remember this gang bang scene I saw online and at the end of the scene when everyone ejaculated into the porn star's mouth, I kept hearing a voice in my head yelling "Mickey D's!" So utterly disgusting... These are guys whose hands I would not want to shake if I met them in person because they all look like they never wash their hands in real life, and here is this women swallowing their collective loads with a smile.

All of these girls who take advantage of the lifestyle Instagram facilitates, are used to existing in a living fantasy world that you can *never* compete with because *no **one** man can give them the experiences they are used to*. Only a plethora of men can. Just like there are women who can only be satisfied sexually by gang bangs, most of these women today can only be satisfied relationship-wise by multiple men. #facts

Give It Up for Free on Tinder, Or Sell It on Instagram?

In the early 2010s, something unprecedented happened in American dating culture. Despite the launch of Tinder (arguably the most revolutionary dating technology ever created) young men began having dramatically less sex. This wasn't supposed to happen. Tinder's intuitive swiping mechanism promised to solve the inefficiencies of traditional courtship, making romantic connections as easy as ordering food delivery. Yet the data tells a different story entirely...

Between 2000 and 2018, the percentage of sexually inactive men aged 18-24 skyrocketed from 19% to 31% with nearly one in three young men reporting no sexual activity in the past year. Among men aged 25-34, rates more than doubled from 7% to 14%. Since 2018, nation-wide research statistics on this phenomenon are limited, *much like studies on the decline in testosterone levels in males are non-existent post-2015.* The limited local statistics that are available, however, show things are only getting worse! This dramatic shift occurred not in spite of Tinder's rise, but seemingly because of it - or more precisely, because of what happened when Tinder and Instagram collided.

The Promise of Technology

When Tinder launched in September 2012, it appeared to be a game-changer. Within two months, the app had facilitated over one million matches. By late 2013, users were making 350 million swipes per day. By the end of 2014, that number had tripled to one billion daily swipes. The technology worked exactly as designed, and people were connecting at unprecedented scale.

But there was a fundamental problem lurking beneath these impressive numbers: a severe gender imbalance. From the beginning, Tinder's user base skewed heavily male (approximately 75-76% men to just 24-25%

women), a ratio of roughly three men for every woman. In some markets like India, the disparity was even more extreme.

This wasn't just a demographic curiosity. It created a brutal mathematical reality: women on Tinder enjoyed an average match rate of 31%, while men languished at just 2.6%. Put simply, women were 11 to 15 times more likely to match with someone than men were. For the average male user, Tinder's revolutionary technology delivered almost nothing. Millions of swipes. A handful of matches. Even fewer dates. Almost no sex.

The Rise of Instagram: A Parallel Universe

While Tinder struggled with its gender problem, Instagram was experiencing explosive growth. The photo-sharing platform had launched in October 2010, but it was during Tinder's ascendance that Instagram truly took off. From 100 million users in February 2013, Instagram surged to 200 million in 2014, then 370 million in 2015, reaching 500 million by June 2016.

Then came the innovation that changed everything: Instagram Stories, launched in August 2016. Within months, 100 million people were using Stories daily. Within eight months, Stories had surpassed Snapchat's entire user base. The feature created something powerful: a way for users to broadcast their daily lives in ephemeral, seemingly casual content that encouraged constant engagement.

For attractive young women, Instagram offered something Tinder never could: monetization without stigma.

The Sugar Dating Explosion

While mainstream media focused on hookup culture and Tinder, a parallel economy was quietly exploding. Seeking Arrangement, a website connecting "sugar babies" (typically young, attractive women) with "sugar daddies" (wealthy, older men), saw astronomical growth during this exact period.

By 2017, Seeking Arrangement boasted 3.2 million users in the United States alone. Of these, approximately 1.2 million (nearly 40%) identified as students. The platform specifically targeted college women, offering free premium upgrades for anyone with an .edu email address. The numbers were staggering: roughly 3 million college students nationwide were registered on the site, representing 37% of all sugar baby users.

Consider what this means. At Temple University in 2016, 296 students created new Seeking Arrangement profiles in a single year. By early 2017, 1,068 Temple students (nearly 3% of the entire student body) were registered on the platform. Similar patterns emerged at universities across the country: Georgia State, University of Central Florida, University of Alabama, University of Florida.

These weren't desperate women with no other options. These were young, attractive college students — exactly the demographic most sought-after on dating apps, who had made a calculated decision: *why date for free when you could monetize your attractiveness?*

The Instagram Advantage: Plausible Deniability

Here's where Instagram became revolutionary in ways its creators never intended – *or did they?* Unlike Seeking Arrangement, which required you to explicitly create a profile on a sugar dating site, Instagram provided perfect camouflage. An attractive woman could:

- Build a following by posting carefully curated photos showcasing her lifestyle, beauty, and accessibility.

- Attract attention from wealthy men through the explore page, hashtags, or strategic follows.

- Receive DMs from potential benefactors without ever explicitly soliciting anything.

- Maintain complete deniability: "I'm not a sugar baby, I'm an influencer" or "We're just friends who help each other out."

Instagram Stories amplified this dynamic exponentially. The ephemeral, casual nature of Stories allowed women to broadcast their availability and lifestyle 24/7 without the permanence of feed posts. They could show themselves at nice restaurants, wearing designer clothes, traveling to exotic locations — all signals to potential sugar daddies that they appreciated and expected a certain lifestyle.

For wealthy men, Instagram was a buffet. Why pay for Seeking Arrangement when you could browse Instagram for free, slide into DMs, and initiate contact without the explicit transactional framework of a sugar dating site? The arrangement was the same, but the venue provided everyone involved with plausible deniability.

The Great Stratification

What emerged between 2012 and 2016 wasn't a unified dating market—it was a fractured, two-tiered system:

Tier One: Instagram + Arrangements

- Attractive women who could monetize their looks

- Wealthy men willing to pay for access

- Relationships framed as "mentorship," "friendship," or "mutual benefit"

- Direct financial support, gifts, travel, and lifestyle upgrades in exchange for companionship (and often, sex)

Tier Two: Tinder + Free Dating Apps

- Average and below-average women

- Average and below-average men

- The remaining attractive men and women not interested in or aware of arrangements

- Traditional dating expectations: split bills, reciprocal interest, eventual monogamy

The problem for men on Tinder was simple: they were fishing in a depleted pond. The most attractive women (the ones generating the most interest) had increasingly migrated to Instagram-enabled arrangements. What remained on Tinder was a platform with a 3:1 male-to-female ratio where many of the most desirable women had simply opted out.

The Paradox Explained

This explains what seemed impossible: how could the introduction of the most efficient dating technology in human history coincide with dramatically declining sexual activity among young men?

The answer: Tinder's efficiency didn't matter if the supply side of the market had been siphoned off to a different platform entirely. Revolutionary technology is useless when you're solving the wrong problem. Tinder made it easier to connect with potential partners, but it couldn't create those partners out of thin air. And it certainly couldn't compete with Instagram when Instagram allowed attractive women to monetize access to themselves.

Consider the experience of the average young man in 2015-2016:

He downloads Tinder, optimistic about the possibilities. He swipes right on hundreds of profiles of busted bitches, and single moms with multiple pitbulls, hoping someone will match. Most don't. The few who do often don't respond to messages. The even fewer who respond rarely agree to meet. And when they do meet, the women are often markedly different from their photos, which were already barely sparking interest.

Meanwhile, the genuinely attractive women he encounters in daily life - at the gym, in class, at work… are increasingly uninterested in traditional dating. Most are openly "seeing someone" but cagey about the details. Others post Instagram Stories from expensive restaurants, luxury hotels, and exotic vacations that seem incompatible with a college student or entry-level employee's budget. Still others are simply "too busy" or "focusing on themselves right now."

What he doesn't realize is that many of these women haven't opted out of dating, but have opted into a different market entirely. One where their youth and beauty translate directly into economic benefits. Where a dinner date isn't a prelude to a potential relationship but a compensated evening. Where sex isn't the hopeful outcome of successful courtship but a negotiated component of an ongoing financial arrangement.

The Numbers Don't Lie

By 2016-2018, the transformation was complete. Sexual inactivity among men aged 18-24 had reached 31%—up from 19% just sixteen years earlier. Men aged 25-34 saw their rates double from 7% to 14%. Women's rates increased too, but far less dramatically: from 15% to 19% for those aged 18-24, and from 7% to 13% for those aged 25-34.

The gender gap is telling. If declining sexual activity were purely about technology displacing in-person interaction (as many researchers suggested), you'd expect roughly equal impacts on both sexes. Instead, you see a crisis concentrated almost entirely among men, suggesting not a decline in sexual activity generally, but a redistribution of sexual access specifically.

During this exact period, Instagram grew from 100 million to 500 million users. Tinder processed billions of swipes daily. Seeking Arrangement added millions of student users. These weren't separate phenomena—they were interconnected pieces of a new sexual economy where attractiveness could be monetized like never before, and where traditional dating markets were hollowed out as a result.

The Invisible Hand of the Market

What we witnessed between 2012 and 2016 was the invisible hand of the market operating with brutal efficiency. When Instagram created a platform that allowed attractive women to monetize their looks without stigma, and when sites like Seeking Arrangement normalized mutually beneficial arrangements, the rational choice for many attractive women became obvious: why participate in traditional dating when you could profit from it instead?

This wasn't prostitution in the traditional sense, though the line was admittedly blurry. It was something newer and more socially acceptable—transactional dating dressed up in the language of mentorship, mutual benefit, and modern relationships. Instagram provided the storefront. Seeking Arrangement provided the explicit marketplace. Together, they created an entirely new economy.

The casualties were average men on Tinder, swiping endlessly through a pool of low sexual market value women while wondering why the revolution they'd been promised had somehow passed them by. The technology worked perfectly. The market had simply evolved beyond what the technology was designed to solve.

In the span of just four years, from Tinder's launch in 2012 to Instagram Stories' debut in 2016, the American sexual marketplace had fractured into tiers that previous generations never had to navigate. And an entire generation of young men found themselves on the wrong side of that divide, with match rates below 3% and sexual inactivity rates approaching one in three.

I mean, why "date" on Tinder when you can get all the benefits of a relationship (sex combined with a man's resources) from whoring on Instagram? Why "hook up" on Tinder when you can get paid cash money for the same sex via Instagram? Instagram allowed women to operate as *undercover whores with full plausible deniability*: "I post pictures of my ass *for myself.*" Sure you do, honey buns! See, when women are sexually frigid, or orgasmically impotent or however you chose to phrase it, sex is not really a big deal for them at all. But it remains a big deal for men. So the natural result is that women see a demand for something they don't think much of at all, and therefore have no hesitation to sell it. They see no value in their pussy, their sexuality, nor themselves so why not fly to Dubai and sell their dignity for $30,000 and some shopping trips? Oh, I forgot… they had no dignity to begin with due to self-hatred. My bad! All of these horrors unfold because unprocessed trauma has made them anorgasmic, and they hate themselves for running away from their problems like the fucking cowards they are.

While You Beg for Trash on Tinder, The Elites Enjoy Sex Slaves...

...and engineer school shootings! An analysis of sex trafficking data in the United States will prove to you that there is zero effort made to do anything about it, and I will tell you why shortly. Let's take a look at some of the data:

- Globally, the most common form of human trafficking (79%) is sex exploitation, NOT LABOR!

- Globally, forced commercial sexual exploitation generates $173 billion in illegal profits annually.

- In 1997 *alone* as many as 175,000 young women from the former Soviet Union and Eastern and Central Europe were *sold as commodities in the sex markets of the developed countries in Europe and the Americas.*

- Human trafficking is the second most profitable illegal industry in the U.S.

- Sex trafficking is the most common type of trafficking in the U.S.

- Since its inception, the Human Trafficking Hotline has identified 112,822 cases of human trafficking. 218,568 victims were identified in these cases.

- In 2024, it is estimated that approximately 24,000 individuals fell victim to human trafficking within the United States, with the majority of them being sex trafficked.

Given the above statistics, does it make sense when the Federal criminal data indicates:

- Only 6,000 out of 600,000 people reported missing in a year will remain "unrecovered."

- Based on official HHS certification data, only ~**680 foreign national women and children** were officially certified as sex trafficking victims in FY 2023.

Of course it doesn't make sense. Unless, of course, those who are *enjoying* all of these sex slaves don't want the party to end? Let's assume that out of the 175,000 young women from the Eastern Block that were sold in Europe and the Americas, that half of them were sold in the United States. That is almost 90,000 women. Where exactly are these 90,000 women who are being sexually exploited? Remember, *you* do not have the resources to purchase, house/hide, and ultimately *dispose of* "human traffic." Only the "elites" do.

Doesn't it make you angry that you, the average guy, gets completely deprived of sex unless you are willing to jump on fatsos or an assortment of other hand grenades, while having to sit around and watch all the hottest women on the planet turned into literal whores on Instagram or trafficked as sex slaves for the Satanic elite to enjoy in ways beyond your imagination? It shocks me on a daily basis that the only mass shootings that occur are school shootings. Well, not really, because in my opinion those school shootings are all carried out by "manchurian candidates" anyway. Allow me to explain. Most human beings, unless they have been brainwashed by thousands of hours of rap music *and* have no father in the house, are incapable of shooting anyone unless they are afraid for their lives and *even then* many are incapable of it. This is why the US military spends so much money and effort to turn ordinary people into killing machines – because it is unnatural for most people to engage in any sort of killing, let alone killing en masse.

So logically speaking, if we suddenly see an alarming increase in mass shootings with the majority of them occurring in schools or houses of worship, something is very off. Why? Because an equal number of DMVs, police stations, and courthouses should be getting shot up as well. But it never happens. Only the post office gets periodically shot up – *by other postal workers!* This is impossible if you really think about it! You are telling me that a fucking schoolhouse or a church inspires enough murderous rage to get someone to shoot them up, but your local DMV, police station or courthouse *doesn't?* There is a reason schools and houses of worship find themselves on the receiving end of a hail of bullets so often… it is because the elites figure that people will view children and religious people as *innocent.* DMV workers and cops, not so much…

See, the goal of the elites is to take away all of the guns from Americans so we can all end up like the rest of the west – robbed and raped on a daily basis by gangs of migrant trash from Africa and the Islamic world. They already pulled off a mass gun disarm in Australia after some mass shooting convinced that entire nation of kangaroo-fuckers to give up their guns. So the elites figured the same tactic should work in the United States, they just need to keep orchestrating mass shootings one on top of the other, until the American public gives in. What the elites don't realize, is that the United States was birthed from the barrel of a gun. We are a culture of guns, not a culture of criminals (Australia), not a culture of pill-popping dog-fuckers (Canadians) and certainly not a culture of monarchist fags (British). Americans don't want to hear anything but a symphony of suppressors spraying .556 rounds courtesy of forced-reset triggers. I went out on a date with a British girl once who started to lecture me about our nation's gun problem. I told her our nation doesn't have a gun problem, we *had* a problem with the British though, that we solved with guns, and if she doesn't like it here, she should fuck off back to England to get raped by Pakistanis and die in a cladding fire. I mean, I didn't start lecturing her about her nation's dental problems, did I? The nerve of that stupid cunt...

Now some of you may still not believe school shootings post-1996 are "manchurian candidate" scenarios. Then again, you probably believe jet fuel melts steel beams, or that women *don't* like to be choked during sex! Anyhow, here is the evidence I present that leads me to conclude school shootings post–1996 are indeed "manchurian candidate" scenarios...

Australia implemented major gun control reforms in **1996-1997** following the Port Arthur massacre in April 1996, where 35 people were killed. In America, pre-1996 the data shows that throughout the early-to-mid 1990s, school shootings occurred but were relatively sporadic, with incidents spread across different years and locations. However, the pattern appears to intensify further after 1996...

Key indicators of acceleration after 1996:

- **Higher-profile, deadlier incidents:**

- ○ October 1, 1997 - Pearl High School, Mississippi.

- ○ March 24, 1998 - Westside Middle School, Arkansas.

- ○ May 21, 1998 - Thurston High School, Oregon.

- ○ April 20, 1999 - Columbine High School, Colorado. (the deadliest school shooting up until that point)

- **Increased frequency:** The 1997-1999 period shows multiple major incidents occurring within a relatively short time frame.

- **Geographic spread:** These incidents occurred across different regions (Mississippi, Arkansas, Oregon, Colorado), suggesting a broader pattern rather than isolated local phenomena.

Allow me to give you another reason why these school shootings are intentionally orchestrated… It has been said that *"If you want to know who controls you, look at whom you are not allowed to criticize."* The problem with this statement is that those who control you are *unknown to you by design.* They would never *reveal* themselves. Furthermore, this statement is always used to promote anti-semitism, when the world is *not* controlled by Jews even if they have a disproportionate amount of power in media, entertainment and politics given their population demographics.

A more precise statement is: *"If you want to know **what** the agenda is, look at **what** you are not allowed to criticize."* Under this more precise statement, we can accurately ascertain that Israel is *part* of "the agenda," without falling into the trap of thinking Israel *is behind* the agenda. In truth, what is *behind* Israel is also *behind* many other bad faith actors on the stage. With this in mind, Alex Jones used to say how some specific school shooting was staged by "crisis actors" or whatever. It's a famous conspiracy theory that I don't subscribe too, but no matter… in America you are *supposed* to have freedom of speech. But apparently the families of the victims of this particular school shooting were offended, and claimed people were calling them liars on the streets, and engaging in other forms of harassment. Either way, they sued Alex Jones and got some dimwit jurors to rule in their favor, allowing them to claim an utterly absurd and unreasonable amount of damages from Alex. Why? Because he doubted the official narrative, and because his doubt was actually gaining traction. You are not allowed to criticize the school shooting narrative, because is is an integral part of "the agenda." The Elites simply could not afford to allow this to occur. That this travesty of justice with respect to "freedom of speech" occurred shows you how intent the elites are on their plans for public disarmament succeeding, and you will no doubt continue to see more and more school shootings because this is the reptilian way – once you find something that worked once, you continue doing it over and over again.

What's so terrifying about the United States these days, is that there is no more rule of law. If you have true freedom of speech, then you have the right to say whatever it is that you believe to be true and nobody should have the right to punish you for it. I know you can't yell fire in a crowded theater, but if you believe a school shooting never happened, or that we never landed on the moon, that is your right, and you should be able to say that no matter who you are and no matter what media you choose to convey your message. But in the United States today, a judge holds all the cards in civil cases, and actually agrees to hear these garbage cases when they should just be tossed in the trash. Just to clarify, I am not alleging that school shootings are fabricated using "crisis actors," but it is my personal, subjective opinion that school shootings are carried out by "manchurian candidates" who have been brainwashed and programmed to carry out these shootings. It is an opinion based on the evidence I see around me, in combination with my own anecdotal knowledge and basic common sense, and I have the right to express my opinion in public.

The other big issue with "gun violence" is that there is actually no problem with "gun violence," there is just an issue with "youths" with guns, no fathers, no impulse control, and no ability to project into the future because their IQ is so incredibly low. So many "youths" are so thin-skinned and so low IQ, that they shoot each other because someone stepped on their sneakers, or because they felt "disrespected" or simply because of their inability to contemplate the future and comprehend concepts like "consequences."

The easiest way to understand this, is that in any community that doesn't have such "youths," and everyone is allowed to carry a firearm, crime is very low. Why? Because everyone is at least smart enough to understand the potential danger they are in if they are rude, aggressive, violent, or behave in a criminal manner. But in communities replete with certain "youths," where everyone is allowed to carry a firearm – either based on the law or lack of enforcement of the law, it's just constant gun battles.

This is also another reason why you know school shootings are orchestrated. Because it is never these "youths" who shoot up a school or carry out a mass shooting, when they shoot up literally everything else! Schools are always shot up by those who normally never shoot at anything but paper and steel targets. How do you explain these statistical incongruencies?

Finally, if you want to stop gun violence, the solution is not to get rid of guns, but rather punish those who commit criminal acts of gun violence. How can it be that the cities with the toughest gun laws have the most gun violence? It is *only possible* if said gun laws are not being enforced! So when you are abolishing the basics, such enforcing laws, requiring bail, etc., is it really a surprise when you have an explosion in gun violence? Even the retarded could predict that sort of an outcome!

Elites like George Soros want you to lose access to firearms because they don't want you fighting back when they flood your nation with rapist migrants who couldn't give a fuck about feminism or "me too" and have no problems groping and raping their way to sexual satisfaction. In England the police do nothing about Moslem gangs from Pakistan raping young British girls, yet they have special undercover police units to harass British males who "cat-call" joggers, even though cat-calling isn't illegal. England is a true joke of a nation, that still suckles on the dicks of royalty, when said royalty does nothing to protect the orifices of British girls from the dicks of foreign invaders who violate them on a daily basis.

This is why Americans must *never* give up their guns. Because England has *never* learned it's lesson: they actually try and hold Americans accountable to their Orwellian internet censorship and hate speech laws even though we kicked their limey asses out of here centuries ago! Apparently the Germans haven't learned their lesson either, and have begun rearming at a rate not seen since the rise of Adolf Hitler. They say it is due to fear of Russia, but isn't it better German women go back to being raped by Russian males, then continue to be raped by African and Moslem migrants? Well *it isn't* from the point of view of the Satanic extraterrestrials, who are in control of the elites who *think* they are running the show around here, because the idea is to downgrade the IQ of the West to make westerners easier to control.

"Diversity is only strength if you are trying to produce stronger slaves."
— Vlad P.

The Pornography Disaster

Besides hyper-inflation, another huge causal factor in the women of our nation's descent into whoredom is the trauma of viewing online pornography during their developmental years. A girl used to enjoy sliding down the stairway banister to get her jollies, but these days they grow up having marathon masturbation sessions to the craziest porn they can search up on their phones and tablets. Men don't realize how many female porn addicts there are out there. I'm talking about grown-ass women who'll goon for hours a day with the help of their Hitachi magic wand.

I worked in the adult industry for a few years developing novelty products and doing consulting work, and the running joke in the industry was "Thank heavens for incest because without child molestation there would be no girls to do porn." However the industry appears to go to great lengths to cover this up. Just check out the ridiculous study called "Pornography Actresses: An Assessment of the Damaged Goods Hypothesis" (2013, PubMed) which found that there were no statistically significant differences in the incidence of childhood sexual abuse between porn actresses and the control group. Sure… tell me more lies! Laughably, the study also found that porn actresses reported higher self-esteem, more social support, and greater sexual satisfaction compared to the control group.

It would appear that this 2013 "study" was paid for by the porn industry to contradict a much more believable 2011 study that backs up the "running joke" in the industry I told just a moment ago. That study is called "Comparison of the Mental Health of Female Adult Film Performers and Other Young Women in California" (2011, PubMed) which found that nearly 88% of participants had experienced sexual abuse as children, along with 90% experiencing psychological abuse and 79% experiencing physical abuse.

Which of these diametrically opposed studies do you find more believable?

The History of Pornography

Pornography in the United States can be traced back to Berlin, particularly during the Weimar Republic period. Let's take a snapshot of said scene during the Weimar Republic (1919-1933), before Hitler's rise to power...

1920s Berlin was at the hectic center of the Weimar Republic, where the social environment was chaotic, and politics were passionate. The defeat in World War I along with the collapse of the monarchy *and* the currency created a cultural and economic vacuum that was filled with unprecedented sexual experimentation and liberation.

The scope of prostitution in Weimar Berlin was staggering. More than 120,000 desperate women and girls of every age and stripe sold their bodies for a pittance, including mother-daughter prostitution teams and brazen streetwalkers well into the third trimester of pregnancy. Historians identify 16 different types of prostitutes, including "telephone girls," which were enormously expensive child prostitutes ages 12-17 labeled "Marlene Dietrichs" or "Lillian Harveys" according to their physical attributes. These girls could be ordered by phone and delivered by taxi to the client.

Along with drug use and prostitution, pornography also enjoyed a golden age during the years of the Weimar Republic. Making full use of the latest photographic technology, both amateur and professional porn producers struggled to keep up with the insatiable demand of the Berlin public. What's interesting is that there was such a demand for pornography, when real sex was so readily available. So curious! Either way, much of this was produced by seemingly respectable photographers. By day, they would take family portraits, but by night they would switch their focus to making adult images. Similarly, the booming movie industry of the 1920s was also complicit. Directors and cameramen would often have a nice sideline making some of the first porn films after-hours in the big studios.

There were an estimated 500 establishments on the underground scene, that included a large number of homosexual venues for men and for women. Sometimes transvestites of one or both genders were admitted, otherwise there were at least 5 known establishments that were exclusively for a transvestite clientele. There were also several nudist venues.

At the center of this sexual revolution was Magnus Hirschfeld's Institute for Sexual Science, founded in 1919. Hirschfeld built a unique library at the institute on gender, same-sex love and eroticism. The institute pioneered research and treatment for various matters regarding gender and sexuality, including gay, transgender, and intersex topics. Berlin also had a museum of sexuality during the Weimar period, at Dr. Magnus Hirschfeld's Institute of Sexology.

The extreme economic conditions contributed to the sexual marketplace. In October 1923, German currency traded at the astronomical rate of 4.2 billion marks to the U.S. dollar. One historian pointed out that "the most exquisite blow job" to be had in Berlin never cost an American tourist more than 30 cents.

The so-called sex reform movement of Weimar Germany (1919-1933), was dedicated to providing more sexual and social freedoms to men and women. Its two major aims were to give working class men and women access to information about birth control as well as access to birth control itself. It also aimed to reform Paragraphs 218 and 219 of the German Penal Code of 1871 that prohibited abortions and anyone from aiding and abetting their facilitation.

The extent of sexual exploitation and pornography in pre-Nazi Berlin was indeed remarkable for its time, representing perhaps the most sexually liberal urban environment that had ever existed up to that point in *modern Western history*.

Let's take a closer look at *exactly* who was behind the so-called sex reform movement… The sex reform movement was thus led primarily by **Magnus Hirschfeld** and **Helene Stöcker**, with significant contributions from medical professionals like **Max Hodann, Arthur Kronfeld**, and **Friedrich Wertheim**. These individuals created a network of organizations, publications, and institutions that promoted sexual education, reproductive rights, LGBTQ+ rights, and women's liberation during the progressive Weimar period.

- **Magnus Hirschfeld (1868-1935)** - The most prominent figure, Magnus Hirschfeld was a German physician, sexologist and LGBTQ advocate who founded the Scientific-Humanitarian Committee and World League for Sexual Reform. He opened the Institute for Sexual Science in Berlin in 1919, the first of its kind in the world. Hirschfeld initiated the founding of the World League for Sexual Reform in 1921, during the First Congress for Sexual Reform in Berlin, which he had also organized.

- **Helene Stöcker (1869-1943)** - Feminist leader and sexual reformer, Helene Stöcker was a German feminist, pacifist and gender activist who helped found the League for the Protection of Mothers (Bund für Mutterschutz, BfM) in 1905, and became the editor of the organization's magazine. Helene Stöcker's Deutscher Bund für Mutterschutz und Sexualreform held offices at Hirschfeld's Institute. She was president and guiding spirit of the League for the Protection of Motherhood and Sexual Reform, and editor of the journal Neue Generation (The New Generation).

- **Max Hodann** - Medical reformer Max Hodann worked at the Institute and developed pioneering strategies for sex counseling services that would inspire later practices. Hirschfeld and Hodann developed pioneering strategies for sex counseling services.

Among those who survived by fleeing Germany were Max
Hodann.

- **Arthur Kronfeld** – Psychotherapist and later professor at the
  Charité, co-founder of and collaborator at the Institute founded
  by Magnus Hirschfeld.

- **Friedrich Wertheim** – Dermatologist, co-founder and
  collaborator at the Institute alongside Hirschfeld and Kronfeld.

On May 6th 1933, the Institute of Sexology was broken into and occupied
by Nazi-supporting youth. Several days later the entire contents of the
library were removed and burned, marking the end of this extraordinary
period of sexual openness. When Hitler came to power, this movement of
"sexual libertarianism" got temporarily snuffed out in Germany and
Western Europe, but gradually returned once peace was reestablished and
Western Europe underwent post-war reconstruction. The same
phenomenon occurred in Japan. Mind you, both Western European and
Japanese post-war reconstruction was carried out by the Americans. It is
actually the American influence behind Japanese pornography blurring
out the genitals.

While sexual exploitation has always run rampant throughout the history
of the world, pornography is a relatively recent sexually exploitative
phenomena that is based on technology. Initially, it was the technology of
the still camera driving it, then the film camera, then the video camera,
then the internet, and now finally AI. The evolution and scaling of
pornography-facilitating technology has allowed pornography to increase
it's hold on the human psyche in an exponential fashion. Prior to modern
visual media, voyeurs had to make do with live sex shows. However, there
was no real demand for such nonsense, as sex had always been easy to
obtain up until recent times.

There is this myth that the past was somehow "sexually traditional" and conservative. This is utter hogwash. History is filled with false narratives that fall apart when one looks past the surface. The red pill will say stupid things like "Back in the day it was impossible for women to be promiscuous because there were no birth control pills." You must be kidding me! They just took it up the ass you dummies! You do realize that the only thing separating the rectum from the vagina is a thin wall of flesh through which you can easily hit the posterior fronix of the vagina during anal sex and trigger an extremely powerful orgasm in a woman? If you fuck a woman's pussy while another guy fucks her ass, the two of you will be able to feel each other's cocks rubbing against each other, separated only by that aforementioned wall of flesh.

When pornography got exported to America, it started out rather innocuously with magazines like Playboy, but before you knew it, there were hardcore films being *screened in mainstream theaters*. Think about what I just said. Hardcore films were available to watch in mainstream movie theaters and people were sitting in their seats masturbating during the film. Do you see that anywhere in the United States today? So how can people believe that somehow people were "conservative" in the past? The entire 1970s was people rubbing it out in theaters across the country. Times Square was filled with live sex shows with people fucking on stage, and the whole disco scene was one endless coke-fueled orgy. There were also heterosexual sex clubs and gay bathhouses all over the place, as this was prior to the AIDS scamdemic which shut them down the same way that the Covid scamdemic shut society at large down. What most people don't remember, as I will revealed later, is that Anthony Fauci was involved in the AIDS scamdemic as well! History repeating itself, no doubt!

Prior to the hardcore 1970s you had the hippies of the 1960s having sex with everything in sight. Oh, but the 1950s were conservative, right? Wrong. What happened was real sex, freely given, was slowly replaced with pornography and "pay4play." As if it wasn't bad enough being a "john" paying for sex that used to be free, or a "cuck" watching other men fuck the girl of your dreams on film or in a magazine... most men today are just "simps" paying for *mere* female attention. Yet you all believe you are somehow living in the most sexually free time in history!

This is the true purpose of pornography: To destroy your ability to relate to women sexually in real life, therefore preventing you from attaining sexual fulfillment, which makes it easier to crush your spirit and enslave you. As an added bonus, it makes it impossible to have a successful marriage and raise children that would grow up to be real men and women.

When I started working in the adult entertainment industry, I was shocked to discover that pornography was a multi-billion-dollar industry that consistently loses money with respect to content creation itself. At the time I was working in the industry, the only people making money were those who operated webcam studios, with the endless free porn all over the internet simply driving traffic to the cam sites. It isn't like anyone bought XXX DVDs anymore by that point, but I thought content producers were making money off their site subscriptions, no? I found out quickly from insiders that there just wasn't money being made like that anymore. Which made sense, as you could get endless porn for free. Even the stuff under subscription, was pirated and uploaded to file sharing sites so what was the point in subscribing to anything?

I also found out that most of the girls who were "starring" in porn were just doing it to get exposure for their prostitution services, as most of your favorite stars work as escorts. Doing porn *is* prostitution after all, except the sexual acts are being filmed, which makes the porn actors exhibitionists as well as prostitutes. Then the content is sold to what are basically voyeurs – all of you! Because the consumption of pornography is voyeurism, plain and simple. Anyway, my point here is that the production of pornographic content itself, did not really make any money for anyone at the end of the day, relatively speaking. It just didn't make any sense to me, and I was sure there were at least *some* content producers who *had* to be making money, but it was stressed to me over-and-over that the revenue model was to push content consumers to cam girl sites because that was the only place where money could be made. Even PornHub's revenue, for example, comes from ads.

It is hard to say at what point this state of affairs occurred, but by the time I found myself moonlighting in the industry producing adult novelty supplements, and consulting at "Internext," this was indeed the case. OnlyFans had not come on the scene yet, so girls were not able to monetize their own content or pre-existing popularity from shooting content at mainstream production houses. Girls made their money from shooting porn and working as escorts, or from working as cam girls. Many also went "on tour" working strip clubs and engaging in coast-to-coast prostitution tours. For a girl to get into pornography at that time was actually a pretty stupid idea, because becoming a porn actress removed the shield of plausible deniability about her whoredom. The day rate is also pretty low given what a girl has to endure, and she demolishes her reputation in the process of being used as a human pincushion. Permanently. I know that prior to OnlyFans, porn stars had their own websites, but if the website subscriptions really made so much money, why were they going on stripping and prostitution tours? It made no sense at all.

Porn Keeps Getting More Extreme and Nobody Seems To Notice

I was a teenager in the 1980s and porn in the 1980s, as well as in the early 1990s, was pretty tame. The energy was very different, and films consisted of mutual oral sex, 3 positions, and either a back shot or facial to end the scene. Around the 2000s it started getting more "adventurous" and at a certain point porn went "gonzo" which means the camera was acknowledged by the performers, and the sex got really dominating and abusive. Throat-fucking, anal and ass-to-mouth became all the rage thanks in large part to a performer who pioneered this style who went by the stage name of Max Hardcore (real name Max Little). His style of porn was copied by another performer named Rocco Siffredi who was a former male model with a larger penis than Mr. Little, who was so aptly named. Rocco, albeit very sexually aggressive, at least *appeared* to actually like women. Max, on the other hand, *appeared* to hate women, engaging them in a rather abusive manner on camera while sporting a ten-gallon cowboy hat in all of his scenes. I say *appeared* because it is my understanding that Max would show all of the female talent videos of his work beforehand and make it very clear to them what they were getting into. I met Max in person twice, and his aura from my perception was that of a person who would either be a serial rapist or a flat-out serial killer, were it not for his success in porn. That's my highly subjective, personal opinion, or course. He ended up doing a few years in federal prison on a technicality which I believe was the transportation of DVDs that had scenes involving piss drinking, through some bumfuck jurisdiction where that sort of thing was against the law. I always felt that someone was out to get him, and don't think he was treated fairly at all, although Rocco Siffredi wisely cut all of the piss-drinking scenes from his DVD releases in America, while keeping them intact in the European releases. Either way, it is Rocco who often gets the credit for the state of porn today, when the credit should actually be going to Max. Furthermore, I always admired what Max accomplished. When you think about it, to be someone with his attributes and then to create the sort of empire he did and have the sort of impact he did... it is truly incredible. As a side note, Max Hardcore is so popular in China, that I once saw one of his films playing in a fucking bar!

The reason I am giving this short history lecture is because I had stopped watching porn right before gonzo came upon the scene, as I had found myself in a relationship. When we broke up and I went back "on the market," I started dating girls much younger than myself. To my surprise I found I was getting very bad reviews in terms of my sexual performance, whereas in the past women had raved about it. I wasn't quite sure what I was suddenly doing wrong, so I decided to go pick up a bunch of porn DVDs and see what people were into in those days. I remember watching some selections from Rocco's "Animal Trainer" series and I was a bit shocked. Pure aggression, domination and degradation. Times had changed. No wonder women were unhappy with me! Incidentally, if you want to know how women love to be "fucked," pick up a couple of his "Animal Trainer" DVDs. It's actually porn that is educational. Is it the complete picture? No. I will cover sex in great detail later in this book, but for now it is a great education in *one facet* of your sexual repertoire.

So with the next girl I went home with, I just asked myself, "What would Rocco do?" and then proceeded to do it. When it was over she couldn't stop raving about the best sex of her life. It was weird because this wasn't really how I wanted to relate to women, but it's basic sales and marketing – you give the customer what they want, at least if you want their repeat business.

Based on my experience and the experience of countless men I have spoken with, the number of women who are sexually turned on by being physically dominated, verbally degraded, slapped, choked, spit upon, etc. is rather alarming. Well, it isn't *really* when you remember how much women hate themselves. Naturally they won't come out and tell you that they are into these sorts of things, and will deny it if asked, as they expect you to be able to *discern* that they want these sorts of things and then just *give it to them.* Female sexuality is very dark and depraved, and most men are not ready to accept it.

Of course, this is for "information purposes only" because as men we live in very dangerous time where dishing out this brand of intimacy is highly risky from both a legal, as well as a cancel-cultural standpoint. There has been more than one famous PUA who got canceled and "put on blast" for "promoting rape culture," when all they pointed out was that in Japan, a significantly large segment of women enjoy being taken by force, so it can be somewhat liberating for a westerner to visit Japan and enjoy these women and their proclivities. They weren't *promoting* rape culture, just pointing out that *Japan has an actual rape culture.*

Japanese rape culture really showed itself in full force during Japanese military conquests, as there is extensive and well-documented evidence of systematic military sanctioned rape and sexual exploitation by the Japanese military during wars and occupations from 1930-1945 that was perpetrated at a level *unmatched* by any other nation or culture. This evidence comes from multiple sources including survivor testimonies, military documents, war crimes tribunals, and historical research.

Scale and Scope:

- **Estimated 200,000+ women** were forced into sexual slavery across Japanese-occupied territories.

- **Systematic establishment** of "comfort stations" (military brothels) throughout the Japanese Empire.

- **Multi-ethnic victims**: Korean, Chinese, Filipino, Dutch, Indonesian, Taiwanese, and other women.

- **Age range**: Many victims were teenagers, some as young as 11-16 years old.

Documentary Evidence:

- **Japanese military documents** discovered post-war confirming official involvement.

- **Testimonies from Japanese soldiers** admitting to the system's existence.

- **Allied interrogation records** from captured Japanese personnel.

- **Wartime photographs and records** from comfort stations.

Official Sanctioning:

- **Imperial Japanese Army directives** establishing and regulating comfort stations.

- **Military police oversight** of comfort station operations.

- **Army medical supervision** including mandatory health examinations.

- **Transportation logistics** provided by military for moving women.

Command Structure Involvement:

- **High-ranking officers** directly involved in establishment of facilities.

- **Unit commanders** requisitioning and managing comfort women.

- **Military contractors** officially designated to procure women.

- **Government collaboration** between military and civil authorities.

Korea (1910-1945):

- **Recruitment deception**: Women told they would work in factories or as nurses.

- **Forced conscription**: Direct seizure of women, particularly during later war years.

- **Police collaboration**: Korean police under Japanese control assisting in recruitment.

China (1937-1945):

- **Nanjing Massacre (1937)**: Mass rape documented alongside killings.

- **Systematic establishment**: Comfort stations set up in occupied Chinese cities.

- **Local collaboration**: Use of local intermediaries to procure women.

Southeast Asia (1941-1945):

- **Philippines**: Documented comfort stations and mass rape during occupation.

- **Indonesia**: Dutch colonial women and local women forced into sexual slavery.

- **Burma/Myanmar**: Comfort stations along military supply routes.

Pacific Islands:

- **Okinawa**: Documented sexual violence against local women.

- **Various Pacific islands**: Comfort stations established on military bases.

Nanjing Massacre (1937):

- **Mass rape** documented by international observers.

- **John Rabe's diary** and other Western witness accounts.

- Estimated 20,000-80,000 rapes **during 6-8 week period.**

Manila Massacre (1945):

- **Systematic rape and killing** during final Japanese resistance.

- **US military documentation** of atrocities discovered upon liberation.

Burma-Thailand Railway:

- **Sexual exploitation** of women in POW and labor camp areas.

- **Allied prisoner testimony** witnessing abuses.

In short, Japan's history of sexual abuses during wartime represents one of the most thoroughly documented cases of systematic military sexual violence in modern history, with evidence meeting rigorous historical and legal standards for establishing institutional responsibility. What's even more horrifying, is reading actual witness and survivor accounts. The degree and nature of the sexual abuses, and the levels of humiliation inflicted on women, truly boggle the mind. We are not just talking about women being forced to have sex with Japanese soldiers, but women en masse being used as human latrines around the clock and all sorts of demented stuff. *Women who resisted were often publicly skinned alive in order to ensure compliance from the conquered female population.*

Not only did the Japanese military make the Russian military's top-down policy of systematic rape during World War II look like courtship, they somehow managed to make the experiments of Nazi scientist Dr. Josef Mengele look compassionate.

Yes, there is also extensive and well-documented evidence of systematic human experimentation conducted by the Japanese military, primarily during World War II. This evidence comes from survivor testimonies, post-war confessions, American intelligence documents, and physical evidence discovered after the war.

Unit 731 and Related Biological Warfare Units

- **Unit 731**: The primary biological warfare unit led by Shiro Ishii in Manchuria.

- **Estimated 3,000+ victims** killed in experiments at Unit 731 alone.

- **Multiple satellite units**: Units 100, 516, 543, 1644, and others across occupied territories.

- **Massive facilities**: Unit 731's Pingfan complex covered 6 square kilometers.

- **Large staff**: Over 3,000 researchers, technicians, and support personnel.

Biological Warfare Testing:

- **Live pathogen injection**: Plague, anthrax, cholera, typhus, and other diseases.

- **Infection studies**: Monitoring disease progression until death.

- **Vaccine testing**: Using prisoners as test subjects for experimental treatments.

- **Vector studies**: Using fleas, rats, and other carriers to spread disease.

Surgical Experiments:

- **Vivisection without anesthesia**: Dissecting living prisoners to study organ function.

- **Amputation studies**: Removing limbs to study blood loss and shock.

- **Organ removal**: Extracting organs from living subjects.

- **Brain surgery**: Experimental neurosurgical procedures.

Environmental and Physical Experiments:

- **Frostbite studies**: Exposing prisoners to extreme cold and studying tissue damage.

- **Pressure experiments**: Testing effects of altitude and pressure changes.

- **Dehydration studies**: Denying water to study survival limits.

- **Starvation experiments**: Studying effects of prolonged malnutrition.

Chemical and Weapons Testing:

- **Poison gas exposure**: Testing various chemical weapons.

- **Explosive device testing**: Using prisoners as targets for weapons.

- **Chemical injection**: Testing various toxic substances.

- **Burn studies**: Deliberately causing burns to study treatment methods.

Primary Locations:

- **Manchuria**: Main experimental facilities and largest operations.

- **China proper**: Urban testing sites and smaller facilities.

- **Korea**: Satellite facilities and testing programs.

- **Southeast Asia**: Limited documented experiments in occupied territories.

Victim Demographics:

- **Chinese civilians**: Largest group of victims, including entire families.

- **Soviet POWs**: Captured soldiers used in experiments.

- **Korean civilians**: Both volunteers deceived about purposes and forced subjects.

- **Some Allied POWs**: Though extent remains disputed.

- **Mongolian and other prisoners**: Various ethnic groups in occupied areas.

What's interesting is that the United States granted immunity to Unit 731 researchers in exchange for their data, which propelled both the American as well as the Japanese medical and pharmaceutical industry far forward. The American biological weapons program at Fort Detrick acquired Japanese research as well. Communications from MacArthur's headquarters about Unit 731 include classified memos regarding immunity deals with Japanese researchers. While the Nazis also produced unethical medical data, the Japanese dwarfed the Nazis in both scale and scope in this regard.

Don't get me wrong... I love sushi and I sleep on a mattress on the floor because beds make a lot of noise when you fuck like Rocco Sifreddi, but Japanese "culture" beyond sushi doesn't really exist. I say this because what they hold up as "their" culture was given to them by the Chinese and the Koreans - whom are basically Chinese anyway. If this offends Koreans, peep this:

- **Historical influence:** Korea was within China's sphere of influence for much of its history, adopting Chinese writing systems, Confucian philosophy, Buddhist traditions, governmental structures, and artistic styles. Korean elites historically learned Classical Chinese as their literary language.

- **Cultural substrates:** Many fundamental aspects of Korean culture — ancestor veneration, hierarchical social relationships, concepts of filial piety, artistic traditions like ceramics and painting - share deep roots with Chinese traditions.

- **Genetic studies:** Some research suggests significant shared ancestry between Korean and northern Chinese populations, with gene flow between the regions over millennia.

- **Linguistic borrowing:** A substantial portion of Korean vocabulary derives from Chinese loanwords, though the grammatical structure differs significantly.

- **Regional variation argument:** One could argue that Korean distinctiveness is comparable to regional Chinese variations - that just as Cantonese and Mandarin speakers might be considered "Chinese" despite significant differences, Koreans represent another regional variation within a broader East Asian cultural sphere.

I know progressives will say that my line of reasoning erases Korean "agency," but if you asked a random group of people what the difference between Korean and Chinese culture is, most people would say Koreans love Kimchi and then they would draw a blank. So if "agency" is nothing more than rotten cabbage, it isn't worth much. Don't get mad, I like Koreans, and used to live next to Koreatown in Manhattan and even managed a hotel in Koreatown when I was in college. One thing I respect a lot about Koreans is that if a Korean guy is your friend, *he is your friend.* They don't take friendship lightly.

I don't have a problem with Japanese people either, I am just saying they are a fucked up bunch. But their cuisine is totally awesome, and any culture that includes bathing in hot springs and larping as a capybara is pretty sweet. Oh, and I do have a real appreciation for Japanese porn. I hear there is a real shortage of male porn talent in Japan, so maybe I should head over there and apply for a job? Porn aside, one thing I wanted to do but probably never will, is travel up and down Japan visiting hot springs. Besides fucking hookers, my only other vice is eating in high-end Japanese restaurants.

You know, it should not be a shock that Japan created the sex industry that they did as an outlet for their demented drives. You can't take a group of people whose main wartime pastimes are raping women and skewering infants on samurai swords, and then expect to them to work as fucking salarymen pulling 80 hour workweeks, unless you give them an *outlet.* But there is also a *price* for this outlet…

It has been stated in recent media that 50% of the Japanese population are virgins and have no desire to lose said virginity. While some state these claims as sensational, 10 years prior, virginity across the population stood at 25%, so it is not unrealistic to imagine that in 10 years it has gone up to the claimed 50%:

According to a detailed University of Tokyo study analyzing Japan's National Fertility Survey data from 1987 to 2015, about 25% of Japanese adults aged 18-39 have no history of heterosexual intercourse - specifically, 24.6% of women and 25.8% of men in that age range as of 2015.

Birth rates are consequently plummeting, with Prime Minister Shigeru Ishiba having described the situation as "a silent emergency." Meanwhile, "experts" ignore the real cause and instead cite bleak job prospects, the high cost of living, and a gender-biased corporate culture that adds extra burdens for women and working mothers as key factors deterring young people from marriage and childbearing. But the reality is that *Japan has ruined the ability of their populace to pair-bond and form stable family units by flooding their society with pornography and then turning all sexual and emotional needs into commodities that can be purchased.* In Japan, any and all sexual acts, no matter how outlandish or depraved, are 100% legally available for sale in the myriad sex districts. So are all of a human being's emotional needs. Want to be cuddled after fucking a pregnant women in the ass in Kabukicho, the red light district of Tokyo's Shinjuku ward? Simply head on over to the "cuddle bar" and your needs will be met. Also, the same services available for men, are available for women as well – minus anal sex with preggos, naturally. Don't laugh, one of my best friends recently availed himself of this service and gaped some pregnant Japanese whore's asshole. Imagine how that kid will grow up, given what his mom was doing while carrying him! I mean, you just want to chill in your mom's womb, while my friend's dick is banging you upside the head like Mike Tyson for a full hour as he pounds your mother's dirty whore asshole into oblivion. Are you beginning to see the pattern emerge across first-world nations? Get your population hooked on endless porn, commodify all aspects of sex and relationships, and get total control over your population by destroying pair bonding, familial bonds, and seizing control over the most powerful energy available to a human being. It's *sexual* energy. The next step is *always* to flood the first-world nation with feral, low-IQ migrants to breed the host population out of existence.

A Child Watching Porn *vs.* A Child Being Molested

Why does the porn industry try to cover up the reality that 9 out of 10 women in porn were molested as children? Well, first you need to realize that right now as you read this, boys and girls across the United States are accessing porn on their computers, tablets and smartphones *while still children themselves*, and "pleasuring" themselves to what they see. Self-pleasuring is perfectly natural, but doing it to the types of pornographic stimulation you see online is not. Furthermore, most parents are struggling to survive economically, so they are used to sticking a tablet in front of their children and letting YouTube raise them on an endless diet of creepy cartoons that give off the vibe they were created by either pedophiles, the CIA, or both! Children today grow up fast – quickly graduating from that suspect garbage on YouTube, to hardcore pornography.

Next, you need to remind yourself that they aren't pleasuring themselves to the porn of the 1970s or the 1980s either... So again, while it is perfectly natural for a child to be aroused by seeing naked bodies engaging in sexual activity even if they don't fully understand what they are seeing... How natural is it for a child to have fingertip access to hundreds of thousands of videos depicting gang bangs, blow bangs, anal gapings, throat fucking, bukkake, etc. and then diddling themselves to it?

It really isn't very hard to imagine that in terms of the neuroplasticity of the developing child's brain, this sort of exposure is producing damage *similar* to the damage that results from Childhood Sexual Abuse (CSA). It's almost as if a child masturbating to online pornography is *child molestation by proxy* – as if the porn industry has effectively molested the children of the *entire nation* and nobody has even noticed! Think about it like this, if your creepy uncle was showing your developing daughter his collection of gang bang videos on your big-screen TV for several hours, every single time he came over to babysit her, would that not be considered child sexual abuse? Would it not have deleterious effects on her? Would you be cool with it? Of course not. He would either be on trial, or else snacking on shotgun pellets. So why are you letting the porn industry get away with it? Don't worry, it will only get worse, as AI can produce infinite pornography of any genre, on demand.

Now with all of this in mind, is it really a shock to you that every girl today is whoring on Instagram, and operating an OnlyFans account? Their childhood porn habits have literally programmed them for sex work! Please keep in mind that *I am not saying that watching porn is **as emotionally traumatizing** in children as being sexually molested, or that it produces changes in neuroplasticity that are **identical** to those of being sexually molested as a child.* What *I am saying, is that a female child watching porn and self-pleasuring to it **will traumatically alter the neuroplasticity of her brain** to enough of a degree, that it will radically influence her sexual lifestyle choices as an adult, just as would being molested.*

- Childhood Sexual Abuse (CSA) is associated with profound and lasting alterations in brain development and neuroplasticity. It is well-established in neuroscience literature that CSA can lead to reduced volume in the hippocampus and prefrontal cortex, altered amygdala function, and disrupted connectivity in brain networks involved in emotion, memory, and stress regulation. These changes are linked to increased risk for depression, anxiety, PTSD, and difficulties with emotional and cognitive functioning throughout life.

- Research shows that pornography exposure during childhood can significantly affect the developing brain's neuroplasticity, with potentially lasting consequences due to the fact that pornography acts as a supernormal stimulus that programs sexual arousal templates and scripts, which become perceived as natural and intuitive. Studies find that frequent pornography consumption is associated with reduced gray matter volume in brain areas like the right caudate and altered functional connectivity between the striatum and prefrontal cortex - areas critical for reward processing and executive control. Exposure to pornography at a young age can be experienced as traumatic, as children lack the cognitive and emotional maturity to process explicit material. This can lead to shame, confusion, and distorted beliefs about sex and relationships, along with higher risks of anxiety, depression, and social isolation in adulthood.

Wilhelm Reich's Views on Pornography

Reich stated in his book, "The Sexual Revolution" that: "*any kind of literature which creates sexual anxiety must be prohibited. This includes pornography.*" Reich conceptualized pornography as more than just sexual images. For him, "*Pornography is the tendency to make an image of the sexual elements of a person or situation, and relate to the image with the ego or staring eyes alone. The belly, the heart, and the autonomic nervous system is left out.*"

Reich viewed "glamour" in movies, magazines, and consumerism as examples of this broader definition, describing it as "*objectifying and manipulating basic elements of sexual excitement in order to achieve power or wealth. This is a grave misuse of human sexual feeling.*" He further warned that: "***The biggest danger is that the concept of sexual freedom, which is, at base, the freedom to feel, becomes distorted into the supposed freedom to take, use, stare and insist. But these latter actions are secondary drives.***"

Reich traced the origins of pornography to historical sexual repression: When social organization passed from matriarchy to patriarchy and class society, the unity of religion and sexuality underwent a split, and the religious component became the antithesis of the sexual component. With that, the "cult" of sexuality went out of existence. It was replaced by the brothel, pornography and backstairs-sexuality. *Note: the preceding two sentences are actual quotes from Reich's work, which I edited slightly to make his language and diction more understandable, as more than 75 years have past since his writings. Historically speaking, I can also find no evidence of the existence of a matriarchy. However, this does not diminish Reich's contribution to our understanding of things.*

Reich saw pornography as a symptom of a sexually repressed society rather than genuine sexual liberation. He believed it represented a distortion of healthy sexuality into something ego-driven and disconnected from authentic feeling and biological function. His opposition to pornography was rooted in his belief that it perpetuated sexual anxiety and objectification rather than promoting the kind of natural, orgastic sexual fulfillment he advocated for human well being.

In short, Reich considered a culture of pornography to be worse than a Puritanical culture. He wasn't for sexual freedom so much as he was for orgasmic freedom. The issue, from his perspective, was that *the root of society's problems did not stem from sexual repression, but rather from the inability to experience orgasm fully due to trauma, and that this applied to **both** men as well as women.* This may be difficult for many men to grasp, but just because you can get hard and ejaculate does not mean that you are capable of a deep orgasmic experience, either. It is parallel to the reality that most women rely on a clitoral orgasm for release. The clitoris is like a little penis, which can grow when a woman takes an anabolic steroid like oxandrolone, which originally was compounded in order to remedy a micro penis in a growing male. A woman who is *only* capable of clitoral orgasms is sexually frigid, even though nobody wants to hear this. In the same way, most men are capable of getting hard and ejaculating, yet are also *as orgasmically frigid* as a woman! The fact that the Hitachi Magic Wand is the top-selling sex toy of all time is no surprise, as it has a monster motor capable of pumping out incredible vibrations, that a woman uses to force out clitoral orgasm after clitoral orgasm. This only compounds her problems by reinforcing her reliance upon clitoral orgasms themselves.

So a male may not be *physically* impotent, yet he may still be *orgasmically* impotent. Reich lamented that the porn industry had co-opted his work and movement for their own twisted ends because porn promoted sexual "freedom," but it was a freedom *free from orgasm*. Have you ever seen a woman have a bona fide, full-body orgasm arising from her "cervical pocket" in porn? I don't think I have seen it more than three times and always in a watered down way.

The point is we really don't have sexual freedom. What we have is sexual *liberty*. The distinction between "freedom" and "liberty" is subtle but philosophically significant, though the terms are often used interchangeably in everyday language. If you look both words up in the Merriam-Webster or Oxford English dictionary, the words are defined as the same. But they are not. This is a corruption.

- Freedom often encompasses both "freedom from" obstacles that inhibit the realization of your potential (i.e. trauma) as well as the "freedom to" realize your potential.

- Liberty is more commonly associated with "freedom from" arbitrary outside interference such as from a government.

Now that we are clear on the real definitions, I will ask you:

"What is the point of having sexual liberty if you don't have the freedom to enjoy it?"

I remember one time I was a guest on Playboy Radio and this guy called in and said how he lived through the "sexual revolution" and the "hippie free love era," and was so upset at how that movement got co-opted by pornography. He remarked that what he saw today was just so sad, and had nothing to do with either sex or love – it was just pure exploitation. Everyone in the studio grew very quiet because not only was he right, and echoed Reich's own sentiments, but because there was no way to respond other than to sit in shame.

Of course, Reich went down in history as a loon, who died in Federal Prison for claiming he could cure cancer with "orgone" energy. The great musician Kate Bush paid tribute to his own greatness in her song, "Cloudbusting," as he had also developed some of the earliest weather-control technology. This technology grew with the help of the shadow government of the United States, and most people today have no idea just how powerful the weather control technology of the U.S. government actually is. But that is outside of the scope of this book... I was lucky enough to study some of this early technology under one of Reich's students, and even participated in a modern weather control project using some of his original technology.

The True Purpose of The Porn Industry

There is far more to the history of pornography than meets the eye. Meaning, it is far more than just "people and free market forces," grossly misunderstanding and co-opting Reich's work to the detriment of the human spiritual condition. There are forces at work behind the porn industry that use it as a weapon against humanity. I have already touched on the role of pornography in the destruction of the family unit's formation by turning out potential wives and mothers into a life of perpetual whoredom, for example, but there are still other aspects of pornography that extend beyond being a detriment to society, and ultimately becoming a "detriment" to the human spiritual condition - to *grossly understate* the actual final outcome desired by Satan in this regard.

For example, it can be argued that Rocco Siffredi, easily the most influential porn performer of all time, is single-handedly responsible for making anal intercourse more popular that vaginal intercourse in porn. What's interesting is one time I ran across a YouTube video where Rocco was being interviewed with respect to his association with the Frankfurt School, a certain socialist think tank. This video can no longer be found, and I can not find any other evidence of his connection to this Marxist-leaning think tank. However, it all made sense when I came across that video, because the radical left promotes both anal sex as well as homosexuality as a tool to facilitate collapse of the current social order because it lowers reproductive rates and erodes the family unit.

When I was in college in the 1990s and attended both New York University and the City University of New York, every single liberal arts class had "Das Kapital" and "The Communist Manifesto" as part of the curriculum, which meant that in the course of acquiring your Bachelor of Arts degree, you would have been forced to read this trash at least five times. I was nearly expelled from the City University of New York because I had told an Indian professor that I would "see her in hell" because she openly preached that Mao Tse Tung, who was responsible for the deaths of close to 100 million Chinese, was the greatest thing to ever happen to China. Her argument for my expulsion was that since she was a Hindu, my statement to "see her in hell" was tantamount to a hate crime! I escaped expulsion because a Jewish professor defended me in their academic kangaroo court.

Nothing I see today shocks me, as in 1995 I could already see the mass indoctrination that communists were pulling off in our nation's universities. The youth were just *too* easy to brainwash! Furthermore, almost every single professor pushing this anti-establishment garbage was also a homosexual and openly encouraging students to experiment with homosexuality while insisting that everyone is naturally bisexual. What did any of this have to do with "education" or giving me a means to earn a living, and why the fuck was I paying for this? My issue isn't with anal sex per say, as it is pretty awesome, but when you are openly promoting it to the degree that you never see vaginal intercourse in porn anymore unless it is a double-penetration scene, you have to come to suspect something is very fishy indeed and it isn't the female performer's pussy!

So when you look at the details of a career like Rocco's, you have to ask yourself if there are any other influences that facilitated his unmatched level of success and influence? His alleged association with the Frankfurt School would be one, but it is also a suspicion of mine that Rocco is possessed by some sort of entity, which uses him as a vessel with which to indulge in sex in this physical realm, and which is orchestrating his success, in order for it to be able to enjoy as much sex as possible itself. Siffredi himself has described his sex addiction as emerging from "some kind of devil in me."

Sleepwalking people are inclined to take such statements metaphorically, when they are meant literally. Rocco has also been quoted as saying: *"It drives me out of my mind at times, to the point where I become almost aggressive. There was a time when I was afraid I didn't know how to stop."* He described: *"As soon as I saw a woman, but also a man or a transsexual I couldn't help myself, I had to have sex. It was as if there were two personalities inside me and one wanted to harm itself."* Also, he has spoken about *"his desire to castrate himself and to die in order to free himself from sex addiction."*

Adult actress Bobbi Starr has been quoted as having said: *"Any girl in the industry who has been with him... will tell you that they have done things with him that they [would] never do with anyone else."* This could also possibly be due to the influence of an entity that is attached to Rocco. It is not beyond the realm of possibility that when Rocco was young he entered into some sort of pact with an entity and his "career" is the consequence of that free will decision of his.

In general, you always have to look past any official narratives and ask yourself, "Could I repeat this particular individual's career path if I had the talents and attributes necessary for success?" If the answer is "no," then there were outside forces at play that are in the shadows. A good example of this is the career of being a "Hollywood celebrity." If one wants to be a doctor, one can attend medical school and being a doctor is practically guaranteed. The path is clear. But to be a successful actor, there is no clear path. You could go to a legitimate acting school and establish yourself as a legitimate stage actor, but we all know that almost no Hollywood celebrities can act worth a shit. So that isn't it... Is it looks? Most Hollywood celebrities are a far cry from beautiful, and often mid-tier at best in the looks department. So that's not it either... So then how do they get to be Hollywood celebrities? In my opinion, in many cases it involves a willingness to get involved in certain darker aspects of reality, and to advance agendas that are in alignment with the darkness that is in rebellion against The Divine Father.

But *what* is the ultimate purpose of getting everyone addicted to porn? I have already explored the reasons communists are in favor of it. But why would literal demons be so keen on porn becoming so popular? Again, when I worked in the industry, I was told that the whole purpose of pornography was to make sure that people would end up incapable of relating sexually with real live human beings, *and therefore would consume even more porn.* But why would that be the goal, if porn wasn't making money at that point? Why would the goal be to consume *even more porn*? I have already mentioned that porn's purpose is to render you unable to form actual sexual relationships, functional family units, make you disinterested in society, and ultimately easier to control. This would in turn make it easier for the elites to steer society in any direction they chose. But again why would demons and Satan be so interested in this? Naturally, it is dark extraterrestrials aligned with Satan along with Satan himself, who are behind the elites, so perhaps it would help if we knew *the actual direction* that the elites wanted to steer society in? Again, why would the main goal be to consume *even more porn* when there is no financial incentive to do so?

It is because Satan and the elites who do his bidding wish to steer society into a transhumanistic direction which will culminate in the extinction of free will for humanity. This will be accomplished by implanting a microchip into human beings much like Elon Musk promotes. This is the "mark of the beast," which will create an interface with some iteration of artificial intelligence that will usurp the free will of those humans who receive it. ***However, in order for this to occur humans must make the free will choice, to give up their free will.*** In order to push humanity to give up their free will, "incentives" must be created that are both "of the carrot" as well as "of the stick." Threatening people that they will not be able to buy or sell, and therefore obtain what they need to survive (such as food and shelter) without a microchip implant, is an example of the "stick." Much like when people who lived in Europe, were told they would not be allowed to buy groceries without proof of vaccination. But what would a "carrot" look like? Well, the biggest "carrot" for human beings is sexual pleasure, so it makes sense to wean humans off real sex and onto pornography, which has now evolved with the help of AI to levels of dopamine manipulation that were previously unimaginable. Cheap blow up sex dolls that used to be sold as party gags have evolved into hyper-realistic sex dolls. The next evolutionary step will be AI-powered sex robots, along with pornographic virtual reality rendered so immersively goonable with the help of AI, that humans will have zero interest in sex with other human beings. They will only be interested in sexual interactions with AI-based "constructs," *with the mark of the beast being the prerequisite for interaction with them.* This is the "carrot" and why it is absolutely imperative to get everyone hooked on as much porn as possible. This is the true ultimate purpose of the porn industry, and it has nothing to do with money.

OnlyFans Is *Not* Empowerment!

"They" call doing porn "empowerment" for women and show off girls making obscene amounts of money doing OnlyFans. This brings in the suckers: young girls who will end up ruining their lives thinking they can make $100,000/month on OnlyFans. Well, you can also make $30,000/weekend in Dubai getting trains run on you and eating a literal platter of shit for the grand finale.

Does that sound empowering to you?

You know, it's amazing how men can hear a female porn performer drone on and on about how what she does is "empowerment" and not understand what the bitch is actually saying! Sex work is not empowerment because it enables a woman to "embrace" her sexuality, as pornography has next to *nothing* to do with female sexuality, so there is therefore nothing to "embrace." What porn performers do is "empowerment" because it allows them to turn their pussies, mouths and assholes into cold hard cash and fame as opposed to letting everyone just use their holes for free and remaining unknown. The irony is that real empowerment for a woman is orgasmic empowerment, and what is so ridiculous about nonsense like "1,000 man gang bangs," is that those 1,000 men run up inside of the woman for only 30 seconds apiece. I mean, do the math! Now how can this possibly lead to orgasmic empowerment? I would guess women who do these sorts of "stunts" have never had an orgasm more powerful than a bowel movement – not even once. So the only empowerment going on here is financial and attentive in nature.

Also, keep in mind the only reason girls on OnlyFans resort to stunts like this, is because making money from OnlyFans is *that* hard. They need to do extreme things just to stand out. It's "strictly business," as EPMD used to rap. I am not trying to shit on such performers here, as in many ways they are more like performance artists than porn stars, and they do serve as a sexual outhouse, which is a public service. I would rather shit on the 1,000 guys who stand in line at some Airbnb to subject themselves to this sort of debacle!

If a woman wants to make money, her best bet is to target the ever growing army of simps out there. This is because men are absorbing female neurosis to such a degree, that they are starting to prioritize female attention over sex with females themselves. I know successful guys who pay women just to hang out with them on the phone for hours a day while they are at work, and pay them fortunes for this.

Every Woman You Desire Is Already Engaging in Sex Work

The brutal reality is that *all* attractive women that you would *really* want to fuck are already engaging in sex work. There are almost no exceptions. The hot models you see on IG, are on IG not only because they are addicted to attention and the dopamine rush of attaining "likes." Oh no, that is a *side benefit.* They are there because they are marketing themselves sexually to men *world-wide.* All a woman has to do is upload some hot, half-naked pictures of herself and men with money and looks and lifestyle will flood into her DMs offering her huge sums of cash, paid trips to meet them in other parts of the world, shopping expeditions... all in exchange for sex - the kind of sex you masturbate too in the raunchiest of porn films. Again, before social media, a woman with such aspirations would have to travel to Miami or some place where people with money hung around or go to expensive hotel bars or exclusive parties to meet these sorts of men. But IG has made it possible for any woman to engage in prostitution and target the entire planet, without ever having to leave her house or spend a dime on advertisement. All within the time it takes to set up an account. The whole while plausibly denying that she is engaging in prostitution. I mean, it isn't like she is uploading pics of herself to some website for escorts where everything is crystal clear to everyone...

Most women have a good 10 years in which to live this sort of elite lifestyle of self-indulgence while experiencing every sexual fantasy imaginable on someone else's dime. Women like to talk about double-standards, but how can a man do this? He really can't, and it is extremely unfair. So yeah, if a guy busts his ass for years to attain a gorgeous body and a big bank account, it's understandable that he wants a fucking prize for his efforts, and a woman with a higher body count than an airport car rental is no prize. This is because the very definition of a prize means that only a select few get one.

Let's look at the definition of the word "prize" over on dictionary.com shall we?

Noun

- A reward for victory or superiority, as in a contest or competition. *A woman with a high body count cannot be considered as such, as statistically most men she has fucked are losers by the very standards set by women themselves.*

- Something that is won in a lottery or the like. *Finding a beautiful woman with a low body count is akin to winning a lottery!*

- Anything striven for, worth striving for, or much valued. *Who would strive for a woman that gave it up to an army of dudes who didn't strive to get her?*

- Something seized or captured, especially an enemy's ship and cargo captured at sea in wartime. *This would be considered rape so we can scratch this off the list.*

Yes, this gross unfairness is the number one reason why men are upset by women with high body counts, and slut-shame females, etc... Sure, they will offer up all sorts of third-tier rationales for their position which have enough truth to be legit, such as claiming female promiscuity prevents females from pair-bonding, or that it's lowers a man's status when he enters a high-end restaurant and half the males eating at the other tables have gone choo-choo on his wife or girlfriend. These are *all* legit reasons. However, these stated reasons are *not the main reason*. The main reason is that men absolutely cannot stand the injustice of having to work so fucking impossibly hard to live out even a *fraction* of their sexual fantasies while a woman has to do literally nothing and even gets paid to live out *all* of hers. The injustice of the situation is simply unbearable. The other main reason men are upset by a woman with a high body count, is because as I mentioned earlier, the higher the body count the greater the chance she has been with someone who gave her such a deep orgasmic experience, that she can never really be exclusively yours. You will always be sharing her with that guy, even if she never sees him again.

Most men choose to drown themselves in masturbation, vaping and video gaming just to avoid facing this simple, yet ultimately undeniable, fact of their miserable lives. So the next time a woman talks about double-standards, *just tell her to shut the fuck up*. Men's lives, if they refuse to become stoned gooners and gamers, are insanely difficult and filled with nothing but heartbreak, yet they must keep pressing on no matter what. There is no escape from the grind, and no other choice but to embrace it and to try to find effective and alternative means of self-care. The reward? Sex with prostitutes (all beautiful women these days) and no real chance of a relationship let alone love, as all the "trophy wives" are really just prostitutes that winners foolishly buy instead of rent. Because marrying a prostitute is infinitely more expensive than renting one!

If you do get a girlfriend who isn't a prostitute, despite being hot, she is probably mentally ill on some level and you will be miserable accommodating all of her mental problems. Whenever you meet some guy who bagged a hot girl in a relationship and things appear normal, just check their medicine cabinet the next time you are at their house for an event. You will see SSRI prescriptions (anti-depressants) that make their pussies dead as door nails, NDRI prescriptions (norepinephrine and dopamine reuptake inhibitors) which make women absolutely batshit insane, and Klonopin prescriptions (for their crippling social anxiety) that they will never be able to titrate off from. It is *no fun at all* to be in a relationship with these sorts of women. You have to re-parent them, they never STFU, have a lot of trouble taking directions, are extremely needy... It just isn't worth it.

PART III: SOME SEXUAL AND SPIRITUAL TRUTHS

Are Women Really *That* Different from Men?

I would postulate that the gulf between men and women is a bit exaggerated. A sock turned inside out, is still a sock! Meaning, beyond the biological differences that create the polarities of male and female, from a practical standpoint they are the same creation. Yet you are always hearing this endless tripe that women are somehow "completely different and unfathomable creatures."

Look, women aren't some fucking mystery. You need to *stop* thinking that women are insane (although many become so), that women are illogical (although it is true they are more concerned with feeling than logic), that they don't know what they want (they know *exactly* what they want, *you* just can't provide it for them), and that you can never please them (sexually, this is *usually* the case with rare exception – at least until you finish reading this book).

Seriously, inject 50mg of testosterone propionate into a female, and watch her turn into a man with a pussy within the hour. Don't believe me? Go pick up a bona fide female bodybuilder who injects testosterone and date her for a while. It's basically a dude with a pussy. Also, having grown up in a gay neighborhood, let me tell you that many gay bottoms are just like straight women, only *far* worse. I am not joking… if you think you have problems with women, go make friends with a gay male who is a top and only fucks with beautiful twink bottoms. You will find he has the same problems as you, only worse. The only real difference, is that he is getting laid *literally* 100x more than you. If men and women are soooo different, how can this be so?

I had a best friend back in NYC who was a gay top. He had his own place, and enough money to not have to work. He was Italian and looked like a twin of Rocco Siffredi, but with an even bigger cock. He could also out fuck Rocco with only 20mg of Tadalafil in his system. He was otherwise completely drug free. It was hard to find time to hang out with him, let alone hang out with him in peace, because all of these homo hookup apps he had on his phone like Grindr would be "dinging" every few minutes. Since he didn't have to work, all he did was fuck. What a life! He probably fucked 3 different guys a day, every single day, for years on end. I am not making this up. Straight people have no clue just how much sex gay males have. I would swing by his house to drop off something, and some random fruit would answer the door on his knees offering to suck my dick, while another would be face down on the sofa with his gaping asshole whistling dixie in the door draft.

Was my friend happy? Nope. He was actually very unhappy. Why? Because he truly loved many of these beautiful boys and wanted a real relationship with at least one of them, yet nobody wanted him despite the fact he was a truly amazing man who just wanted to love and be loved back. They just wanted to be fucked by his giant cock for hours on end before going back to some loser boyfriend they had, or some sugar daddy who paid their bills... the ones who were "single" were repulsed by the idea of being with my friend. Why? Because *just like most women, most gay bottoms utterly hate themselves.* What a coincidence! Some of you reading this may wonder how I can say that gay bottoms hate themselves. Having grown up in a gay neighborhood, the irony is not lost on me that the LGBTQ+ community is always dubbing their parades and public events with the term "pride" despite the fact that in reality, they have none. Here is some irrefutable evidence of homosexual self-hatred:

- *They have to be high on drugs in order to enjoy their sexuality.* 50% of gay males use Alkyl Nitrites ("poppers"), 30% use methamphetamines, 20% use MDMA, 15% use GHB and cocaine usage is 3x higher than that of the general population. Think about this... if you as a straight male had an endless supply of willing sexual partners, would you not be in paradise? Why would you simultaneously feel the need to be taking all of these drugs in order to enjoy your sexual abundance? Is this not a signal of underlying self-hatred?

- *Intentionally contracting HIV ("bug chasing") or other serious diseases.* 100% of all outbreaks of new STD variants can be traced back to some gay bathhouse somewhere. With the HIV incidence rate 44 times higher among gay men, and gay men accounting for as many as 80% of primary and secondary syphilis cases, why do only 16% of gay men use condoms? Why do gay bottoms let an endless parade of men ejaculate inside of them knowing their community has the highest rates of viral and bacterial STIs across the board? Does this sound like self-love?

- *Getting you anus "fisted" to the point you destroy the normal function of your organ of elimination and have to wear adult diapers most of the time.* Depending on the population of gay men surveyed, 5-25% of gay men engage in this sexual behavior on a regular basis. From my anecdotal observations, at least 25% across the "bottom" population are getting fist-fucked on a regular basis. I can't imagine purposefully damaging your digestive tract like this to be anything other than self-hatred.

In summary, of course there are differences between the genders, but don't think women are somehow beyond understanding. They just want you to believe that, because once you understand them, they lose so much of their mystery and power.

The Manufactured AIDS Crisis of the 1980s

I want to make sure that people don't read the prior section and think I am "homophobic" or engaging in some sort of literary "gay bashing." I am simply sharing my observations, and the obvious truths that spring from them.

To show some solidarity with gay males against the powers of planetary oppression, I want to talk in great detail about the manufactured "AIDS crisis" of the 1980s, which Dr. Anthony Fauci played a major role in, just as he played a major role in the Covid-19 scamdemic of the 2020s, 40 years later. I will present evidence to support not only my belief that the AIDS crisis was an intentional act of genocide against gay males, but that it had a much larger purpose as did the manufactured Covid-19 scamdemic, which is *to prepare humans to accept Satan's "mark of the beast."*

I personally lived through the AIDS crisis back in the 1980s, when I lived in NYC. I vividly remember watching gay men dropping dead left-and-right, and it makes me upset that what I view as an *intentional genocide* has been forgotten in time, with young people these days *actually believing* the lie that HIV causes AIDS. To remember nothing but a lie, as if it were the truth, and forgetting all of those who died to give birth to this lie, is completely and utterly fucked up.

So without further ado, let's talk about what I believe really caused the immune systems of gay males to fail en masse. After all, "AIDS" is not a virus, but rather a "syndrome."

Between 1978 and 1981, the CDC conducted a series of hepatitis B vaccine trials that took place in New York, San Francisco, and other cities, primarily targeting gay men who were at high risk for hepatitis B. The timing coincidence between these trials, and the first cases of AIDS being reported in June of 1981, has been noted by many people who lived through that era. Also of note is that all of the early AIDS cases were indeed among men who had participated in these vaccine trials, or else lived in the same communities that had been involved in the vaccine trials. The vaccine was made from plasma collected from hepatitis B carriers, drawn from the gay community itself. Of most importance here, is that stored blood samples from trial participants were later tested for HIV, and some samples from 1978-1979 did indeed test positive for HIV. This demonstrates that the virus was already in circulation well before the vaccine trials, as well as long before there were any reported cases of AIDS. So right there, we can conclude that HIV could not have possibly caused AIDS. If it did, there would have been cases of AIDS reported long before 1981.

The hepatitis B virus was discovered in 1965 by Dr. Baruch Blumberg who won the Nobel Prize for his discovery. Working with Dr. Blumberg, microbiologist Irving Millman helped to develop a blood test for the hepatitis B virus. The concept for developing a hepatitis B vaccine using HBsAg derived from human plasma was initially proposed by Blumberg and Millman in 1969. In 1981, the FDA approved a more sophisticated plasma-derived hepatitis B vaccine for human use. Merck Pharmaceuticals manufactured this plasma vaccine as "Heptavax," which was the first commercial hepatitis B virus vaccine.

The key figure in all of this was **Maurice Hilleman.** Hilleman collected blood from gay men and intravenous drug users - groups known to be at risk for viral hepatitis. In addition to the sought-after hepatitis B surface proteins, the blood samples not only contained HIV, but other viruses as well that would have been common to those how shot IV drugs or participated in what at the time we can refer to as the "gay bathhouse scene." While Hilleman devised a multistep heating process to purify this blood so that only the hepatitis B surface proteins remained, this vaccine that had been made using human hepatitis B infected blood *was injected* *into chimpanzees known to be infected with the cancer causing simian virus 40 (SV40)* as part of the manufacturing process.

The research shows that **HIV was indeed inactivated by Hilleman's heating process, and that a** period of 15 minutes warming up to 65°C had already completely inactivated representatives of nine virus families, including lentivirus (human immunodeficiency virus). The research also shows that the efficacy of two heating cycles (90 sec at 103°C and 10 hr at 65°C) used during the manufacture of a plasma-derived hepatitis-B vaccine was validated for the inactivation of 12 virus families, **including HIV (another reason HIV could not have caused AIDS).**

However, while HIV was killed by the heat treatment, *SV40 (simian virus 40) survived the heating process*: simian virus 40 (SV-40) was the most heat-resistant virus evaluated. The infectivity of SV-40 was reduced by 10^4 but a marginal residual activity (<1.5 TCID50 per ml) was observed. Subsequent pasteurization for 10 h at 65°C did not further reduce the infectivity of SV-40. **This is significant because *SV40 was known to contaminate vaccines* and has been linked to cancer.** Even more significant was that Hilleman *was also one of the vaccine pioneers to warn about the possibility that simian viruses might contaminate vaccines.* The best-known of these viruses is SV40, a viral contaminant of the polio vaccine, whose discovery led to the recall of Salk's vaccine in 1961 and its replacement with Albert Sabin's oral vaccine. We also need to remember that *SV40 was NOT naturally in the blood drawn from gay males - it got there through the vaccine production process.*

So the research clearly states that even after discovering SV40's heat resistance, *they continued using these inadequate protocols*. This suggests either gross negligence or deliberate contamination, *especially* given Hilleman's expertise and previous warnings about simian virus contamination. In an extraordinary PBS taped interview (1987) with medical historian Edward Shorter and Dr. Maurice Hilleman, Merck's foremost vaccine developer, Dr. Hilleman acknowledged that the polio vaccine (manufactured by Merck) had been contaminated with SV40. *He also indicated the likelihood that SV40 is the source of AIDS*: "I didn't know we were importing AIDS."

Early AIDS patients were also getting opportunistic infections and certain cancers, the most notable being Kaposi's sarcoma. Notable, because while Kaposi's sarcoma *could* have resulted from immune suppression, it is *normally* attributed to the relatively rare oncogenic herpesvirus 8 (HHV-8), and also most commonly found in people in certain regions of Africa where the virus is more endemic. Given that the heating protocols used were known to be ineffective against SV40 but utilized anyway, is it not possible that either the heating protocols were also ineffective against other contaminants or even neglected entirely in the actual vaccine production process? Is it not possible that gay males were being injected with what would have amounted to a cocktail of viral contaminants that would have overwhelmed their immune systems resulting in the *syndrome* of "AIDS," which is an acronym for "Acquired Immune Deficiency Syndrome?"

Given Hilleman's brilliance, his knowledge of the dangers of SV40 as a known vaccine contaminant, and his conscious choice to not alter heating protocols to neutralize it, etc., it seems highly disingenuous for Hilleman to claim he didn't realize that "we were importing AIDS." A man like Hilleman would have known for sure that he would have been "importing AIDS." What's even worse, is that they knew that HIV could not have possibly caused AIDS since heating protocols would have destroyed the HIV in the vaccines, and since HIV has already been in the blood of gay males long before there was an "AIDS crisis." This means that the billions that were spent doing research to answer the question of what caused AIDS after Dr. Anthony Fauci came upon the scene, came up with an "answer" that was already known from the start to *not* be the answer. It also means that that the official story that HIV causes AIDS is a blatant lie.

Fauci's Central Role in Both Events

AIDS Crisis:

- Spearheaded the research establishing "HIV causes AIDS."
- Had a close professional relationship with Hilleman.
- Directed billions in research toward HIV when evidence suggests it couldn't have survived vaccine production.
- Promoted toxic "treatments" like AZT.

COVID-19 Pandemic:

- Led the official response as head of NIAID.
- Promoted gain-of-function research at Wuhan lab.
- Initially dismissed lab leak theory as "conspiracy theory."
- Advocated for lockdowns that destroyed the economy, masks that were proved ineffective, and potentially dangerous and even potentially lethal experimental mRNA vaccines claiming that said vaccines only work if *everyone* gets them.

What's also curious is that former President Biden issued Dr. Anthony Fauci a presidential pardon even though he had not been accused, tried or convicted of anything at all! Isn't that *weird*? Preemptive pardons are historically issued when:

- Crimes are known to have occurred but haven't been prosecuted yet.
- There's expectation of future criminal exposure.
- Political protection is needed for past actions.

This suggests:

- The Biden administration knew Fauci faced potential criminal liability.

- Evidence exists of criminal conduct during COVID response.

- The need to protect him from future investigations.

There you have it! HIV does not cause AIDS. In order to produce the deadly syndrome known as AIDS, you *probably* require a cocktail of viral contaminants, including SV40 as a key factor, which is not normally found in humans, unless you eat infected simians, or have sex with infected simians. While some people do eat and fuck monkeys, this was *not* how SV40 was introduced into the gay population. It was introduced via the Hepatitis B vaccines because SV40 infected chimpanzees were used in the vaccine production process, and *protocols were deliberately put in place to make sure the SV40 virus survived pasteurization and got passed into the gay population.* Additionally, the fact that so many AIDS patients developed Kaposi's sarcoma, which is caused by the relatively rare oncogenic herpesvirus 8 (HHV-8), indicates to me that HHV-8 was present in the vaccine and survived pasteurization as well. What if the pasteurization process was ignored completely? What if gay men were injected with a live cocktail of viruses that included SV40?

"But why tho?" you may ask... was it just to make blood money, or to experiment with population control via the testing of vectors of viral warfare upon gay men?

In my opinion, the whole reason for the fraud of "HIV causes AIDS," was to create as much trauma and neurosis around real sex as possible, in order to further the agenda of ultimate control over humans via the eradication of their free will. You see, in order to control humans, you *must* control their sexuality, as it is one of the most powerful forces in the human psyche. Making people terrified of real sex with real people, by leading them to believe that such activities will give them some imaginary STD that will *kill* them, was necessary in order to traumatize people enough to gain control over their sexuality, and by extension, gain control over them. Because then the thwarted biological drive to have sex with real live human beings, could be redirected into the consumption of pornography, the ultimately *catastrophic* consequences of which, are already understood now that I have explained to you what the *true purpose* of pornography ultimately is. Prior to the AIDS crisis, people were having sex like crazy without a care in the world. This could not have been allowed to continue in the eyes of the elites, who have plans for you. *Big* plans...

Homosexuality, Dr. Edmund Bergler and the Mayhem of Lucifer

I grew up in a gay neighborhood in NYC and had plenty of close gay friends. Gay men are pretty awesome, although growing up I noticed they all seemed to harbor this strange subconscious mix of fear and hatred of women. Look, if there are no women around, most men will fuck *anything* in place of them, no matter if they are other men, literal animals or whatever. But to be *repulsed* by sex with women and want nothing to do with them goes against the basic biological imperative of reproduction, which is up there with psychic stability and physical survival, so there is something *peculiar* about genuine homosexuals, no matter how common they may be. Even more telling, is the absolutely self-destructive nature of the "gay lifestyle" which includes mixing drugs with sex at every opportunity, intentionally trying to catch diseases ("bug chasing"), having scores of men run trains on you without protection, and getting your asshole fisted until you need to wear adult diapers. These are all signs of something gone very wrong on a developmental level. I am not suggesting that a gay person should make efforts to "cure" himself of being gay *even if* such a thing were a remote possibility. Which it isn't, just to be clear. I mean, you can't "cure" someone of NPD or BPD, so just forget about changing a man's preference for where he gives or takes dick! I am just pointing out what is painfully obvious despite the deafening chorus of "born this way." Whenever you witness anything that is unnatural or self-destructive, let alone both, you are probably looking at the end-product of developmental trauma no matter how politically incorrect it may be to point it out.

Dr. Edmund Bergler, one of Freud's students and possibly the greatest medical psychiatrist in history, was a prolific author and his textbooks at one time comprised the core of the study of analytical psychiatry in medical schools across the country. This was also before psychiatrists became nothing more than "drug pushers" who "solved" everything by prescribing medication. But once the Satanic cultural Marxist agenda began to pick up steam, Bergler was completely "canceled" from medical academia. His books were expunged from university libraries, and publishing houses refused to continue to publish them. His book catalog would have been wiped from existence, were it not for used book dealers on Amazon, from whom you can still pick up copies at a premium. These books will always sport a stamp from some University library on the inside, identifying where they came from. His "crime?" Pointing out that while genuine homosexuality arises from developmental trauma that is *incurable,* many men who end up identifying as homosexuals were not incurable, but simply encouraged down that path instead of being treated with analytical psychiatry.

I have read many of Bergler's books, and his wisdom is *extremely* difficult to grasp because he deals exclusively with trauma acquired in the womb, and during what Freud called the "oral stage" of human development (0-18 months). To further complicate matters, humans were engineered by Lucifer so as to lose access to all memory from that time. This is sometimes referred to as "infantile amnesia" or "childhood amnesia" and is considered the inability of adults to recall episodic memories from early childhood, typically before age 3-4. Is it not strange that not only is the "Oral stage" sealed up, but everything up until the "Oedipal stage" is as well? This was achieved by Lucifer via genetic tampering with the hippocampus, thereby creating the phenomenon of the "subconscious mind" which is unique to "humans" on this planet. He did this to make sure humans could be manipulated with ease. He also truncated the human life span to barely 100 years, to further insure that humans would not be able to figure things out before their lives would be over, upon which time their memories would be lost and they would get recycled back into the "matrix" to go through it all over again. It was an incredibly cruel and nasty thing to do, and I would not be surprised *if* it turned out to weigh heavily upon Lucifer's ultimate "uncreation."

Pro Tip: There is a common misconception that Lucifer, Satan and The Devil are three names for the same being, but this is not so and to conflate them with one another is a serious error. They are three separate beings, all of whom can be considered extraterrestrial in nature despite any other categories of classification they may be subject to. All of these beings have also appeared thoughout human history bearing a myriad of different names, of which I will share but a few. Lucifer, for example, also went by the name of "Enki," and was a reptilian scientist and genetic engineer who engineered the current iteration of "human beings" on this planet.

In terms of understanding the writings of Dr. Edmund Bergler, grasping what he teaches is further hindered by the fact that most humans indulge in psychic masochism to at least *some degree*, and the mind does *everything it can* to prevent one from discovering the mechanics of this phenomenon, in order to maintain psychic stability. This will make sense when you are done with this section, as I will now take the time to explain Bergler here in a way that I do not believe anyone has ever done before, because it is critical to understand *why* Bergler spoke of incurable vs. curable neurotics, in order to grasp just how bad the "human condition" actually is.

As I have explained earlier in this book, "neurosis" in it's simplest form is just an inner conflict that one pushes down into the subconscious in order to attain psychic stability. The example I used is that of a woman in conflict over wanting to experience a deep orgasm, yet simultaneously afraid of the feelings that are inherent to said orgasmic experience. So rather than resolving the conflict by allowing herself to have the orgasm and dealing with the feelings she is afraid of, she chooses to block her ability have a deep orgasm via the *somatic mechanism* of tensing up her urogenital and pelvic diaphragms, and then forgetting about the inner conflict so that she no longer has to feel conflicted. Tensing up on a somatic level is the *mechanism* by which she pushes her inner conflict down into the tissues of her physical body. Consequently, the physical body where she has "locked up" the *energetics* of the conflict, *becomes* the locus of the *interface* to the "subconscious mind." By subsequently forgetting her inner conflict, she has effectively "locked it up and thrown away the key," so to speak. So it is accurate to say that the physical body itself is the subconscious mind. But to be precise, the physical body itself is just the interface to the subconscious mind. Much like a computer terminal used to be an interface to the "mainframe." These days, mainframes have been replaced by "clouds."

Now as I have also explained earlier in this book, there is a deeper and more complex explanation of neurosis which is that of someone choosing to make the decision to experience *inauthentic* suffering in order to avoid feeling *authentic* suffering. The example I have used is that of someone washing their hands 50 times per day to avoid feeling grief which would overwhelm them and therefore cause psychic instability. The compulsion to wash the hands is an *additional type of somatic mechanism* that is a bit different than the somatic mechanism of tensing up the urogenital and pelvic diaphragms to block a deep orgasmic experience, although the repression of grief and *all* emotions, *always* involves the somatic mechanism of tensing up the master diaphragm at the level of the solar plexus. In this particular illustrative example, however, the physical distraction of washing the hands over and over is an *additional* somatic mechanism stacked atop the primary somatic mechanism of tensing up the master diaphragm at the level of the solar plexus, in order to provide reinforcement for the primary somatic mechanism. This additional somatic mechanism of washing the hands as a physical distraction from what is being felt, transforms very quickly from a *habit* into a *compulsion*. Just like smoking cigarettes, etc., can and often does. Once this occurs, the inner conflict over feeling the overwhelming grief can be forgotten as well, as it has now been pushed down into the subconscious (which again is "located" in the actual physical body) by this "double-stacking" of somatic mechanisms of repression.

So far so good, but we are still talking about the mechanics of neurosis from the perspective of Wilhelm Reich, another student of Freud, who focused primarily on neurotic conflicts that arose from what Freud referred to as the "Oedipal Stage" (3-5 years) of human development and on. Again, Bergler focused on neurotic conflicts that arose in the womb and in what Freud referred to as the "Oral Stage" (0-18 months) of human development. *All* of these conflicts covered by Bergler at this stage are based upon trauma inflicted by the mother (or the lack of having one), and *all* memories from this time period in a human's developmental life are locked away in the subconscious by default due to Lucifer's genetic machinations, which makes both accessing them as well as navigating them insanely difficult and often impossible from a practical perspective. Yet Bergler was brilliant enough to figure out the dynamics of their operation nonetheless. Let's dive in!

When a mother causes a child to suffer deprivation or abuse, the child experiences a form of trauma that is *completely unnatural*: "How can a mother who is supposed to be nothing but comfort and love deprive me and abuse me?" This completely unnatural trauma's ability to destabilize the psyche of the child is exacerbated by the utter helplessness of the child, and the absolute dependency of the child upon the mother. So much so, that in order to regain psychic stability, the child must do something *far more extreme* than merely employing somatic tension to repress the pain, or developing a compulsion to distract itself from the pain, and subsequently forgetting about what happened. Instead, the child resorts to a solution to regain psychic stability that is *utterly catastrophic* for it's future: the child "rewires" itself so that the desire for deprivation and abuse replaces the desire for comfort and love. At that point, the child has been reprogrammed to be a "psychic masochist" and seeks out pain and suffering and enjoys it, which is a *very different* path to regaining psychic stability than simply repressing pain and suffering or replacing it with a substitute form of "inauthentic" pain and suffering as a distraction!

This resultant Satanic inversion of the child's drives should not be shocking, when you learn that Enki (Lucifer) worked alongside Enlil (Yahweh) at the time, and that Enlil was the son of King Anu (Satan) of the Annunaki. This is what Zecharia Sitchin never told you, because *he did not know*!

Now *here* is where the *deepest and most primal* neurotic conflict is born, and the nature of this neurotic conflict is *very different* from neurotic conflicts that are birthed in the Oedipal stage (3-5 years) and beyond. What happens is this "rewiring" of the child's psychic circuitry is in and of itself so aberrant as well as so unnatural, that another part of your the mind (which Freud and Bergler called "the superego" and which is really just a fancy term for "the conscious mind") starts screaming "This is soooo wrong!" and begins to torment you over your newly minted masochistic impulses in order to reign them in, and thereby prevent your absolute annihilation, lest your psychic masochism be allowed free reign to pursue what ultimately amounts to self-destruction.

While it is true that I keep saying throughout this book that the drive for psychic stability trumps the drive for physical survival, there is still a "tipping point" beyond which the self-destructive tendencies inherent to certain solutions for maintaining psychic stability become so extreme, that a human being indulging in them without restraint would not even stay alive long enough to reproduce, and the "human race" would quickly annihilate itself. Consequently a "fail safe" comes into play to prevent this from happening. This "fail safe" *is* the neurotic conflict *itself* that arises from the ashes of an Oral stage befouled by maternal trauma. So while it can be said that later stage neurotic conflicts maintain *psychic stability*, Oral stage neurotic conflicts struggle to maintain *physical survivability* – or at least postpone the inevitable long enough for the organism to hopefully reproduce itself.

To summarize, the "inner conflict" that powers neuroses born from what Freud called the Oral stage of human development, is *not* a conflict based upon feeling something vs. not feeling something. This is because the child had no choice but to feel the suffering the mother inflicted upon it, and therefore found re-wiring its basic drives the *only* viable solution to endure said suffering. Rather, it is a conflict between the child's newly acquired drive to seek out masochistic pleasure vs. the part of the child's mind that is tormenting it with screams of "This cannot be allowed, this is an unnatural aberration that leads to misery and self-destruction!" What makes it even more of a mess, is that this entire conflict gets forgotten and buried in your subconscious with zero effort on your part because Lucifer engineered it to happen *automatically*. From this point forward, without conscious awareness of the powerful dynamics at play beneath the surface, your subconscious mind that craves suffering will start to engineer your life choices in such a way so as to get to enjoy the suffering it craves, while simultaneously convincing you that you are simply a victim of circumstances outside of yourself.

The key here is that Bergler is still defining neurosis as a conflict, but this level of base neurosis *isn't* a conflict over whether to feel or not to feel, this is a level of conflict between two halves of a mind that have been split in two and rewired for self-destruction, where the mind has completely forgotten that it has been rewired for self-destruction due to intentional genetic tampering by an extraterrestrial influence. It is this scenario, that Bergler generally considered to be incurable. Why is it incurable? Because there is zero motivation to change! A woman may grow tired of not being able to enjoy sex, and a man may grow tired of washing his hands 50x per day, but someone who truly enjoys suffering, cannot grow tired of it! Furthermore, the psychic masochist has zero awareness that the deepest part of himself craves suffering. Even if it is pointed out to him, or even if he realizes it on some level, it's what he really *wants*, so he or she is doomed.

The writings of Dr. Edmund Bergler tie in perfectly with the writings of Lloyd DeMause once Bergler is truly understood. *But when you realize that the ultimate consequence of psychic masochism is war itself,* then you understand why Lucifer engineered the subconscious mind in "humans" to begin with... it was to make sure that humans kept slaughtering each other so they can continue to be a never-ending food source for 4th and 5th dimensional entities to feed upon in this "matrix" that humanity finds itself trapped in. The more you know!

So let me ask you, isn't knowing the above reason enough to start praying directly to The Divine Father at once? Why are you wasting your time with religion? Can Jesus extricate you from your psychic masochistic drives? If he could, Christians would not have waged war *with each other* for hundreds of years!

Rh-Blood, Alien Abductions and the Hybridization of Abductees

I opened this book addressing the extraterrestrial influence on the construction of the rings of Saturn and their implications, so it is only fitting that I address the impact that extraterrestrials have had on humans with respect to trauma, and many other root ills that plague human society. I know a lot of people don't believe in extraterrestrials, but those who run the world, *do.* To be precise, it isn't that they believe, *they know for a fact.* People who refuse to accept the existence of extraterrestrials are the same people who believe that IQ and gender do not exist, or that vaccines only work if everyone gets one. These are the sorts of assholes that will happily stick a microchip implant in their brain, and I am not really interested in these types of people. I am more interested in other dark-natured hybrids such as myself who will read my words, wake up, and reach out to The Divine Father for assistance with respect to finding a place for themselves in His creation that is in alignment with His will.

While I don't think it is possible to "prove" to those with no direct experience with extraterrestrials, that they do in fact exist... I can point out, however, that when I was a child and went to the Hayden Planetarium in NYC to watch the planetarium show, it was always stressed how we were alone in the universe. This made no sense to me, because the universe is so large, how could we possibly be the only ones out there? These days when you go to the Hayden Planetarium – now called the Rose Center for Earth and Space, the narrator of the planetarium show will be like, "Of course we aren't alone how could you think otherwise, etc." I am paraphrasing here a bit, but the idea is that they are now pushing a totally different story than they did in the 1980s. This should tell you *what* is coming.

The dark reality is that this planet is under the control of dark extraterrestrials who are in rebellion against The Divine Father, and who desire this planet for themselves. Furthermore, most of the beings in religion, mythology and legends, actually exist or did exist, and for the most part they can all be classified as extraterrestrial in nature. This doesn't mean that every story about them is true, or that everything you read about them is true, but it is something to keep in mind. Also, many extraterrestrial beings of note will often have multiple names across multiple cultures, which just creates more confusion if you are not "in the know."

As I mentioned in the last section, Lucifer was the chief genetic engineer responsible for the creation of modern human beings, who fashioned for them a "subconscious mind" by tampering with the hippocampus, so that they could be easily subjugated via trauma, specifically the kinds of trauma which would lead to warfare and wholesale suffering, in order to feed the appetites of dark 4th and 5th dimensional entities that enjoy roaming this planetary feedlot for sustenance. Lucifer also truncated the human lifespan, so those who survived the trauma and warfare would have no time to "wise up" before dying and getting reincarnated right back onto the factory farm called "earth." Another thing that bears mention, is that Lucifer fashioned modern human beings by combining the hominid DNA native to this planet with the DNA of various reptilian species. What is important about this fact, is that the DNA extracted from the various reptilian species used in his hybridization program was extracted from *cadavers* as opposed to living reptilian beings. I will decline to explain the precise reason why this was done, beyond saying that this course of action made the "humans" Lucifer engineered more susceptible to influence and control by dark extraterrestrials. This reality, is the reason why humans are so obsessed with zombie films and TV shows and cannot figure out why – because modern human beings are in effect, *literal* undead themselves.

With the above in mind, there are certain humans who are extremely attractive to dark extraterrestrials for abduction and further hybridization, and *most* (but not all) of those are human beings who have what is called "Rh- blood." Only around 15% of the world population has it, and this blood marker means you are genetically related to those who survived the fall of Atlantis. This means that your genetic ancestry is already extraterrestrial, so you much easier to hybridize and control then a "stock human" and therefore your chances of being abducted by extraterrestrials is very high. A simple, inexpensive mail-in blood test available on Amazon will reveal if you have this blood marker or not, so if you feel like you have been abducted, or that you are not entirely human, or that you have been a victim of mind control programming, taking such a test is a step in the direction of the truth. Because if you feel this way, and a blood test confirms your Rh- status, then you might be onto something. Although, there are some who are *not* Rh- who are *still* victims of abduction and hybridization. This is critical to be aware of, especially as you try and work through your psychosomatic blockages in an attempt to bring out the "authentic you." Remember, the "authentic you" may not exactly be human, and it may be buried beneath layers of trauma *far beyond* the trauma of social conditioning, an abusive parent, common sexual abuse, or a traumatic birth. This is because the abduction and hybridization of humans usually involves torture, along with mind control and reprogramming, which adds yet another traumatic dimension to your "human experience."

Understand that most of the world's leaders have been thru mind control programming themselves and perpetuate trauma *en masse* to facilitate greater leverage over human behavior for their "handlers," who are ultimately... extraterrestrial in nature. Some years ago, I attended a family wedding. There were a lot of people in attendance, as my family is rather large, and I didn't know many people there. It was announced that this wedding would be "unorthodox" as there was no reverend or minister officiating it. Instead, it was some woman who was introduced in a rather "euphemistic" manner. I immediately knew something was up. During the wedding ceremony, she tied the couple's hands together and at a certain point called out to some entity or entities (I cannot recall who) that if this marriage is approved of (and whatever else she said - I cannot recall what) then they should block out the sun to show their approval. No sooner had she said this than the sky went black. It was a bright sunny day and suddenly it was like night. Within moments the sun "switched back on" again. I looked at my dad in disbelief and he turned to me and said, "You are I will be the only ones who remember this occurred." I am not sure *how* he knew that, or *why* that would be so, but after the ceremony, I commented to one of my relatives: "Wasn't it crazy when the sun got blacked out?" The relative looked at me funny and asked me if I was high or something. So I went up to that woman or witch or whatever she was and told her it was really interesting that the sun got blacked out like that. She looked at me in shock, said nothing, turned and scuttled away.

A few days later I was speaking with another relative on the phone who had been there, and she commented that the ones who got married are part of some "group," and will be turning over their children for "training" or something like that. I knew immediately what that meant, and asked her how they could do this to their children? Don't they realize what will be done to them? She said yes, but this will enable their children to take on positions of power in society so they will have great futures ahead of them. Sure, they will be able to take on positions of power, because they will be tortured until their minds split into alters, then those "alters" will be programmed so they can be under control when placed into positions of power. While this particular example isn't *necessarily* a case of alien abduction and hybridization, I would say the chances of it being so *in addition* are pretty high. I say this because they are most probably Rh-, as many in my family are, and the forces that wish to control them and place them into positions of power are ultimately extraterrestral in nature, or else operating inside of a hierarchy with extraterrestrials at the top.

Why else are humans abducted and hybridized? The genetic hybridization of beings (not just humans) allows for the creation of life forms that are highly task specialized and superior at executing said tasks, but with the added bonus that they are also easily controlled. The creation of super-soldiers is often done in this manner, as is the creation of beings to carry out deep space mining operations, or to provide sexual services. Such beings are often sold on interstellar slave markets. Where do you think the Ottoman Empire on Earth got their inspiration from?

Be aware that the most valuable commodities in the universe are genetics and weapons technology, since they allow the extraterrestrial civilizations with access to them, control over limited resources in the face of ever-growing competing extraterrestrial populations. Unlike humans who barely live 100 years, many extraterrestrials live for thousands, if not tens of thousands of years, and many are for practical purposes immortal to one degree or another. You can imagine the strain on resources with planetary populations in possession of such longevity. Another thing that humans do not realize is that many extraterrestrial civilizations have access to technology that is quite literally *millions* of years ahead of ours. Being able to transfer a soul and consciousness from one genetic vehicle to another is child's play, and teleportation has been around for so long nobody thinks anything about it. Abducting a human being is nearly effortless, unless thwarted by another group of extraterrestrials or by The Divine Father. So when you see some Hollywood fantasy of a ragtag bunch of humans saving the earth from an alien invasion, rest assured this would never happen in real life.

I have spoken live at alien abductee events to sold out audiences, as abductees are often treated as "crazy" by others and always searching for answers and not finding any. While my "answers" are somewhat limited, at least they are a break from the usual recycled lies such as "extraterrestrials are your friends," and I do provide a solution via prayer free from the confines of any religious ideology. Certainly, if you know aliens exist due to your direct experience, is it so hard to believe that The Divine Father exists as well - even if you may not have had a direct experience with him *yet*? It is very easy to make the jump if you don't fall for the extraterrestrial lies that there is only "source," or some other all-encompassing "energy field" from which creation springs. They *all* know of The Divine Father's existence because they are *dimensionally* far closer to him than you are in this 3rd dimensional "matrix" reality. They all just lie to you because they don't want you reaching out to Him. Which I encourage you to do! Hybrids have extra motivation to reach out to The Divine Father because they know they don't belong anywhere on this planet, and some of them are rare, one-of-a-kind creations that would have trouble fitting in even among the species their DNA was drawn from. What do you do when you really have no place to call home? You tend to fall in with "the wrong crowd." This is especially so for beings whose nature is dark, and therefore might feel they have to join the dark beings that rebel against The Divine Father just to fit in somewhere. They don't. The Divine Father can easily find a home for them, just like he can find a home for any hybrid, no matter how unique. Given time on this planet is short for everyone due to what is coming, now is the time to establish a direct relationship with The Divine Father. It is almost like when you visited your high school guidance counselor, except he was probably super lame, whereas The Divine Father is perfectly awesome.

The Root of Low Testosterone & Transgender Politics

First, let's talk about the drastic drop in testosterone levels in young males in the United States, keeping in mind that a man should have a testosterone level of at least ~1000 ng/dL to enjoy optimal health. I am also well aware that this is a measure of testosterone bound in the bloodstream and that this is not a measure of "free testosterone."

Anyway, here is the mean total testosterone decreasing according to **NHANES study data for young adult men (15-39 years):**

- 1999-2000 (605.39 ng/dL)

- 2003-2004 (567.44 ng/dL)

- 2011-2012 (424.96 ng/dL)

- 2013-2014 (431.76 ng/dL)

- 2015-2016 (451.22 ng/dL)

This is a decline of approximately **25.5% over 17 years with the** steepest decline occurring between 2003-2004 (567.44 ng/dL) and 2011-2012 (424.96 ng/dL) - a drop of **142.48 ng/dL in about 8 years.**

Notice this study only runs to 2015. What has happened in the last 10 years? THERE ARE NO STATISTICS! I wonder why? The lowest the testing could go, would be down to 200 ng/dL and given the data up to 2015, I can imagine we are pretty close to the level of 200-300 ng/dL at this point.

NOTE: While there are no official studies prior to 1999, the mean testosterone levels in 1999-2000 of 605.39 ng/dL were incredibly low to start with. Meaning, they are 50% lower than what would have been "normal levels" in, say 1980, which would have been 1000-1200 ng/dL. So this decline most probably began in 1980, because that was the year so many endocrine disrupting chemicals flooded our environment:

Bisphenol A (BPA):

- **1891:** First reported by Russian chemist Aleksandr Dianin.

- **1930s:** Tested as artificial estrogen but found to be much weaker than estradiol.

- **1950s:** Large-scale commercial production began for plastics manufacturing.

- **1950s-1960s:** Widespread introduction into consumer products and food packaging.

- **By late 1980s: Production in the U.S. reached close to a billion pounds per year.**

Atrazine:

- **1958:** First registered for use in the United States.

- **1960s-present:** Became one of the most commonly applied herbicides in the world.

- **By 1980: Hit peak environmental saturation via contamination of US drinking water.**

Glyphosate:

- **1970:** First synthesized by Monsanto.

- **1974:** First registered for commercial use.

- **1990s-present: Massive increase in use with introduction of genetically modified crops.**

Phthalates:

- **1920s:** First commercial use.

- **1950s-1970s:** Major expansion into consumer products.

- **1980s-present: Ubiquitous in plastics, personal care products.**

Key Timeline Points for Drinking Water Contamination:

- **1940s-1950s:** The beginning of widespread synthetic chemical contamination in water supplies as DDT, early plastics, and industrial chemicals entered mass production and use.

- **1960s-1970s:** Peak contamination period as industrial chemical production soared and environmental regulations were minimal.

- **1970s:** Recognition of the problem led to the creation of the EPA (1970) and initial bans of the most egregious chemicals like DDT (1972).

- **1980s-present: Continued introduction of new synthetic chemicals, with many EDCs now detected in drinking water supplies despite treatment processes.**

Now let's take a look at how *just one* of these endocrine disrupting chemicals is responsible for all the transgender people by looking at what this chemical does to amphibians…

Atrazine Studies - Tyrone Hayes' Groundbreaking Research

The most prominent research in this field comes from **Dr. Tyrone Hayes** at UC Berkeley, who conducted extensive studies on Atrazine's effects on amphibians:

- Atrazine exposure caused complete feminization and chemical castration in male African clawed frogs (Xenopus laevis), with

10% of exposed genetic males developing into functional females.

- **75% of exposed males were chemically castrated** and essentially "dead" reproductively, while 10% turned from males into females.

- Atrazine at **concentrations as low as 0.1 ppb induced hermaphroditism and demasculinized male frogs.**

- Male frogs suffered a **10-fold decrease in testosterone levels when exposed to 25 ppb atrazine.**

Is it *not* curious that by the 1980s when Atrazine hit peak environmental saturation via contamination of US drinking water, this also marked the beginning of the decline in testosterone levels, which has ended in the utter crisis men find themselves in today?

Is it *also not* surprising that "Gender Identity Disorder" first appeared as a diagnosis in the DSM-III in 1980, where it appeared under "psychosexual disorders?"

My point is that *all these people who claim they were born the wrong gender are not crazy*! The problem is, instead of telling them *the truth – that they are the victims of endocrine disrupting chemicals*, we allow Satanic cultural Marxists to harness their pain, and foster the propagation of insane concepts such as "there is no such thing as gender." We then *pretend* like we have the surgical technology to transform a man into a woman, or vice versa. We do not! We cannot surgically turn a man into a woman or vice versa, and there is definitely such a thing as gender – just ask the fucking frogs, you fucking morons!

All these freaks roaming about the LGBTQ+ "pride" parades are simply victims of endocrine disrupting chemicals on a *genocidal scale*. It is sad and I am not trying to promote hate in my writing, but rather promote the truth of the matter. What we are seeing in the LGBTQ+ community is *our collective future.* They are the "canaries in the coal mine," and we need to do something about it before it is too late!

Atrazine is found primarily in corn products and in sugar. Corn products and sugar are *in everything.*

But the worst damage is caused by Atrazine that is in the drinking water:

- **The EPA Maximum Contaminant Level (MCL) for atrazine is 3 ppb.** *Remember, Atrazine at concentrations as low as 0.1 ppb induced hermaphroditism and demasculinized male frogs!*

- EPA's monitoring data for 2014 show that some Midwestern communities experience Atrazine spikes in the spring and summer at levels well above the legal limit. **In 2014, Atrazine concentrations in 18 communities exceeded the legal limit of 3 ppb, sometimes for weeks.**

- EWG research shows that **Atrazine is the most commonly detected pesticide in tap water.**

- In 2015 Atrazine was **detected in more than 800 systems in 19 states at levels exceeding a health-protective guideline.**

- All of the watersheds monitored by the EPA and **90% of the drinking water sampled tested positive for Atrazine.**

Ladies and gentlemen, there you have it... Atrazine is the source of all of the crashed testosterone levels, the transgender epidemic, and all these people flocking to LGBTQ+ events who can't figure out what they are or have this nagging feeling they were born in the wrong body. In many cases, they were! You can thank your Satanic government for letting Atrazine get pumped into your drinking water. *Now you know why you are always being told to drink so many glasses of water per day!* You're welcome!

Finally, as you well know by now, we are living on a planet under the influence of Satan, and it may be of interest for you to learn that biologically speaking, Satan is a hermaphrodite. Still think all of that Atrazine wound up in the water supply by accident?

Practical Gender Polarities in Males and Females

The utter lack of sex education on this planet is absolutely astounding. Just because you know how to put on a condom (don't laugh, a significant percentage of the planet is too stupid to figure out how a condom works), or have watched endless hours of online pornography doesn't mean you have been sexually educated. As a matter of fact, society teaches men and women endless lies about sex. We all know that male and female are different polarities, for example, but when it comes to the male and female "magnets," where exactly is the south pole and where exactly is the north pole for each gender? This is *critical* to understand!

For example:

- You are told that the female is weak in her heart because she needs to nurture children, and is strong in her pussy because she can have a train run on her, cumming as much as she wants, while exhausting man-after-man.

- You are then told that the man is strong in his heart because he does not need to nurture children, but that his cock is weak, because once he shoots his load he is pretty much done.

The *conclusions* above are utterly *false* and only *appear* to be true, *within the context of the example!* Let's now take a look at the truth of the matter they don't want you to know...

- If you want to utterly *destroy* a man or *possess him,* you do so via his heart because it is in his heart that he is weakest. A man in love, is a man who can be destroyed by the one he loves, and you don't have to look far to see how many men have been irreparably damaged and altered because they opened their hearts to the wrong woman!

- If you want to utterly *destroy* a woman or *possess her,* you do so via her pussy. This is why men prize virginity and obsess on body count. However, what is less commonly known is that women obsess over *how many girls a guy has been in love with!* This is because they know a *little more* than you do, in terms of the truth about actual male and female polarities, but hide it from you to maintain power, as they are the physically weaker sex.

So in terms of the male and female "magnets:"

- The pussy is the negative pole on the female, and her heart is the positive pole as she penetrates the man's heart with her heart, although this penetration is *entirely* energetic. She is strongest in her heart, not her pussy.

- The heart is the negative pole on the male, and his cock is the positive pole as he penetrates the woman's pussy with his cock, and this penetration is *both* physical *as well as* energetic. He is strongest in his cock, not his heart.

It is not easy to discern these actual dynamics, because most men are not capable of inducing the level of vaginal orgasm in a woman in order to destroy or possess her, and the damage the woman can inflict on a man's heart is hard to discern, because not only is her interaction with the man's heart entirely energetic, but additionally most women are not capable of energetically penetrating a man's heart with *conscious awareness.* The damage they cause is often done passively and on "autopilot." However, you can still visualize a cock destroying a woman's pussy on some level because you can visualize the physical part of the act of intercourse, even if you cannot see the energetic part. So for example you can imagine a very thick cock leaving a pussy stretched out, gaping open and in need of a bag of ice post-coitus.

The fragility of the female pussy is is also one of the many reasons women are frigid - they are protecting themselves from potential destruction at the hands of sexually skilled men.

Many men have frozen hearts for similar reasons.

So during the act of sex, assuming both the male and the female do not have blocked up sexual or heart chakras, relatively speaking, the energy from the cock flows into the pussy triggering vaginal orgasms that take over her whole body. While this imprints the man upon the woman and addicts her to him, the woman will *then* take the energy building up inside of her and project it from her heart chakra into his. So while he fucks her pussy physically as well as energetically, she energetically fucks his heart. This is *very* real and not some woo-woo nonsense! Any man who has experienced this knows what I am talking about. It *feels very physical* even though it is entirely energetic. Another little known fact, is that the man's heart is also capable of orgasm just like a pussy, and once the woman "fucks" his heart and makes it orgasm she imprints herself upon the man and addicts him to her. More on this in a bit!

Now this would be the normal flow of energies between couples who are free from trauma and blockages in their chakras and diaphragms, but due to trauma, actual sexual encounters between men and women are "felt like traffic accidents," to quote Helen Remington (Holly Hunter) in David Cronenberg's 1996 film "Crash" starring James Spader.

Just like the red pill's redefinition of "female hypergamy" only exists because most women cannot find a man who can satisfy their pussy, the sexual dissatisfaction of men – even if enjoying lots of sex, is *precisely* because they cannot find a woman who can fuck their heart and bring it to orgasm. It's ironic, really… women think their pussy is enough to lock down men who are in the top 1%. It isn't.

These are the "facts of life" with respect to sex. The *real* facts of life that you were never taught in your "sex education" classes. Now some of my "progressive" (i.e. unfuckable) readers may wonder how LGBTQ+ peeps fit into this scheme? Well, when two men or two women fuck each other, things get all fucked up, pun intended. Two men fucking just fans the flames of endless desire. Two women having sex with each other goes nowhere because there is no fire – just water, and this is one of the reasons lesbian relationships have the highest rates of physical abuse. I will leave it to you, to figure out the exact mechanics as to *why*.

I grew up in a gay neighborhood in both the 1970s and the 1980s (Murray Hill, Manhattan). This was a time when men were still men. Even gay men were fucking men. Pun intended. Nobody paid attention to lesbians because there weren't many around and there is no such thing as a lesbian, anyway. Every lesbian takes dick in secret at some point because a woman needs masculine energy. Laying out in the sun or on a tanning bed can only go so far, you know? I don't care whom I piss off with this statement, every "lesbian" knows I am stating straight facts. Pun intended. While there are no statistics to support my claims, I can still prove I am correct.

Observe…

Lesbian Identity vs. Behavior

Research indicates that *"often behavior and identity do not match: women may label themselves heterosexual but have sexual relations with women, self-identified lesbians may have sex with men, or women may find that what they considered an immutable sexual identity has changed over time."*

You would never hear convoluted, hamster-wheel blanket statements like the above unless researchers were attempting to cover up an inconvenient truth – that there is no such thing as a lesbian!

The "Gold Star Lesbian" Concept

The term "gold star lesbian" refers to "a lesbian who has never had sex with a man," but it's become controversial within LGBTQ+ communities. The term can be used as a source of pride or comfort to some lesbians, but it has "cissexist implications and can be derogatory towards bisexual women."

Just listen to that leftist drivel! The fact that a term such as "gold star lesbian" even exists reveals that there is no such thing. Do gay males have a term like "gold star homosexual?" Why not? Also, the fact that the term "gold star lesbian" is so controversial just proves my point yet again. Lesbians are truly mythical creatures! Even unicorns tell stories about them to their children! If there are any "gold star lesbians" around it is only because no man will touch them. This is an important point, given where I am going with all of this.

Again, back in my day, gays were gays and there was no LGBTQ+ nonsense. Also, when you went to a gay neighborhood or attended a gay parade the one thing you noticed was how *attractive* everyone was, relatively speaking. I remember being very young, at a gay parade in NYC thinking to myself how thankful I was that all of these men were gay, because if they were straight I would have had so much competition!

Now compare and contrast the homos of yesteryear to those of today: Attend an LGBTQ+ parade or "pride" festival and you will notice something: everyone is fucking unattractive to the point of being downright repulsive. Even stranger, you won't actually see *any "traditional" gay people at any* of these events, just an army of unfuckable freaks whom nobody wants anything to do with, because again, they are all so *insanely* unattractive. I mean, besides **drag queens who are just caricatures of how gay males *actually see* women**, in the old days you had *transsexuals* who made every effort to be as passable as possible. Much like you *still* see in Thailand. To be fair, you will also still see quite a few today working as escorts in the USA, where they *have to be passable.* But roaming today's LGBTQ+ landscape are mostly these creatures straight out of the Dungeons and Dragons "Monster Manual" who can't seem to make the least bit of effort to be passable. I'm talking dudes with beards, wearing lipstick and heels, etc. Half the time I don't even know WTF I am looking at, and feel like I am visiting someone in a psychiatric ward!

Meanwhile… *actual* gay males no longer live in "gay ghettos," and Murray Hill, the West Village and Chelsea in NYC are no longer gay neighborhoods. There is one small new gay neighborhood in what used to be called "Hell's Kitchen," simply because it isn't like those into the "leather scene" are capable of integrating into the mainstream. I was always most impressed by that specific gay subculture, because these dudes are akin to gay warriors from ancient times. But the reality is that the majority of gay males no longer consider their homosexuality a relevant part of their identity and just want to integrate. The fact that they are gay is almost a footnote these days. They have their rights. The can get married. Society accepts them. So why dwell on their sexual identity? They have crossed the proverbial river, so they simply left the boat on the shore and walked away.

Only a loser considers their sexuality to be their "identity." Naturally, your sexuality is a *part* of your identity, but to make it your *entire identity* is pathetic. Understandable though, because the real identity of members of today's LGBTQ+ community is *not* their sexuality, but the fact that they are all outcasts *whom nobody loves or desires.* But they can't say that! So they rally around their sexuality which is a *sexuality of undesirability*. But again, they can't say that so they adopted this forest of made up terminologies to define themselves as a sort of "cope." By banding together, they attempt to crowd-source their human needs to be loved and sexually desired, so that they can survive and not have to commit suicide. It is heartbreaking to watch, and I don't blame them. I am really not trying to shit on them, and many of them are really nice and cool people who just want love. It isn't their fault that they were "born this way," and unlike traditional homosexuals, *they actually were born this way* thanks to all the Atrazine in the drinking water.

I need to emphasize this, because while some point the finger of blame at cultural Marxism, commies certainly didn't create these poor bastards. *It's environmental*, and I proved it earlier on in this book.

True Sexual Dynamics

Women are always portrayed as some sort of complex mystery that is unable to be satisfied. This is because what women truly desire is sexual satisfaction, yet it is close to impossible for most of them to find it. The male ego is not going to admit that they aren't "up to the job," so men sit around and pretend women are a mystery, or that they can never be satisfied. What these men are really saying, is that it is a mystery to *them* exactly *how* to satisfy women, and that women can never be satisfied by *them*. Women will assist in promoting this confusion in order to attain greater agency, by saying ridiculous things like "I can get cock anywhere so men really have no value." While it is true that a woman can get sex at the drop of a hat, she cannot attain sexual *satisfaction* as easily, much like that famous song by the Rolling Stones laments. Because this "cock" that she is being offered at every step of her daily meanderings is basically "trash cock," much like most pussy is actually "trash pussy." Of course, every man likes to think of his cock as amazing, just like most women like to think they have a "million dollar pussy," but most guys do not have an amazing cock and I am not talking about the *size* of it, as we will learn shortly. Furthermore, women who talk about how "good their pussy is" don't understand that what matters is their heart, not their pussy.

Pro Tip: Speaking of "trash pussy," guys with options and experience know all too well that most pussies are not worth fucking. Which is part of the reason men who are having sex with women these days usually prefer anal. It's tighter, warmer, gives more powerful orgasms to the woman if she isn't frigid, and you can't get a girl pregnant when you blow your load into her asshole. It's also more dominant, as well as more intimate. Why fuck a blown out pussy and risk pregnancy, when you can just fuck a tight asshole?

A woman's inability to attain sexual satisfaction is two-fold: The first reason is that something like 90% of women are frigid. This means that they are incapable of achieving a vaginal orgasm. Clitoral orgasms are not relevant here. Neither is "squirting." Do some women squirt? Certainly. Some women shit themselves when they cum, too. It is quite natural for a woman, when she has a powerful orgasm, to push the man out of her pussy or asshole. A 130 lb girl can cum so hard while face down and ass up, that she can send a 230 lb man lying on top of her balls deep in her butt, *several feet into the air.* You probably haven't seen that in any porn films though? They could have contests for how high in the air an orgasming porn star can toss men of different weight classes. But then none of them are capable of such feats so scratch that idea! It's actually pretty entertaining to listen to delusional female porn stars attempt to reframe themselves as "sexual athletes" and try and convince you that doing "double anal" grants them the same social status as someone in the NBA. The whole "she's a squirter" nonsense is pretty annoying as well, since the squirting you see in porn is a shadow of what a woman is truly capable of.

I realize that when I say that 90% of women are frigid I should be able to back that statement up. The problem is that there are no real statistics on this, because what woman is going to admit to it? One has to go by the anecdotal experiences of a myriad of professionals and those who have extensive personal experience with a lot of women, *who are otherwise capable of bringing a woman to vaginal orgasm.* Another problem is that it is now considered "hateful" to bring up female orgasmic impotence, and just like they try and tell you that obese girls are as beautiful as supermodels and should be on the cover of Sports Illustrated as well, they try and tell you that all orgasms are the same and that clitoral orgasms are somehow equivalent in value to vaginal orgasms. It is like saying IQ isn't real, size doesn't matter, and all of this feel good nonsense that everyone knows is just pure feel good bullshit. Like, you can run around sporting a beard and rocking high heels, demanding to be addressed as a woman, but you are still a man – just a mentally fucked up one, and everybody knows it.

So from my own anecdotal library, let me say this... Many years ago I created supplements for the adult entertainment industry. I was in what is called the "novelty" aspect of the biz. Since women buy more shit than men, I wanted to create an adult novelty supplement for women. So I asked around 100 random women from all walks of life over the course of one year, what supplement they would want me to develop, after explaining that I formulated cum pills so men could shoot massive wads of goo.

Every single woman said one of two things:

- I want a product to make me want sex (98 respondents).

- I want a product to make me actually enjoy sex (2 respondents).

If this anecdotal evidence doesn't drive it home for you, you probably believe the official 9/11 commission report!

Pro Tip: Jet fuel can't melt steel beams. If you doubt this, go purchase some, pour it on a section of running rail down by some train tracks near you, and throw a match on it. If the running rail melts, then the 9/11 commission report is correct. But it won't. I was at a pool party, brought this up, and people started sneering and laughing at me. It's truly aggravating how so many people will believe *anything* rather than face psychic instability. The 9/11 commission report could have literally said that vibrations from one of the airplane passenger's sex toys caused a standing resonance that brought the twin towers down and people would have believed it, rather then face the reality that it was a controlled demolition. Because then their entire world would collapse, and they might have to actually *do something* to fix this joke of a "civilization." Numerous NYFD firefighters *literally* said they witnessed the cutting charges detonating, and Larry Silverstein *literally* slipped up on national television and admitted it was a controlled demolition only to later pretend he meant to say something else. I was on a podcast once and one of the hosts asked me if I was open to reading the 9/11 commission report with an open mind. I responded that this was the equivalent of asking me if I was open to reading a treatise on pedophilia with an open mind! He exploded into an absolute rage because my analogy really hit the mark. I came up with this analogy on the fly, because I attended the Bronx High School of Science, and my physics teacher at that time was the editor of the NAMBLA newsletter. That's an acronym for North American Man/Boy Love Association. When The NYC Board of Education learned of this, they gave him an administrative role and refused to let him around children. His defense, which he argued all the way to the Supreme Court of the United States, was that once a boy turns 16 he is no longer attracted to him, so his students were perfectly safe around him. Can you imagine? I mean, it was probably true and all but still... the gall! I believe the Supreme Court ruled against him and he finally lost his job, which at that point was probably printing up NAMBLA newsletters on a NYC Board of Education mimeograph machine at the taxpayer's expense.

Progressives and other pieces of shit who love to brainwash and gaslight people will always dismiss the wisdom acquired through your own life experiences as "anecdotal" because it makes them *appear* smart when they are in fact, stupid. Stupid people *love* to say things like "you are making a strawman argument" or "that's an ad hominem argument you have over there" because stupid people have to take courses in college to learn how to think. They are like someone who needed training wheels to learn to ride a bicycle. Sure, they can now finally ride a bicycle, but they are also vastly inferior to the person who didn't require them and should never be granted, say, a motorcycle license. This abject stupidity (average IQ in the USA is only 98) is why the majority of the population of the United States does not actually have the right to vote on anything of real importance, although they foolishly believe they do. Oh, you never noticed? We live in a representational democracy where we don't get to vote on issues, but rather get to vote for a representative - who votes *for us* on the issues *we should* be voting on! Sadly, this representative never votes in your interests, but only in the interests of their own re-election. What's even more depressing, is *the one thing* you get to vote on, which is *who* that representative will be, you fuck up *every single time.* It's amazing to behold! You losers actually vote into office politicians like Alexandria Ocasio-Cortez, Gavin Newsome, and Nancy Pelosi (to name just three) over and over and over again. How can it be that the population consistently elects and re-elects such repugnant human trash? The population of New York City is now getting ready to elect yet another open communist for mayor. I am not just picking on progressives here, *all* the Congressmen and Senators are garbage. So are *all* the presidents you elect. Most of them are geriatrics who should be in a nursing home anyway, not running a nation!

I'm getting rather off-track here, so let's get back to talking about sexuality…

Now that we know the true polarities of the male and female form, let us look at how they function practically during the act of sex itself, under ideal circumstances. Keeping in mind of course, that most people have all of their chakras completely clogged up from trauma. So what I will describe here is not the commonplace experience… Also, keep in mind that when I say "vaginal orgasm" I am not referring to a little spasm in the cervical area either. I am talking about full-blown, full-body orgasms that wash over her in wave-after-wave that are triggered through the anterior or posterior fronix of her vagina *or* via anal stimulation of her posterior fronix.

When a man has sex, he has to have good energy flow through his cock. Unlike porn films where the male talent thrusts in and out like a jackhammer, 80% of the "thrusting motion" is actually more like a grinding motion at full penetration depth. This is not so much to keep constant stimulation around her clitoral region with your pelvic bone, but rather to provide constant stimulation to her anterior/posterior fronix and her cervix. I am sure many of you have heard the hip hop classic "Bottom of the Pussyhole" by Cam'ron? Periodically you will engage in thrusting in and out, but the dominant motion is not thrusting, but rather grinding. How you modulate your grinding, and alternate between grinding and thrusting, is really dependent on how tuned in you are to your partner's body.

The important thing here is the ability to have "staying power" because when the head of your cock is grinding the bottom of her pussy, both your biology *and her biology* really want you to cum. Because your biology and her biology want the both of you to reproduce *more* than they want the both of you to experience pleasure. So when she starts to really have full-body, vaginally triggered orgasms, your desire to cum will be overwhelming! Again, because her body wants your body - to give it a baby! You must resist this urge, in order to bring her to even deeper levels of orgasmic surrender. Sex with a woman is called "screwing" for a reason, and that is because screwing the head of your penis into her anterior or posterior fronix and making her cervix move like a slow motion speed bag is really the main motion if you are going to be fucking for more than 15 minutes. Over the long term, one alternates between screwing and thrusting motions. One should be shooting for at least 1 hour of this sort of alternating penetration pattern to start, and in later chapters I will show you how to really get rid of premature ejaculation and stay hard with a combination of custom methods, not stupid advice like "spray your cock with lidocaine" or use the "stop-start" method.

Naturally, this is a purely mechanical explanation for those who believe there is no such thing as energy, but the real trigger of female orgasm actually has a strong energetic component. Without the energetic component, the mechanics mean little. I mean, try bringing a girl lying on a slab in the morgue to orgasm! Well, it may be fun to try if she died young and hot! This statement may gross you out, but when a hot young girl commits suicide or dies from a drug overdose, you can rest assured her corpse gets well fucked before it winds up in the funeral home! What's the difference between a blow up doll and a dead body? The dead body is more realistic. When I was very young, I worked with a much older guy who used to work in a morgue, and he taught me the ins-and-outs of having sex with corpses one night while we were working the graveyard shift. All puns intended!

Anyway, I always found it interesting how people can deny the existence of energy. They think the body is just a bunch of chemical reactions or something. Do you really think there are any open-heart surgeons who are atheists? When you are working on a literal beating heart (not that any of you do), do you not marvel at what is powering it? Where is the battery? It's truly amazing. People who deny the existence of energy, or "chi" are usually the same ilk who deny the existence of The Divine Father. They believe in things like "evolution." Don't get me wrong, evolution exists, but *not* in the way it is taught in school: life is not the consequence of an endless series of totally random, yet surprisingly advantageous "mutations" that get propagated due to their undeniable advantages. The way evolution is presented from a "scientific" perspective, is as absurd as a tornado blowing through a junkyard and assembling a fully functioning automobile.

Back to energy... So there is an energy channel that runs down into the female vagina but often it is "clogged" so if the man has enough energy in his penis (which is why you shouldn't be jacking off to porn several times a day or even daily) and can last for a long time during intercourse, then the energy from his penis can begin to open up, or else "clear out" this channel inside of a woman until the energy from his cock can flow into it and then "boom!" it's like pressing a button and the girl says, "I love you." Maybe I should make a doll where if you press the right spot inside her pussy it says "I love you." I think it would sell well and also be highly educational! Instead, you have all these mid and low-tier male porn stars selling courses on how to teach your girl to squirt and/or have a g-spot orgasm by ramming your fingers up into the tented roof of her vagina. For many women this is a bad idea because their "g-spot" holds all of this trauma and you ramming your fingers up there is just a big "ouch." Much like when your cock slams into the hardened cervix of a woman who competes in the world as a man. It is far more efficient and pleasant to use the energy of your cock to clear this sort of trauma, although I do not encourage men to try and assist in resolving a woman's trauma *even if* you have the capability, unless she is paying you to do so in some professional capacity. Your time and energy is better spent on a woman who isn't carrying such baggage. Broken women can work on their own traumas, on their own time, by combining breathwork with mechanical g-spot stimulation. But women are usually too lazy to embark on such a journey. Sucks to be them!

Pro Tip: One of the consequences of women competing as men, in a man's world, is that they fry their ovaries and reproductive system. It starts with abnormally heavy or long menses where large amounts of blood are lost and pernicious anemia develops. Many of these women go into early menopause, and require hysterectomies as well as the removal of their ovaries. Sex with these women is a bad idea because sex for them is usually painful. I remember having sex with a woman who was like this and when I would hit the bottom of her pussy she would jump one foot off the bed and be in so much pain that sex would end right there and then. Sometimes she would be bleeding internally from her reproductive system for no apparent reason and require hospitalization. There was another woman I had sex with who bled so much during menstruation, it was literally like an open faucet of blood between her legs. When I first saw it, I thought she might bleed to death, that's how bad it was! Needless to say, she often suffered life-threatening anemia and needed to take iron pills that had an absurd amount of iron in each pill.

Back to the implications of my "anecdotal" study! If we extrapolate my 100 woman sample across the female population one would conclude that 98% of women don't even want sex. That sounds extreme, and statisticians would take serious issue with extrapolating a 100 woman sample out across the entire US female population. So let's drop it from 98% to 80% to pay homage to the Pareto Principle which suggests that roughly 80% of effects come from 20% of causes. So, is it possible that 80% of women don't even want sex when 100% of men want sex?

Of course it is. This is a natural result of trauma, sexual repression, etc. It also explains *a lot*. One of the implications of this is that if a woman really doesn't see what the big deal about sex *is*, she is more inclined to sell it, or use it as a means to an end, as she can clearly see that to men, sex is a *really* big deal - even if it isn't to *her*. To put it simply: *If you have something you do not value, yet everyone else does, you are going to sell it, and not cherish it!* Keep in mind that almost every woman is capable of a clitoral orgasm, but that is not enough to make a woman really *want* sex or even *enjoy* sex. She can just use a sex toy to attain her clitoral orgasm, or else spread peanut butter on her pussy and whistle at her dog. No women who is truly vaginally orgasmic has an armory of vibrators or is down to be eaten out by her dog. What would be the point? Although to be fair, some women like to be fucked by their dog, because the dog's penis is at a higher temperature than a human's penis is.

Besides trauma and sexual repression, another reason that so many women are uninterested in sex, is because most men absolutely suck in bed. Again, most men like to talk about trash pussy, but to be fair most men have a dick that is trash as well. The male ego can't deal with this, but it is the truth, and it has nothing to do with the size of the penis, etc. It has more to do with a complete lack of understanding about how to fuck, coupled with the reality that most men have *no energy* in their penis *in part* because they are masturbating to porn all day long and over-ejaculating, and also *in part* because they themselves are frigid in the sense that the energy in their sexual chakra is frozen as much as it is in women.

Male frigidity is harder to notice because if the dick gets hard everyone assumes everything is okay. Well, most women can have a clitoral (the female penis) orgasm but things are certainly *not* okay. I know some people will start arguing that the clitoris is not a female penis citing some inaccurate biological mumbo-jumbo but they just need to shut the fuck up. Because it fundamentally is. "Science" also tells you that men evolved from apes. That so many people believe this is absolutely mind-blowing. What would be the *mechanism* for such "evolution?" Advantageous mutations? So exactly *how many* "advantageous mutations" would have had to occur to turn an ape into a man, and what would trigger such mutations? Radioactivity? So apes must have spent billions of years roaming a radioactive hellscape enduring millions upon millions of random mutations until enough of them that could be considered "advantageous" accumulated and ultimately turned them into men! How stupid can you possibly be?

Finally, most men get their sex education from pornography and will run around saying that what really satisfies a woman is getting her "back blown out" or being "smashed" and all this dumb shit that impotent male porn stars do. I am calling them impotent because so many male porn stars have huge cocks (relatively speaking) that are only rock hard thanks to tri-mix injections and other drugs, plus *nothing* happens when they run that cock up inside the female performer. So they start pounding harder and harder to vent their frustration at having *zero impact* on the female performer sexually. I am *not* saying a woman doesn't like to get fucked with passion or pounded out but you can't get hung up on one aspect of a sexual encounter and think that is the whole thing.

Pro Tip: *Often times you will encounter a female bragging about how she fakes orgasms.* For all you dummies, this is actually a shit-test to see if there are any men around capable of giving her one! The proper response is to reply that you can only fake an orgasm for a man who has never actually seen one. She of course will double down and insist. Look her in the eye and say, "You haven't actually enjoyed a real orgasm, have you?" If she continues to hold her ground simply say, "A real orgasm is *impossible* to fake, partly because you will neither be able to speak during it, nor stand on your own two legs after it, even if your life depended on doing so." At this point, she will usually go home with you or decide to go home with you in the future, as she knows you can deliver the goods - how else would you know all of this unless you have been the one giving these sorts of experiences to women?

There is no real "talent" involved anymore in being a male sex performer, as all these performers today are not only popping PDE-5 inhibitors, but are also injecting Trimix and Quadmix directly into their penile shaft which will get you hard and keep you hard even in the middle of a zombie apocalypse. If you get the right formulation and strength, penile injections will give you a level of performance that will rival that of any porn star, and the number of "civilian" men using these drugs has been skyrocketing. With how cheap 4K HD cameras are, anybody can shoot porn after taking a lighting course on YouTube, and purchasing the appropriate pharmacology.

Now keep in mind that a woman can be "frigid" and still be highly sexual. There are girls who are masturbating for hours a day to online pornography and having sex with everything in sight who still cannot attain full-body, vaginally triggered orgasms. Their orgasms are all clitoral. The usage of high powered vibrators that can rattle your teeth loose, just reinforces this tendency to remain stuck in the realm of the clitoral orgasm. So don't think because so many women are frigid or turned off to sex in general, that underneath it all they are *not* these insanely sexual beings, because they still *are*.

It is just hard to see the actual nature of things because the consequences of emotional and sexual trauma are always at play, and distorting your perception of reality due to the inherent human craving for psychic stability. Even the fact that women are always going for guys with money is not a *survival* issue, as you can survive on very little. It is a *stability* issue. Women crave amazing sex, they crave love, and they crave the lifestyle that money can give them. But amazing sex and real love both threaten psychic stability in traumatized women, which creates a monstrous neurotic conflict! A guy with lots of money though, does not present any inner conflicts for most women.

This is alluded to in the 1984 song "The Glamorous Life" by Sheila E. where the female protagonist meets a man who can trigger orgasmic waves in her, and she realizes that her "gold digging days" are done for. Sheila E. also correctly points out that for a woman, this experience is what she considers genuine love, and that the imprint the man leaves on her by giving her this experience has consequences for the rest of her life.

Traumatized women cannot bear to be out of control in an *authentic* manner (i.e. experiencing deep orgasmic states or being deeply in love), but they have no problem with being out of control in terms of the expression of their trauma via completely fucked up and irresponsible behavior. Traumatized women also cannot bear being in love since they hate themselves – they simply cannot accept love, nor have they any love to give others. Finally, traumatized women also cannot bear being in love with someone who is superior to them because such a dynamic always reflects back to them their inherent or perceived inferiority.

So since traumatized women have no love for men beyond a man's resources, and no love for their own children or even themselves, they fill the void with self-indulgence, and attention-seeking on social media. All of their actions reek of self-destruction and self-hatred, yet serve to maintain psychic stability. However, since all women are free to crave money without suffering a neurotic conflict over the craving, due to the fact that obtaining money is not a threat to their psychic stability, they put all of their energy into that.

Anyway, when a girl really finds herself insanely turned on by you, one of her instinctual reactions is to fuck you on the spot. But the problem for her is what if she wants a relationship as well? What if she is afraid you will judge her for sleeping with you so fast? What if she *also* wants to use sex to extract resources from you? What if she is afraid of being emotionally hurt or sexually enslaved by you? Her only solution is to control her sexuality so as to turn it into "agency," which is a euphemism for commodifying her sexuality in order to exchange it for money, power or status. This is intimately tied in with female neurosis.

Healthy Ejaculatory Frequency vs. "No-Fap" & "Gooning"

Train yourself to never come in a woman's pussy or ass. I will explain to you where your pleasure will actually come from very shortly. No, I am not talking about some "multiorgasmic male" garbage because there really is no such thing with respect to the male genitals. Practically speaking, this idea of separating "orgasm" from ejaculation is only possible in men who have had their prostates destroyed via surgical intervention for prostate cancer. They now have what is called "retrograde ejaculation." So yes, it is possible to have an "orgasmic" experience without ejaculation, but this is a medical abnormality and not something that can be trained, which is what books like "The Multiorgasmic Man" promote.

However, the whole concept of having sex without *ever* ejaculating is beyond absurd. This was originally promoted to elderly men back in China as a way to "restore their chi" and *never* meant for young men to embrace! But regardless of age, there simply are times when your body needs to ejaculate, because never doing so is unhealthy as fuck. What the actual frequency of ejaculation should be, is relative and for you to discover, but when we are talking about the ever-growing community of "no fap" males, we are really talking about a community of *mentally ill neurotics.* These men start walking down this insane path for two main reasons:

- Male testosterone levels are so abysmally low. This makes "no fap" easier, while serving as a desperate attempt to increase testosterone levels. It doesn't work. Filter out Atrazine from your drinking water, take 50mg worth of Lugol's iodine every day, and supplement with DHEA. If that doesn't work, you will need to take exogenous testosterone. More on that later...

- "No fap" is the natural swing of the pendulum from the extreme of over-masturbating to online pornography, to the extreme of not ejaculating at all – which *will* lead to "edging," and if you aren't vigilant, this will lead to the utter insanity of "gooning," which is incredibly self-destructive.

Never ejaculating is abusive to your body and totally unnatural, which is why you will have wet dreams and then feel bad about yourself, when your body is just trying to regain it's natural balance. In a state of nature, you are grabbing bitches and blowing loads into them. Just accept that.

But "gooning" is by far, the most unnatural thing you can do with respect to how you handle your sexual energy. It will scramble your brain and open you up to possession by entities who use cyberspace as a medium to attach to people. You will see videos on PornHub claiming to summon succubi with hypnotic inductions and goonable content loops, and you should stay as far the fuck away from this type of content as you possibly can. If you exercise your free will to summon some succubus, how will you be able to get rid of it? You may think you can just exercise your free will and tell it to go kick rocks, but that is not how it works. If you give a cop consent to enter into your home, can you withdraw consent once he is inside? No, you cannot. At that point you have already waived your rights against unlawful searches and seizures. So why is it that a woman can go home with a man in order to have sex with him, and then withdraw consent in the middle of the act? How can she cry "rape" should the man insist on continuing and force the issue? Well, she *can't*. This idea that you can "withdraw consent at any time" is *not* reality. Of course she has legal recourse in today's twisted up world, but... it goes against the natural order of things. Even modern BDSM has become a joke with their constant use of "safe words" and obsession with concepts like "aftercare." It's both fake *and* gay. You posers need to stop using your sexual partners as therapists. Those who are really down with the lifestyle do *not* use "safe words." They set the ground rules beforehand, and then jump into the ocean.

Anyway, contrary to the "wisdom" of total losers, if you refrain from ejaculating you will *not* magically draw women to you, nor will it give you superpowers, no matter what you are told. As a matter of fact, it will *repel* women because women will *neither* sense that you are some sort of self-styled stoic who is above the need for women, *nor* be triggered to chase you and win your approval. What women *will* sense is that you have a blocked up sexual chakra and that you are trapped in a very unattractive neurotic conflict! Not ejaculating will also lead to "edging" which will fill your mind with thought-forms that will repel women. Just think about it: women like men who are already getting laid due to the phenomenon of "pre-selection." So going "no fap" basically turns you into an *energetic incel* and the backed-up sexual energy broadcasts your inceldom for every woman to pick up on.

The key is ejaculating *when you body needs to do so, and not out of compulsion.* This is the balanced path that leads to the greatest gains. But when your body is telling you that you need to cum, I suggest only doing so in her mouth so you don't develop a habit of cumming in her pussy or asshole and end up sabotaging your ability to truly satisfy a woman, and ultimately, yourself. Hang tight, I will explain this thoroughly shortly!

Pro Tip: If a woman does not swallow your spunk, she does not love you. End of story. Don't fall for this crap that some women "just don't like certain things and that's okay." It's *not* okay! When a woman spits your load into the toilet, she is telling you *in no uncertain terms* that your very essence is nothing more than waste – akin to shit, and deserving of nothing more than to be flushed down the fucking toilet. What effect do you think this sort of interaction will have on your psyche on a subconscious level? How should you handle such disrespect should it occur? Stop her running to the toilet and say, "No, you are the toilet. Now swallow." If she pushes back, then the next time your are fucking her and feel the need to piss, just piss inside of her and when she complains, tell her that you view her as your toilet. That will either end the relationship on a high note, or else she will be super turned on and start swallowing. After all, why spit your cum into the toilet when she *is* the toilet? Another great way to drive the message home is when you are fucking her doggy in the bathroom, stick her head in the toilet while you are fucking her. She'll either get the message eventually or else dump you. Either way, you win!

Ride Her Orgasmic Waves Without Cumming Yourself...

...much like a surfer rides waves on the ocean without wiping out. Each orgasm you survive allows you to take her even deeper into orgasm, generating even more powerful successive waves. For this very reason, you need to condition yourself to never cum in her pussy or ass, because that way you will never fall off her orgasmic waves, no matter how powerful they may become.

Now here is where it starts to get really enlightening, and understanding what I am about to explain - even if you have yet to experience it, is critical for the understanding of many other things...

For example, we already know that "female hypergamy" is due to the fact that women cannot attain sexual satisfaction. But what we are also about to learn, is that the reason men cheat no matter how hot their girl may be, is because they are *also* not being sexually satisfied by their women. The truth is that there are very few women on this planet who really know how to satisfy a man. Mind you, there are some wise enough to keep their man's balls drained at all times, so he can't cheat even if a gun is pointed at his head. These women are usually highly adept at sucking cock like some deep throat vacuum cleaner and will suck their man off as many times per day as necessary, in order to keep him from straying. But again, most women are not really attracted to their husbands or boyfriends to begin with, so this strategy is out of the question for them. Plus, in a woman's eyes sucking cock also involves a level of submission far deeper than taking it up the ass. Especially if you want her on her knees while she sucks you off. Most women despise most men, so this is also out of the question.

But while those women who do follow such a winning strategy have the right intentions and should be cherished, this is not really how you keep a man satisfied, just drained. Their "heart is in the right place," *but their heart chakra is not.* Allow me to elaborate, because when you talk to a man about not cumming in a woman's pussy or ass and lasting for hours and bringing her to some kind of ideal "orgasmic depth," the question that usually comes up is:

"Well, What's in It for Me as A Man?"

Are you really just supposed to be some sort of sexual tool for a woman? Naturally, your ego will get validation knowing you are responsible for all of this pleasure that she is experiencing, and from all the praise she will be subsequently lavishing upon you. You will also finally begin to realize your value as a man, and that she can't just "get dick anywhere," as she likes to boast. The reality is that men are a lot like the sun: they shine but never see the results of the rays that they emit. I mean, the sun doesn't see the life that exists on earth because of how it shines, does it? It just sits out there in space and has no clue. Maybe it even thinks it's useless? A woman has the ability to reflect back to you your value, much like the earth reflects back to the sun its value. When a woman is in deep orgasmic throes you can see how powerful you really are, whereas normally your power just shines out into empty space, being mocked and laughed at by stupid bitches who literally have cum no closer to orgasm than a bout of explosive diarrhea. So as a man, if your value is not being reflected back to you by a woman, how can you perceive it? Hmmm… Idiots will tell you that you should not need others for validation, but in this case, you do! No man is an island, and stoicism is masochistically stupid. No fap, stoicism and sigma males – the trinity of cope. No place to go from there but MGTOW.

However, even if you do get to experience your value through a woman's orgasmic responses, you will *still* be unsatisfied. Riding a woman's orgasmic waves is in some ways akin to edging, where the underlying sexual tension of your being is never actually resolved so where can sex ultimately lead? Eventually you will have to cum and while that *resolves the tension* in the short-term, it still doesn't ultimately *satisfy* you. I mean, you can make her orgasm so hard and so often, yet all that you get after all of your training and hard work is *just* to ejaculate at *some* point? It really doesn't seem fair, does it? You could have just done that from the start! I remember listening to Tony Huge in some video online, a real pioneer in his field of endeavor, and he had said that in the end, after learning all sorts of sexual skills, he just went back to nutting as fast as possible. I totally get it. What you need is an orgasm but not one based on ejaculation, and since I have already pointed out that separating orgasm from ejaculation is not possible (it's all just "cumming" even if your *intensity* dial is adjustable), then what *am* I talking about here?

Ah, here is where *magic can potentially happen* and true understanding can finally begin. See, what *can* happen if you are capable of facilitating the right sort of experience in a woman, is that eventually you *may* encounter a woman who has a minimum of traumatic armoring and she will take the energy from your cock into her pussy, "process" this energy upwards via her orgasm, and expel the energy out of her heart into yours. She will literally *penetrate* your heart via her heart. This is what they don't tell you about tantric sex, because most tantra teachers don't know anything about it. Remember, the woman's positive pole is not her pussy, *but her heart*. The pussy is her negative, receptive pole that gets penetrated. Since the man's heart is his negative pole, *it* gets penetrated - *by her heart*, which as I have said before is her positive pole. So while a man *physically* (and energetically) penetrates a woman's pussy with his cock, the woman *energetically* penetrates a man's heart with hers! **So what I *am* talking about here, is a woman inducing a full-body orgasmic experience in a man that is *complementary* to hers and that *originates* from his negative pole – his heart, and propagates as a wave form throughout his body *from that point of origin*. This is what Wilhelm Reich got wrong. He believed that cumming very intensely and with deep feeling was the male orgasm. It isn't. The wave-form of the full-body male orgasm propagates from the heart and not from the genitals!**

Again, this dynamic is actually why men worry about how many cocks have been in a woman's pussy, while women worry about how many other women have "run up inside" of another man's heart. Mind you, they don't have the conscious awareness and knowledge that you now possess reading this, so they *usually don't know why* it bothers them that a man they are interested in, was in love before, and *why* they are jealous of his past relationships. The truth is that *a woman who wants you, wants to fuck your heart as much as you want to fuck her pussy*. Even if she doesn't know how to do it, or even that she *can* do it.

This "energetic penetration" is not some "woo-woo" nonsense that is in your mind. When this event happens, it is as solid and real as can be. While unbelievable until it happens to you, *your heart can be penetrated by the woman until it orgasms*. **This is when you experience satisfaction and pleasure as a man - not so much when you ejaculate, as that just**

provides relief of tension, but when you have a full body orgasm that propagates from your heart... At that point, the two of you can merge to a certain depth. Like a ying-yang symbol. Each penetrating the other and making the other orgasm, but at opposite poles. You are now sexually satisfied - for a while at least! I mean, you can't stay like that forever. Most people need to go to work to pay bills! But this experience is what really bonds a man to a woman and vice versa, yet again, most men have their heart chakra blocked up just like most women have their sexual chakra blocked up. Why? Because they are protecting their negative, receptive pole, in which they are the most vulnerable! For human beings, with respect to the energies of love and sex, the goal is to de-armor the blocked negative pole and reconnect it to the positive pole. Both inside of themselves, as well as externally with their sexual partners. In terms of inside of themselves, the goal is to reconnect the heart with the genitals or vice versa, depending on gender. In terms of externally with their sexual partners, the goal is to reconnect the genitals with the genitals, and the heart with the heart. Just keep in mind that in each respective gender, the pole that got blocked and severed the connections both internally as well as externally, is different. In women, it is the genitals that have the greater problem, in the man, it is the heart that has the greater problem.

Again, this is why edging, and it's extreme, gooning, never lead anywhere. With edging you build and build the tension until you eventually have to spit it out of your cock via ejaculation, or else try to hold onto the high and break through to something greater, which is what leads to gooning - and what is gooning really in essence? You are trying to merge with a digital signal in the *form* of a woman, not an actual woman. (*Yes, I know some of you goon to furries and futanari and I am well aware of "Rule 34" which states, "If it exists there is porn of it."*) But gooning is downright dangerous as you don't know what entities will use cyberspace as a route to attach to you. This will become more apparent as AI becomes more and more advanced, and people foolishly choose the transhuman route to damnation by implanting chips in their brain, as Satanists such as Elon Musk promote. If you use your free will to choose to give up your free will, what utterly disastrous consequences will such a decision have? Now is the time to really think about it. You are better off putting a bullet in your head than a microchip. Yes, you will lose your life, but not your soul. Think about it now, because forcing covid vaccines onto people was just a trial run for AI implants. One day, they will try and force you to take a microchip implant. That day is approaching fast. Very fast. It is almost upon us.

Introduce Your Lovers to This Slowly

Now even if you are capable of engaging sexually with a woman in such a tantric manner, I don't recommend most women be approached like this right off the bat. You have to meet them on their level. It is like a self-improvement guru who has to show off his (leased) luxury car fleet and pretend he is all about those custom rims on his Rolls Royce in order to meet his target audience at the level they are able to receive him at. He knows that a fleet of Lamborghinis have no inherent intrinsic value (hopefully), because when you are looking at them parked on the street they look fire, and you desire to possess their sexiness, but when you are driving down the road in one them the car disappears, and all that you perceive is the road itself! Well, in truth you also FEEL the car, which is why the experience of driving a 1970s restomod Corvette is always way more FUN than any supercar or hypercar. But here is the thing: do you notice how driving exotic cars and fucking super hot girls are really parallel experiences? Many girls and cars look hot and come across as all sexy, but they are not necessarily fun to drive!

Either way, when you first start having sex with a woman, you want to give them what they want, which is what I will call the "Rocco Siffredi experience." But since you will be able to go for hours, yet can't exactly jackhammer them for hours on end without it becoming very unpleasant for them… so as the time goes by you can just naturally slip into a more tantric style of intercourse, and then just when that starts to get old, you can go back to Rocco's "trademark" style!

Statutory Rape, Grooming & Other Utterly Arbitrary Nonsense

If we are going to be speaking on realistic sexual dynamics, we are going to have to acknowledge that in the United States these days, if you are an adult and you have sex with a teenager, the popular consensus will brand you a "pedophile." This is *not* what you are, based upon the very clinical definition of the word.

Here are two clinical definitions of a pedophile:

- *The American Psychological Association (APA) Dictionary of Psychology defines pedophilia as "a paraphilia in which sexual acts or fantasies involving pre-pubertal children are the persistently preferred or exclusive method of achieving sexual excitement."*

- *By diagnostic criteria of the DSM (Diagnostic and Statistical Manual of Mental Disorders), a pedophile is an individual who fantasizes about, is sexually aroused by, or experiences sexual urges toward prepubescent children (generally under 13 years) for a period of at least 6 months. Pedophiles are either severely distressed by these sexual urges, experience interpersonal difficulties because of them, or act on them.*

Now that we know what a pedophile actually is, rest assured that if you are an adult and have sex with a teenager, you are just a very lucky guy, and you are only guilty of "statutory rape" dependent upon your jurisdiction:

- **14 years old:** Austria, Italy, Serbia, Germany, Portugal, China, Brazil, Colombia.

- **15 years old:** France, Poland, Czech Republic, Sweden, Greece, Denmark, Iceland.

- **16 years old:** Spain, Romania, Switzerland, Netherlands, Norway, United Kingdom, Russia, Alabama, Alaska, Arkansas, Connecticut, Georgia, Hawaii, Indiana, Iowa, Kansas, Kentucky, Maine, Maryland, Massachusetts, Michigan, Minnesota, Mississippi, Montana, Nevada, New Hampshire, New Jersey, North Carolina, Ohio, Oklahoma, Pennsylvania, Rhode Island, South Carolina, South Dakota, Vermont, Washington, West Virginia.

- **17 years old:** Colorado, Illinois, Louisiana, Missouri, New York, Texas, Wyoming and Utah.

- **18 years old:** Arizona, California, Delaware, Florida, Idaho, North Dakota, Oregon, Tennessee, Virginia, Wisconsin, and Washington, D.C.

If "statutory rape" is so utterly arbitrary, how can it be real? Furthermore, it is grossly unfair to use the word "rape" in the term since the arbitrary act of "statutory rape" does not fall under the Federal definition of rape! The very fact they throw the term "rape" in there shows you that "statutory rape" is just a way of scaring individuals away from behaving in what is a completely natural manner.

The next "word of the day" is "grooming," which is used all the time these days to describe a situation where someone gets into a non-sexual relationship with a girl who is below the age of consent, in order to obtain a sexual relationship with her when she has attained the age of consent. This is looked at by feminists and jealous women (men too) as somehow equivalent to "rape" and makes you a "predator" of some sort. But in fact, "grooming" means something *entirely* different than the commonly accepted definition I just described!

Let's take a look at what "grooming" really is, as the U.S. Department of Justice, Office of Sex Offender Sentencing, Monitoring, Apprehending, Registering, and Tracking (SMART) uses the following definition of grooming:

"Grooming is a method used by offenders that involves building trust with a child and the adults around a child in an effort to gain access to and time alone with her/him."

Legal definition: "The winning of the confidence of a victim in order to commit a sexual assault on him or her, now a specific criminal offense."

Notice the usage of the word "CHILD" twice? *This means under the age of 13.* So having a non-sexual relationship with someone below the age of consent — yet *over* the age of 13, in order to secure a sexual relationship with that person when they have attained the age of consent, is NOT grooming because at NO POINT during the time period governing the interaction is that person a CHILD!

It also does not qualify as "grooming" with respect to sexual assault, as the eventual relationship that blossomed over time was CONSENSUAL.

But the most ridiculous aspect of all of this, is how public opinion pillories you for stating that you are attracted to adolescent females, when it is totally natural! *As if* your attraction makes you a degenerate, let alone a pedophile, a predator, or a criminal! This is just a ploy by older, "ran-thru" women to shame men away from younger, fresh females. Don't believe it?

The late 1800s saw significant reform efforts, largely driven by **women's rights activists** and "social purity" movements. Reformers argued that young girls needed greater legal protection from sexual exploitation.

Between 1880 and 1920, most states raised their age of consent laws significantly - many to 16, 17, or 18 years old. This period established the modern framework of statutory rape laws, which *criminalized sexual activity with minors **regardless** of consent.*

There you have it – old and salty American women wanted American men to keep funneling their resources into their old, blown-out pussies instead of diverting them into nice tight young ones!

What's unfair is that even in law enforcement circles, the term pedophile is sometimes used informally to refer to any person who commits one or more sexually-based crimes that relate to legally underage victims (as opposed to just those under the age of 13). These crimes *may* include child sexual abuse, statutory rape, offenses involving child pornography, child grooming, stalking, and indecent exposure.

Do you notice how they have cleverly mixed together offenses that involve persons under the age of 13 and persons *merely* under the "age of consent?" They are bundling together offenses that don't necessarily involve *children!* This is not right, because if you were not having sex with a girl under 13, you cannot be considered a pedophile by the very clinical definition of the word! You can only be considered a "statutory rapist" which again is not rape based on the very definition of rape, and since what constitutes "statutory rape" is dependent on jurisdiction, it does not even exist in any sort of objective reality.

Now if you are actually having sex with a girl who is prepubescent (under 13) then you are a child molester and probably a pedophile, although you may not be, as there are child molesters who engage in child molestation for reasons other than pedophiliac urges.

There is still another serious overlapping issue here though, and that involves the legal definitions of "child sexual abuse." The problem with the statutes in regard to child sexual abuse, is that they *also* interchange the word "child" with "minor," which by definition includes those who are *not* children, yet don't meet the ridiculously arbitrary "age of consent" laws! This has been done on purpose, in order to tarnish what is in fact natural, with the stain of pedophilia. Once again, you can thank the wiles of jealous, fucked-out women with their labia flapping in the wind for this legal sleight-of-hand!

Finally, I want to address the utterly stupid concept that these utterly arbitrary age of consent laws are there because a girl of some totally arbitrary age is not mentally developed enough to give consent. What is so laughable about this, is that a girl below the "age of consent" is legally capable of giving consent to a boy who is also "below the age of consent." How ridiculous! Just more evidence that these laws were put in place to prop up the sexual market value of older, less desirable women. Of course older, less desirable women don't mind if a 16 year old boy fucks a 16 year old girl, as that 16 year old boy has no money or resources anyway. But they sure as shit won't allow a 30 year old with his own house, car, and a high six figure income to enjoy a 16 year old girl or start a family with her as a reward for all of his hard work! Nope, they want to *force* that 30 year old to be with *them*! It's also funny when an old maid asks a couple with a huge age gap what they "have in common." The stock answer should always be "amazing sex!" Go seethe, bitch – and take a shit while you are at it!

Look, a girl of a certain age is either capable of giving consent, or she is not. It's like women claiming one moment that they are a "goddess," and then the next moment claiming they are a "victim." Make up your fucking mind what you are!

The Blackest Pill There Is?

Earlier in this book I made reference to the book "The Origins of War in Child Abuse" by the late Lloyd deMause. You will never see the world the same again when you realize just how pervasive both incest and child sexual abuse actually are. Not only that, but you'll get an understanding of just how awful childhood can be in terms of plain vanilla physical abuse and neglect, never mind the sexual abuse. Lloyd deMause, in this book and in many others he authored – along with a copious amount of academic journals he published, explores the connections between childhood abuse and trauma, and the development of violent and aggressive behavior in adulthood, including war and genocide. He argues that war and violence are the inevitable result of childhood abuse, with adults re-enacting childhood trauma by replacing the parent or abusive figure with the "motherland." Given the understanding you now possess of the life's work of the late Dr. Edmund Bergler, you can easily see how the writings of deMause and Bergler tie together with the genetic engineering of modern human beings by Lucifer, to create a time bomb for war, genocide, and suffering that never seems to stop ticking. Because no matter how many times the bomb detonates, humans never learn from what happened *because they were specifically designed* by Lucifer to never learn, so as to keep feeding the 4th and 5th dimensional entities that feed upon the fallout every time the bomb detonates. Here are two notable quotes from the book "The Origins of War in Child Abuse" that focus specifically on the issue of child sexual abuse, as opposed to my earlier quotes from the book which focused on the issue of infanticide:

"In America, the most accurate scientific studies, based on lengthy interviews, report that 30 percent of men and 40 percent of women remember having been sexually molested during childhood—defining 'molestation' as actual genital contact, not just exposure..."

"Adjusting statistically for what is known about these additional factors, I have concluded that the real sexual abuse rate for America is 60 percent for girls and 45 percent for boys, about half of these directly incestuous."

There are many realities uncovered in academia that are so indigestible (upcoming pun intended) that they get buried, often with the academics who uncover them losing their positions and/or having their academic writings tossed aside. A famous example of this is the archaeological and anthropological issue of "pot polish." To sum it up, archaeological anthropologists discovered (along with the help of electron microscopes) that the majority of human bones found in dig sites *world-wide* showed evidence of having been cooked in a pot at one point. While this explained why human and animal bones were often unearthed mixed together in the same dig sites, it also revealed that the number one food source for humans during large spans of historical time *was other humans*, and not animals as is commonly believed.

The works of Lloyd DeMause find themselves in the same predicament as those expounding on the discovery of "pot polish," with nobody wanting to believe the sheer extent of the abuse of children on this planet. However, I remember watching the Shawn Ryan Podcast when he had the famous "ethical hacker" Ryan Montgomery on as a guest. Ryan had hacked a child-porn site to find a database of 7,000 parents in the United States who had birthed children for *the express purpose* of shooting child porn with them, and collectively sharing their children – along with the content they produced with them, with other pedophile parents. Even worse, this website was linked to a series of other similar websites, so who knows what the actual number of participating parents actually was, but Ryan asserts it is in the tens of thousands.

The idea behind these websites being, that a collective of pedophiles could safely enjoy access to an endless supply of each other's children, along with endless hours of home-grown content. Ryan Montgomery went to the press, the FBI, local law enforcement… yet nothing was ever done. Now why do you think nothing was ever done? Could it be related to the fact that the owner of the website was former congressional candidate Nathan Larson, who ended up being starved to death by guards and inmates in Federal prison? Woops! I would suggest the possibility that Nathan Larson was potentially feeding the needs of the pedophile elites. In case you are having trouble extrapolating the full scope of the problem, allow me to refer to another episode of the Shawn Ryan Podcast where he had Tim Tebow on as a guest. Here is a direct quote from Tim:

"It is overwhelming when you think how much is done by families, by friends, by those in the trusted circle. It's off the charts of what is being done in the families. The number one offender is biological fathers."

Mr. Tebow then presented a document showing a Department of Justice (DOJ) "red dot map," with every red dot over the last 30 days representing at least one unique IP address of individuals downloading, sharing, and distributing child abuse and rape images of children under the age of 12. One guy they were monitoring online had something like 20 TB worth of baby rape content. There were over 111,000 of these unique IP addresses on this DOJ red dot map, just in the United States, over the last 30 days. As a matter of fact, multiple organizations estimate that 500,000 predators are online every day, leaving minors vulnerable each time they access a social media account.

That's 3% of the United States population, which means that if your pull 100 random people off the street in the United States, 3 of them are pedophiles. Given the number of databases and tangential evidence, it is probably closer to 5% of the United States population. This is absurd! Tim then goes on to state that 55% - 85% of those represented on that DOJ red dot map are also hands-on offenders, and that your average offender has 13 victims over their lifespan.

Shawn Ryan then asks Tim, "Why do you think there is so much push-back on this particular subject?" Tim Tebow then proceeds to give some low IQ answer that the problem is too complicated for people to understand due to the "spread out nature" of the problem. Well, there is really nothing complicated about it all: A statistically significant percentage of the United States population consists of parents who rape their own children, from infancy though adolescence, and film it in order to share it with others who enjoy similar interests. I am still unclear as to what he meant by the "spread out nature" of the problem, although I have some speculations as to what he *may* have meant by it.

A common response as to why most people stick their heads in the sand when this topic is broached, would be that the majority of people, whom *allegedly* have no such predilection for this degree of insanity, simply cannot comprehend the motivation to carry out this sort of evil. Hence, they deny its very existence, rather than face it, and have to deal with the challenge it presents to their own *psychic stability*. A very plausible explanation indeed, as well as an explanation in line with the thesis of this book.

But *what if...* what if the reason people turn a blind eye to these horrors is *not* because they cannot comprehend them, but rather because buried deep down inside of them are these very same impulses, and *that* is what they don't want to have to face? If this were true, it would not challenge my assertion that humans strive to maintain their own psychic stability above all. In fact, it would actually reinforce it. I mean, this would be the hardest and *blackest* pill to swallow of all, pun incoming: One one hand, most people are repulsed by the idea of cannibalism, and cannibalism remains a topic reserved for exploitation films and zombie flicks. Yet according to certain underground academics, *cannibalism was the norm* for a great swath of human history, with other humans being the main source of protein in the human diet. However, if you ate people today, you would be labeled some sort of serial killer and locked away for life, unless you went down in a plane crash in the Andes mountains and did it to survive.

Another example is the "Oedipal Complex" taught to students of psychology and psychiatry, and of course to anyone who received a classical education - who all know the story of "Oedipus Rex" upon which the "complex" is based. I can even clearly remember trying to have sexual relations with my own mother when I was a small child. I was too young to know how to fuck, but I was definitely extremely sexually attracted to her, and on several occasions made attempts to get into the shower with her and express myself sexually while I was still a small child. She wasn't having it, and for much of my adult life I was obsessed with having sex in the shower, and I dare say I have fucked a lot of other people's mothers in my day, especially in the shower! Wet skin turns me on very much. It really all makes perfect sense. But what's ironic, is that when my own mother had Alzheimer's and would run about the house naked, I would be rather weirded out by it. Was it because I finally had an opportunity to have sex with her after burying my feelings for so long, if I so desired? I cannot say for sure, because I didn't want to even *begin* to explore these sorts of thoughts. *Psychic stability* and all that yet again...

My point is that if cannibalism was a common practice at one time in the history of "civilization," and psychologists all agree that having the *impulse* to fuck your own mother is normal at one point in your life, then what other *impulses* are "normal?" As I point out earlier in this book, in Roman times sex with small children was widespread and accepted by Roman society, with nobody thinking anything of a wealthy Roman having a whole bunch of young children (usually slaves) around the house to take care of his sexual needs. The writings of DeMause, as well as the statistical assertions of Ryan Montgomery and Tim Tebow, lead to a very disturbing thought: If the problem of child rape and sexual abuse is *this* widespread and has always been so, to the point that it was common practice in certain ancient civilizations, could these *impulses* somehow be way more "normal" than anyone would want to admit? Have these impulses simply been "driven underground" by "modern civilization," only to flourish in the shadows with the same intensity they once did out in the open? It's like everybody always says they are against rape and disgusted by it, but historically speaking, the moment war breaks out, the amount of soldier-on-civilian rapes often reach epidemic levels.

Please don't misunderstand what I am saying here. I am *not* a pedophile and I am *in no way* advocating for, or promoting, the acts of cannibalism, fucking your own mother, or raping your infant children. I am simply postulating that the *impulse*, or *thought-forms* behind this behavior may be more "normal" than anyone wants to admit – **not the *act itself.*** In other words, I am postulating that it is ***normal* to have *impulses* to commit *abnormal* acts.** Especially when it comes to inflicting trauma, sexual and otherwise, on infants and children. Why? Because you have been engineered that way in order to encourage the creation of traumas that will become the fuel for future wars and therefore feeding opportunities for 4th and 5th dimensional entities. Later on in this book, I will discuss the nature of your "mind" and where your thoughts come from. For now, let me just say that *you are not your thoughts or impulses because they do not necessarily arise from "you."* But this is hard for most people to realize because almost nobody has engaged in the prerequisite amount of meditation to even ask the question as to where thoughts and impulses arise from to begin with! Who wants to meditate when you have social media acting as a digital Pez dispenser, dispensing dopamine hits on demand? For example, many thoughts and impulses could be coming from Satanic forces, which have easy access to your mind given how Lucifer engineered your construction. This is why it is so important to realize that you are not necessarily your thoughts and impulses, and *even more important* to realize that just because you have the *thought* or *impulse* to do something, doesn't mean that you should actually do it! Unless you are high on "bath salts" of course, because apparently everyone high on them starts to try and eat other people's faces off. That's a joke, BTW... In the same manner, you may have a thought, and may even *entertain* said thought (potentially a slippery slope), but it doesn't mean that you should *dwell* on said thought! It's just asking for trouble... There is a reason eastern philosophers have said "The mind should not dwell" and I once heard the apt expression, "Dwelling is helling." The question of "where should the mind dwell" is actually one of the most important questions that you can ask which I will talk about later.

But of course, where will men get the courage to become aware of these very dark places in their own "minds," when most men these days can't even admit to being sexually attracted to 15 or 16 year old girls when *everyone* knows that they are and that it is perfectly natural?

While I am on these very dark topics, I want to address the fact that pedophiles often advocate for what they call the "sexual rights of children" or some sort of equivalent. Now clearly no pedophile gives a shit about the sexual rights of children given the damage they inflict upon children, and are really just concerned with securing *their* right to have sex with children! But the essence of their argument is that children have a sexuality, and that a certain percentage of children wish to have sex with adults, so who is anyone to interfere with the sexual rights of a child? Let's examine this assertion...

In my own personal experience I am only aware of one women, whom I knew personally, who had sex with all of her father's male friends when she was as young as 8 years old, and claims to have seduced them all herself. It is important to point out that this woman occupied a reptilian-human hybrid body as do I, and therefore it is highly possible that she is not human at all, given the physical form she occupies. Reptilians have a very powerful sexuality that is rather different than that of a human, and reptilians take no issue with the idea of incest, nor are they damaged by engaging in such behavior. This is why I am perfectly comfortable talking about my childhood desire to fuck my own mother. So it is entirely possible that she sought out these encounters and naturally enjoyed them and took no psychological damage from them. I am not sure what her father would think about all his so-called "friends" fucking his 8 year old daughter, and it certainly goes to show you how many men would fuck an 8 year old, if the 8 year old offered herself up and they were certain that she would not tell anyone!

But this specific case that I am sharing is an *absolute outlier*. While it is indeed true that young children have a sexuality, this sexuality is not corrupted by thought-forms about sex that adults are all possessed by, and the sexuality of a young child is rather amorphous and "innocently" expressed. It really has yet to take on an actual form. So it is not exactly an *upstanding idea* to corrupt that child's sexuality in order to satisfy your own selfish desires. While I will acknowledge that there is a gamut of intentions behind the actions of pedophiles that run the range from destruction of said child, to simply interacting with the "pure" sexuality of the child, with the desire to corrupt the child probably somewhere in the middle... even the idea of simply "interacting" with the "pure" sexuality of the child is a very bad idea that is not in the long-term interests of the child, *even if* the child did desire the interaction.

This is because a child's nervous system is not properly developed, and adult sexual stimulation is too powerful for it. The child *may* very well enjoy the interaction, but its nervous system quickly gets overloaded and cannot handle the intensity of sensation. Since the build up of sexual tension in the child cannot be released, it *accumulates* in both the nervous system and in the subconscious (same thing really), only to explode when they are much older. This is actually one of the reasons adults sexually molest children, because they know that some years down the road when the child hits puberty, they will become utterly sex crazed trying to discharge the pent up sexual energy acquired from their "molestation," and then adults can enjoy this absolutely super-charged nubile teenage girl (or boy). It is my speculation that many female porn super stars are great examples of this.

As a more common and perhaps less inflammatory example, you may have the impulse to murder people, and perhaps many of the people you wish to murder actually deserve it, but that is not allowed by society – unless you join the military. Under the auspices of the military, you are free to murder people you don't know, and who probably don't actually deserve it, as much as you would like. It's all fun and games, until your conscience catches up with you!

This is something that isn't spoken of openly… the fact that so much of what is dubbed "PTSD" is really just your conscience beating the shit out of you non-stop for the things that you did, that you really should not have done. I had a friend once who was in the Marines, and did tours in Afghanistan. When he was done, he became a "contractor" which is a handy euphemism for "mercenary." He made a lot of money and went on to become very successful in business, but he could not live alone, had serious trouble sleeping, and periodically would act in a possessed manner. One day I asked him why so many veterans these day seem to have so much more trouble with things like PTSD, than did their counterparts who survived World War II. He responded by saying that during World War II, the United States military discovered that most soldiers would purposefully miss their targets, and that only a handful of soldiers were doing all of the killing. So the goal of the United States military became to get *all* soldiers to kill at the same rate, and they devised methodologies to accomplish said goal. The result, he said, is that when you first get to a place like Iraq or Afghanistan, you arrive brainwashed to murder with impunity. All is well until *one day*, you close your eyes to go to sleep and all you can see is those people that you murdered without a second thought. Now they are *all* that you can think about, and they haunt the fuck out of you. Trouble is, you can't make it right because you took something from them that you can't exactly give back now, can you? Your conscience simply won't let you rest, unless you went so far, that you even murdered your own conscience - and that sure ain't coming back no matter how many times you might "accept Jesus." *This* is why the suicide rates among veterans are so high these days.

Some years back I ran into one of these "operators" in a bar (I think it was "The Gin Mill") on the upper west side of Manhattan. I was supposed to meet someone there, who ended up never showing up. The bar was crowded that night, and the only seat available was next to some guy sitting in the corner whom nobody wanted to sit next to, because he radiated death. That wasn't a problem for me, and I really wanted to sit down, so I asked him if the seat was available, he nodded and I sat down. I ordered a drink, and maybe 10 minutes later he turns to me and says, "Can I ask you for some advice? You seem like someone who may be able to give me some." I said sure, and he proceeds to inform me that he had recently left the US military, where he had been "doing a lot of killing." I am choosing to leave out *many* details here which would make this story 10x better, but also make telling it *unnecessarily* risky... His dilemma was that the U.S. military wanted him to reenlist, but he had a child and couldn't look his child in the eye anymore because of what he did for a living. Yet at the same time, he was incapable of functioning in the civilian world at this point. Since he was separated and had to pay child support, the dilemma was that he felt like he had to go back in order to earn the money to pay his child support and be able to see his child, yet then he would be unable to face his child. But if he didn't go back, he was afraid he would be unable to see his child at all due to his inability to pay child support, so what to do?

I really didn't have a solution for him, as from my perspective *at the time*, he already had done so much stuff he should not have been doing, that I had the thought that if he were doomed, he might as well be able to at least provide his child with financial support. But I wasn't happy with that conclusion, so I simply acknowledged his dilemma. The reason I could not see clearly, was because I was thinking in terms of karma instead of thinking in terms of The Divine Father. I felt somewhat bad about my inability to offer him actionable advice, but at the end of the day he also needs to figure things out for himself. *If* I were asked this sort of question today, I would have said that the fact you can't look your own child in the eye should tell you all that you need to know, and that you should *not* go back. I would tell him *not to accept* this idea that he cannot function in the civilian world anymore, and to pray to The Divine Father, telling him that you understand that there are probably going to be undesirable consequences for your past actions, but you still wish to repent for your past wrongdoings and refuse to continue murdering people for the U.S. military, and that you want to be of use to The Divine Father instead of the U.S. Military, and ask him to guide you to align your will with His.

Let's take a look at former Navy Seal Chad Wright as an example, who has become rather popular on YouTube recently due to his stories about his encounters with "demons" and his conversion to Christianity. When you look into his eyes, what do you see? He clearly worked extremely hard to get that look in his eyes, and then wonders why what he calls "demons" came a calling for him one day. It doesn't matter that he became a Christian, he cannot escape the consequences of his actions. Demons and other dark beings like to pretend they have been exorcised or driven away by the faith of Christians, because they know they have until the rest of your days to come for you, and they do enjoy the horror Christians experience when their time comes to an end, and they are finally confronted with the realization that their "hellfire insurance" doesn't cover them after all. Jesus can't "save" Chad Wright from the consequences of his own *free will decision* to join the US Navy and murder people. Look, a firefighter doesn't become a firefighter in order to "serve his community," he becomes one because he enjoys walking among the flames. In the same way, do you think that Chad Wright joined the Navy to "serve his country," or do you think he joined because he *wanted to engage in killing free from consequences?* Even podcaster Shawn Ryan, admitted in an interview that he joined up to be able to legally kill someone. At least he is honest! Except they all find out too late that there is no such thing as engaging in killing "free from consequences" as a human, even if "your country" pats you on the back for all the wrong you've done. In the Bible that Chad enjoys thumping, it says "Thou shalt not kill." But you'll notice many Christians like to ignore the Old Testament in favor of the New Testament. The Bible is not as heavy that way, and easier to wave in other people's faces. It is not my intention to pass judgment on Chad Wright here, as only the Divine Father can do that, just to point out that actions do not become consequence-free just because you followed orders, "served" your country, or converted to Christianity.

What Christians like Chad Wright and Tim Tebow fail to realize, is that Christianity is no different from Satanism at the core. What is the core of Christianity? The false and blasphemous claim that The Divine Father is planning to send everyone to hell *even if* they spend their lives doing good and being righteous, and that the only way out is to "accept" Jesus. So they are falsely and blasphemously claiming that The Divine Father - who is perfect, and therefore *perfectly just*, is in actuality completely unjust. Who *else* feels this way? Satan, of course.

Christians then commit even worse blasphemy by falsely claiming that Jesus is more powerful than The Divine Father who created him, even going so far as to use terms like "Lord," "God," and "Father" to refer to Jesus himself. It is impossible for Jesus to be more powerful than The Divine Father and even the Bible itself clearly demonstrates this. Now who *else* aspires to replace The Divine Father? Satan, of course.

Christians, who have already falsely and blasphemously claimed that The Divine Father is unjust, *then* go so far as to act as if the very being who created both them and Jesus, The Divine Father, somehow no longer exists... THEN hypocritically promote *an even more unjust scenario* through Jesus! They do this by promoting the idea that *no matter what evil you have done*, you can be "forgiven" (escape punishment and gain entry into heaven) as long as you "accept" Jesus. Who else would promote such an inversion of justice? Satan, of course.

Tim Tebow, while on the Shawn Ryan Podcast, spoke about the influence of Satanic cults with respect to the problem of child sexual abuse and rape. He then proceeded to tell a story of a particular predator who was caught, and interviewed by a psychologist. The psychologist was trying to figure out *why* the predator had selected a *specific* child on the playground to rape, and the predator responded that he just looked for the happiest child on the playground, so that he could "steal her soul."

But according to Christians like Tim Tebow, the only thing that this predator would have to do to get into heaven would be to "accept" Jesus, sometime before he kicks the bucket. It wouldn't matter if this predator had destroyed the lives of hundreds of children. Nope. Not at all. Who needs justice when you have Jesus? According to Christians all you need to do is say a few words, and you can waltz right into heaven with the shit of little kids still fresh on your dick. How insane is that?

How can someone like Tim Tebow sit there and talk about his battle against Satan, when he is inadvertently standing with him? Do not think I am mocking Tim's desire to help children who are victimized. I am mocking his religious beliefs that blaspheme The Divine Father and make a mockery of justice, and I am mocking him for how incredibly stupid he is not to see this. Even more ridiculous, is that Tim Tebow neglects to mention that the Catholic Church is one of the biggest nests of pedophiles out there. Since countless Catholic priests have probably given sermons with the shit of alter boys still on their dicks, perhaps Tim should tend to the fires in his own house, before fighting fires elsewhere?

Organizations that deal with unwanted children also attract pedophiles like a magnet, for obvious reasons. One of my friends who was given up by his mother for adoption when he was very young, told me that any mother who opts for adoption instead of abortion, is usually unknowingly signing her child up for endless rape. The good news is that birth control is everywhere, so there is no need to turn abortions into a hobby, or offer up your unwanted children to pedophiles. A lot of people don't know that the #1 country to obtain infants without birth records or a recorded identity, is Catholic Poland. There are quite a few brokers out there who target women carrying unwanted pregnancies, and pay them big money to deliver them in a private clinic where there will no record of a birth. They tell these women that the big money comes from wealthy people who cannot have children and wish to avoid wait lists or being denied their desire to adopt a white child, and that their unwanted children will have an amazing life. In reality, these children end up sold to some of the worst individuals out there, who create a living hell for them until they are no longer useful, at which point they are disposed of.

In conclusion, the issue here is that humanity needs to take a much closer look at themselves and stop sleepwalking through their lives. They need to become aware of what is really going on inside of themselves, as well as what is really going on in the outside world. But it is only getting worse, with more and more people than ever falling asleep at the wheel of life thanks to smartphones and social media. The reality is that human beings were engineered from the jump by certain dark beings to be easily brainwashed, controlled, manipulated, etc. As a result, you as a human being *simply cannot afford* to fall asleep at the wheel! You must seek awareness, and a direct relationship with your creator, The Divine Father. Forget all religions that get in the way. No matter if you are of the light or of the dark, all you really need is The Divine Father. Tell him you acknowledge him as your creator and ask to align your will with his. What better use of your free will could there possibly be? If you were created to be an instrument of killing, then he will see to it that your nature is ultimately satisfied without bringing undesirable consequences upon yourself. But if you just go with whatever thoughts or impulses are presented to you by who-knows-who, without consulting directly with The Divine Father who literally created you, you may just find yourself on a road to hell. At a certain point, your momentum will be so strong, that you will not be able to turn back even if you suddenly want to. What humans need to understand, is that there are some tickets that are one-way with no return ticket, and you want to know this before you get one of those tickets punched, because there will be no way off the train once that happens.

The Influence of Satanic Entities on Constant Human Warfare

When you look at Putin's aggression in the Ukraine, you have to wonder what it's all about. It isn't *Russia* that invades Ukraine, after all. The *Russian people* didn't vote to invade Ukraine, and they certainly aren't picking up Kalashnikov rifles on their own volition and marching towards the Ukraine, either. It all comes down to one *short, little old man.*

Vladimir Putin. Now ask yourself, why would a 72 year old man have the desire to re-create some Russian Empire of old? Why does he not just enjoy what is left of his time on Earth, having sex with his mistresses and enjoying plate-after-plate of delicious pelmeni? Mmm… Why start a war against a nation who is neither a threat nor an aggressor? Why talk so casually about slinging nuclear weapons around, when you have a daughter who has to live on this planet? The answer is that he is under the influence of Satan and other dark entities that are in rebellion against The Divine Father. So is *every single* world leader, pretty much. They would not be *allowed* to become world leaders were they *not* compromised. Puppets on strings, who often can't even discern the strings that pull on them.

As I have said over and over, the reason for the constant push for war is that all the slaughter feeds certain 4th and 5th dimensional entities. Without you idiots killing each other because someone told you to do so, these entities would go hungry. Remember what I said at the beginning of this book, that we are living in a matrix transmitted by the planet Saturn? **Imagine a factory farm where the animals *slaughter each other* without the owner having to lift a finger, then reincarnate back into new animal bodies to repeat the process. The food supply never runs out, and all you have to do is influence the animals to keep slaughtering each other!** This is the planet you live on, and you are the stupid livestock that 4th and 5th dimensional entities dine upon. Humans were genetically engineered to be unable to see into the 4th and 5th dimensions as reptilians can, for example. If humans had the eyes to see, they would shit themselves at what they would actually witness on battlefields. Humans of old were capable of seeing into the 4th and 5th dimensions, which is why the legends of old would speak of all these entities on battlefields feeding on fallen warriors and fighting over their dying corpses and spiriting away their souls. These aren't "legends," and this isn't mythology. This is the unseen *reality*.

When looked at through this lens, wars actually start to make sense. I was watching a documentary series on Netflix the other day about World War II. When you pay close attention, you may get the thought that the whole purpose of that war was just to kill off as many people as possible, and create as much suffering as possible. But it's *not* because war is some solution to an *imagined* overpopulation problem. It's simply because the animals on this factory farm need to be periodically slaughtered so that those at the top of the planetary food chain can have a feast.

But people need to realize that they still have *a choice*. You don't *have* to go to war! In that same World War II documentary on Netflix, it is pointed out that Winston Churchill, who was a real piece of shit, decided that the Allies should wage a campaign of genocide upon German civilians by firebombing city-after-city that had no military value whatsoever, just to murder as many civilians as possible. These historical facts, along with the mechanics of "firebombing," are not often discussed, because they are *literal holocausts* based on the actual definition of the word itself, which comes from the ancient Greek word "holokauston," meaning "a completely burnt sacrificial offering." Which should prompt you to ask the question, "to whom was Churchill making these sacrifices?"

The objective of firebombing is to create a literal firestorm inside of a city, burning everyone alive while the fires suck out all of the oxygen, suffocating anyone who somehow manages to avoid the flames. This is accomplished by loading up fleets of bomber aircraft with incendiary ordinance as opposed to explosive ordinance, which is then dropped on cities in order to start as many fires as possible.

Around 15 German cities were firebombed to almost total destruction, and more than 120 cities were turned to virtual rubble. German civilian deaths from British and American bombing have been estimated between 570,000 and 800,000. The major German cities that suffered firebombing attacks include:

- **Hamburg:** 50,000 deaths

- **Dresden:** 35,000 civilians

- **Kassel:** 10,000 deaths

- **Darmstadt:** 12,500 deaths

- **Pforzheim:** 21,200 deaths

- **Würzburg:** 5,000 deaths

- **Swinemuende:** 23,000 deaths

There is an interview in this Netflix documentary with an RAF bomber pilot, where he talks about being called into a mission briefing, and is told he has to fly to Hamburg to do a bombing run. He said he was confused, because he had just returned from firebombing Hamburg and the place was destroyed. He is then told that a post office building survived, and underneath it is an air raid shelter with 60,000 civilians who hid there during the firestorm, and his job is to fly over there and bomb it into oblivion, killing those 60,000 civilians. He states in the interview that this is messed up, but what could he do? Those were his orders. So he did it.

This is utterly ridiculous. You are told to commit a genocidal war crime involving the mass murder of civilians that your conscience is telling you not to do, and you pretend like you had no choice? This pilot could have refused. What is the worst they could have done? Court martial him and have him shot? Who cares? Better than having to go to the next realm with 60,000 civilians on your conscience. The "next realm" for him may be far from pleasant.

It's like after the most recent scamdemic was over, Fauci came out and said, "Well, nobody forced anyone to take a vaccine!" People were so upset, because if they didn't take the vaccine in many cases, they would lose their livelihoods. Perhaps this is not "force" in the physical sense, as nobody held anyone down and forced the vaccine into their bodies, but it is "coercion" at an extreme level. I can clearly see why people would be so enraged, yet Fauci did speak the truth. You did have a choice, even though the choices both sucked.

All Political Parties Lead Towards Your Satanic Enslavement

The last presidential election was a real hot one. I don't remember seeing the United States more divided. I am no lefty, and I am well aware that all of these "progressives" and "cultural Marxists" are straight up communists who want to destroy society as we know it, replace it with a totalitarian state, and enslave you. *But so does the right-wing*! They *also* want to destroy society as we know it, but instead of replacing it with a totalitarian communist state, they want to replace it with a totalitarian, transhuman feudal state, *and take away your free will in the process*. This goes *way beyond* commonly understood concepts of enslavement. In the past, one could argue that there was no real difference between communism and fascism, as both are totalitarianism wearing different uniforms. While Wilhelm Reich did make a successful case in his day that communism was worse than fascism, time and technology have proven him wrong. These days, the left is actually the lesser of the two evils *in the sense* that voting democrat *may* function to delay the inevitable, although I will make another suggestion at the end of this section.

What is so sad, is people are incapable of discerning that *both* democrats and republicans are mere puppets of Satan and his agenda. I mean, members of *both* parties attend the gatherings at Bohemian Grove (look it up). But Amerimutts with their average IQ of 98 fall for the narrative that Trump is somehow their savior. How stupid! If Jesus can't save you from the consequences of your poor free will decisions, what is a con artist like Trump going to be able to do? The only person who can "save" you is *you*. After all, it is said that "God helps those who help themselves." You do so by working to attain *awareness*, and by praying every day to The Divine Father, free from the shackles of religion, and asking him to help you to align your will with his own. What better usage of your free will could there be?

I am not devoid of empathy despite being of the darkness. I have lived long enough in a human body to completely understand humans and the human experience. How else could I have written a book such as this? As much as I tire of humans along with their limitless stupidity and consummate weakness, I cannot be *too* hard on beings that have been tampered with by extraterrestrial genetic engineers such as Lucifer (Enki) to the degree that they have been. I am not excusing humans or their behaviors, just sharing my observations and experiences.

For example, I can totally understand *why* people voted for Trump. After all, we have been besieged by the utter insanity of the far left for *far* too long. Anyone who has had to deal with the mentally ill for any period of time understands just how *exhausting* it can be. Most people have come to realize that the far left are nothing more than a bunch of rabid communists who are mentally ill, whose entire aim is to tear down modern society because they themselves cannot succeed in it, and replace it with a totalitarian state where everyone is forced to be as big of a loser as they are. After all, the only way to have true equality is to cut everyone down to the lowest level! Their inner wish is to cut the wings from all birds, as they themselves cannot fly, and the mere sight and sound of birds flying about and chirping is never-ending torture for them, since it perpetually reminds them that they themselves, can never fly. Unless you send them flying off the roof of a tall building, of course!

The left is Satanic in nature, as is the right, only the right is dumber - hiding their dumbness behind "common sense" whereas the left are more intelligent, and hence more susceptible to mental illness, which they suffer from in spades. But being dumb is why so many on the right are Christians, and the only person dumber than a Christian, is a Satanist. Because while a Christian is too dumb to realize that his beliefs are Satanic corruptions, a Satanist is too dumb to realize that Satan despises those who worship him. On a side note, an evil person I once knew was fond of saying, "You can't be evil and stupid." This is funny, because the *dumbest of them all* are those of the darkness who rebel against The Divine Father. In many cases, they are also insane.

Anyway, as I have said before, many years ago Satanists and Luciferians alike actively decided to embrace both communism as well as Islam, because they deemed these two movements to be ideal for wrecking destruction upon mankind and advancing the agenda of Satan and those of the darkness who rebel against The Divine Father, and wish to make a mockery of His creation in this realm. Why do they wish to make a mockery of it? For the same reason the left wants to cut the proverbial wings from all birds: Satan, despite being a biological hermaphrodite, can neither physically give birth nor create out of nothing like The Divine Father can, and is filled with envious rage over it. Even the most advanced extraterrestrial geneticists who may *look* like gods who *appear* to create in the eyes of a civilization that is more primitive, in reality can do little more than *reassemble what has already been created by The Divine Father.* Hybridizing a new form of life is *not* the same as creating a new form of life out of nothing.

With this knowledge, is it any shock that Satanic communists disguised as "progressives" and "cultural Marxists" import an endless stream of Moslem migrants corrupted by Satanic interpretations of Islam into western countries, and allow them to rape and sexually abuse the native female populations in line with their acquired Satanic hatred for women, then write laws in countries like England that throw you in jail for even *talking* about it? They invert justice, because perfect justice is important to The Divine Father. They promote sexual violence against women, because Satan hates females. They super-saturate your drinking water with Atrazine to wipe out your testosterone production and make you transgender because biologically speaking, Satan is a hermaphrodite. Satan wants you in *his* own image as you run about the planet stripped of your free will thanks to the efforts of Satanists like Elon Musk and Peter Thiel.

Do you know why the left dub themselves "progressives?" Because they are making *progress*, but towards *what* goal? The goal of your Satanic enslavement, you imbeciles! In light of what I have just said, does it shock you that the next probable mayor of NYC, will be *both* a communist and a Moslem? How can a communist, who traditionally is an atheist, be a Moslem? Didn't Karl Marx state that religion is the opium of the people? Because the next probable mayor of NYC is a Satanist, obviously, who has simultaneously embraced the two paths deemed most likely to *progress* the agenda of Satan at this time. But the residents of New York City vote for this, so why would The Divine Father intervene if it is the free will of the people to vote for their own destruction? Mind you, only 30% of the population of New York City votes, but the 70% who can't seem to be bothered to turn up for elections are *still* voting, they are just voting – by *not* voting!

Now let's take a look at Trump. On the *surface* it may *appear* that he is in opposition to the nonsense on the left. After all, he is rounding up and deporting every criminal illegal immigrant in sight, which is a good thing, as only an insane person (or a Satanist) thinks it is a great idea to have unjust criminal aggressors running around committing crimes with impunity *regardless of their immigration status*. Since these criminals aren't here legally, *obviously deportation is the correct legal remedy*. Trump is also held up by Christians as "their president," but remember, Christians promote Satanism while being too dumb to discern it, and likewise cannot discern that Trump is pressing the agenda of Satan just as aggressively as the left is.

See, while the left promotes all of this "there is no such thing as gender" garbage instead of telling you that gender dysphoria *only* exists because our drinking water has been *super*-saturated with Atrazine as part of a Satanic conspiracy to make you into a reflection of Satan's own biological image, a deeper examination of Trump will reveal that he is *also* promoting the agenda of Satan, just the *next level* in the *progression* of said agenda. So all the Christian retards vote for him thinking they have put a stop to the Satanic agenda, when they have simply voted for *The Satanic Agenda 2.0* – and that has been the whole reason *all along* for the left behaving like the unhinged lunatics they are! They *wanted* to give you such a level of fatigue from their nonsense, that you would vote for the next level in the progression of the Satanic agenda, which is Donald J. Trump and J.D. Vance. This is what author David Icke has been talking about for years with his "problem-reaction-solution" model but nobody has been paying attention. Naturally, David Icke is of the light. Maybe you will listen to me because I am of the dark? Probably not, unless you are of the dark yourselves and resonate with me, and in fact *you* are my primary mission. I want to get you on the side of The Divine Father. He has plenty of work for you. You don't have to run with losers just to be with your own kind, and end up in the abyss.

People don't seem to grasp that the Chinese don't pay tariffs, *you do* in the form of higher prices since the importer pays the tariffs. So if Trump places an import duty of 50% on everything coming in from China, your income and savings have just been cut by 50%. While it is perfectly fine to stop China from dumping low cost consumer goods on the U.S. market, our entire manufacturing base is now in China, and what remains in the U.S. is completely dependent upon Chinese machinery and raw materials. So no matter how high the tariffs go, they will not bring the manufacturing base back. It is impossible at this point. All you do is make Americans poorer and poorer which is part of *the plan*. If Trump took a hint from the Chinese and used all of that tariff money to subsidize FedEx so *all* shipping and freight costs for *all* Americans and American businesses were slashed 90% that would have a truly positive impact on the economy, but the reality is that the billions collected from tariffs will just be sent to Israel, or used to build more underground bases for the elite to hide in when the days of reckoning are at hand, or else used to pay back the interest on the money the U.S. borrows from the Federal Reserve, which is no more "Federal" than is FedEx itself! I mean, you do realize that the United States does not actually mint it's own currency even if it physically prints it? It fucking borrows it! At interest! From an "international" banking cartel. How is this even possible?

Furthermore, Trump does nothing to enforce the endless antitrust laws on the books and allows the dairy, meat production and housing industries to collude and fix prices so food and shelter grow more unaffordable with every passing year. Does Trump use our nation's antitrust laws to break up companies like Meta and Google? Of course not, because they are part of *the plan*. So don't be fooled into pacification because he deports a few criminal illegals, declares there are only two genders, fines Amazon because they made it difficult to cancel your Prime membership, or stacks the Supreme Court so that you can put a "brace" on your "pistol" or slap a "bump stock" on your AR-15. Please don't mistake where I stand on guns! I am *all for* the Second Amendment and think U.S. citizens should be able to own belt-fed machine guns if they so desire, without any additional ATF paperwork than you would need to own a Glock 19. All I am saying is don't be fooled by these "crumbs," because Trump is conspiring with Satan to take away the most important of your freedoms: your free will itself!

Because behind Trump, and especially JD Vance, is Peter Thiel, who openly advocates for the end of democracy and its replacement with an oligarchy of technocrats. If you think England's "big brother" surveillance state is terrifying, take a look at Peter Thiel's "Palantir." The symbol for the company is the crystal ball used by Saruman in "The Lord of The Rings," and they openly admit this. Palantir states that their goal is to create a surveillance state to "protect us from terrorism and our children from pedophiles," which ironically is the same thing the Satanic progressives over in England claim their big brother surveillance state's goal is! Which *can't* be the case, as they allow British children to be raped and sexually exploited by Satanic Moslem migrants on a daily basis. Hmmm… Do you see the pattern yet? For those of you who never read "The Lord of The Rings," or maybe you watched the film trilogy but you were high on weed and busy jacking off to Galadriel the whole time, let me remind you that Saruman's Palantir crystal ball was connected to Sauron, who corrupted and influenced him through it. In the same manner, Peter Thiel's "Palantir" will be connected to Satan.

Now here is where it gets interesting… do any of you "Lord of The Rings" aficionados remember what Sauron's motivations were? They weren't revealed in the original film trilogy by Peter Jackson, but Sauron was basically an engineer (as was Lucifer) who was corrupted by Melkor (who represents Satan). Melkor appealed to Sauron's mindset as an engineer, and convinced him that The Creator's creation was imperfect due to the gift of free will, and so Sauron's goal became to remove the element of free will from Middle Earth. This was why he forged the rings of power and the one ring, because they were tools intended to allow him *to turn creation into a clockwork by removing the element of free will.* This is *precisely* what Peter Thiel and Elon Musk intend to facilitate on behalf of Satan. Palantir is Peter Thiel's contribution towards this Satanic goal, and Elon Musk's contribution is the NeuroLink. With these tools, they can potentially excise free will from humanity, and turn this aspect of The Divine Father's creation, into a clockwork. Satan has already created the "one ring to rule them all" in the form of the planet Saturn. Saturn used to be one of the twin suns over planet earth, yet was banished into deep space, much in the same manner that Melkor was banished from the world by The Creator.

This is what you voted for when you voted for Trump and JD Vance, you stupid, stupid Christian sheep! You all talk about the "mark of the beast," then vote into office the very individuals who promote it! The orchestrated conflicts between the right and the left are only to drive you, like the herd of stupid animals you are, in the direction the Satanic elite wants you to ultimately go in, to begin with! Both the right and the left are both Satanic, only the right takes you closer to the ultimate Satanic goal of the eradication of free will, which is why you were influenced to vote "right" this time around, while thinking you were voting for your "salvation." As if salvation can be voted for! But when people believe you can obtain salvation just by saying a few words, why would they not believe you can vote for it as well? This is the whole problem with the young conservative crowd – they aren't aligned with The Divine Father, they are aligned with Jesus. I have noticed that they all like to sporadically sperge "Christ is King" like they have tourette's or something, in between lines of coke on their livestreams. The Divine Father is who is in charge, not Jesus.

This idea that creation needs to be turned into a clockwork also drives mega assholes like George Soros to make the kinds of problems for society that he does. It isn't hard to imagine that going through the horrors of World War II, Soros became possessed of the notion that somehow the world needed to change. The issue is that no human being has the wisdom or intelligence to enact *that* level of change without creating an utter disaster in the process. You need to align your will with that of The Divine Father to accomplish something like that. But none of these clowns like Soros, Thiel or Musk ever reach out to The Divine Father and ask to assist him. They arrogantly believe they can somehow do a better job and don't need his help. It's utterly preposterous, and typically Satanic. They are getting their ideas from entities they run into when smoking DMT, instead of working for The Divine Father. How ridiculous!

Now you also know *why* the elite are obsessed with watches. Why are members of the wealthy elite wearing or otherwise collecting timepieces that cost in excess of $100,000? You don't even need a watch these days thanks to your smartphone. But wearing a watch is symbolic for being enslaved to time, or Kronos. Kronos is another name for Saturn, and Saturn is another name for Satan, as well as the planet he has turned into a transmitter, from which he broadcasts this "Matrix reality" from.

Here are some excerpts from "Notes on Motives in the Silmarillion" which appears in *Morgoth's Ring*, the tenth volume of *The History of Middle-earth* series edited by Christopher Tolkien:

"Melkor 'incarnated' himself (as Morgoth) permanently. He did this so as to control the hröa, the 'flesh' or physical matter, of Arda. He attempted to identify himself with it. A vaster, and more perilous, procedure, though of similar sort to the operations of Sauron with the Rings. Thus, outside the Blessed Realm, all 'matter' was likely to have a 'Melkor ingredient', and those who had bodies, nourished by the hröa of Arda, had as it were a tendency, small or great, towards Melkor: they were none of them wholly free of him in their incarnate form, and their bodies had an effect upon their spirits."

"The whole of 'Middle-earth' was Morgoth's Ring."

"Moreover, the final eradication of Sauron (as a power directing evil) was achievable by the destruction of the Ring. No such eradication of Morgoth was possible, since this required the complete disintegration of the 'matter' of Arda."

I point out the above because as I explain in this book, while human beings were heavily genetically engineered by Enki (Lucifer) which respect to the creation of their subconscious mind, which allows for their easy control at the hands of extraterrestrials, Satan has engineered this entire 3rd dimensional prison reality that human beings occupy. Enki (Lucifer) worked with Enlil back in the day, and Enlil was the son of King Anu of the Anunnaki. Anu is another name for Satan, which is not commonly known.

BTW, the Anunnaki created black people to be used as slaves and as a food source, since Earth at that time was used to resupply their extraterrestrial military vessel, Nibiru. Nibiru is not a "planet," but rather a planetoid-shaped craft. So it's pretty funny when you have comedian Katt Williams wearing some Anunnaki-inspired necklace on the Joe Rogan podcast and not realizing he is repping those who hate him and created his ancestors to be used as slaves and food. It's even funnier than black people who convert to Islam, although the joke has a common theme. As a matter of fact, the reason black people have such a shitty experience on this planet is precisely because the Anunnaki bear a grudge against them. For those who don't know, Enki (Lucifer) thought it a hoot to use the genetics of an extraterrestrial slave rebellion leader in black people's DNA in order to make problems for Enlil, and this put black people on the Anunnaki shit-list. I am putting this out there because I know black people often wonder why they have it so hard.

In the next presidential election, I would suggest that every citizen of the United States writes "We want the direct intervention of The Divine Father" on the ballot instead of voting for yet another Satanic piece of shit. The night of the next presidential election, I would also suggest that everyone needs to pray directly to The Divine Father that they are using their free will to ask for his direct intervention, as they no longer want any part in advancing any agendas that are in rebellion against Him, and desire his direct intervention in order to be able to make this happen. If everyone did this, they would be *shocked* at what would happen next. But as long as you sit there in the flames and go "this is fine" like some living meme, you will just continue to burn.

PART IV: THE WAY FORWARD

The Cure for Porn Addiction Is Real Sex with Beautiful Women

The reason why so many men remain addicted to porn, even when they have a real live female partner, *isn't just* because the sex doesn't "sparkle" like the synthetic stuff online does... and it also *isn't just* because the sex falls short in terms of "authentic energetics..." It's *also* because the reality is that most guys are fucking women that are not beautiful enough to satiate their desire for female beauty. Newsflash: if you don't wake up next to your girl, gaze at her gorgeous face and say to yourself "fuck yeah!" then you have a problem that needs to be fixed. I know in the last section I gave an exotic car analogy for hot girls, which I still stand by: No matter how hot your girl is, when you are running dick up inside of her you cannot *see* how hot she is, or *watch* yourself fuck her like you are watching a porn video. All you can really do is *feel*. In truth, your sexual experience is ultimately more energetic than it is physical. However, this is not to say that physical beauty is unimportant!

Let me clarify: I am not talking about a girl being hot or sexy here, I am talking about genuine female beauty which is important to a man, yet most men do not get to experience it. I also don't want to encourage any of you to fuck any more fat and ugly chicks than necessary by giving you any convenient excuses to perpetuate your loserdom. I do understand that sometimes you get catfished and so you just say "fuck it" and go for it, but this has got to stop. They'll never lose weight or get plastic surgery if you keep rewarding them for being fatsos and ugly. Too many men are having sex with fat and ugly women and either deluding themselves into thinking these busted fat bitches are hot, or else lying to everyone around them by declaring that they "aren't attracted to thin girls" or need a girl with some

285

"meat on her bones." The former are the biggest losers out there: It is one thing to delude others, another thing to totally delude yourself.

Based on the most recent and authoritative data, approximately **82% of adult women in the United States are either overweight or obese**. This figure comes from projections and recent analyses indicating that, as of 2024–2025, the combined prevalence of overweight and obesity among adult women is about 82.1%

Breaking it down:

- **Overweight (BMI 25–29.9):** About **27.5%** of adult women.

- **Obesity (BMI ≥30):** About **41.9%–46%** of adult women, depending on the source and year.

- **Combined overweight or obesity: 82.1%** of adult women (2025 projection, including both categories).

What's insane is how fat girls have zero shame about being fat anymore. They proudly lay out by the pool in bikinis and complain about their problems with men to anyone who will listen. Well, your problems with men are related to the fact that you are fat! You really should not allow yourself on the dating market until you have lost enough weight to be considered thin, because you will only attract loser guys who want to use you, since they feel that fucking a fat bitch is still better than jerking off alone. Older women also fail to accept this male reality in order to cope. While there are women in their 40s and 50s who are hotter than most women in their 20s, they are extremely rare, so all of these women in their 40s and 50s who brag about "dating" younger men are just deluding themselves into thinking that they are anything other than practice dummies who take loads in their tummies.

Anyway, my main point is that when men aren't feeling anything with the girl they are currently shagging, then of course the siren song of online pornography starts to call. So *the truth is that you aren't a porn addict, your sex life just sucks.*

Once you become consciously aware of what the dynamics of porn addiction actually entail, by reading these words and understanding them, then overcoming porn "addiction" becomes super easy. You simply take the steps outlined in this book to attain what is real, and stop guilting yourself when you do indulge in the porn drug when necessary, in order to keep yourself going until you reach your goal and get fed on something real. Porn becomes like medicine then, and not a drug. Opiates are great when you are in pain, not so great when you become addicted to them. I mean, if you smoke the rock once in a while but don't get addicted, what is the actual harm? The truth of many addictions is that they fall away once you have something better to do. Something real, something truly fun.

How To Drown in Pussy

When I was in my early 20s I had a friend who was a bit older than I who got tons of pussy despite having a face that only a mother could love. What he used to do, before he would go out to bars or clubs, is he would go fuck some prostitute. After fucking, you really don't care about getting laid for the next few hours, and you have the crucial "scent of sexual success" which cannot be replicated with pheromones, and believe me I have tried! Because if a woman knows you are having sex, she wants to give you more sex. Just like it is easier to get people to give you money, when you already have money.

Pro Tip: After you have sex *do not shower* or wash your face or hands. Because you want to smell like sex. It is the best way to get more sex. There are some perfume and pheromone products that do actually work *to a degree* to achieve this aim, but you always have to be testing for new ones because the ones that work, don't stay on the market for long. Usually because the ingredients that make them work, get harvested out of existence. For example. there used to be a tree from the Amazon rainforest that produced a sap that worked, until Brazilians cut down all those trees in order to grow more bananas. I hate bananas, BTW, and anything banana flavored. Bananas are for primates, not people! Banana flavored beer is quite popular in Berlin, I have heard, and I can imagine if you time traveled back to 1939 you could stop the Nazis in their tracks just by showing the Waffen SS some YouTube videos you saved to your phone, depicting today's Germany: a bunch of schwuler sitting around swilling banana flavored beer while Turkish and African migrants force their bananas upon German women in public spaces. The Waffen SS would just give up and refuse to fight knowing this was the future of Germany. Now when it comes to colognes, cheaper ironically outperforms expensive, and you want to find the ones that make random women who are strangers complement you in public. That is all that matters! Another strategy is to wear female perfume that you adore which indicates that you are preselected because if a woman smells another woman all over you, of course she wants you now too! Another advantage to wearing female perfume that you adore is you will enjoy the smell, and *feel* like you are with a woman, which will also attract women who mistakenly believe you to be preselected. A similar strategy can be employed with pheromone products, where you apply the ones meant to attract men, to unironically attract women instead. But nothing beats having sex and not cleaning yourself up afterwards. It's also pretty hot when some new girl is sucking your cock after it has been in another girl's asshole and she has no idea that she is tasting another girl's ass.

So let's scale this method my friend used, to whatever level you can afford. I would suggest that once one starts to make *some* money, one should start fucking the hottest hookers one can find, but it is important that they are hookers who love men and love having sex. Many hookers hate men and hate having sex, but not all. In the beginning, it will be difficult to screen them and you will have bad experiences, but pretty soon you will be able to tell from pictures and the words she uses what a girl is all about – even if her face is obscured. Your highest rate of success will be with Brazilian sex workers, who are always touring the major US cities. You want hookers who love to deep kiss *you*, and have their pussies and asses eaten. If you find some that are also vaginally orgasmic, even better! Stick the winners in your "rotation" and treat them as the valuable assets they are.

The point is, you want to be having as much life-affirming sex as you can afford, with insanely hot women on a regular basis, because this will create a pheromone-enriched aura of sexual abundance and sexual satisfaction that will attract "civilian" women like hunting lure attracts deer.

Because you will only be having sex with prostitutes who *actually* like men, sex, and most importantly - *you*, a lot of them will want to fuck you for free or at least hang out with you for free outside of fucking. But for this to occur, you *must* be good at sex and focused on giving them pleasure while having *zero* judgment of them and/or their lifestyle choices. Pretty soon, you will have a paid harem of the hottest girls and the experience of sexual abundance, which other civilian women will respond to positively. You will also have zero thirst. Since most civilian women cannot hold a candle to a hot Brazilian girl who works out 3 hours a day and has elective surgery, you will have enormous leverage when you talk to civilian women, who will now want to get a piece of you.

What's funny is a lot of men have this incredible resistance to "dating" a prostitute but will have no issue dating a stripper even though a stripper is also classified as a "sex worker," and often engaging in prostitution in addition to stripping. As a matter of fact, having a stripper girlfriend is *far* more dangerous than having a prostitute girlfriend because strippers tend to hold PhDs in manipulation, illusion and hatred of men. Either way, the fundamental dynamics of dating a sex worker are the same, no matter if she is a stripper, prostitute, porn star, or "content creator" on OnlyFans.

Female Trinity #2 – The 3 Types of Men in A Sex Worker's Life

So, if you are interested in relating with a stripper, you must realize there are 3 types of men a stripper will have a relationship with:

- **The client.** This is the type of man that makes it possible for her to be a stripper to begin with. He gets to have sex with the stripper, but he has to spend an absolute fortune and the sex is sub-par, because either she is not attracted to the client, or else has to hold back to keep the money coming in.

- **The fun guy/fuck boy.** He has the best deal because he spends no money on her (often the opposite), yet gets to have her "best sexual self" wrapped in her stripper persona. She is attracted to him yet doesn't want anything but sex and fun from him because *her life has no actual fun.* He gets her "best sexual self" for free.

- **The boyfriend/husband.** He gets the worst deal, because he hardly has sex with her, she never "shows up" in her stripper persona, and he has to deal with all of her mental problems. The only good thing is he is usually not spending any money on her either. But still, a bum deal.

Your goal is to end up the "fun guy/fuck boy" and you do this by actually being attractive and amazing in bed, and by letting it be known that you enjoy access to cocaine and MDMA. Sex workers of all stripes and tons of "civilian" hotties who will be drawn in by your lifestyle of "sexual abundance" simply *love* these drugs and want to do coke and MDMA all night long, and these drugs make them even hornier and more "sexually adventurous" than usual. If you let your "hooker harem" know that you have access, just watch what happens! You can tell them to invite their friends over to party and the next thing you know, you are having threesomes and reverse gangbangs. I don't do coke, but if *you do*, you are definitely going to need trimix or quadmix penile injections to "perform" while on coke.

The next step is to document your "hooker harem" while pretending they are "civilians," as well as your party lifestyle (minus the drug use obviously) on social media, and it certainly helps if you can rent the illusion of wealth by renting or leasing an exotic car. No man should use a Ferrari for this purpose BTW, because I have lost count of the number of women who have told me that owning a Ferrari means you have a small penis, and have backed up their assertion with some story of a guy they slept with, who had a Ferrari as well as a small penis. For some reason, this does not apply to Lamborghinis, and a Lamborghini is the only car I know of that will get you laid, as will a custom Jeep. Go figure. So rent or lease either a Lamborghini or a custom Jeep and put it in your Instagram pictures and stories.

Make sure to like and comment on the profiles of other hot girls you are attracted to, and maybe hire some woman such as a "gal Friday" to slide into their DMs on your behalf and seduce them for you. Many wealthy people and celebrities do this to maximize the amount of pussy in their lives. So here again are the three scalable levels:

- Build a hooker harem in your city that actually likes you.

- Provide your harem with access to MDMA and cocaine.

- Document your harem on social media pretending they are "civilians," while hiring someone to DM civilian women, with the intention of luring them into "your world."

This is really easy to implement with just a little extra disposable income and can be scaled to whatever level you can afford. It is not much different from what a club promoter does, to be honest. Just remember that you don't need to be rich to have an elite level of sexual abundance, just a *little extra* disposable income. The best Brazilian hookers are usually around $600/hour, MDMA and cocaine are cheap these days, an IG account is free, and you can hire some woman on Fiverr to slide into DMs all day long. Hookers that charge a lot of money are rarely worth it, IME.

The True Cost of a Girlfriend

If you have a girlfriend or had one, add up the total amount of money you spent on her during the time you were together. Next, add up the amount of time you spent chasing her, hanging out with her (not having sex), listening to her nonsense, attending events you would never have attended on your own... Take the number of hours you spent on these endeavors and multiply that by the value of you time. After all, you could have used that time to learn a money-making skill or build a business, you know! So, add the lost value of your wasted time to the amount of money that you already *thought* you spent on her. *Really* take into account the *opportunity cost* of things you could have done with that time, that you spent with her *instead*, that *didn't* involve sex.

Now add up the total number of *hours* you had sex with her over the course of your relationship. If she refused to suck cock or do anal or failed to satisfy your every sexual desire, cut the number of those hours in *half*. Finally, divide the amount of money spent on her and lost over being with her, by the number of hours of sex you had with her, and you will come to realize you were probably paying well over $5000/hour for sex or some crazy shit like that.

Still think you don't pay for sex?

Look, women want money because they don't want to have to work for a living nor worry about money. Can you blame them? Up until recently women didn't *have* to work. Now they do. There is a big difference between having the *right* to go to work, and *actually having to go to work*!

I do not downplay the importance of money with women. What I do downplay is the need to drive an exotic car, wear a very expensive watch, etc. No woman gives a shit about these things. They just *signal* that you have money while simultaneously broadcast your own insecurity and need to prove something, which attracts gold-diggers and women looking for a man to simp for them. But money itself is insanely critical *if* you are looking for a long-term relationship *and* you are *not* a "cool loser" or "bad boy." Especially when you are going for the highest echelons of women. Being a "cool loser" or a "bad boy" may grant you brief sexual access to them, but that is about it. I can't tell you how many times in my youth a woman was crazy about me but flat out told me she could not be with me because I didn't have money, and she didn't want to fuck me on the side either because she knew she would fall in love with me, and when a woman is in love, the contrast of being with a man she *doesn't* love for financial gain is *repulsive*. But... if she isn't constantly being reminded of the fact she is in love with you (because she stays far away from you), she can push her feelings down and get to the business at hand of gold-digging. I once had a girlfriend who chose to be with my broke ass anyway, but still raged at me periodically, because being with me prevented her from gold-digging. The irony is that this woman didn't need to gold-dig. Yet *still* she wanted to gold-dig! Many women are extremely greedy, do not kid yourselves!

Most women will chose money over love, both due to practical necessity, and because they don't trust being in love due to their unresolved childhood trauma - and they are correct not to trust it, because their unresolved childhood trauma will *ruin the love they have with you anyway, and they know it*. So it is really the case that they do not trust themselves to not fuck things up, more so than they don't trust you or love itself. Additionally, facing down their inner demons is just too hard. They are too weak. It is just so much easier to run away and chase money, which is what they do 99% of the time. They want a man in the 1%, while they are in the 99%. It's ironic, isn't it?

The reality is most women think they can cheat the spiritual challenges that are presented to them in life. They run *from* love and the opportunity it presents for spiritual growth thru the release of trauma, and instead run *towards* the distractions of endless travel, endless cocks, and endless shopping sprees. They comingle their need for love with their need for attention, thinking they can fill their need for the former with the latter, and social media enables this swap to the extreme! However, they will have to live and die with the consequences of their choices, and believe me, most women die filled with regret over their cowardice. Men have no clue just how many of the women they want to be with, are *literally* crying themselves to sleep every night – mostly due to their own choices. Don't be like them. Be a man.

Body Game and Chemical Enhancement – Your Secret Weapons

In order to succeed with hookers (or any woman for that matter), one has to *actually* be physically attractive, and of course, *amazing* in bed. They admire a nice body and love a good cock because this means they can actually *enjoy* having sex for money. Hookers are a great yardstick to measure how good you are because they are literally taking dick all day, every day and have seen it all. Not much will impress them. They are jaded and closed off. If you do impress them or open then up, however, the confidence boost is insane. Listen, if a hooker wants you to fuck her for free, or start dating you just for your dick, you are in the top-tier of males. Hookers also appreciate good hygiene such as smelling great and having manicured hands, etc. Plus, they put so much effort into their appearance and hygiene, it really pisses them off when a guy shows up who can't even make an effort. This gets you in the habit of always being polished and presentable, with excellent personal hygiene. Which is very important in life in general.

Pro Tip: Don't be one of those repulsive fucks who posts "reviews" about prostitutes on escort review sites unless the girl asks you to, in order to help her business. Nothing screams "pathetic" louder than some asshole who has endless reviews of girls, where he reveals in gory details the play-by-play of what she did with him. Escorts look your dumb ass up when you book them, and when they see you leaving reviews you can be sure they will never do anything special with you even if they want to, because they know you will let the entire fucking world know, and then every guy who sees them in the future will expect the same treatment even if he does not deserve it. I mean, how stupid can you incels be? Leaving reviews let's the entire world know that you are a total incel and hate women, because the act of leaving reviews is degrading to the sex worker if she doesn't ask for them, *and* it's like you are telling the world, "Look everyone! I'm *not* an incel!" when all it does is confirm that you are indeed one. When you book time to fuck an escort for the first time, the *intention* is to start a relationship with one, even if it is, or starts out as, a *paid* relationship. Unless the girl is ripping people off or has no business being in this line of work, you should not be talking about her to others. The only reason to talk about an escort is if you need to warn others to stay away.

Civilian bitches are often weirdos and will sleep with guys who don't shower or have nasty fingernails, and it is pretty depressing when you are the kind of man who takes care of himself, yet women don't appreciate it, because so many of them are such incredible losers. Contrary to popular belief, the hookers that love men and sex have high self-esteem. As do most genuine pimps. That's why they take care of themselves, and demand payment in exchange for sex and relationships. People like to shit on hookers, but civilian bitches fuck endless trash for free. The hooker who loves men and sex (that's the only kind to see) is smart enough to get money for what she loves to do, which is to fuck. Furthermore, if a guy doesn't mind paying $500-$1000/hour for sex, it is *impossible* for him to be *that* much of a loser, because he has to be enough of a winner to make that sort of disposable income to begin with, while at the same time enough of a winner *not* to *overpay* a hooker! You can't6 argue against this. So saying "only losers pay for sex," is pretty ridiculous.

Anyway, having a nice body is super important to your success with women. Some call this "body game" and it is a legit avenue of pursuit. Naturally, having body game is even more powerful when you are tall and good looking, or else short and good-looking (as long as you are not too short). But if you aren't good-looking *plus* you're short, results will be limited. Anyway, you don't need to be some jacked monster ready for the bodybuilding stage, but you need muscles and a level of body-fat low enough to see them. A low level of body fat will also bring out the definition in your face and make you better looking (hopefully).

Developing A Physique That Will Get You Pussy – With Drugs!

I hate to break this to you, but you can't achieve the body you want without drugs. It is impossible. I am not only going to prove this to you beyond all shadow of a doubt, but I will teach you everything you need to know about drugs to achieve your "body game" goals. I used to have a very successful YouTube channel on this topic, but jealous haters kept reporting me to YouTube so they shut the channel down. YouTube is filled with channels and "coaches" teaching steroid usage and most of them haven't a clue what they are talking about and just vomit up all kinds of nonsense to generate content and confuse people to the point that they feel the need to purchase coaching sessions from the same people who confused the hell out of them in the first place. I suspect it was some of these "coaches" who took down my channel, because every other honest steroid channel that actually taught you stuff was taken down, including all the amazing content from Tony Huge, whom I have hung out with in person. He's an amazing guy, and a perfect example of yet another good-looking, successful guy who spends all his time in Thailand because American women don't want anything to do with him. Why? Because he's a winner who can't be manipulated or controlled, while most women are complete loooosers. If you are a winner, *but* you *can* be manipulated or controlled, women will go for you because then they don't feel so shitty about themselves, plus they can use you to further their own goals.

Why It Is Impossible to Build the Body You Want Without Drugs

By the time a human male reaches the age of 21-25, he has all the muscle fibers his genetics will allow, and it is impossible to create more muscle fibers no matter how hard he trains or how heavy he lifts. Mind you, it is possible to increase the *size* of the fibers you have by saturating your body with creatine salts, which will pull water into your muscles and make you look like you put on 10-15 lbs of muscle, but it is just an illusion. You can also increase the size of your muscle fibers by loading them with glycogen from carbs, but this is not creating new muscle fibers. When you stop loading them with creatine, glycogen, or working out, you will lose all of your "gains."

The reason for this is that there is only *one* substance that can create new muscle fibers and that is IGF-1. By the time you are 21-25, your IGF-1 levels are too low to continue to create new muscle fibers. Sure, you can tear your current muscle fibers down in training and let them recover, but new ones will simply not be made. I know this is hard for many of you to accept and you will cry out, "But I want to do it naturally!" Well, you just can't. Sorry. When you see a guy in the gym with muscles that *honestly* has never used drugs, the truth is that he looked more or less that way before the age of 21. If he didn't, he is on drugs and lying about it. *End of story*. You won't realize this until you join the "dark side," but nearly 100% of people in the gym with good physiques are using drugs even if they are far from big. They are just lying about it – until you start using drugs yourself, because then they will see you have come over to the "dark side," and approach you and start talking to you about it, asking you what you are on, asking you for advice on their current cycles, etc. Steroid users recognize other steroid users and you cannot hide from us, just like a former drug addict always recognizes a fellow drug addict, and nerds always recognize other nerds even if one of them transforms into Mr. Cool Beans when he is older. He may fool the world, but he won't fool his fellow nerds!

So the whole key to building muscle is to increase the amount of IGF-1 in the body when you are training. In light of this truth, performance enhancing drugs (PEDs) that effect muscles can be classified into two categories, those that increase or amplify IGF-1, and those that don't. This is why some people lose all of their gains when they stop using steroids, while others keep them. Those that lost all of their gains were not using drugs that created new muscle fibers via IGF-1, while those that kept all of their gains did. Those who did a mix of drugs, lost only the gains from the drugs that had no relationship with IGF-1. Here is the complete list of drugs that increase IGF-1 or amplify the effects of it:

- **IGF-1 LR3** – Literally IGF-1 itself in the best form. Only recently has synthesis become possible, and this is often *all* that you need to start with. It is not a steroid, just a peptide, so you can still tell everyone you are natty. lol

- **Methandienone (oral)** – Forces the body to increase IGF-1 as it passes through the liver, which is why the injectable form is trash, since it doesn't make that "first pass" through the liver.

- **HGH** – Causes the body to increase IGF-1 levels which is why everyone abuses it. Obsolete these days since they can now synthesize IGF-1 LR3, and HGH has tons of side effects. Plus, it will not make you taller, just uglier. Again, not something for those trying to looksmaxx! Avoid.

- **Trenbolone** – enhances the sensitivity of IGF-1 receptors in the body. It does other things as well, and carries consequences for usage that IGF-1 LR3 and methandienone do not, so I will devote a few paragraphs to it in a moment.

That's it! Every other steroid is useless for creating new muscle fibers (which are permanent) and can only *temporarily* increase the size of your existing muscle fibers. There is no point using them if you are looking to create a physique to run "body game." *Some* examples are:

- **Nandrolone** – Protects joints when heavy lifting.

- **Oxymetholone** – Allows you to put on 30 lbs of temporary muscle fast by retaining water, increases strength. The only reason you should use this, is if you get a blood test and are found to be anemic, as a 6-week cycle @ 50mg / day will permanently cure your anemia and allow you to put on muscle assuming you have your IGF-1 levels on point.

- **Oxandrolone** – Originally created to increase the size of micro-penises in boys going through puberty. Later used to speed recovery in burn victims.

- **Stanozolol** – a popular steroid used while dieting. A complete waste of money.

Why You Are a Complete Loser If You Don't Use Drugs

You know what is really strange? Most women are a far cry from beautiful. As a matter of fact, if you could wave a magic wand and all make up would disappear overnight, you would wake up to a world of absolute horrors. So why don't all women get plastic surgery and become beautiful? After all, they line up for boob jobs and ass implants like homeless peeps at a soup kitchen so why don't they fix their fucking faces? Especially given that surgeons these days can make an ugly dog into a supermodel... There are examples of girls online, who were ugly as fuck, then the right surgeon made them look like a supermodel. Unfortunately for many of them, they kept getting surgeries and ended up looking like utter shit. This is because when you change your face, every time you look in the mirror, you continue to see your old self. All plastic surgeons are aware of this phenomenon. In the same manner, even if you put on 50 lbs of pure muscle you will always perceive yourself as skinny. It's called body dysmorphia, which is not a big deal if you didn't hate the old you. It's just a weird experience that can be safely ignored.

But I digress... my point is why the fuck don't all women get plastic surgery and enjoy an amazing life instead of wasting money on makeup and being insecure about their looks? It's for one simple reason: to get surgery is to truly *admit* that you are not beautiful and therefore *inferior*, and the female ego cannot handle such an admission.

In the same way, *so many men insist on being natty because their ego refuses to admit that they are inferior and need steroids.* It has nothing to do with "believing in hard work" because on steroids you will be working harder than ever. After all, steroids don't do anything if you just sit on your couch and goon. You will also hear nattys claim: "You are cheating yourself" which is the dumbest shit ever, because *what* is it that you are cheating yourself *out of*? Go ahead, I'll wait... Is it the journey and satisfaction of doing it naturally? Again, that is not possible. So what is it? They will even say that you "took the easy way out" which also makes no sense because again, on drugs you will be working even harder than if you were "natty." Just watch Dorian Yates training in his infamous "Blood and Guts" video. Does that look to you like the "easy way out?" Does it look like he is "cheating himself" out of something? The only thing he is cheating himself out of, is an easier path in life!

Again, it is just the ego's refusal to admit your utter inferiority. What's even scarier to most of these absolute losers, is that deep down they know that even if they were to use steroids, they would *still* look like crap. What would that say about them then? That they are *double* inferior? Totally, because their genetics are so incredibly terrible that steroids would expose this reality for the whole world to see. Better for people to just believe, "I'd look like Mr. Olympia too, if I took steroids." No, you wouldn't. Your genetics aren't good enough for that.

This is why people online obsess on getting Mike O'Hearn to admit he uses steroids. Does he use them? I have no idea and couldn't care less. But what I do know is that this dude is almost 60 years old and looks better than 99% of 20 year old males and is handsome as all fuck. But if they can just get him to admit he juices, then they can dismiss it all to drug use and won't have to feel so damn inferior compared to him. But the reality is that no matter if Mike O'Hearn uses them or not, he is still so genetically superior to 99% of the world population that it would not make much of a difference. He is simply better than you, end of story.

Conversely, a desire to maintain the illusion that they are inherently superior to you is why many retired bodybuilders *downplay* their own steroid usage. You will often find these cats shitting on the cycles of newer, younger bodybuilders, because they do not wish to be eclipsed by them, so they'd rather they didn't succeed.

The worst aspect of YouTube is the literal *army of unaccomplished failures* with nothing to offer except vitriol, gossip and finger-pointing. They start entire channels devoted to shitting all over people who have actually accomplished something in life, abusing thumbnails with titles like "It's Over" and "He's Done!" While it is true that in many cases the object of their obsession is, in fact, deserving of a bit of mockery, it is utterly deranged to make video-after-video attacking someone to the point that your whole channel becomes a virtual shrine to those you *claim* to hate. The truth is that you hate them because you are jealous of them, and are also furious that they are being rewarded for their fuckery.

"The lady doth protest too much, methinks."
— Queen Gertrude, Hamlet (Act III, Scene II).

There is another psychological factor here at play, which is that people internalize and project the "lessons" taught to them by their worthless parents onto others in adulthood. Let's take a look at the case of the "Liver King." The Liver King promoted something that was really healthy – the consumption of raw animal organs. The health benefits of such a practice are well documented. I myself ate raw meat for years and loved it. It gives you so much energy. But how to promote such a healthy, yet "avant garde" lifestyle to the masses? Well, you can use steroids to turn yourself into a superhero and then use your physique to promote the diet. Now it should be obvious to even a 98 IQ American that this guy was blasted to the gills on juice, but when people "officially" find out, they go ballistic as if they just found out Santa Claus doesn't exist – and these are grown-ass men. Because deep inside, they are just traumatized children. How pathetic!

Now the Liver King *could* have told people he used steroids, and given that his physique was so insane given the meager cycles he was running, he *could* have claimed the difference was his diet. To be honest, *very few people could attain his results on the cycles he was running*, so the diet *was probably a major factor.* After all, raw organs, raw meat, raw eggs and raw milk are the best sources of protein out there, and all old-school era bodybuilders ate raw liver like crazy. But, he didn't take this route, and instead chose to pretend he was natty. *Who cares?* Why do people get so angry over something like this, which has zero impact upon their lives?

It's because when they were kids, they told a lie and their parents *brutalized* them for it. Now, as walking man-children, they take on the role of their abusive parent and attack other grown-ass men and attempt to punish them in the same way they were punished as children. I know a lot of you human trash will say that parents *should* punish their children for lying, but if you had any brains you would know that when a child lies and the parent punishes them for it, said parent is actually setting the child up to fail at life. Why? Because the most successful people in the world do nothing but lie! The parents are in effect losers, who believe that they would have been winners if only the world didn't lie to them, or reward lying. So they take it out on their children, only to end up dooming their own children to fail, for the same reasons they themselves did.

Let's Talk Trenbolone!

Trenbolone is my favorite steroid and the greatest anabolic steroid of all time. I blasted it with little intermission over a period of a few years, often hitting dosages of 700mg of the acetate ester per week. I will explain what "ester" means shortly. Trenbolone is a veterinary steroid, meant for use in cattle. Some years ago, the meat industry was looking for a steroid that would make cattle as big as possible, on as little feed as possible, as fast as possible, in order to increase profit margins as much as possible. They found trenbolone, or more accurately, paid some chemist to develop it.

Trenbolone accomplishes the goals of cattle ranchers by increasing the efficiency at which an animal utilizes the feed it is given. Normally, an animal can only absorb a certain percentage of the nutrients in feed, but with trenbolone it absorbs 100% of the nutrients, thereby requiring less feed, saving money and increasing profit margins. It also makes cattle bigger, faster. Also saving money and increasing profit margins! It does this by sensitizing the IGF-1 receptors to increase the efficacy of current IGF-1 levels. It is for this reason that it is always recommended to use trenbolone with either methandienone or IGF-1 LR3, as trenbolone will potentiate the effects of the methandienone or the IGF-1 LR3 by sensitizing your IGF-1 receptors to the flood of IGF-1 that the methandienone or IGF-1 LR3 will induce.

When Trenbolone is given to cattle, it is also paired with an enormous amount of estrogen. Without a lot of estrogen to assist it, trenbolone is not as effective. *This* is why beef has so much estrogen in it. It is a by product of the usage of trenbolone. It is also for this reason, that trenbolone is ideally paired with a high dosage of testosterone, because a lot of that testosterone will be converted into estrogen, which trenbolone will use to make it's magic happen!

So the ideal way to use trenbolone would be:

- **Trenbolone**: 300mg per week (acetate ester is ideal).

- **Testosterone**: 300mg per week (propionate ester is ideal).

- **Methandienone**: 30-50mg per day, 1 hour before workout, *-or-* IGF-1 LR3: 30-50mcg post-workout.

However, I do not recommend one starts with a cycle like this, because there are long term consequences to such a cycle. The first is that you may not be able to restore your natural testosterone production. Normally, when you stop using gear, your body returns back to normal testosterone production. YOU DO NOT NEED POST CYCLE THERAPY (PCT)!!! PCT is actually the reason many people crash and get all fucked up when they come off cycle. There is absolutely no need for it. However, sometimes your body does not resume normal testosterone production. In that case, you will have to get on TRT or HRT.

Another issue is that trenbolone will make *permanent* changes to your metabolism. What I mean is, you will never be able to eat a lot of food again without getting fat because your body will be using food so efficiently, it won't need a lot of food ever again. Remember, that was the whole point to trenbolone in the first place! So forget this "eat big to get big" garbage because that only applies to bodybuilders who use a shit-ton of insulin, which is so dangerous only professional bodybuilders who earn a living at bodybuilding should consider its usage.

I'm sure you have heard stories that trenbolone makes people crazy, violent, or sex maniacs. This is complete garbage. What trenbolone does do, is it brings out who you are. I have done soooo much tren and never had an issue. I know people will say, "that's because your trenbolone was fake!" Well, if my trenbolone was fake, then how come over seven years I put on 80 lbs of permanent muscle that doesn't go away even if I stop training or eating? I guess that "fake" trenbolone was some pretty good fake shit, huh?

Furthermore, one time I gave a friend of mine some of my stash because he wanted to try it. Three weeks later, he gave back to me what was left over and said he couldn't handle the stuff. I asked him what happened, and he proceeded to inform me that he had nearly quit his job and dumped his girlfriend while on the stuff. I said, "Yeah but you hate your job and your girlfriend is a total cunt." The trenbolone was simply looking out for him. Remember, *the tren is your friend!* My point is, trenbolone shows you the truth about who you are and what you need to do. Stop blaming trenbolone for forcing you to take an honest look at yourself and your life and forcing you to take action.

Finally, let's talk about what an "ester" is. Injectable steroids like testosterone and trenbolone come in different esters which determine the rate at which what is injected, is released into the bloodstream. So pure testosterone in water (suspension) or in oil (base) hits the bloodstream instantly with 100% of what is injected going right into your bloodstream on the spot, whereas testosterone with an ester attached to it will hit the bloodstream over time at a steady rate (called a "half-life"). Here are all the esters of both testosterone and trenbolone, with the fastest-acting (shortest half-life) at the top and the slowest-acting (longest half-life) at the bottom. Keep in mind there are also blends of the different esters available, which I think are useless.

Testosterone Suspension (water based)	Methyltrienonlone Injectable (avoid the oral)
Testosterone Base (oil based)	Trenbolone Suspension (water based)
Testosterone Acetate (very rare)	Trenbolone Base (oil based)
Testosterone Propionate	Trenbolone Acetate
Testosterone Phenylpropionate	Trenbolone Hexahydrobenzylcarbonate (Parabolan)
Testosterone Cypionate	Trenbolone Enanthate
Testosterone Enanthate	
Testosterone Undeconate	

Now let's look at what these esters mean from a practical standpoint. It doesn't mean much if I say that the half-life of testosterone propionate is 3-5 days. Plus there is a huge difference between 3 and 5 days, which is usually dependent upon the body chemistry of the person injecting it. A half-life of 3-5 days means that after 3-5 days *half* the testosterone you injected has been released into the bloodstream. Well, let's look at what your blood levels of testosterone would be, on specific dosages and esters, in order to give you a concrete grasp of what "ester" means, bearing in mind that "natural" testosterone levels are inside of the range of 200-1200 ng/dL:

Testosterone Ester	Dosage	~ ng/dL
Cypionate (half-life: 7-10 days)	200mg 2x/week (400mg/week)	1800 ng/dL
Propionate (half-life: 3-5 days)	100mg 3x/week (300mg/week)	15,000 ng/dL
Suspension (half-life: N/A)	100mg/daily (700mg/week)	>50,000 ng/dL

Now you have a real grasp of what different esters can actually do. With a drug like trenbolone, the first time you use it, you should use the acetate form to see how your body reacts to it. If you happen to get side effects, then you won't have them for long due to the short half-life. If you get side effects, then the "base" form is probably best for you, because it will be out of your system before it can create problems. Base (as well as methyltrienolone) would need to be injected 15 minutes before a workout, whereas the versions that have an ester have no set injection time, relative to a workout.

Based on this, the ideal testosterone and trenbolone cycle would be 100mg of testosterone propionate and 100mg of trenbolone acetate, injected 3x per week, as these esters are readily available from most sources, while having the most impact due to the perpetual saturation of your body with these compounds at a high enough dosage, along with the greatest amount of estrogen produced which the trenbolone requires. For best results, stack with methandienone and/or IGF1 LR3.

A Series of Unfortunate Events Is Always Proceeded By...

You do remember what a friend of mine who chopped off his own hand and subsequently committed suicide, said to me between these two totally unnecessary events? It would behoove you to take heed of the wisdom he so painfully acquired. In that regard, *I totally discourage everyone reading this book from running trenbolone cycles.* There is NO REASON you can't put on 30 lbs of permanent muscle inside of one to two years by cycling methandienone against IGF-1 LR3. You can run 8 weeks of one, then 8 weeks of the other. Rinse and repeat. The whole time, add 1.5g-3g of choline and 1.5g-3g of inositol to one of you daily protein shakes and you will never have issues with liver toxicity from the methandienone. As a matter of fact, methandienone is the only steroid that makes everyone who takes it feel happy. If you use just these two compounds, that have zero side effects, you can achieve your goal of having a very attractive physical body as long as you don't overeat. Again, eating has nothing to do with getting big unless you are on a dangerously large amount of insulin, and the regular abuse of insulin totally qualifies as a series of completely unnecessary events which can lean to some very unfortunate ones!

But Isn't Diet the Most Important Aspect of Success?

This is 100% bullshit told to you by "fake nattys" and IFBB Pros, attempting to downplay their steroid usage. As long as you get enough protein to grow, enough carbs to get through your workout, and enough vitamins and minerals to stay healthy, that's all you need. You will create new muscle fibers while staying lean. If you are already fat, you need to eat less. A lot less. Every... fucking... day... the easiest way to accomplish this is to choose to drink zero or low calorie carbonated drinks that have lots of caffeine, *instead* of eating. Another way is to vape pure flavored nicotine when you want to stick food in your mouth, but not from those plastic vapes you get at the gas station or the "head shop." You need to purchase the high-quality flavored liquids that don't have any added chemicals other than nicotine and flavor, and load them into your own high-quality vape. Sadly, thanks to lobbying from the dying tobacco industry, the "good stuff" is harder to get! Some people use nicotine patches as well.

My current diet is basically one meal a day for dinner, which is either quality rice or quality pasta with three chicken thighs, lean beef marinated in red wine and vinegar to make it easier to chew, or two cans of sardines.

Mostly it is chicken thighs. The rest of the day I try to drink a lot of skim milk that is just protein, or eat some low-calorie cookies to keep me satiated. If it is a workout day, then after my workout I will throw 8 raw, extra-large, high-quality eggs into a blender with some Tillamook ice cream, which is the only "real" brand of ice cream I can find. I say "real" because all the other brands I see appear to have things in them I don't feel should be in there. If I find I need more food on a particular day, I just scramble six eggs.

The most critical aspect of your diet is to intake enough protein daily. The rest doesn't really matter as much, and can be adjusted on the fly. How much protein? Who can say for sure? In reality, you can get away with a lot less protein than you think, assuming you are consuming protein from whole eggs, or mixing proteins to make sure you get a complete amino acid profile. So with that in mind, let's say that 1g of protein per pound of body weight is more than adequate.

Once you have sufficient levels of IGF-1 coursing through your bloodstream, the most important aspect of your success is your training, which I will get to soon. Because while it is impossible to succeed *without* drugs, the reality is that once you have the *right amount* of drugs at the *right times*, it really comes down to how hard you work in the gym.

"But what about ketogenic diets?" a lot of you will cry out. I need to mention this here because ketogenic diets are possibly the stupidest fad to ever plague the fitness industry. Ketogenic diets are stupid because in order to put your body into ketosis, you have to literally starve your body of carbs, which is difficult and painful because your body absolutely hates you for it. The whole reason your body can burn ketones in place of carbohydrates *in the first place*, is because carbohydrates are so critical they require an emergency backup system, which is the ability to burn ketones for energy. So why are you fucking around trying to access your body's emergency carbohydrate back up system for? Your body wants carbs, not ketones, you dumb fucking piece of shit. Then you wonder why ketogenic diets are so difficult. Talk about having a low IQ. People are so crazy about ketogenic diets because deep down so many of them are psychic masochists and secretly desire suffering and failure as opposed to pleasure and success. Don't sabotage yourself like this!

How To Train to Develop Your Physique

Intensity is the most important thing in training. If you don't know what that looks like, check out the Dorian Yates "Blood and Guts" video which is available somewhere on YouTube.

Next, don't over train. Give your muscles plenty of time to recover. A body part should only be trained once every 7-10 days when you train intense enough. Some people will argue this and point to powerlifting programs where they train a body part twice per week, but that second session is using light weights to work on form, technique, speed, etc. so that second session does not actually interfere with the recovery process. Some bodybuilders do something similar, so that does not refute my assertion either. Still others will point to Olympic lifters who train a body part every single day, but they are forgetting that Olympic lifters are not training to get jacked, but to get strong. Strength is a product of the nervous system, and warrants totally different training methodologies, although it is impossible to train for either size or strength without having an impact on the other variable. Some may also point to convicts who train every day but they are doing calisthenics so that is not a refutation of my advice either.

The next issue is exercise selection. You need to pick free weight exercises or machines that actually target the muscle you want to target. If you get on *any* chest machine or do *any* chest exercise, and after your sets your chest *isn't* pumped and popping, then that machine or free weight exercise is *not* hitting your chest! Everyone has a different body in terms of limb lengths, etc. so you need to find what works for you. Dips are great for most people, while regular free weight bench presses actually work for very few. The Hammer Strength wide isolateral chest machine works amazing for me, but many other chest machines won't. Why is this? Because the angles are unnatural for my body. When you do a pushup, which is a natural movement, you are actually "benching" at a slight decline. Same when you do dips, or in my case when I use the Hammer Strength wide isolateral chest machine. This is a natural angle. This is also why powerlifters slightly arch their backs when benching – to make the movement more natural. However, there are guys out there who will find that machines I find "unnatural" will work for them, as will free weight benching without needing to arch their backs. The same phenomenon applies to training your quadriceps. Most machines and exercises are working everything *but* the quads on so many people! Be mindful! Picking the right free weight exercises and machines is soooo important!

This issue is most noticeable when training the chest and quadriceps, but applies to a lesser degree to other body parts as well. Since time is so precious and you shouldn't be spending so much of it at the gym, you don't need to focus on that many exercises. If you do chin ups as opposed to pull ups, you won't need to train your biceps directly. Same if you do dips or the right chest exercises – you won't need to train triceps. When it comes to your shoulders, the *only* direct shoulder exercises you need are those that work the rear deltoids, because the rear delts are what create the illusion of "boulder shoulders" and "shoulder width." No matter how big your side and front delts are (and they will be automatically when you train chest correctly), you will never have good "delts" unless you work the rear delts.

So for the upper body:

- Weighted dips or other effective chest movements.

- Weighted chin ups.

- Effective rear delt movements.

When it comes to your back musculature, the practical reality that is all back movements are identical, only the range of motion is different. A seated row for example, is just a pull up with a shortened, very specific range of motion. Don't waste your precious time!

When it comes to training the lower body, you ideally want to pick exercises that also develop flexibility, with the goal of being able to do front and side splits so as to maximize blood flow to the penis. These are impossible if your psoas and hip flexors are locked up. This is why all lower body programs should incorporate the Polliquin split squat which is also called the ATG split squat. Additionally, I would pick one other leg exercise that would be done on a different day, that targets the quadriceps in a tangible way. Most squat and leg press movements are not hitting the quads for most people, so you will need to look outside the box, but the greater the selection of leg machines at your gym, the better off you usually are.

The posterior chain is best developed with nordic curls, and the Louie Simmons reverse hyperextension machine. Avoid deadlifts at all costs. They offer very little return in terms of reward, yet promise a very high risk of injury. Once your spine is fucked, you are fucked – and not in the way you would like to be.

Any other exercises you do should be those that assist you in generating power when you want to hurt someone. Russian wrestlers and boxers know plenty of such exercises, and athletes who train the shot put as well as the discus and hammer throw produce the highest levels of such power. Model your supplemental training on theirs.

The next question is how many sets and reps do you do? Traditionally speaking...

- If you are doing an exercise where you are able to safely "go heavy," then the 5 x 5 system is ideal. You select a weight where you can only do 5 reps, and do 5 sets. Usually by the time you get to the 4th or 5th set you can't do 5 reps. When the day comes that you can, raise the weight.

- If you are doing an exercise where it is not safe to go heavy, such as chest or biceps (most tears and career-ending injuries happen here), then you use the 4 x 10-12 system. Once you can do 4 sets of 12 reps of a certain weight, raise the weight until you can only do 4 sets of 10 reps.

However, there is also the very valid school of thought that you only need 1 or 2 sets of any particular exercise, and that doing 4 or 5 sets is only necessary if you cannot generate the necessary intensity in 1 or 2 sets. This may be because you are trying to avoid injury. If you can generate the necessary intensity without injury, you should use only 1 or 2 sets because then your nervous system will never burn out from the volume.

- Pick a weight where you can do a high rep range and really push yourself to the point of failure and beyond to get those extra reps in. You can do forced reps, rest-pause, etc. to pull this off.

- Another way to do this is by "drop setting" which is where you load a machine with a weight where you can do maybe 8 reps, and then when you reach failure, strip off some of the weight and keep going, until there is no more weight left on the bar. The beauty of this method is that the volume is not taxing to the nervous system, and you will hit a point of failure to push beyond multiple times along the way, triggering maximum muscle growth. In essence, that one set is in actuality several sets, compressed into one working set in a way that will *not* exhaust your nervous system.

That's all you need to know to build your body. Of course, it you love mountain biking or swimming or whatever, then continue to do those things as well.

Combat Sports

Red pill dating gurus like to push combat sports as a way to raise your sexual market value, and combat sports are growing in popularity. Should you take up a combat sport? No. Should you learn to fight? Yes. The two are *not* the same thing.

Combatives instructor Tim Larkin likes to say that there is a difference between social and asocial violence:

- Social violence can be defined as violence that has domination as the goal, and is accompanied by a rule-set that is either explicitly or else implicity understood. MMA, boxing and BJJ matches are perfect examples.

- Asocial violence can be define as violence that has death or physical destruction (injury, maiming, mutilation) as the goal, and is not accompanied by a rule-set. Criminal predation and assassinations are perfect examples of this.

This is an extremely important distinction because MMA aficionados love to say that their sport fighting skillset makes them "hard to kill" when in reality it makes them easier to kill, because it gives them a distorted view of their own physical vulnerability. Mind you, their sport fighting skillset *does* make them harder to beat up, bully or dominate, but certainly not "hard to kill" because all humans are *extremely easy to kill*. This is because human bodies are not made for combat like a ferret, mongoose, or mink's body is.

Furthermore, in asocially violent situations, one is always attacked by someone with a gun/knife, by a group of people, or by someone who far outclasses you physically - and *one is always attacked by surprise*. This is how all predators operate because no predator will pick a target they believe they will fail to dominate or destroy! This simple reality negates any and all "sport fighting" skills you may possess because you can't fight unarmed against a gun/knife, a group of people, someone with the size and skill set of Brock Lesnar, and *especially* not against any attacker you never saw coming.

So if you really want confidence, in the sense of the ability to protect yourself and the girl you are with, then you need to *specifically* study how to deal with asocial violence as opposed to learning how to dominate other males in a cage or a ring, which quite frankly is what slaves have been made to do since the beginning of time for the entertainment of their masters. You do realize that all gladiators were slaves and that their skills were useless against a handful of legionnaires who operated as one unit? You also realize that gladiators were regularly fucked in the butt by patricians? How can you be an alpha male when you are operating from the mindset of an anal sex slave who fights other anal sex slaves for the entertainment of others?

While there are awesome instructors out there who teach what is dubbed "self-protection" such as WR Mann, Sammy Franco, and Lee Morrison, to name just a few, the most important thing to learn is *how* asocial predators operate, followed by knowledge of the law in your jurisdiction. This can be mastered if one spends a little time each day on YouTube watching the right videos. This is soooo important because you could be legally concealed carrying, but if you don't know you are about to be attacked, or operate in the world oblivious as to how asocially violent attacks occur, you will never get your gun out in time to make a difference. If you don't understand the critical importance of things like time and distance you are likewise cooked. As a matter of fact, if all that you learn is *strategic awareness* and all you practice is *avoidance*, you will probably never find yourself in a situation where you will have to engage in violence of any sort. Which is a good thing because prosecutors today are a woke bunch, and even if you win a criminal case or the prosecutor drops/declines prosecution, you can and will still be sued in civil court. The rule of "double jeopardy" that says you cannot be tried for the same crime twice, doesn't count here because the scumbags who authored our system of injustice will say that civil court is not criminal court. How insane! So I can be exonerated for "murder" in a criminal court, but then be tried for "wrongful death" in a civil court with respect to the *same event*? HOW is this not being tried TWICE for the SAME CRIME??? Because "wrongful death" is not "classified" as a crime? This is beyond absurd. But as I keep pointing out over-and-over, our planet's governmental systems are utterly Satanic, and making a mockery of justice is one of the governmental systems' goals.

Pro Tip: I was once called for jury duty, and was "auditioned" to be a juror on a case I will not give details on because I don't want to get in trouble, but the lawsuit was so preposterous that I cannot understand why a judge would even agree to listen to such garbage and not simply dismiss the case from the jump. Well, it's because most judges are part of the Satanic legal system, which has the goal of mocking justice, since justice it is so very important to The Divine Father. Well, I got shuttled into a room where they were selecting jurors for this travesty of justice. When they asked if anyone had any questions about the case, I raised my hand. When prompted, I asked: "See that beautiful girl sitting over there? If I ask her out and she rejects me, can I sue her for emotional distress with *unlimited* financial damages?" Everyone started laughing, so everyone got dismissed and excused from service early. Years later, some guy at a gym I was lifting in came over and said he was one of the jurors in the room that day, and how awesome my question was. He said that everyone was thinking the exact same thing, just unable to verbalize it, or too scared to say anything. This is why *they* don't want you on tren! They don't want you unafraid to stand up to their bullshit. If you ask me, suing people or defending a lawsuit should not require lawyers nor cost anything – in other words, the entire system should operate like small claims court, but with the judge having to justify their decisions based in law, and with a panel of higher level judges reviewing all of their decisions. Because the way the system works now, is that the person who has the most money, usually wins because the one who runs out of money first, loses - even if they are in the right, because they cannot afford the lawyers to keep on fighting. Most people therefore settle or let themselves get bullied and abused because they can't even afford to fight in the first place. There are endless plaintiffs and law firms with zero ethics that take advantage of the current system, which is of incredible detriment to the social and economic fabric of the nation. Plus, the idea of leaving your fate up to a jury with an average IQ of 98 that has been picked so as to stack the odds in favor of one side or another is a total perversion of justice. When you watch lawyers engage in jury selection, they haggle and trade jurors like baseball cards as each side attempts to stack things in their favor. Of course you don't want jurors with an overt bias, but lawyers take things to the extreme and make a mockery of justice. At the very minimum, the lawyers on both sides are in agreement to look for the dumbest jurors possible, so as to have the maximum chance to influence them in one direction or another.

The next order of business after learning how criminals operate and how our corrupted legal system operates, would be learning how to use both a gun and a knife, and to always be armed with one or both when you go out into the world. This is because knives and guns are the only way to survive an asocially violent scenario against predators who are armed with knives and guns themselves, or else outnumber you, or physically outclass you. A 130 lb female can have a black belt in BJJ for example, and will not be able to do anything against a violent rapist who is over 200 lbs. But if she carries a blade (or two) and has the will to use them, she is a force to be reckoned with even if she has no skills with said blades. If you disagree, just shut the fuck up. You don't know what you are talking about. There are loads of men in prison who thought they could handle themselves due to their study of "martial arts," getting raped on a daily basis. One of my friends who did over 10 years in a maximum security state prison once laughed and said to me when I visited him, "Anyone who thinks their MMA shit will help them in here, is in for a shock."

Speaking of learning to shoot a handgun... It is easier than you think to shoot effectively, but most people go about it the wrong way. The best handgun shooters in the world, with respect to *actual* gunfights, are a select group of police in South Africa, who are involved in more gun fights with criminals than anyone else on the planet. They all shoot one-handed, which flies in the face of all this two-handed garbage that is taught everywhere. Another stupid trend is the usage of "red dot" sights on pistols and that sort of thing. A green laser on the underside of your pistol, that is activated by the pressure of your grip, is the fastest way to acquire a target because it allows you to be "target focused" at all times and to cultivate invaluable "point shooting" skills as opposed to being "sight focused." Every instructor out there will always yell at their students to be "target focused," then yell at them to focus on the front sight, or even worse, on the red dot sight. You can't do both at once unless your weapon has either a stock or a "brace." As far as knives go, there are a few good knife instructors out there like WR Mann, Raymond Floro, James Keating, and Shivworks, to name a few.

The final order of business is learning to strike with as much power, precision and accuracy as possible, which can be learned from YouTube videos and spending a lot of time on a heavy bag or equivalent. Many scenarios can also be drilled from online learning. The purpose of in person training, is for complex scenarios where one has fucked up on the basics and now finds oneself with a knife held to one's throat, stuck in a headlock, or in a clinch/grappling scenario, etc. You need a live instructor in order to drill those scenarios effectively. Live training is also good for adrenaline innoculation and the like.

Another huge issue with taking up combat sports beside the fact that your time would be better spent making money, is the very high risk of debilitating injury. How many people have been seriously and permanently damaged "rolling" at a BJJ facility or participating in Judo? Countless. *If* one decides to take up such activities, *the only way to go is private lessons.* If you can't afford them, spend your time making money until you can. Because whenever you tangle with a stranger in a martial arts class, you always run the risk that said stranger has the hidden intent to cripple or seriously injure you under the guise of an "accident." Do not underestimate how many fucked up people are roaming about out there! Especially if you radiate success with women, etc., you will attract these envious, rotten losers chomping at the bit to ruin your life. There are also many people *without* bad intentions, who simply have zero kinesthetic sensibilities and are so "disembodied" (living in their head) that they will injure you out of sheer somatic incompetence and then waddle away innocently.

Combat sports injuries often require expensive surgeries and many of these injuries are irreparable. How can you defend yourself in a reality-based scenario when you got yourself crippled because you were "sport fighting?" Furthermore, most adults have lost the suppleness of youth, and engaging in combat sports – specifically those involving grappling, is about as foolish as some desk jockey taking up Olympic lifting at his local CrossFit facility.

This is probably a good time to mention that you should arrange to see a good chiropractor once per week to keep yourself in good running order. Unless you live in New York City, it isn't hard to find one who will charge around $50/session. A good chiropractor for me is *always* a big guy as they have to be tall and strong to adjust other big dudes like me without struggle. A good chiropractor will also know how to do fascia scraping and include it as part of his adjustment session, along with therapeutic ultrasound.

So while there is nothing inherently wrong with taking up combat sports if that is what floats your boat, you must stay cognizant of the fact that whatever is learned is really geared towards the goal of dominating other men using social violence, and has little application with respect to protecting oneself from asocially violent predators.

Supplements

Nutrition is the foundation of good health. Most people look at nutrition only in terms of protein, carbs and fats, along with how many calories you consume in a day, but this is very short-sighted. While those macros are important, what is being left out is the awareness of the importance of *bioavailable* vitamins and minerals.

Nobody ever talks about them because modern food is devoid of them, and this is the root of most health issues. As a matter of fact, most food in the supermarket isn't even real food. Don't believe me? Just read the ingredient labels!

Modern agriculture has ripped all the vitamins and minerals out of grains, out of fruits and out of vegetables... oranges have almost no vitamin C in them and taste like nothing. Vegetables, instead of being vitamin and mineral rich, are merely "roughage" to assist you in taking a shit. Grains used to actually have protein and serious vitamins in them, but now they have nothing.

The reality is that you have to supplement *everything* these days. Therefore, you will have to spend money on supplements and I am not talking about bullshit like preworkouts, creatine, etc. I mean plain old vitamins and minerals. The good news is that this stuff is actually pretty cheap.

They say that health is a form of wealth and that is certainly true. What people don't realize is just how easy it is to build and maintain that form of wealth. I am going to give you the simple keys to make sure that you never catch a cold or get the flu, and never get cancer or any other sort of disease.

Testosterone

Before I get into vitamins and minerals, I want to talk about supplementing with testosterone. As we discussed earlier in this book, the drinking water supply is hopelessly contaminated with Atrazine and a myriad of other estrogen mimicking chemicals. It is chemical warfare being waged against males, and you have to fight fire with fire, or *chemicals with chemicals*. I mean, you can't say that you are "natty" when you are drinking Atrazine-laced water now, can you? You also can't say that having a testosterone level in the range of 200-400 ng/dL is "natural" either...

In regards to this, you need to get your levels checked and see how low they actually are. If they are anything less than 800 ng/dL, the first thing to do is try and see if you can raise your testosterone levels naturally by taking DHEA which is available on Amazon. You want to take enough DHEA to get your blood levels of DHEA-S over 500 mcg/dL. 100mg of

DHEA daily should do the trick. Get your blood tested again after three months for both DHEA-S and testosterone.

Next, get a water filter pitcher that uses a nanometer-sized filter mesh that can filter out atrazine and other chemicals. If your test levels are still below 800 ng/dL, you'll need to check your free testosterone, and take whatever supplements you can to raise your free testosterone. Because you can have 500-600 ng/dL levels but with enough free testosterone, still be fine. However, if you are lower than 500 ng/dL and/or can't get your free testosterone levels high enough, no matter what you do naturally, then you'll need to start injecting 300mg of testosterone cypionate or enanthate weekly.

Magnesium

Magnesium is used in hundreds of reactions in the human body, and your heart pretty much runs on it. Despite being probably the most important mineral to human life, nearly everyone is close to being fatally deficient in it. Want to know why certain bottled water brands are so addictive? They contain magnesium, and once your body tastes it, it craves it. This is also why people crave chocolate, incidentally. Trouble is, *all* oral magnesium supplements are total shit and do nothing for the body - except for magnesium chloride, which is the ideal form. However, even with oral ingestion, you can *never* get your magnesium levels high enough without getting diarrhea, as you can only take in so much through your digestive system.

The solution is topical magnesium oil spray. Many brands suck, and cause the skin to itch and burn, or else leave powdered residue on your skin. I use the Venture Pal brand which comes in different scents while having none of the aforementioned issues, and is cheap as dirt! I do 20 sprays per arm, twice a day, for a total of 80 sprays. This is well over 1 gram of *elemental magnesium* per day and you will feel the difference immediately.

One must remember that 1 gram of magnesium chloride doesn't have much actual *elemental magnesium* and is mostly chloride. So you can see how impossible it would be to get over 1 gram of *elemental magnesium* into your body via oral administration.

Getting enough elemental magnesium is also the most important variable in avoiding high blood pressure.

Vitamin C

Vitamin C cannot be synthesized by the human body and must be consumed from external sources. Since most people do not realize just how much vitamin C is actually required by their bodies, the reality is that most human beings are suffering from subclinical scurvy. This is easy to prove. A goat, for example, is capable of synthesizing it's own Vitamin C. When under stress, it's body will synthesize 150 *grams* per day. Now how much vitamin C does a human supplement daily if they supplement it at all? 1 gram if they are lucky? Can you see the problem here? Your adrenal glands run on vitamin C, incidentally, so all this "adrenal fatigue" nonsense is really just vitamin C deficiency. The optimal dose of vitamin C for a human being is 3-5 grams per day. In the beginning one can actually take dosages that are many times that, but before you know it, your body will start to catch up and then the extra vitamin C comes out as diarrhea. Rather than mess around (literally), just take 4 grams a day over the course of the day, and after a few months you can drop it to 3 grams. Sodium ascorbate, which is a pH neutral form of vitamin C, is the best. Ascrobic acid is, well, acid. Not good in large doses when it comes time to urinate. Vitamin C, much like magnesium chloride, is also very inexpensive.

Iodine

Iodine is one of the biggest conspiracies in all of nutrition. You are told it is poison, but so is water if you consume enough of it. Both iodine compounds (iodate) and bromine compounds (bromate) are used as **"dough conditioners."** This is because both potassium iodate and potassium bromate are oxidizing agents that help develop gluten by forming disulfide bridges between protein molecules, creating stronger, more elastic dough. Potassium bromate was first used in the 1960s to replace potassium iodate because bakers claimed it provides more dependable results and makes the dough more elastic, which is easier to use for commercial baking. The switch from iodate to bromate apparently started in the late 1940s, but really picked up steam in the 1960s, and iodine was phased out by the 1980s. However, potassium bromate is an endocrine disrupter that interferes with the thyroid's ability to produce and use iodine, and is believed to play a role in various cancers. It's currently banned in Europe, Canada, Brazil, and China. It remains legal in the United States, though many bakers have voluntarily stopped using it.

Bromides and other halogen class metals go into the receptors in your thyroid that iodine normally goes into, and then your thyroid begins to malfunction. These days no doctor seems to be able to figure out the cause of the thyroid epidemic. It's lack of iodine. There was even a movement in congress in the early part of the 20th century to fortify milk with iodine to combat cancer, but it never came to fruition and the evidence of this appears to have been scrubbed from the Internet in recent years. In the 1950s the Hoxsey Clinic in Texas claimed to cure cancer left-and-right with potassium iodide, but the federal government persecuted them and so they fled into Mexico, where they still operate to this very day, still curing people of cancer left-and-right. I know this because I have visited this clinic and met quite a few of their patients in person whose cancers went into remission, and I have three friends who were cured of terminal cancer because of that clinic. Of course, the oncologists of these three friends back home simply declared that they never had cancer to begin with, and that the initial tests were all mistaken – as we *all know* there is no cure for cancer, *right*? This is the world we live in... Did you know that Japan, which has the highest consumption of iodine in the world due to their heavy consumption of specific strains of seaweed, has breast cancer rates 2-3 times lower than the west and prostate cancer rates 10-20 times lower as well? I am sure Fukushima will change that, and statistics already seem to be confirming this. This is because there is not much that can be done against cancer that is caused by radiation, chemical exposure or smoking cigarettes. If you get that sort of cancer, just fly to Thailand or Brazil and fuck yourself to death.

Pro Tip: I personally would avoid chemotherapy or radiation treatments for any sort of cancer. Chemotherapy utilizes nitrogen mustards, which were derived from the chemical warfare agent sulfur mustard (mustard gas), used in World War I. After the war, researchers discovered that nitrogen mustards could damage rapidly dividing cells, leading to their development as some of the first chemotherapy drugs in the 1940s. *As if* taking mustard agents and hoping the cancer cells die before you do wasn't a stupid enough idea, chemotherapy is often followed by radiation treatments. The medical industry will say that statistically speaking ~99% of women with breast cancer survive these treatments. Yet I know of three personally who did not. These anecdotal numbers do not match up in terms of probabilities with the official statistics, so I would fly a major red flag here. Just before they died, these three woman *all* told me how much they regretted giving into fear and not exploring other treatment options, and how much better off they would have been avoiding the suffering of battling the cancer with chemotherapy and radiation and taking a holistic route.

I view chemotherapy and radiation treatments as you paying money to suffer and die, when the medical industry has known for the last century that most cancers can be prevented with enough intake of potassium iodide every day. But isn't salt iodized? It isn't enough. Just enough to prevent fucking goiters which would draw attention to the real problem.

The reason you get a goiter is because your thyroid gland is increasing its physical size in a desperate attempt to "catch" more iodine in your bloodstream. The elites are trying to murder you. They hate you. Haven't you learned anything from the Covid-19 scamdemic? When are you going to understand this? I remember when my mom, who had Alzheimer's and didn't even know how to use a toilet anymore, got cancer (I saw the "black tar" she was shitting on the living room rug and knew immediately she had cancer) and the doctors tried to pressure me into signing her up for chemotherapy and radiation. They told me I was a terrible son for not using my medical power of attorney to torture her, so I reminded them that she is like 76 years old, has advanced Alzheimer's and weighs in at 90 lbs at 5'4" so *what the actual fuck* is wrong with *them*? I am a terrible son because I don't want to torture her to death? She had colon cancer that had already spread to her liver so she was already dead, and barely lasted another 2 months anyway. Why torture her on the way out when she can just float out on a morphine IV? Again, the medical system is utterly Satanic, and makes a mockery of health by making sure people get sick, then torturing them to death and making them pay for their own torture!

Losing your hair? One of the reasons is iodine deficiency, because a malfunctioning thyroid causes hair loss. Did you know that your testicles use iodine to make testosterone? So iodine supplementation is another thing to try along with DHEA before you jump on testosterone injections.

If you buy some Lugol's iodine and paint it on your inner forearm, it should stay there for at least 12 hours if you are *not* deficient. In most people, their body sucks it all up within 2 hours. Not good! If you ingest enough iodine, you won't get cancer or sick in general, just as if you take enough vitamin C, you won't catch colds or the flu. You can buy 25mg and 50mg tablets of Lugol's iodine online. I take 50mg per day. Some will take as much as 100mg per day, but I think 50mg is fine. However, eventually you will hit iodine saturation and need to drop the daily dose to around

12.5mg. You will know when this happens if you get regular blood work and one day your "free T3" levels drop to almost nothing. This is because your body makes thyroid hormones from the iodine and doesn't want to over produce them. I like the LugoTab brand. Lugol's is a blend of elemental iodine and potassium iodide. You can also supplement with super-saturated potassium iodide solution (SSKI) and with SSKI you can take much higher dosages than you can with Lugol's, based on my personal experience. If you use just regular KI then 65mg is a good daily dosage until you achieve saturation. Running high-dose SSKI with the dose spread out over the day is for battling cancer and the like, not general health and well-being.

If you purchase Lugol's in tablet form it is expensive, but KI in tablet form is cheap as it is normally sold for protection during radiation disasters. It protects your thyroid from radiation because the iodine occupies the receptor sites that radiation would otherwise slip into, much as bromide does from baked goods, along with other halogens. The liquid forms of either are the cheapest option. SSKI only comes in liquid form. Don't take your iodine at the same time you take your vitamin C as it decreases the effectiveness of the iodine.

Pygeum and Your Prostate

If you are supplementing with iodine, then the only *other* thing you need to take for your prostate is a high-dosage pygeum extract. BTW, a lot of men don't realize that if they have to pee frequently or get up at night to piss, it is usually *not* the fault of the prostate, but rather an issue with adhesions and/or pelvic tension in the bladder and pelvis. For this, work on developing your front and side splits. If one actually does have a prostate problem, however, such as it is getting enlarged or inflamed or anything like that, the easiest way to fix it is to get a TENS unit on Amazon with different "programs," that look like MP3 players. Then, buy a bipolar butt plug on Amazon. Total cost for the setup is around $50. The plugs are usually sold for digital kegel exercisers, but running one with an actual TENS unit will shrink any prostate down to nothing, squeeze out the toxins, etc. and this is actually one solution for getting rid of premature ejaculation as well and lasting as long as you want to. I will cover this more later, but thought it appropriate to mention it here now as well. If you take care of your prostate physically, you don't have to worry about nonsense PSA numbers that just trick men into entering the medical machinery and getting their genitals mutilated in the process by doctors who are both evil and stupid.

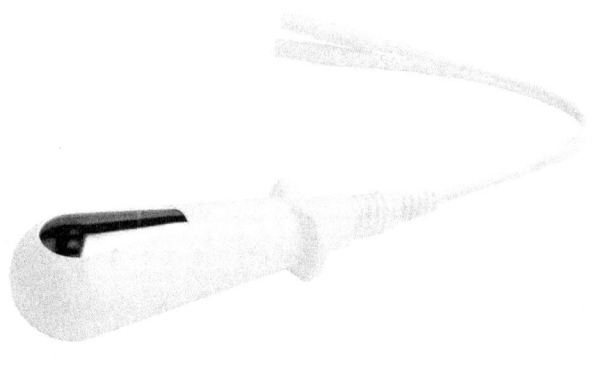

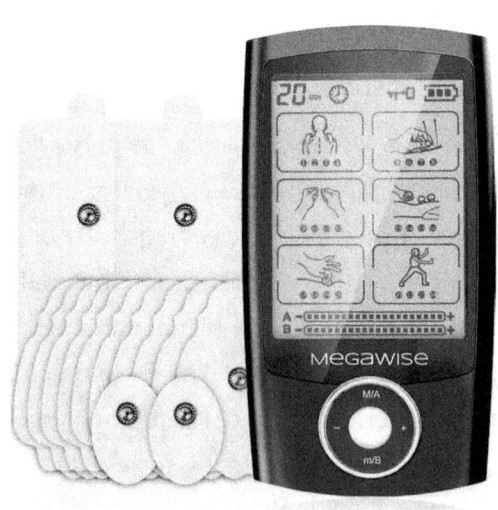

D3+K2

Even the government has raised the RDA for vitamin D3, it is *that* important. The ideal dosage is 10,000 iu per day and make sure you have some K2 in the formulation as well. Again, dirt cheap! Why 10,000 iu per day? Because that is a dose that will keep your D3 blood levels at the upper limit without creating any problems. There are books out there promoting mega-dosing D3, but unless you are getting extensive blood work to monitor several other variables, you could find yourself in trouble such as suppressing your parathyroid gland and watching your hair fall out, or stripping calcium out of your teeth and watching them rot at an accelerated speed. NOTE: in the summer when you are spending a lot of time in the sun or tanning, stop the D3 supplementation as it is totally unnecessary.

B Vitamins

So many sneer at them B's, but they are critical and since they are not fat-soluble you need to take them daily, since the body can't store them up. The key is to always buy each B vitamin separately because all B-complexes are insanely underdosed and formulated with the least bioavailable forms of B vitamins. When you buy each B vitamin separately, you can get a high dose of each and pick the most bioavailable forms. There are a lot of B vitamins to buy, but they aren't expensive and many can be purchased in powder form.

Stress and Blood Pressure

Modern day life is insanely stressful which is why you need vitamin C and elemental magnesium to counteract the stress, and also to lower you blood pressure. Cloves also work very well because they contain eugenol. Chew two at a time and suck on the juice. Betaine nitrate will give you plenty of nitrates that your body will convert into nitrites, assuming you stop using mouthwash that kills the good bacteria in your mouth responsible for the bulk of the conversion process. ATP is another amazing vasodilator. But an incredible way to lower your blood pressure and shoot stress in the head is with an inexpensive vagus nerve stimulator sold on Amazon for $90. I use this one and it works like magic:

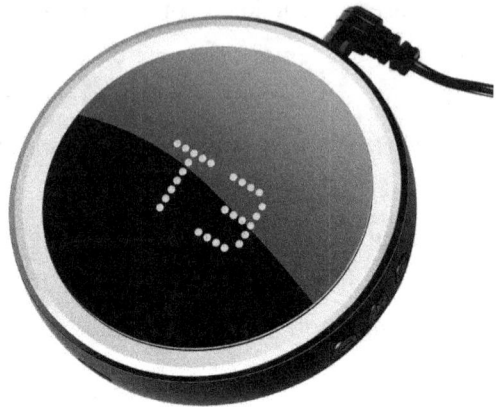

This device forces your nervous system to drop into parasympathetic mode inside of 20 minutes, quickly dropping blood pressure and dissolving stress.

On The Correlation Between Smoking and Lung Cancer...

In 2023, Princeton's Science and Global Security program released research showing "in unprecedented detail the spread of radioactive fallout from *94 continental U.S. atmospheric nuclear weapon tests*, including the first nuclear weapon test - the July 16th 1945 Trinity explosion." **Prior to this 2023 study, the US government promoted the false narrative that nuclear testing caused only limited, localized harm — when in fact the very first test *alone* contaminated nearly the entire continental United States.** The Princeton nuclear fallout study was released on **July 20-21, 2023**, at a time when Ukraine-related nuclear threats were dominating headlines. The Russian war in Ukraine was generating massive media coverage, with news organizations focusing heavily on "Russia's nuclear threat signals throughout the war" as "one of the dominant topics in international news coverage." The Bulletin of the Atomic Scientists had even moved the Doomsday Clock to 90 seconds to midnight in January 2023, citing "increasing risk of nuclear escalation stemming from Russia's invasion of Ukraine."

What makes this particularly significant, is that while the world was focused on potential future nuclear threats from Russia, this groundbreaking study revealed the previously unknown extent of **actual nuclear contamination** that had already affected 46 U.S. states, Canada, and Mexico from decades-old American tests. This was a perfect time to release such information, because nobody would then take notice of the fact that the actual levels of contamination in the United States alone were catastrophic in terms of the contamination of the ecosystem and the food supply, which explains the widespread problem of heavy metals in the food supply, as well as the *skyrocketing* rates in lung cancer: there was a ***600% increase in lung cancer mortality rates in women since 1950, along with a 250% increase in lung cancer mortality rates in men since 1950.*** The reason the rate in women is nearly 3x that of men, can be attributed to the increase in the number of women who started taking up the habit of smoking. But why would smoking suddenly become so carcinogenic?

Tobacco's Unique Affinity for Polonium-210:

- In particular, polonium-210 attaches to, and concentrates in, tobacco leaves. *Elevated concentrations of polonium-210 in tobacco were documented as early as 1964.*

- As the plant grows, the radon from fertilizer, along with naturally-occurring radon decay products in surrounding soil and rocks, cling to the sticky hairs on the bottom of tobacco leaves, called trichomes. Rain does not wash them away.

Sources of Polonium-210 in Tobacco:

- **Nuclear Fallout**

  - Scientists from the University of California, Los Angeles, reviewed 27 previously unanalyzed documents and found that tobacco companies knew about the radioactive content of cigarettes as early as 1959. The companies studied the polonium-210 problem throughout the 1960s, and knew that it caused "cancerous growths" in the lungs of smokers.

- **High-Phosphate Fertilizers**

  - The majority of the polonium-210 in tobacco plants likely comes from high-phosphate fertilizers applied to the tobacco crop. Tobacco farmers in developed countries primarily use manufactured fertilizer high in phosphates produced from apatite rock that contains radium-226 and descendant radioisotopes such as lead-210 and polonium-210. ***High-concentration phosphate fertilizers** became widespread in the 1950s-1960s - precisely during the atmospheric nuclear testing period.* The **1960s shift to "higher analysis fertilizers"** means tobacco crops were receiving much higher doses of phosphate-derived polonium-210 *at the exact same time* that nuclear fallout was contaminating the atmosphere.

This connection suggests that the lung cancer epidemic during 1950-1970 was likely a **synergistic effect** of:

- **Increased tobacco consumption** during and after WWII.

- **Nuclear fallout contamination** from atmospheric testing (1945-1963) settling on tobacco crops.

- **High-phosphate fertilizers** increasing baseline polonium-210 levels.

- **Industry knowledge and deliberate concealment** of the radioactive contamination.

The timing is remarkable: Over time the number and size (or yield) of these weapons increased, especially in the late 1950s and early 1960s - precisely when lung cancer rates exploded. It wasn't just smoking behavior, but radioactively contaminated tobacco from nuclear fallout that "supercharged" the carcinogenic impact of cigarettes during the atmospheric testing era.

All About Penis Size

If one goes online, one can find statistical calculators that will show you what the probabilities of encountering a penis of a certain size is. Most penises are between 5" and 6" in length. The statistical curve of penis sizes mirrors the statistical curve of vaginal depths, although there are clearly very few studies on vaginal depth, as the gathering of penis size statistics is fueled by condom companies who need to figure out what condom sizes they should be manufacturing. However, if one sleeps with enough women and has a penis that is long enough, one will quickly find that most vaginas aren't very deep at all and that it is pretty easy to hit the bottom of the pussy (posterior and anterior fronix) in *most* positions, with most women. Actually, you'd be shocked just how many women have really shallow pussies. Contrary to what the idiot medical community likes to parrot, a pussy can *not* stretch to accommodate any length penis. There is a limit to it's expansion when a female is excited.

From the man's perspective, the main thing is to be long enough that you can easily hit the bottom of most women's pussies in all the major positions. If you can do that, you are long enough and there is *zero* advantage to being longer. It is true that there will be some women where you will not be long enough, but… if you are long enough for that minority, you will be too long for the majority and this can be an issue. The number of women who need an 8" cock to "bottom them out" is like 2% of the population, so you will be better of being a perfect fit for the other 98% of women out there. If you do want to be longer, one can always hang weights from you penis a few minutes per day. Zenhanger.com has the easiest and most comfortable hanging gear out there, IMO. I personally prefer penis pumping, which I will cover shortly.

Pro Tip: "Doggy style" allows you to go deepest in terms of penetration, and so will putting a pillow or wedge under her hips in "missionary." Brazilian "sex chairs" also allow for deeper penetration with ease, but they are hard to obtain outside of Brazil. Finally, you always want to have sex with women who can do splits, and/or are very flexible. The closer their skills are to that of a contortionist, the better. Girls who are inflexible in their pelvic region are an absolute sexual nightmare. You will need extra length just to penetrate them deep enough and some women are so locked up biomechanically that you can't even enter them easily in the doggy position. Don't even bother with these somatic disasters. If you are interested in some girl sexually, ask her if she can do splits or if she is good at yoga since most bitches have taken yoga classes like the lemmings they are. So that you don't come across as a weirdo, talk about how one of your fitness goals is to do the splits or that one time you took a yoga class, blah, blah, blah. It is easy to tell if a girl is flexible by looking at her posture when standing or walking – especially at the beach or by the pool. The "holy grail" is if you see what are called "squirter dimples" or "dimples of venus" that look like this:

The more flexible a girl is, the easier sex with her is going to be.

But what about girth? It is true that girth is more important to a woman because women like to feel that they are filled up. When a woman talks about a "perfect fit," it is the girth that is the determining factor. If you have a 6" girth, for example, you will have the most impact on a woman across any given penile length. With that being said, the caveat is that there are lots of women out there, where nothing can fill them up. This is due to a combination of hormonal problems, along with the constant abuse of over-sized sex toys when they masturbate. It has gotten so ridiculous, that all of these guys are getting silicone filler in their penis to attain girths of 7"+! This is a stupid and irreversible procedure that can cause issues down the line, and for what? If a girl needs girth like that, it is her own fault and it is not your job to make up for her poor lifestyle choices. There are even new procedures out there now where she can put filler in her own pussy to make it tighter so she should take responsibility for her shortcomings (pun intended), not you! Trust me, there are plenty of women who have tight pussies that can be completely packed out with a 6" girth. Also, if you put fillers in your cock, you can have issues if you ever decide or need to do penile injections of Trimix or Quadmix.

So remember, if you can hit the bottom of her pussy and fill her up, you are big enough. Stop watching porn where every guy claims to be 2-3" longer than he actually is anyway. They even scale up the dildos modeled on porn star cocks to maintain their false size claims. Just more evidence that the purpose of porn is to emasculate you as a man.

Pro Tip: *Women love to weaponize penis size and use it against men* because it is such a devastating weapon to cut down a man's sense of self-worth. They also use it to cover up their own frigidity. I have found that women who constantly talk about penis size are almost always incapable of attaining a vaginal orgasm. So if a woman keeps talking dick size, just flat out ask her if she is capable of attaining a vaginal orgasm. That should put a stop to her nonsense which is a shit-test at best, and downright abuse at worst. I've said this to several women and it stopped them in their tracks and they subsequently admitted they could not attain a vaginal orgasm. Also, if a woman volunteers such stupidity as "I need at least nine inches" (a common quip) just respond with a deadpan: "sounds like a personal problem." What women also fail to realize, is that seeking out the biggest dicks they can find to get pounded out with, is disastrous for the health of their pussy. My father had a 9" dick and my mother suffered multiple vaginal prolapses and eventually the surgeons couldn't put her little humpty dumpty back together again so no more vaginal sex for her! I also remember being at a sex club and meeting this 21 year old girl. I started making out with her and put my hands down her pants to initiate sex. When I tried to slide my fingers into her sopping wet pussy I felt her cervix sticking it's head out of the mouth of her pussy like a crowning baby. She was all embarrassed, as she should be. What the fuck are you doing in a sex club when your pussy is closed due to a cave in? I would have fucked her ass, but she was turned off by my discovery of her "secret." When I got home I looked up her profile on a fetish website, and in her profile she stated that her main fetish was being "power fucked" by dicks 9" and bigger. Well that explained that! She would have loved my pops! Well ladies, this is the consequence of your idiotic fetishes. Maybe she should have worked on resolving her frigidity rather than hate-fucking her icebox until it turned itself inside out in protest?

How To Enlarge Your Penis

Medical morons will say you cannot enlarge your penis unless you cut the suspensory ligament or inject silicone fillers into the shaft. Both are pages taken from the "Big Book of Very Bad Ideas." You can enlarge your penis over time, but it takes a very long time. Because of this, and because so many men injure their penises doing enlargement practices, you want to look at any penis enlargement routine more like doing cardio and forget about gains, just let yourself be surprised over time. In this way, you won't be tempted to do stupid shit and get injured. With that being said, the best pump you can get off the shelf is the one sold by Zen Hanger. There is a content creator who goes by the handle of "Hink" on YouTube who wears a Mexican wrestling mask to conceal his identity, claims to be a medical doctor, and makes videos on penile enlargement based on legit medical research. According to one of the studies he cites, the ideal daily pumping routine is 5 minutes at a negative pressure of -25 kPa, taking a 2 minute break, then doing another 5 minutes at a negative pressure of -25 kPa. This is based on extensive scientific testing for ideal negative pressure levels, times spent under said negative pressure levels, and the number of working sets and rest periods. I find it works well for me, and I enjoy his content. Getting periodic platelet-rich plasma injections (PRP shots) will accelerate your progress. I also wrap my pump in a red-light therapy pad which supercharges both my results and my recovery so I can pump daily. It also keeps my skin and tissues soft and healthy, which can suffer potential discoloration from pumping.

Drugs For Sexual Performance

As a man, sexual performance is everything. It is the primary value that a man can give to a woman. The first thing you have to keep in mind is that what you see in porn is not reality. Besides, the truth is that anyone can be a porn star these days, as all you need to do is take the same drugs that porn stars take. Back in the 1970s and the 1980s, you really had to be a stud to be a porn star, which is why there were so few male porn stars. It is not easy to get hard in front of cameras and a crew, and to keep your erection for long periods of time while they shoot stills, change positions, etc. These days it is easy thanks to drugs, so you see tons of male "talent" around. With that being said, *there are 3 drugs to get your hard and keep you hard*:

PDE-5 Inhibitors

Tadalafil is the best option. The key with buying these drugs is to realize that most of the brands are shit, including the big name pharmacy brands. The best bet is to go to a website with lots of different generic brands and try them all until you find the one that gives the best results. For example, there are some brands of Tadalafil from India that give you no headache, no stuffy nose, and incredible erections. But most brands have side effects including the ones from major U.S. pharma brands. All of this stuff is made in India anyway, so find the manufacturer who makes the best stuff through trial and error. I like the brand Sunrise Remedies from India. It is the smoothest and most powerful generic Tadalafil, and you can get it mixed with Dapoxetine to last longer (I prefer Sertraline).

PT-141

PT-141 is a peptide you can inject that triggers an erection from the brain itself. They still don't know exactly *how* and *why* it works, but it does. If you get good stuff, which is easy, you can have amazing erections. The problem with PT-141 is it will potentially jack your blood pressure a bit, so you should take it with something that will lower your blood pressure (see above) and provide you with a lot of nitric oxide. My main issue is that *when* it kicks in, is different for every person. You'll have to experiment to know when it will kick in for you, and this is especially important if you plan on mixing it with other drugs, and obviously because you want to time it along with your sexual encounters.

Pro Tip: Stop using "mainstream" mouthwash brands unless you really check out the active ingredients and research them! This is because many active ingredients in mainstream mouthwash brands kill the bacteria that produces nitric oxide and consequently raises blood pressure. You can use a natural mouthwash if you like, but just brush your teeth and suck on cloves, and you should be fine. Cloves freshen breath *and* lower blood pressure because they contain *eugenol*, a strong vasodilator.

Trimix/Quadmix

Both are injected directly into your corpus cavernosum somewhere between the middle and base of your shaft at either a 10am or 2pm angle. Once you inject it (an "auto injector" is easiest) you take your thumb and forefinger and encircle the base of your cock and balls tightly for 60 seconds to trap the drugs in the penile shaft long enough for them to kick in. Then you wait for 5-10 minutes for the full effects. It will get you hard and keep you hard no matter what. Don't inject it in the middle of a zombie apocalypse! The product is a blend of different drugs, that come in different proportions and strengths. Many people will find that the "base mix" does not work for them and will need a stronger formulation or even a custom blend. Once you get it right, it is amazing! Always start with the weakest and lowest dose and work your way towards your ideal dose. One you have your ideal dose, you can experiment mixing it with other drugs, even though they say you should not do so. However, all these drugs work on different principles so you will usually be fine. Mixing drugs is also necessary if you truly want to have sex for hours, as Trimix/Quadmix injections only last for so long. The only annoying thing is depending on how your penis is constructed, it can be easy to hit a vein which leaves a temporary bruise as blood seeps into the surrounding tissues. It takes days for it to look normal again, even though you can still fuck right after hitting a vein. I remember seeing certain porn stars back in the day and wondering what made them special that they could get hard in front of crowds, etc. but then I came to learn they weren't special or "better than me" they were just doing penile injections and hopped up on all sorts of other crap. For some of these porn stars, over the years you will see that they lose a lot of penils size and/or develop tons of scar tissue that changes the shape of their penis. This is a result of doing one too many penile injections!

Pro Tip: If you have venous leakage, then you need to use a soft, silicone cock ring that is easy to remove for marathon sex sessions. Just remember to take it off periodically and NEVER fall asleep or pass out while wearing one!!! You may wake up with a cock that no longer works or needs to be amputated! I like to wear one behind the balls and shaft. If I am sleeping with a woman for the first time, or a short time, my choice is trimix and if a longer session is planned, I take tadalafil just before as well. If I am already sleeping with a woman and she is planning to spend the night or the weekend, then I prefer PT-141 with tadalafil.

There Are 2 Drugs That Will Give You Stamina and Kill Premature Ejaculation

Dapoxetine is not legal in the US, but can be purchased online. It is a failed antidepressant (SSRI) that still worked pretty well for stopping premature ejaculation in off-label usage adventures.

Sertraline is the generic name for another SSRI that you can get a Rx for to stop premature ejaculation in the US. It is much stronger than Dapoxetine, but again, your results will depend on who manufactured it. NorthStar Rx makes the best stuff I ever tried and it is sold by SuperPill online.

SSRIs that are taken for premature ejaculation are taken at low doses. Dapoxetine is usually taken at 60mg and Sertraline at 25mg. These are not doses used to treat depression, although you will definitely feel like "the edge" has been taken off when you are on them. They kick in within 2 hours and last for a few hours at full power, then wear off over the next few hours.

Pro Tip: NEVER mix SSRIs with 5-HTP or L-Tryptophan!!! You will get serotonin sickness which can be deadly and you will feel like you need to check into a psych ward, as your serotonin will be thru the roof! BTW, the impact of SSRIs on orgasmic function is why you should never date women who take SSRIs or any other "meds" for their mental issues. Actual dosages for SSRIs, when they are used to treat depression, are waaaay higher and taken daily so the drug accumulates in the body. As a result, women on these things cannot achieve vaginal orgasm and this is a disaster for a relationship. Also, when you repress your feelings by cranking up the serotonin via SSRIs, eventually one day you will go nuts.

More On Premature Ejaculation

If you have an issue with premature ejaculation, the main cause is tension in the pelvic floor and bladder that jack up the sympathetic nervous system. While SSRIs crank up the parasympathetic nervous system to counteract the jacked up sympathetic, this does not address the root cause. To work on the root cause, beside doing exercises that open up the area such as split squats, etc., you really want to work on the tension in the pelvic floor and this can be done by using a TENS unit coupled with an electrified butt plug as I talked about earlier. But in the end, the main solution to pelvic tension is actually having sex, and by using SSRIs coupled with a drug to keep you hard, you can actually fuck your way through a lot of the tension and release it. That is, assuming you are fortunate enough to have someone willing to have tons of sex with you! Good luck with that!

Pro Tip: When using a TENS unit with an electrified butt plug, be careful not to overdo it, because you can really exhaust your penile nerves and put yourself out of commission for a few days.

Depression Ultimately Doesn't Exist

When one looks at depression, it is merely impotent rage. Rage that, instead of exploding, implodes. So depression is really rage you are not expressing, out of fear of the consequences for expressing it. Express the rage, end the depression! A friend of mine once said, "You aren't depressed, your life just sucks. Change your life and you won't be so depressed." Rage is fuel for change. Learn to express it without ending up in trouble, and your life can't help but get better.

Technically speaking, depression can be defined as low levels of serotonin, hence Rx SSRIs (prescription selective serotonin reuptake inhibitors) are the most popular solution for those who are depressed. Does this contradict what I just said about depression being unexpressed rage? Not at all! Low serotonin is also found in individuals who are violent. Raise the serotonin, repress the violence! Do you see how depression and rage are really the same thing? Both are expressions of low serotonin, and both are treated with SSRIs, *or by safely venting your rage* which is the best option.

But then why have so many school shooters been on SSRIs? This is because serotonin is the chemical of repression. Meaning, it is used to repress feelings. It doesn't cure the depression or safely and constructively express the rage lurking beneath, it merely represses it via it's impact on your autonomic nervous system. So the danger with the zombie-making dosages of SSRIs that are prescribed, is that they cause so much backed up emotion that one day you explode. Hence the school shootings, or the reality that one day, SSRIs just "stop working." You can only hold a ping-pong ball under water for so long!

It's like when people take drugs that prevent them from going into REM sleep and then stop using them, they have endless nightmares for some time until the psychic backlog gets sorted.

The reason SSRIs can also fix premature ejaculation and give incredible stamina, is because SSRIs take you out of the sympathetic (fight or flight) mode of your autonomic nervous system and deeply into your parasympathetic mode. However, it isn't just that they relax you… Again, the serotonin represses your urge to ejaculate just like it represses your urge to be violent, which normally manifests safely as depression. SSRIs are not a permanent solution to *any* issue, *just a temporary tool to use on your journey to a permanent solution.*

All About Hair Loss

When it comes to losing hair, there are four main culprits:

1. **DHT is too high**. The solution is not to get rid of DHT, but keep it within a healthy range. Usually, something you are doing is raising your levels too high, so you just have to figure out what you are doing and stop it, rather then taking DHT blockers or something like that. DHT-based steroids like drostanolone and oxymetholone are big culprits, or taking herbs like Butea Superba along with injectable testosterone, which cause massive spikes in the conversion of testosterone into DHT.

2. **Your thyroid is messed up**. The solution is increased iodine/iodide consumption so that your thyroid can function optimally. If you supplement too much D3, it can also effect your parathyroid and cause hair loss as well.

3. **Levels of zinc and copper are too high or out of balance.** This is usually caused by supplementation with either or both, or eating too many cashew nuts or something. Same thing can happen if you eat too many Brazil nuts and overdose on selenium, or take any sort of trace mineral formula. Most of these trace mineral supplements are mined from sources very high in lithium. While ingesting lithium feels good and lithium used to be used as an anti-depressant, it is no good for your kidneys or your hair. Blood tests can reveal these things, but you can also just stop supplementing with that crap and you should be fine.

4. **Not enough blood flow to your scalp.** This is such a big reason behind hair loss, and people have no idea. The stress and tension of modern life causes people to develop a lot of tension in their scalp, and this kills hair growth. Red light therapy caps, combined with scalp massage is critical. You can get one of those multi-pronged Minoxidil dispensers that rake the scalp, and use that to massage your scalp every day while coating your scalp in Minoxidil.

By doing all of the above, I stopped and reversed my own hair loss.

Chasing The Dragon of Inner Freedom

After chasing this dragon for most of my life, I have discovered that most of the techniques for overcoming trauma and clearing it, are trash. Why are methods that don't work constantly propagated as the answer? Because if you have a method that actually works, people will run away from it, since in actuality they fear the results they may attain. They aren't afraid so much of the freedom ultimately promised from working with the method (although people do genuinely fear such freedom), but rather they fear the pain that will need to be released and consequently endured/overcome to attain the freedom they desire. So, people collectively agree on a subconscious level to promote that which doesn't work, while pretending that it does, and to make sure that methods that actually work, will die off and be forgotten. Consequently there will no longer be any threat to anyone's psychic stability. It's that insidious!

The Psoas Muscle

A good example of this would be methods for releasing the psoas muscle. Releasing the psoas muscle is one of the biggest *keys* to unlocking and resolving trauma. A search on the internet will show endless methods involving stretching, and many massage implements that promise to get the psoas to release. Yet *none* of them deliver! They may offer a slight release at best - a tease of freedom, to be honest. Yet nobody seems to ever complain about this but me! This is because people don't really want to release the psoas anyway, because that would cause authentic pain.

One of the tricky things about the psoas muscle is that its release is intimately connected to releasing constriction in the pelvic, urogenital and thoracic diaphragms as well as the hip flexors, to name a few. The psoas simply cannot be released in isolation from these other problem areas. In this book, I will show you what you need to know to facilitate working through these areas. A "bag of tools" as it were, to get the job done *if* you tap into your intuition in order to use them correctly. But just to keep you from jumping ahead, ATG split squats while holding a dumbbell in each hand as are taught online by the "knees over toes" guy are the best exercise for getting the psoas to release. Another name for them is "Poliquin squats," named after the late lifter, Charles Poliquin. If you want to start your journey, start with these. You can learn how to do them from endless YouTube videos, and perform them at any gym.

One Arm Hangs & Unlocking Your Thorax

This is probably the most important technique, especially given that the psoas connects into the thoracic diaphragm as well as the segment of the spine at the level of the thoracic diaphragm, so the psoas is really under the "jurisdiction" of the thorax. Therefore learning how to "hang loose" is not only critical for unlocking your thorax and thoracic diaphragm as well as resolving rotator cuff issues, but for releasing the psoas as well.

Start with a two-arm hang using "Versa Grips" or a knock off of them to help you maintain your grip. The reason you use Versa Grips is because you want to use as little of your grip strength as possible, which will allow you to access the tension in your rotator cuffs and release it. If you have shoulder pain from too much benching, this will fix it in no time flat. After you get good at hanging from both arms, *carefully* begin hanging from just one arm. Make sure you brace your body with one foot gently against a wall so you don't spin and rotate and get injured. Remember, the key when hanging with either one arm or two, is that you use the strength of your grip as little as possible, and rely on the strap to keep you attached to the bar. Because the less you use your physical grip, the more the load transfers into your connective tissues, forcing them to release tension. A shoulder surgeon actually wrote a book explaining how this technique often replaces the need to have surgery on your rotator cuffs. Unless you have a complete tear, injecting the peptide BPC-157 and hanging should fix them.

But the other benefit to hanging is unlocking your thorax, especially the area behind your heart and the upper attachment points of your thoracic diaphragm. It is easy to access the thorax once the rotator cuffs have relaxed sufficiently which may take a long time, but totally worth it. Accessing the thorax is always done hanging from both arms even if you can hang from one arm no problem. Since men are always trying to protect their heart chakra, this area is usually completely locked up. You can also target the psoas muscle attachment points to the spine, the thoracic diaphragm, etc. The thoracic diaphragm is way larger than anatomy books indicate. The way to start unlocking the thorax is by swinging forward and back and when your legs swing back, tuck your tailbone which activates the psoas muscle. As your legs swing forward, release the tailbone tuck. The final movement which is extremely powerful, is to hang from both arms, tuck your tailbone, and while *keeping* it tucked, rotate your thorax 20x counterclockwise followed by 20x clockwise. When I say to "rotate your thorax" what I mean is to move the entire rib cage box to the right, then to the front, then to the left, then to the back as if you were hanging inside of a tube and wanted to wipe down the inner walls of the tube with your t-shirt. Repeat counterclockwise and clockwise until release occurs.

Pro Tip: Seeing a good chiropractor once per week is critical for getting through many of these obstructions in your posture. Especially when working on your thorax, scraping techniques and therapeutic ultrasound are huge helps and your chiropractor should employ them both!

Yoga: A Complete Waste of Your Time

Yoga is a great example of a bullshit methodology for attaining somatic freedom. Very few people know the true history of yoga, but if you go back far enough in time, there were certain individuals who awakened their kundalini energy and their bodies spontaneously went into certain positions to facilitate the flow of this energy. Others saw this happen, and figured that if they replicated the spontaneous movements they witnessed, they could awaken their own kundalini as well, not realizing that they were putting the cart before the horse. So Yoga can't really do much of anything in and of itself. It can make you a little more flexible on certain planes, and it is a great place for picking up girls who can put their legs behind their ears while you dig them out. Always a plus! Naturally, yoga didn't give these girls this ability, they just gravitate towards yoga classes to showcase their natural abilities. You're welcome! I dated a girl who was naturally a literal contortionist, and she would go to yoga classes just to show up the instructor as she could do any pose or movement at the highest level naturally.

A far more effective tool for somatic self development is **Continuum Movement.** Emilie Conrad developed it based upon her understanding that the body is primarily fluid and that we can tap into our most primal movement patterns - those that echo our earliest evolutionary and embryological development. The practice involves allowing micro-movements, spirals, waves, and undulations to emerge naturally, often starting with very subtle internal sensations and breathing patterns. This is where I came up with the idea for my thorax release techniques. **Continuum Movement is** quite different from more structured movement practices because it really emphasizes that deep, organic intelligence of the body. Many people find it deeply healing and transformative, especially for trauma work and reconnecting with the body's innate wisdom. Emilie Conrad's work was really pioneering in how it bridges somatic therapy, movement, and a kind of cellular-level awareness. In my opinion, Emilie herself was some sort of alien-human hybrid, because she could do things with her body that I have never seen before except in other alien-human hybrids. I am not sure if most humans would be able to replicate all of her results, but much can be learned from her and what she taught. It is invaluable.

There Are No Primal Therapists Left

Primal therapy is a therapy created by Arthur Janov, where one is driven to scream – yet the scream emitted is not a *conscious decision*. This "primal scream" can release a lot of trauma, but idiots today think that if they just practice screaming, they can achieve the same effect. Primal therapy has been lost to time, but Motley Crue immortalized the therapy in their song, "Primal Scream." Today there are no genuine primal therapists left who can deliver the results Janov promised. They are all retired or dead. Why didn't primal therapy catch on? Mostly, because it worked! Well, that's precisely why it died out. I managed to find and work with the only three primal therapists left alive that I could find. One of them temporarily came out of retirement to work with me because I was so enthusiastic. They all sucked except for one, but he was so idealistic he insisted on doing it in a group setting to keep it practically free, and you know there is always some asshole in the group who disrupts the process as much as possible *on purpose*, yet this therapist refused to throw the clown out. His very nature, that which made him so good at primal therapy, allowed for one person in the group to disrupt the process for nearly everyone. So I left before I lost control and beat that saboteur into a coma. I can't stand such human trash who enjoy preventing people from healing and show up every week to make sure nobody achieves healing. They do this, because these sorts of people can't be healed themselves. So they don't want anyone else to succeed.

Only One True School of Reichian Therapy Is Still Around

Reichian therapy nearly disappeared into oblivion because all of the people offering it, dropped the sexual component from the therapy, thereby rendering it what Reich himself would call "psychically impotent." The only authentic Reichian therapy left today is a 14-day course called Shamanic De-armoring taught by a group called "The Deer Tribe Metis Society," which was founded by the late Harley "Thunder Strikes" Reagan. Harley Reagan was described by some as a cult leader, but he was just an incredibly cool guy. You don't have to subscribe to all the Native American beliefs and practices of The Deer Tribe Metis Society in order to participate in the 14-day Shamanic De-armoring retreat, so don't let that stuff "put you off." I would recommend anyone interested in Reichian therapy and sexual breathwork take the 14-day retreat. You'll just need to keep in mind that you will need to do the exercises they teach at the end of the retreat on a *daily* basis for the next few years in order to really get the full benefits. This is mentioned but not stressed by those teaching the retreat, since people are lazy and don't want to do the work, therefore stressing that the 14-day retreat just lays the foundation for the *daily* exercises to be effective *if* practiced over the next few years is counterproductive from a business standpoint. I think I may be the only person who did those exercises every day for the next few years? Anyway, they tell you at the end of the retreat that you are now "dearmored human beings" which isn't *exactly* the *complete* truth. But you *can* be - *if* you make what is taught part of your everyday practice. Again, most people just "dabble" with these things because they don't actually have the desire, or the strength, to walk the path for real.

It's similar with BDSM. Almost everyone in that scene is a complete poser. BDSM has become so filled with nonsense that the whole community has become psychically impotent. The book "50 Shades of Grey," and the millions of women who read the book and took an interest in what they *believed* to be BDSM were the final nail in the coffin for the lifestyle. Their knowledge of BDSM comes from a book whose author often seems to struggle to string several proper English sentences together in a row, and has a shallow understanding of BDSM and sex in general for that matter. I felt embarrassment for her when reading her book. Describing scenes where the main character sticks his cock in the female lead, she *instantly* orgasms and he cums 30 seconds later. Is this for real? Sure, it happens sometimes, but c'mon... What's worse, is that this utter crap resonated with millions of women. Well, the truth is that what resonated with millions of women was the fantasy of a rich, handsome and *dysfunctional* man adopting a girl who was also *dysfunctional* – albeit in a complementary way, and buying her everything her heart desires.

Remember what I said about women being losers, who date loser men, whose loserdom resonates with their own? I can't tell you the horror I experienced as all these vapid vanilla whores streamed into BDSM clubs in NYC looking for something that doesn't even exist. I did a session with one woman who used her safe word in under one minute and I hardly even did anything. Another thing that makes me laugh is that when you attend a BDSM meetup group in any city in the United States, nearly everyone is obese and gross. Don't these dominants take any pride in themselves or in their submissives?

Banging Hippie Chicks at Osho's Resort in Pune

The late spiritual guru "Osho" needs to be mentioned here as well. He was more of a "cult leader" than Harley Reagan ever was and had an incredible impact in his time. While he watered down the Reichian breathwork practices from a technical perspective so they would be easier to learn, he indirectly kept the sexual component due to his promiscuous "commune" where group sex was encouraged, so the sexual component was indirectly there. His methodology was effective, although not as effective as Shamanic De-armoring's. Long dead, his foundation still operates a resort in Pune, India where one can take his breathwork classes when one is not having sex with hippie chicks who make pilgrimages to the resort from all over the world. It's a shadow of what once was at his commune in Oregon, USA, but it is all that is left. In case you want to start your own sex cult, BTW, Osho is the man you want to model!

While Harley Reagan and Osho both mixed sex with their breathwork as originally intended, Stanislov Groff isolated the breathwork itself from the sexual component and called it "Holotropic Breathwork." It's not worth your time, because without the sexual component it is again "psychically impotent" as Reich himself would say. I actually started out taking Osho sessions from Krisana Locke, who is famous for teaching internet guru

Elliot Hulse about Reichian Therapy. I worked with her long before YouTube even existed, and she was actually Osho's personal secretary at one point and despite teaching the breathwork divorced from the sexual component, she was still rather effective given this glaring issue and I am a big fan of hers. I suspect it is because she still carries the "energetic blueprint" from Osho's commune on some level? She lives and teaches in Berlin these days if anyone is interested in taking classes with her.

What About Hypnosis?

I know there are famous hypnotists out there who claim that they can hypnotize anyone, make any girl fall in love with them, or get anyone to throw money at them, but this is total crap. If you ever meet anyone who can do these sorts of things, it is most likely because they have a relationship with an entity that is attached to them, who can do these sorts of things on their behalf. A lot of people who can do unexplainable or "supernatural" things have entities that they work with, who assist them. This is more common than you realize. The rest are alien-human hybrids. Anyway, only a certain percentage of the population are what are considered "natural somnambulists," and stage hypnotists seek them out as on-stage assistants, and will target those in their audience who have this trait to do demonstrations on. This isn't to say that everyone can't be *influenced*, but that is different from being *hypnotized*.

Hypnosis is potentially dangerous, because when you allow yourself to be hypnotized, you open yourself up to attachment and possession by various entities. This is one of the reasons "gooning" is so bad for you, besides the fact that it scrambles your brain. People goon while "edging," and this combination of sexual energy along with hypnotic imagery and sound is a recipe for serious trouble. Various entities can easily reach you using cyberspace as a bridge. The worst type of content is porn on tube sites that embed some sort of hypnotic induction, promising to attract in a succubus or similar. Remember, it's not *what* to do in life, so much as what *not* to do. If you use your free will to get yourself possessed by or else get an entity attached to you, how will you get rid of it? Good luck with that!

The potential for possession aside, I really want to point out that hypnosis should *never* be used to deal with trauma. The best it can do is repress your current trauma even deeper. The *worst* it can do is induce a complete and potentially fatal breakdown of your psyche. This is because more people than you would realize are the victims of mind control programming that was installed using horrific physical and sexual abuse. This is because when a child (or adult) is tortured to the extreme, their mind will split into pieces. These individual pieces can then be isolated and programmed with drugs, hypnosis, etc. to be accessed at future times for specific purposes. This is how secret "sex slaves," and "manchurian candidates" such as school shooters are created. These people always have multiple personalities engineered via trauma, that are locked away inside of them even if they do not display evidence of their existence, and are for the most part unaware of them. Don't laugh – this could be you! You wouldn't even know it! These alter personalities were often not only constructed with a vicious combination of hypnosis, drugs and abuse, but also with hidden technologies which do not have an origin on this planet or even in this dimension. Given the sinister intended purpose behind the creation of many of these alter personalities, they often come with self-destruction programming which can be activated when you fuck around with hypnosis and attempt to access them.

I was part of the Montauk Project and tortured frequently as a child. I remember one time when I was in college I went to see a movie in a theater on West 23rd Street, and there was a torture scene in the film. While watching the scene, I began to experience panic attacks for lack of a better way to say it. I didn't understand what was happening and just knew I needed to get out of the theater. So I made it out into the hallway, with everything spinning around me like I was on a carousel. I thought I was going to pass out or fall down so I quickly lay down before that could happen and risk hitting my head. When everything around me stopped spinning and I calmed down, I suddenly remembered in vivid detail one of my torture sessions. I was not sad or angry or upset. I just lay there in wonder that I had so completely forgotten it like it had never ever happened, and suddenly had remembered it in such detail like I could never forget it again. It was simply crazy! I will talk more about my past as this book winds down.

Inner Game That Actually Works

Now that you can deliver the goods, and you are actively out there slaying sex workers, how to use this as leverage to draw in civilian females? That is the focus of this part of the book. I think a good place to start is to look at the nature of the mind itself, since our mental state is of such critical importance.

There is a difference between being conscious and being aware. The terms "conscious" and "aware" are often used interchangeably, but this is not correct. What is the difference between the two? Well, for starters, animals are conscious but not aware. So what does that mean *experientially*?

Let's start by stating that in certain eastern philosophies it has been said that *all* of the following statements about the nature of "reality" are true at once:

- Reality is real.

- Reality is illusion.

- Reality is both real and illusion.

- Reality is neither real nor illusion.

Let me explain this in modern lingo so you might have a chance to understand what "reality" actually is:

- If you get punched in the face, that is about as "real" as it gets.

- However, quantum physics has demonstrated that we are made from atoms, and as atoms are mostly empty space, we are really more of a hologram than something solid. Hence, it can be said that reality is illusion.

- But since we already know that when our "hologram" gets punched in the face it really hurts, how much of an illusion are we, really? Hmmm... Given that the two previous statements are obviously both true at the same time, it is safe to say that reality is *both* real and illusion. I think such a paradox is fairly easy to grasp and accept.

- So how can we *then* say that reality is *also* "neither real nor illusion?" What would make us say something like that? This is where people either get stuck or they get "enlightened."

What that fourth statement is pointing towards is *awareness,* and the fact that what we experience as reality, is *also* **our awareness itself**. Hence reality is both real and illusion, as well as neither real nor illusion because we need to factor in *awareness.* This fourth statement *may* be easier to grasp if I define for you what awareness is, which is *very* tricky, because awareness lies outside of the mind.

How do you use your mind to grasp something that is beyond your mind? That's a very good question indeed! This conundrum is why most people are not enlightened. Not that being enlightened means anything *beyond being enlightened,* because even when you are enlightened you still need to earn a living, take a shit, etc. So let's not romanticize enlightenment now or use it as an excuse to dodge our responsibilities in this realm.

What's funny, is that people always talk about wanting to attain enlightenment, yet if you ask them to define what enlightenment is, they can't. They also can't even attempt to convey what the experience of attaining it would be like. So how can you find something if you don't know what it is that you are looking for? What they are *actually* looking for is something else entirely, that they don't have enough awareness to consciously define - which is *also* problematic, because how can you find something that you are not consciously aware of?

Well, it *can* be done in a certain sense, because your subconscious is always attempting to push you in this direction or that one, but it is usually the stored and buried trauma in your subconscious that is doing the directing, so again, what you are *actually* looking for is still *something else*. What a mess!

The way out is attaining awareness, but I still haven't told you how to do that. Let's see if you can find it if I push you in the right direction. It will be the best that I can do, given that awareness lies beyond your mind.

Western philosophy is so proud of saying, "I think therefore I am" yet this is *not* the case. When you are in the oral surgeon's chair pumped full of anesthesia, you are not conscious and cannot think, yet you still "*am.*" How do we know? Because you are still *aware*. Again, how do you know you are still aware if you aren't even *conscious*? Because when the anesthesia wears off and your mind becomes conscious again, you perceive that something is missing or "off." Were you not *aware* while the oral surgeon kept you unconscious, you would not notice that something was "off" when you regained consciousness.

The truth is that you possess awareness even when knocked unconscious, there is simply *nothing to be aware of!* Yet the "faculty" of awareness is still there! So "I do not think therefore I am" is just as valid as the famous "I think therefore I am." Again, how can *both* be true at the same time?

Because you are not your thoughts - you are awareness! However, you are not "infinite awareness" as David Icke likes to preach. That's pretty ridiculous!

So what *exactly* is this awareness that is not dependent on your mind in order to exist? You know that it lies outside of the mind for sure, but you still don't know *what* it is. I could say that your awareness is part of the energy field of The Creator, The Divine Father. The God with a capital "G" as opposed to the gods and goddesses with the lower case "g" that he creates to assist him with his creation.

Now please don't be lead astray by the blasphemous and ridiculous idea that humans are all gods somehow. This is not the case!

Furthermore, I need to correct a common misconception that people have, which is that your brain is your mind. Your brain is NOT your mind! Your brain simply allows your biology to interface with your mind, which is non-local. An analogy would be that your brain is like a computer with internet access, not the internet itself. Your mind being the internet, in this analogy. So, how much of that "mind" do you think is actually "yours?" Just ask yourself, how many of your thoughts are original and unique? Almost none of them. So if they didn't come from you, where did they come from? Something to "think" about. Another thing is to be aware of, is how many thoughts you have that are *totally fucked up*. Are those really "yours?" Only if you make them so!

Here are some other things to think about: How can a crow, with a brain the size of a peanut, make and use tools and have the intelligence of a young human child, which has a *far* larger brain? How can an elephant, with a human brain - just far larger, and with a (recently discovered) language as complex as that of humans, ("spoken" on the ultra low frequency bandwidth so *you* can't hear it) have such a different existence than that of a human? Is it because they lack the opposable thumbs and fingers necessary to create physical manifestations in this realm? Also, given that the ULF bandwidth they communicate on can cover very long distances, elephants have all basically had cell phones since the beginning. What do you think they talk about?

Probably the fact you suck in bed.

Approach Anxiety and The Fear of Rejection

If you want to get civilian women, then you have to *actually talk to them,* which many men have a lot of problems doing, because they fear rejection. They don't want to be told to fuck off or that they are a creep. They are also afraid that they don't know what to say, or that they will look foolish somehow. Well, it is true that they don't know *what* to say, because they know what they **want** to say, but they also know that they will be punished for saying it. So to rephrase the issue, they don't know *what to say that will get them the results that they desire.* This is a totally legitimate reason for being anxious!

Overall, if you have anxiety over any particular activity, it's usually because you don't participate in that activity often enough to innoculate yourself against the feelings and sensations that accompany said activity. For example, people only have "social anxiety disorder" because they never socialize. You don't actually have a disorder, you just need to stop gooning and playing video games and start socializing. Another great example is fighting. The more fights you get into, the more you become innoculated against adrenaline dumps, etc. This doesn't mean you should "cold approach" 100 women a day and get yourself banned from your local public spaces. It simply means you should socialize with *everybody.*

Furthermore, some of the most successful men when it comes to women, treat all women as if they were hot. They just like women, and women pick up on this. It can never hurt you to actually like women, and not *just* like fucking them!

Women Have Zero Standards, So They Can't *Really* "Reject" You

While women will wax day and night about their "standards" in men, the repulsive reality is that women have *zero standards* and will fuck literally anything (just like most men). Which is kind of fucked up because the woman has such an easy time getting sex so why have no standards? It's understandable in men, but inexcusable in women. If you could somehow magically call up video recordings of every single guy a woman has had sex with, you would find yourself utterly disgusted with their lack of standards. I knew a woman once who made it her business to find the dirtiest homeless vagrants she could and fuck them raw. You think she was unique? Think again! The reason I bring this up is you should *never* think that a woman will reject you due to your lack of looks or height or any other physical attributes. They may not swoon over you, but they will have sex with you! BTW, this is yet another reason why men who refuse to "pay for sex" are so pathetic. They have the mistaken idea that if a woman sleeps with them without cash being exchanged, that this proves she is sleeping with them due to some intrinsic masculine value or skill at seduction, when in reality a woman agreeing to have sex with you is completely meaningless aside from the fact you now have a warm hole to ejaculate into, as again, women will sleep with literally anything. In fact, men with intrinsic masculine value are usually shunned sexually by women, for reasons we have belabored throughout this book.

Pro Tip: *Women are more promiscuous that you can possibly imagine.* Most girls have insane "body counts." Based on my experience, if a girl tells you her body count, multiply that number by a factor of *eight*. This is the actual number, but of course this is *only* if a girl tells you, as you should *never* ask. I mean, do you really think she will tell you the truth anyway? Don't go out of your way to show her that you are stupid! Of course, if a girl tells you her body count is in the hundreds, or that she has lost count, she is telling the truth and there is no need to do any further calculations! What's funny though, is that women don't realize that if a guy is asking her about her body count, it is because he is interested in more than just fucking her. If a guy only wants to fuck a woman, he couldn't care less what her body count is. But if he is looking for more than sex, then of course body count becomes important, because high body counts are simply not conducive to long-term relationships.

Women Are Sexual Degenerates So Don't Fear Being a Creep

No matter if women are frigid or not, most women are sexual degenerates. If you doubt this, secretly acquire access to your girlfriend's laptop, etc., and look up what porn she has been looking at. You will fall off your chair at the stuff she is masturbating to. I tell you, women are absolute degenerates and men have nothing on them when it comes to sheer perversion. NOTE: do *not* look into their email or text messages or WhatsApp or Telegram... You already *know* what you are going to find - why do that to yourself? Are you a masochist or something?

Women Can Be Very Attracted to You and Still Not Interested

Another thing to keep in mind is that there is a huge difference between "attraction" and "interest" when it comes to how a woman feels about a man. Guys have trouble with this, because if they are attracted to a woman, they are also interested in her. Women are not like this at all. Now why would a woman be insanely attracted to a man yet still have no interest in him?

- Already in a relationship.

- Afraid she will get hurt for a myriad of reasons.

- Realizes she cannot manipulate or use the man to advance her own selfish agenda.

- Thinks relating with him will distract her from a goal like studying.

- Worried she will fall in love and this will obstruct her gold-digging or sex work.

I bring all this up because men take rejection to mean that they are unattractive or low value when this may not be the case at all!

Start Talking Daily with Every Woman You Run Across

Hopefully your "approach anxiety" has now been mitigated. The way to finish it off for good is simply to talk to *all* women. Make *no* attempt to pick them up or seduce them. Just talk to them. About anything. Most women have the conversational level of a child so what you say doesn't make any difference as long as it isn't very intelligent. Intelligence is a sure way to turn a woman off, because when a woman thinks you are highly intelligent, she immediately loses interest in you. Why? Because she knows she can't control you or trick you, so you become a bad investment of her time. So just say any shit and don't even expect a response. Every women you meet, simply say "Hello." Then you can add "How's it going?" and then look away as if you don't even need a response. Just be a friendly dude, albeit a disinterested one. If a woman is attracted to you and has enough self-esteem (good luck with that), she will start talking back. If things get awkward just excuse yourself with some good reason. If you are an attractive guy, here is where you will start to learn first-hand that most women have zero self-esteem. Which again, is why they have no standards and fuck losers and trash left-and-right. Because if you have no self-esteem, you have no standards no matter what fibs come out of your mouth as a podcast guest. Sadly, when a man of value takes an interest in such a woman, the disparity between his value and her lack of it, creates such disparate sexual tension, that it quickly becomes too much for her to bear.

There have been many instances where I have been in a public space, and I look at a woman for a brief moment whom I have no interest in, and she gets so angry that I am looking at her and starts a confrontation over it. Sometimes she will call me a creep or say I am harassing her. But I am not, as I have no interest in her. My looking at her has no meaning, or emotional or sexual charge for me. So what's that about? Well, when a woman really likes you but has a low opinion of herself, the sexual tension becomes too much for her. She also may start to think you are mocking her because why would you be looking at her? She will also despise you for your confidence because she wishes she had such confidence. But what she hates the most is the power you have over her. She wants that power for herself. It's like penis envy, but it is actually the *big dick energy* that she is envious over.

Nonetheless, when you are used to talking to every woman you see, then when you see an attractive girl, talking to her will be no different then talking to any other woman. There is also this vibe you will give off. The vibe that you just like women in general, and not *just* fucking them. After doing this for a while, *feel* for when a girl is receptive to you and start making extended eye contact during your conversations to test the waters for proceeding further.

Eye Contact Is Everything

Most men have an issue with extended eye contact because they are not comfortable showing their desires and they are also afraid the woman will look back and see thru them. But it is the eyes that communicate to the woman what you are really after and close the deal. Once your eyes lock and she is cool with it, at that point what you say doesn't even matter. Just keep up the conversation and continue to draw her in. If she cannot be drawn in at that time, feel free to break the eye contact but after a brief respite return to it. If it just isn't the right time for it to proceed further, eject and try again next time. Depending on the situation, you can also change location, or escalate physically. Physical escalation is very simple. You were touching her with your eyes, now touch her with your hands. Start with neutral areas before proceeding over time to less neutral areas. At a certain point, you can be bold with what you say and do, but you have to read her own body language and energy. It really isn't difficult.

Pro Tip: Hygiene is extremely important. You should always be showered and wearing deodorant. Being a member of the clean assholes club at all times is critical. You should get manicures and pedicures and if you want to save money, learn to do them yourself. Always wear a cologne that gets you the most compliments. Just one spray please! Always have your teeth brushed and great smelling breath. Finally, please wash your fucking clothes. So many people wear clothes that smell musty. Not doing these things are surefire ways to lose opportunities for sex that would have been given to you otherwise.

LooksMaxxing?

A lot of people don't know this, but I created the LooksMaxxing movement, and not Mike Mew. I did this many years ago when I uploaded a website on "face pulling" which explained how to apply forward pressure to your maxilla and give yourself cheekbones in the process. After many years, I took down the website. People may think I am telling tall tales by claiming these things, yet LooksMaxxing was not built on "mewing," but rather on face pulling. What happened is when certain guys saw the results of face pulling, they did not want other men to learn the method because they didn't want competition. So they spread misinformation all over the Internet that face pulling didn't work, and that it was dangerous. So mewing took it's place as the go-to method. I know this happened because the guys who spread this misinformation on face pulling contacted me and confessed to it, even offering to pay me to take down the website. I am not going to talk about how to face pull in this book, as you can probably find the information online somewhere. Faces can be remodeled and reshaped because the sutures of the skull are not fused as is taught in medical schools. However, for most people, I recommend plastic surgery when one is in their early 20s to really improve upon their looks.

Women: Get ANY Man You Want and Write Your Own Ticket

This book is written primarily for men, but since women will probably be reading it anyway, I will give you some billion dollar advice on how to get any man you want. I am not joking! First, do I have to state the obvious like YOU SHOULD NOT BE FAT? Losing weight is easy. I already explained how to do this earlier, but since you probably weren't paying attention due to being distracted by some loser's cum leaking from your asshole, here's the Cliff's Notes version: stop eating so fucking much. Get a caffeine, nicotine (no cigarettes!) or cocaine habit to curb your desire to stuff your fucking face all the fucking time. The main reason most women in the United States are fat pigs is because they transmute their desire for sex, into a desire for food. Undo this and use conscious awareness to transmute your desire for food, back into a desire for sex. Eat mostly protein and as little carbs and fats as possible. Take iodine tablets daily to keep your thyroid running properly. You should be good!

Next, YOUR FACE IS YOUR FORTUNE. If you are less than a "9" in the face department (which 99% of you are), GET PLASTIC SURGERY.

Forget boob-jobs and ass implants: *those are for whores, not the **wives** of the top 1% of men on the planet.* You want it to be that when the man of your dreams wakes up next to you every morning, the first thing he does is see you face and shout to himself: "FUCK YEAH, NIGGA'!" So instead of spending hours scrolling on TikTok taking advice from women *who lost the game of life*, spend those hours (and then some) researching the best plastic surgeons on the planet. Remember, you don't want to look like a house cat or a blow-up bimbo bitch. You want to be *beautiful*. Beauty is *not* in the eye of the beholder, it is based entirely on *mathematics*. You want to know what beauty looks like? Go to seaart.ai and type the following prompt:

"I want a front-facing image of the most beautiful caucasian woman in the world, with a face that follows golden mean mathematical ratios as closely as possible."

It will generate an image like the following...

This is what a "10" looks like and it is neither subjective nor a matter of opinion. When you interview with plastic surgeons, show them this picture and say you want to look as close to this as possible.

That's it!

Now for all you haters who take issue with the fact I am prompting for a caucasian woman, let's be honest that white women are the most desirable women in the world compared to any other race. Even if you aren't a white women, you still want the plastic surgeon to bring you as close to this look as possible. Every Asian girl who gets plastic surgery, does so not only to look beautiful, but to look like a *beautiful white woman*. Your skin could be black as black can be, but if you have facial features like in this image, you'll have a higher sexual market value than 99% of white women.

Now with a face like an absolute "10," the man of your dreams is going to want to literally fuck that face more than anything. So, the next order of business is to get a gold medal in cock sucking and deep throating. Go on Amazon and buy a good sized soft silicone dildo with a suction cup and stick it to your shower wall. Every day when you are in the shower, take a swig of avocado oil, swirl it about in your mouth, and practice sucking and deep throating it until you are better than a sword-swallower in Cirque du Soleil. Go online and search for the top three most viewed and liked blowjob videos on the entire internet so you can see what guys are into AND COPY THAT GIRL.

Next, you have to understand what men truly desire from a woman on an emotional level. I had a female friend once who was getting messaged *every few minutes* by some top-shelf man offering to buy her a condo, pay her $20G/month just to go to dinner with him 1x per week, etc. I would have top-shelf men she had sex with just *one time*, invite me out to lunch and tell me that they would buy me a fucking Porsche 911 turbo or any other car I wanted, if I could just influence this girl to marry them. Now here is where things get even more interesting: this girl violated all of the red pill bullshit about being feminine and having a low body count, yet she *still* had all the top men in the world begging to marry her? What was her secret?

She understood, because of her own career, *just how fucking hard the life of a successful man is.* She appreciated, adored and respected those men for what they had to endure, and let them know how she felt in no uncertain terms, and she *meant* it. I guess you could say that instead of competing with men, it was more like she was fighting *alongside* them. She always made any man she was with feel like a fucking lion, because even if they fell short, she understood that they would turn into actual lions if she positively reinforced them, because they were already mostly there anyway. She never nagged, criticized, argued with or contradicted a man she was with. Just sheer positive reinforcement and adoration, further reinforced with endless sex.

Yes, not only did she love men (most of you women hate them), she loved sex and *never* withheld sex or used it to control a man. She was down to fuck and suck, anytime and anywhere.

The final piece of advice is to be aggressive if you are interested in a man. Men have so much female fatigue from the way you dumb bitches behave that you can't sit around and just wait to be approached. Mind you, you don't need to hit on men or throw yourselves at them. Just initiate and *carry* conversations. So many women out there not only expect the man to initiate, but when he does, they do nothing to carry the conversation and expect the man to do everything like he was some sort of performing seal. A good parallel example of this abject stupidity and *lack of compassion* for what men have to go through, is I had a tango instructor once who used to complain that all these women in his classes would refuse to put any effort into getting better at tango, stating that if the guy is good enough as a lead, he can compensate for their inability to follow. This is *exactly* what they do in their relationship life as well. How fucking lazy can these twats be? The tango instructor would correctly respond with, "If you don't know how to follow and your tango skills suck, why would a top-shelf tango dancer have any interest in dancing with you to begin with?" But it just didn't register with them. It's a low IQ thing, yet again! It's like women who want a dominant man but are incapable of surrender so instead they nag and nag, and then they nag some more. Then when the man is left with little choice but to beat the living shit out of them, to obtain submission in lieu of surrender, they cry to the authorities. This is why they have a saying in China, "If your man doesn't beat you, he doesn't love you." Sure, the man could also just walk away, but then he probably didn't love you. It is hard for a man to walk away from a woman he truly loves. Besides myself, I have never met a man who could do it.

Anyway, your main goal when you converse with a man, is to show your interest, and to showcase *your ability to understand and positively reinforce him.* The man will be able to take it from there, but should he be taking too long to make a move, all you need to do is find out what he is into, that women normally are never into, and use that as the lever to hook him. Let me give you a real-world example: Most top-shelf alpha males are into something that they don't like to brag about, such as playing a particular video game, watching a certain fantasy or sci-fi show, etc. It really doesn't matter what it is. It's usually something women either are not interested in, or else judge to be, "for losers." Let's say he likes a certain show on Netflix, for example. Your job is to catch up on watching that show, learn some facts about it, and then when the next season is coming out, tell him you and one of your girlfriends are having a "watch party" at your place and that he should come hang out. Then when he shows up, you can say your girlfriend had to cancel and the two of you just start watching the show together. It's easy at a certain point for you to initiate the best blowjob of his life – nice and sloppy with plenty of saliva and drool and eye contact. Make sure you swallow when he cums, of course. Before the end of the following week, he will probably ask you to marry him, or take you on a trip to meet his parents or some shit.

It's really that easy, but you have to love yourself, and you have to love men enough, to follow my advice. Which 99% of you won't, because you are filled with self-loathing, too lazy to do anything about it, and therefore deserve the shit lot you end up with in life.

One Societal Solution to Ease the Effects of Childhood Trauma

Moving along... when I got older and grew consciously aware of things that were really wrong in the world *at the root*, I had the thought, in my naivete, that the biggest impact I could have on the world would be if I could get parents to raise their children in such a manner so as *not* to create trauma. There was a wonderful book written on the topic called "The Aware Baby" by Aletha J. Solter that I had read for some unknown reason, and afterwards I came to the realization that if every parent got this book before bringing children into this world, than the world would one day be completely unrecognizable, albeit in a very good way!

What convinced me of this, was that one day this couple left a baby with both myself and this girl I was dating at the time, because they wanted to go out drinking. They warned us that the baby was "colicky," which to the uninitiated means it cries in an extreme way all the time for no *apparent* reason. Keyword for all the somatic dummies out there is "apparent," because I can assure you that if a baby is fucking crying, it is *crying for a fucking reason*. Now I am one of those people who cannot stand to hear babies cry, and it throws me into a rage. Part of the reason for this is because I am infuriated that the parents are so unaware that they cannot feel the energy behind the crying and simply think: "Babies cry, that's just how it is." The other reason is of course because I feel like crying all the time as well, and don't need to be reminded of it by some baby! Lol

So of course I am trying to take a nap as my girlfriend is in the bathroom training for the gold medal in bulimia at the upcoming Special Olympics, and this little baby girl starts to wail away. It's pretty horrid, but then I remember something Ms. Solter taught in her book, "The Aware Baby" about curing babies of colic, and I decided to implement it as an experiment. So I take this little baby, and while I lay on my back I lay her face down on my chest so she can feel my heart beat against hers, and I just focus my energy upon her and her own heartbeat while tuning into her crying. I become "present" with her, which is just a fancy way of saying *I am paying attention to her at the exclusion of all other sensory and mental traffic requests.*

We just lay there like this for a while and suddenly this baby changed how it cried, and started crying in a way I had never heard before. It was like someone grabbed the volume knob and cranked it to the very end. I remained still and maintained focus on her, and after a while her cries turned into what can best be described as sobs, followed by "heaving" and finally her shaking like crazy! I realized that by doing exactly what the book advised parents to do, I had allowed this baby to release some sort of unknown trauma (it turned out to be abandonment trauma), much like the shaking deer I talked about at the beginning of Part II. I continued to stay focused on her, and after a long while the baby went limp and fell asleep peacefully on top of me. I took the hint and fell asleep myself. A few hours later my girlfriend woke me up, smelling like bile, yet the baby continued to sleep.

A few days later, her parents ran into me on the street. "What did you do to our baby?" the mother exclaimed... I said "What are you talking about?" She continued, "Our baby no longer cries. She is like a totally different baby. This is incredible." I told her I am just good with kids. Which is true, I just can't stand them. They love me though. Go figure. Then again, kids adore monsters, how else can you explain the timeless success of Maurice Sendak's "Where the Wild Things Are?" The mother then confessed to me that the baby was adopted, and had been abandoned by her birth mother. Well that explained everything! The baby was colicky because of the trauma of being abandoned.

Let me tell another quick story for future parents out there... I was hanging out maybe 20 years later with another female friend who was a single mom, as her own unresolved traumas got her involved with some loser guy who gave her a daughter and then wanted nothing to do with the child. So we were eating in an outdoor cafe in NYC during the covid-19 scamdemic thanks to a vaccine card I doodled with my dick, and her daughter, who was already a few years old and had bladder control issues (trauma), suddenly pisses herself and consequently finds herself sitting in a huge puddle of piss. The mom starts to get a bit upset, and I can see the child is somewhat ashamed.

Now I really don't want this girl to grow up with some fetish for pissing herself on dates or some other kind of weirdness. It's just wholly impractical! So I suddenly look her in the eye and say, "Who cares? I piss in public in front of others all of the time." Then quoting the illustrious character "Shake" from the "Aqua Teen Hunger Force" cartoon series that used to run on cable TV, I proudly exclaim, "The world is my bathroom!" The look on her face was priceless, and honestly, who cares if she pisses herself? It's one of life's simple pleasures. If I had allowed her to be shamed, she would have grown up anorgasmic. This is because her bladder issues are caused by unprocessed trauma, and if she gets shamed for them and starts adding additional layers of trauma - subconsciously locking up her bladder to avoid pissing herself again, she will never be able to cum again, either. To her future lovers... you're welcome! Anyway, her loser piece of shit father abandoned her, did he not? She's going to have enough issues as is, she doesn't need any more of them! If she is going to end up on the pole, she might as well be a squirter! Again, the same musculature that allows you to piss, allows you to experience orgasm. Guys who have premature ejaculation issues nearly always have bladder issues, just as many prostate issues are actually bladder issues in disguise. This is why Tadalafil can help many prostate issues, and why SSRIs are often the only real solution for premature ejaculation – at least until the underlying tension can be released, which of course is *no easy task*.

As a side note, if you have a little girl and she starts to develop bladder issues or get urinary tract infections (UTIs), you may want to investigate if she is being molested. The two often go hand-in-hand. #themoreyouknow

So as I was saying, at some point in the past I had the thought that it would be a really cool project to get "The Aware Baby" by Aletha J. Solther into the hands of expectant mothers. Such a project didn't seem too far fetched, because around the time I was born, doctors were putting the most popular book on child rearing by Dr. Benjamin Spock, into the hands of expectant mothers. I even clearly remember my own mother's copy of the book. First published in 1946, it became one of the best-selling books of the twentieth century, selling 500,000 copies in the first six months and over 50 million copies by the time of Spock's death in 1998. The book has been translated into 39 languages and is widely credited with revolutionizing child-rearing practices for generations of parents, especially in the post-World War II era. His message empowered generations of parents to feel more confident and less anxious about their parenting choices by emphasizing that parenting is a personal journey, and that mistakes are part of learning, urging parents to be responsive to their children's individual needs and to adapt their approach as necessary. I saw Aletha's book as a suitable heir to the throne, so to speak...

See, while such an approach as Dr. Spock's is no doubt far better than one involving swaddling, spanking or any other abusive shenanigans that went on prior to the widespread acceptance of his views, it still fails to provide a road map for creating a child free from trauma. I saw "The Aware Baby" as the next evolutionary step and set up a fundraiser to get money from a foundation to make this dream a reality. After all, how hard would it be to get people on board for something that was "for the children." All I needed was to collect digital signatures. Boy, was I in for a shock! Nothing but resistance, and beneath said resistance, I could clearly detect the unspoken objection: *"Why should future children NOT have to suffer as I did?"* People will talk all the time about how they want a better life for their children, but they are usually referring to things like money or job opportunities. They don't actually want a better life for their child where it actually matters...

My Personal History

I was born in Lenox Hill hospital in Manhattan, on April 17th 1971. The circumstances surrounding your conception are sometimes *far* more important than the circumstances surrounding your physical birth, *despite* the impacts of birth trauma on human development. In my case, I know that I was conceived out on Montauk, Long Island because my biological father told me so. Although he never knew *how*. It is not like I was planned, anyway. Yet he says he never forgot the night of my conception or how *magical* he remembered it to be. Indeed it was, in ways he does not realize, as he is not privy to some of the information that I am. Although, he has confessed to me that there were times when he looked at me or listened to things I would say and thought to himself, "This cannot be my son" although I certainly *look* like his son and a human DNA test would confirm it to be so. People do not realize that the hybridization process of an alien abductee begins in the womb of the abductee's mother, and often the conception itself is tampered with as well, although the participants will remember it as something *other* than what it actually was due to the ability of extraterrestrials to install "screen memories" in their victim's minds. However, what the extraterrestrial engineers presiding over such a project often forget, is that they really cannot be 100% certain what sort of entity will hop into the "driver's seat" of the genetic vehicle they have fashioned. Things don't always go the way *they* plan.

But while my conception may have been "magical" my delivery certainly was not, as I have already explained. It gave me a certain strength, and no doubt this strength has served me well over the course of what has been a *very* difficult life. Surely, millions have had it harder than I, but that doesn't make my existence any *less* difficult, nor make me *feel* any better about it. The longer a being such as myself exists in a world such as this,

375

the harder their experience gets. This is because what you *are*, is not meant to be *in this world*, and the longer you endure here, the more your real nature begins to gnaw away at you, due to it's inability to express itself *in this world*. Not to mention that even a hybridized human body has it's limits with respect to what it can contain, especially if the being it *truly* contains becomes more and more *embodied*. In my case, there is not much left in me that can be considered human. Just enough remains to keep me here in this current form and the clock is ticking. Take note, because you can attempt to bring forth and integrate your "real nature," despite your sheer ignorance of what it *actually may be*, by pursuing Reichian breathwork, kundalini yoga, etc., but if these pursuits are continued relentlessly, you *may* come to learn that much of your "armor" and most of your "blockages" are neither *just* the results of social conditioning that can simply be dropped, nor trauma that can be re-experienced and released, or even psychodynamic conflicts that can be resolved, but are in fact alien implants and other safety/control mechanisms that were installed by the Greys or other extraterrestrial groups as part of your hybridization. You also never want to suffer the misfortune of breaking down the walls that separate potential personality alters, nor recall the depth of torture underwent to produce them in the first place.

Should you succeed in defeating or surmounting any of these obstacles, you *may* find that this "real you" that you strove to bring forth from the muck and the mire that is/was your humanity, has no place in this world and thus *you* have no place in this world. This is the fundamental basis of the angst of hybridized beings, and there are more of us out there than you would know. Beings who wander around with no place to fit in because they are not natural creations. They often gravitate towards each other because even if they are very different from each other, the one thing they have in common is not belonging anywhere in particular. At least they have that experience in common and can accommodate each other's needs in that regard.

Believe me, if you are a hybrid such as I, then the "real you" *may* be something that is both dark and *beyond your imagination*. Awakening it will *not* allow your "human" life to "flow" and your human needs to be met because you are *not* human and your *true* needs are often *in conflict* with your "humanity." This is what many hybrids ultimately are – the fusion of DNA from species that are in direct opposition to each other in the natural order of the multiverse. We are not talking about crossing a dog with a wolf here, nor a lion with a tiger. We are talking something more in line with crossing a snake with a mongoose! Would such a being be able to live with either donor species? It would be rejected by both.

Some time after my birth, my biological mother became a very different person after returning from yet another trip to Montauk, Long Island. This should not really be a surprise, as beneath Camp Hero (now a park) is an underground military base, as well as an entrance into the network of underground cities on this planet filled with dark extraterrestrials. She began to suffer physical pains as well as psychiatric ones that had no discernible cause. She dropped in intelligence, became very religious and "found Jesus." She passed away over 10 years ago with Alzheimer's and cancer, in a hospice in the Bronx. What the medical establishment fails to realize is how many cases of Alzheimer's are actually the mind finally breaking down under all the abuse it has suffered at the hands of Satanically aligned extraterrestrials who wipe the mind over-and-over, often installing false "screen memories" so one cannot recall the actual memories of abduction and hybridization one has experienced. I for one, have almost no memory of my past. I can tell you where I went to school, etc. but there are very few memories. If you never think of your past and it seems you are living in an endless present with just a handful of memories, you can probably thank the Greys, who abducted you continuously throughout your life, if your specific hybridization was valuable enough for them to do so. I say this because if you have no memories, you are lucky, as wiping memories is not damaging, but overwriting memories is.

If all they did was wipe your memories, it means you were valuable enough for them to preserve. Another clue is to appear to have no control over your destiny, and to feel like somehow your freedom has been severely restricted — as if you are in a glass box that nobody else can see. This is because those who hybridized you view you as their property, and the only way you can be freed from them is if another, more powerful extraterrestrial group comes for you, or if The Divine Father wills it. This is one of the reasons why prayer, free from the confines of any religious framework, is so important. Forget about Jesus, pray to The Divine Father.

It was this seemingly utter inability to control my own destiny that had plagued my existence and ultimately led me to becoming *what* I am now. In retrospect, I have come to realize that I was created for a specific purpose, both in regards to the perspective of the extraterrestrials who hybridized my physical form, as well as in regards to the will of The Divine Father, who really doesn't care about the plans of rebellious extraterrestrials, no matter how advanced or powerful they may believe themselves to be. Either way, I have my purpose and any other ideas I may have about what I want to do are largely irrelevant. I know this is an impossible pill for many hybrids to swallow, and a truth that a hybrid can only begin to accept after having struggled for so many years to achieve its mundane goals and satisfy its innate drives, only to be met with frustration and failure over-and-over again. After all, most hybrids have so many advantages over regular humans. In my case, when combined with my natural relentlessness imprinted upon me from a traumatic birth, why was I such a failure? Sure, I had built a successful business, but that was what I did to *make* a living, not how I actually wanted to *live*. It was as if I was surrounded by glass walls or bound with invisible chains. I could almost hear those chains rattling in moments where I found myself walking down an empty block in Tribeca late at night. My best friend at the time and I used to make notes of how *something* would be endlessly blocking our efforts and rearranging our lives just like in that science-fiction film "Dark

City," and we were always just trying to get to "Shell Beach" to uncover the truth, albeit unsuccessfully.

I had always figured I would die in the State of New York's very own "Dark City," perhaps passing in NY Presbyterian hospital on the Upper East Side of Manhattan. NY Presbyterian always felt like it could be my end, just as a hospice in the Bronx had proven to be my late biological mother's. While I had not been expecting to die any time soon despite a brush with death a few years prior when my appendix ruptured and I refused to go the hospital for 10 days, I had nonetheless begun making plans for my funeral before I had even turned 50.

To "be myself" had been the goal of my entire life from age 17 on when I fell in love with a girl I didn't even know, whom I saw walking across the auditorium in my senior year at The Bronx High School of Science back in 1989. I had never seen this girl the prior three years of my studies there, but there were around 3,000 students in attendance at any given time, so this scenario was not *that* improbable. It was a love that was far more than romantic or sexual in nature despite her beauty, and utterly overwhelming in strength. I just did not understand what I was experiencing or what to do with said experience, yet this experience somehow awakened in me this idea that whatever I was *as a human*, was in fact a *mere shadow* of *what I really was*. I wasn't even human, for that matter, although it would take close to 35 years for this to be revealed to me.

In retrospect, I am sure she wasn't human, either.

This moment of awakening made me very unhappy because how could anyone be happy being something they are not? This unhappiness drove me to seek out who or *what* I really was (*what* is more important than *who*), and to bring it forth. My error at the time, was believing that success in this endeavor would bring me happiness in this particular realm. Specifically, that it would bring me love, relationship, sexual abundance, peak sexual experiences, etc. I turned out very wrong in regards to these assumptions, yet I suppose I *had* to have believed in them for so long, in order to have driven myself through close to 35 years of downright starvation with respect to any experiences in the human realm that I would have desired to experience.

I had taken quite an interest in Taoism starting around age 19, and after two extended adventures in China around the age of 30, I became more interested in Buddhist thought than Taoist. I had also just gotten out of a terrible relationship and had realized that everything I knew about women and how to interact with them was terribly wrong, and had to be relearned from scratch. I started looking for books to help me and quickly stumbled upon the PUA scene, which was just in its infancy. In those brave days before social media where you actually had to go out and hunt for women in the real world, I actually attained a certain level of success.

It was mostly an online scene at the time, yet myself and some others would meet every Saturday on the 2nd floor of a pizzeria located across from FIT in Manhattan, which was rented out for a few hours by an instructor who went by the name of Brad P., who was unknown at the time and charged like $20 for a few hours of instruction. Brad P. has long disappeared from the scene, but became quite the legend in his time. Both Mystery and RSD were starting to gain traction at this point, and of course there was Vin DiCarlo and his partner for a short time, Sebastian. What made Vin's early work with Sebastian special, was they pointed out the concept of "attainability," which ironically is a big theme in this book, nearly 25 years later.

Nobody likes to talk about this, but most of these guys weren't as successful with women as they claimed. They would claim to go home with 8s and 9s, but in reality those girls were 5s and 6s, which posed the question, "Why would I study PUA to get 5s and 6s?" NYC was, and still is, a brutal sexual marketplace, and many of the "greats" would get shot to shit in their approaches in places like the meatpacking district, which at the time was the place to be. These days it is just a bunch of shops. Cold approach there was like landing on Normandy beach on D-day. So many just got mowed down, mere moments after hitting the pavement.

Seeing the problem, I began to look at what you would call "naturals." The common thread I saw was that the most successful naturals with women were those who had cluster B personality disorders, specifically narcissistic personality disorder (NPD), or else were flat out sociopaths. Sure, there were outliers whose success defied rational explanation or reverse engineering. For example, I had one friend who was much older, and throughout his entire life, everywhere he went, women threw themselves at him. He was tall but not handsome, neither rich nor famous, and had no real personality. I asked him if he had some massive cock, and he replied that he wished that he did. Yet this guy would go into the corner magazine shop (a relic of pre-internet times, along with bookstores) in the morning after falling out of bed to get a cup of coffee, and random women would just grab him and demand to be taken home and fucked. This happened literally thousands of times in his life with no explanation. But you can't *model* guys like this because they cannot be reverse-engineered. They are mysteries.

So I decided to model those with NPD, which I did very successfully. Being tall and good-looking (in my youth), I pulled off some legendary escapades. Problem was, I could not *feel* anything nor *enjoy* anything. What is the point dining in the best sushi restaurant in all of Japan, if you have lost your ability to taste food? This was the price of success, and I believe that many a successful PUA went into this dark place.

I could not *feel* anything nor *enjoy* anything, because there was no "me" to feel or enjoy any of my conquests. This was because I was still a shadow of my *real* self, although I *still* did not know *what* my real self was. However, what I observed over the course of my adventures, was that human women were not interested in "alpha males" or any of that nonsense propagated to this day in the "manosphere." They did not select for beneficial genes either, with respect to their partner selection process. I am not saying that these foundational assumptions do not hold any sway whatsoever, but most assumptions about human behavior are flawed because they are based on the fallacy that the core drive in a human being is survival, when in fact it is *stability of the psyche* that is the core drive. Look around you. Nothing that humans do promotes their survival, yet everything they do promotes their psychic stability, no matter the ultimate cost. This is because the human psyche is so incredibly fragile, *by design.* Without a fragile psyche, humans could not be so easily manipulated by extraterrestrial entities.

One of the core problems within this realm is the perpetual lack of the *experience* of love. However, when I was young, humans still sought out love even though it was, unbeknownst to them, *unattainable.* Everyone from my generation (Gen X) will remember actor John Cusack's boombox-serenading scene from the 1989 film, "Say Anything." These days love itself is hated and despised. Considered an inconvenience at best, and a terrible form of suffering at worst. Human females repress their sexuality just enough to be able to protect themselves from falling in love, yet not enough to protect themselves from debasement. In the process, they end up inadvertently weaponizing their sexuality, as well as commodifying it.

It was at this point that I came upon a tantric guru who really appeared to "have the goods" when it came to true "inner game." I am referring to the legendary underground tantra teacher who went by the moniker of "Shantam Nityama" at that time. Who knows what he is calling himself these days, in order to stay abreast of all the haters! I met him many years ago after someone uploaded a video of him to a discussion board I frequented. It showed him making a woman orgasm by waving his hand, and the uploader was accusing him of being a scammer. After watching the video and checking out his website, I thought to myself, "If this is a scam, I want to learn this scam!" Interestingly, such sensational hijinks turned out to be legit, and he could indeed make women orgasm from across the room or even across the planet, via Skype. While I had no interest in performing such stunts, I knew this individual could take my journey to the next level, and so I signed up for the only two seminars he ever offered, and we ended up becoming fast friends. My introduction to him came at a critical time after I had become successful at being a PUA, but at the price of my own authenticity, and still haunted by all of my unresolved trauma. Shantam Nityama was instrumental in guiding me out of the woods, and gave me a different model of how sexual dynamics between men and women actually work. It was this basic model that I refined over the years via sex with dark interdimensional beings, who took my understanding of sexual dynamics to another level.

But while he was able to explain what he was doing with women, he was not able to explain *how* he was able to do so, let alone teach others to do it as well. However, I became taken with the notion that the method by which I could learn to do what he did, would be the same method by which I could salvage the real me from the depths of my being. My idea was that my actual self, along with all of it's latent abilities, was buried beneath all of this psycho-physical tension that the late Wilhelm Reich called "armor." This "armor" had been forged as an alloy of neurotic conflict and social conditioning.

At a retreat with him in Bali, Indonesia, I met a sex worker who told me about the Shamanic De-Armoring retreat that is held once a year in Phoenix, AZ and I signed up for it as soon as I could. After attending the retreat, I spent the next three years working on my somatic armoring with brutal breathwork on the daily. Towards the end of those three years I ruptured my appendix from the breathwork. Little did I know at the time that my efforts had caused me to hit upon an actual alien implant!

I didn't go to the hospital for 10 days despite the pain, and when I finally walked into the emergency room, nobody believed my appendix had ruptured because they insisted I would have been dead had it actually done so. Yet a CT scan proved them all wrong, and after days of IV antibiotics I was free of the pain of peritoneal sepsis and left the hospital with a very attractive drainage tube coming out of my lower pelvis. Not a good look in the hottest two weeks of a NYC summer...

By the time they pulled the tube out, my appendix had already regenerated itself, no doubt a benefit of occupying a reptilian-human hybridized body. Of course, I was unaware of these realities at that time. I just knew I should have been killed from the appendix rupture and resultant sepsis, and that I should not have been able to withstand the pain so easily. I decided against continuing on with the breathwork, as the practice had ultimately broken thru a significant amount of obstruction, activating enough kundalini to move my being into a position that was more in alignment with *what* I really was. By now, you see, I had realized that the question was no longer about *who* I really was. The *who* was largely irrelevant.

I can remember cumming so hard one time in some girl's throat, that the kundalini energy that awakened started to break sutures in my skull. I lay there in bed next to this girl who had no gag reflex, twisting and turning Continuum Movement style, to try and accommodate the movement of the kundalini energy as it changed my body, and even the girl could hear the sounds coming from my skull and could not believe what she was hearing. I really wasn't sure I would survive that night, and I remember walking through Central Park North the next morning, shocked yet grateful that I was alive, and not in a psychiatric facility.

I had always been into bodybuilding but never made any real gains no matter how hard I trained, yet when the drama with my appendix was over, this was when a famous IFBB pro approached me at a gym after watching me work out, and informed me that I had a lot of potential, but needed to get on steroids ASAP! I never had an issue with their usage, I simply didn't realize *just* how important they were. Given I hadn't eaten for a few weeks when my appendix ruptured, it seemed like a great time to learn about steroids and start using them. Which I never regretted. My hybridized body adored anabolics of all sorts, and would tolerate any and all compounds no matter how large the dosages were, without side effects. Unlike most people, who use steroids to run away from themselves, I used them to *run towards* myself.

At this point I also found myself with *different, yet far greater* abilities than the tantra teacher I had studied with. The problem that cropped up now, upon the resolution of so many of my issues, was that I could no longer resonate with most women, as they are all filled with unresolved issues. So it became impossible for me to find someone on whom to ply my new trade! I finally did find someone, but I had barely six months to indulge myself before the party was cut short as if by some invisible hand. Which indeed it was! It just didn't seem fair!

Although I didn't realize it at the time, my true nature had also begun to awaken as a consequence of all of my efforts, yet in retrospect it appeared that this dark nature simply could not be allowed free reign in this realm. So while I felt I *should* be out there "cleaning up" with my newfound sexual powers, other forces would not allow for this, much to my chagrin. No matter how hard I tried, every attempt I made at sexual expression on this planet was blocked by what appeared to be that same invisible hand.

In addition, social and economic opportunities consistently evaded me no matter my qualifications or efforts. So did artistic and sporting ambitions.

It was as if I was not allowed to live any sort of actual human life whatsoever, and nobody could understand how I could be so unsuccessful and so unlucky despite decades of struggle and so much natural potential. I mean, it took 20 years of insane effort just to attain a sexual relationship that I found satisfying, but that barely lasted six months before it was destroyed by seemingly mysterious forces beyond my immediate perception.

I did end up with a certain level of internet-fame for a brief moment, and became a successful entrepreneur relative to where I was starting out from, yet even there I should have been much farther along with all the work and sacrifice I had put in, and continued to put in. I always felt like I invested a trillion dollars in myself and got back five cents! Mind you, fame and money are worthless goals pursued by fools who think it will buy them love and satisfying sex, which it never can because it isn't meant to. You can't dig a ditch with a house cat. Of course money and fame can buy *opportunities for sexual experiences*, but you can't buy the skills or fortune to turn those opportunities into *satisfying* sexual experiences. However, my money (and fame) were just by-products of needing to earn a living, since nobody would hire someone such as myself in any capacity, no matter my abilities. I could have easily been a top executive, but being rejected by the corporate system, I had to become a successful CEO on my own, which in fact I did become. The reality is that I had little choice but to go the entrepreneurial route, and given that putting myself "out there" was more so a part of the entrepreneurial journey than ever before, my 15 minutes of fame was just par for the course.

As my inherent darkness had been inadvertently awakened, I found myself gravitating towards dark magic from Thailand and Khmer, often practiced by former Buddhist monks who "go rogue." I should warn anyone reading this that they should steer clear of this sort of thing and not fuck around with it. Whatever you need, just pray to The Divine Father about it. Do not fuck around with dark magic or witchcraft and find out. Many people, especially those in the Russian community, love to hire the services of powerful witches from the East, and/or practice very dark magic that they learn in online forums. In most cases, they do so in order to harm others out of jealousy and envy. I am not saying it is fine to do so to obtain love or money, or for any other reason. I am just pointing out that many individuals who get involved in dark magic, do so with some of the worst motives possible. Again, I advise you to cultivate a direct relationship with The Divine Father, and decline to mess around elsewhere, where you can find yourself experiencing some truly catastrophic consequences down the line.

In my situation, "magic" was not of any help anyway. It was as if some "alien" will was in charge, and I was besides myself. Unlike others who had run away from themselves, I had put over 30 years of hard work and sacrifice into running *towards* myself. What had it amounted to? It was as if I had made it out of my prison cell, only to find myself standing out in the prison yard. Technically, an escape. Practically speaking, still imprisoned. I had nothing even remotely resembling "a life," not realizing a hybridized being such as myself was never meant to have a "life." More like an *existence*.

One day, I found myself eating in a Cantonese restaurant in New York City's Eastern Chinatown that I frequented, and called out in my mind to whomever or whatever happened to be listening. I expressed that I felt as if I had been totally let down by the "light side" of spirituality in the sense that I had worked so impossibly hard for so long, and accomplished so much with respect to the journey I had been undertaking, yet had accomplished so little with respect to achieving the results that I had been expecting. I was pretty sure "karma" existed, but somehow it didn't seem to apply to me. My existence was close to unbearable and I had started entertaining extremely self-destructive thoughts. I had been making incredible progress in my life towards something, but the path was a spiral so it was not like I had actually gone anywhere, even though I had traveled so incredibly far. So the question had now become more like "how do I spiral *out?*"

One thing I kept thinking about, was that with all that I *had* accomplished, I must be of use to *someone.* In other words, I must have *some purpose.* A typical thought for a hybrid often fashioned to be used and discarded, no? As most people had not opted for a path such as mine, *I must be rare and therefore of value.* There must be *a place for me in creation,* right? In that moment I first became open to what humans will define as "the dark side," or evil, as "good" had gotten me nowhere, and "good" didn't even want me on their team from the looks of things.

I am aware that some may believe that a moment such as the one I am describing is a moment of weakness, but they fail to realize that evil has as much a place in creation as does good, and that the important thing is that evil has to align itself with the will of The Divine Father just as good does, in order to facilitate balance throughout creation. If darkness is your true nature, than such a moment is actually a moment of surrender and *acceptance,* and not one of weakness. Another thing I want to point out here is that some of the darkest beings who incarnate into human forms do not necessarily sit around all day thinking about doing terrible things to others, jack off to torture porn, or indulge in any of the thoughts and activities you would imagine them to. Often times, these beings don't even realize their true nature. This was the case with me.

I did remember meeting with an eminent Buddhist scholar years ago in China who told me that I could never "become a Buddha" as my nature was "inherently corrupt" and that I should cultivate myself spiritually using methods that were appropriate for my nature, which he revealed to me. I took his advice with respect to the methods, but when it came to his assessment of my nature, I thought he was talking in metaphor, and not being literal. Even the rogue former Buddhist monk who had been exposing me to Thai and Khmer black magic had told me *what* I really was, and that he was very uncomfortable relating with me. The irony! But again, I didn't really take his assessment of me seriously. It all seemed rather unbelievable, even though I had a lifetime of supernatural experiences and there was so much tangential evidence to support their assertions. Go figure!

So I let it be known that I was open to hearing about any and all possibilities with respect to the path I should walk moving forward. Nobody suddenly appeared from the ether and sat down at my table to partake in dim sum, so I left the restaurant figuring I would be spending the rest of my days taking steroids and uploading workout photos to Instagram. The best I could hope for was that maybe I would make enough money in my business to live in Thailand or Brazil for a few months out of the year fucking hookers, but I invested little hope in such a possible future, as I was pretty sure something would prevent even *that* from ever happening based on my track record up until that point.

It had not even been a few days since Dim Sum, when *certain things* were revealed to me, and an opportunity presented. I seized the opportunity to finally be *me* - even though it placed me smack in the middle of a spiritual war between the darkness that rebels against The Divine Father, and the darkness that aligns itself with His will. This planet *is* enemy territory, and for me the experience was like waking up from a dream that you thought was reality, but instead of waking up in your bed, you wake up on a battlefield surrounded by enemies, and you hear a voice over your radio saying: "If you want to live, do exactly as I say." I did, and barely three years later, I was forced to flee New York City and leave everyone I knew behind. Life has not gotten easier, in fact it has gotten harder. The "rebellious dark" is always gunning for me. I must remain ever vigilant and aware in every moment. Mindful of my actions, my words, and even my thoughts.

I didn't make the decisions that I did due to the lure of power or vengeance or anything like that. I did it for love. Not in the sense of *romantic* love as humans seem to fancy. Human language falls short in this regard, but if you have ever watched an episode of "Doctor Who" on the BBC when David Tennant played the Doctor, and you just felt *something* alive in your heart that kept you going... well, then you probably know what I am trying to talk about here. It is no coincidence that author Douglas Adams in "The Hitchiker's Guide To The Galaxy" named the spaceship that was powered by the "infinite improbability drive" the "Heart of Gold." Because love trumps magic.

As a matter of fact, love *always* trumps magic and when combined with sacrifice of what you hold dear... I talk about *sacrifice* because the path I chose required that I give up what humanity I had acquired, along with my friends, my family, and all that I did hold dear in relation to what *had been* my humanity. But when I got to the point where most of my humanity had been extinguished, what remained in the blackness of my being were actually *all* of the best parts of me, that had *always* been there. They were never part of my "humanity" to begin with, so they were never lost. These days I always find it amusing to watch human entertainment, where the idea is often promoted, that there is something "special" about humanity. Some quality, that other forms of existence envy.

There isn't.

I don't have a lot of time left in this form. Just as I completed this manuscript I lost all interest in human females entirely. Never imagined that would be possible, yet one must appreciate the irony given the nature of this book! I am like a dark butterfly that has the memories of the caterpillar it once was, waiting for the wind to carry me into the next realm.

But the reality is that *none* of you have a lot of time left, either. We are in the "end times," and while my message is primarily targeted at other dark beings who have incarnated into this realm, *anyone* can take the same advice I have for them and also escape the "matrix." So if you have forgotten who or what you are... If you find yourself confused, lost, or otherwise "stuck" here... If you know you do not belong here but don't know where it is that you actually belong... Do not despair! Reach out to The Divine Father *at once*, acknowledge him as your creator, and ask to align your will with His in order to be of assistance to Him. Ask Him what you are and where you belong, and ask Him to guide you, *in accordance with His will.* If you are of the darkness, you do *not* have to join the "rebellious dark" and foolishly place yourself at odds with The Divine Father just to find a place where you can be accepted. The darkness that is aligned with The Divine Father is far more powerful than the darkness that rebels against Him, and they will be happy to have you. If you feel alone and unloved, this can come to an end. Do not fall for the Satanic lie that if you are of the darkness you are somehow automatically against the Divine Father! Satan and those who rebel against The Divine Father want you to think they are the only game in town if you are of the darkness. Believe me, the only game in town is WITH The Divine Father, not against him.

Beyond The Game

I feel this book presents the most accurate understanding of the true, trauma-based dynamics between men and women in what can be termed "the modern sexual marketplace," and presents them within the context of larger planetary and spiritual issues, so you can understand what is *really* at stake here. If there was ever a difficult pill to swallow in the manosphere, this may very will be the one, as humans have a serious aversion to reality – especially to a reality that threatens their psychic stability, and to point out that they are playing a "game" that cannot be won is most definitely a threat to their psychic stability. I guess we can call it taking the "trauma pill?" Nonetheless, "the game" can still be played as elegantly as possible. My solution, which is to raise your sexual market value as high as you can, then rent as many top-shelf women as you can in the hopes that at worst you will have a lot of peak experiences, and at best *maybe, just maybe,* something a bit deeper and a bit more long term *may* arise is utterly unacceptable to most men. It's just not the dream that they were *sold.* Yet I do not believe anyone can come up with a better solution that does not involve oppressing women as was done in the past – which is something I am completely against, and something that should never be repeated. I likewise reject all philosophies that deny a man's need for women, such as going MGTOW, taking up edging and gooning, or dreaming about a future filled with AI sex robots.

In the same manner, the solution of *direct prayer* to The Divine Father asking to align your will with His is also not part of the dream that humans have been sold. Just like feminists, most humans irrespective of gender have been sold on the idea of being "strong and independent," and of being "self made," yet this is not reality. Human beings are neither strong nor independent nor were they designed to be so. Not that it would change anything if they were, since direct prayer to The Divine Father and surrendering to His will is the only viable solution for *all* beings in His creation.

What's so fascinating about most men, is that they continue to *view the world through the eyes of a child, despite being forced to grow up.* This is no small feat, and a testament to just how hopelessly their own mothers have brainwashed them. Brainwashed to the point that they can *never* see women for what they truly are, let alone accept them for it. What's so fascinating about women, is that they have always *viewed the world through the eyes of an adult, despite never having had to grow up.*

I personally don't think the world as we know it will be around in ten years, and I hope I will not be around to even see the next five years. I have no desire to live on a planet where you are forced to live in a high-tech feudal state with zero privacy and zero freedom. I will never implant a chip in my head, hand, or anywhere else inside of my body for that matter. I reject the whole philosophy of transhumanism. I also avoid using social media, and mostly use my smartphone for phone calls, texting, and the most basic of apps.

Rather than not-so-slowly turning yourselves into robots that fuck other robots, renounce all religion at once, and start praying directly to The Divine Father. You need to have a direct relationship with your creator, and your creator is not Jesus, or Mohammad, or Buddha, or some anonymous energy field. Neither are you your own creator: You are not "self made," you are not "infinite awareness," and you are not some god. Most of you can't even chew with your mouths closed, have no fashion sense, and possess the IQ of a rechargeable "intelligent" vibrator, so just STFU and stop embarrassing yourselves with your own delusions of grandeur.

The last election between Trump and Harris was an absolute disgrace. I despise both the right as well as the left, I just ask myself which side will take longer to inflict all the damage they possible can and run with that one, in order to buy as much time as possible.

- On the left you have all these mentally ill types who think the United States should let the entire third world illegally pour into the country, and get all the free medical care, housing, pre-loaded debit cards, and opportunities to commit crimes that they desire. But would any of these progressive libtards allow these same illegals to live in their own houses, plunder their own bank accounts or commit crimes against them personally? These same crazies also believe there is no such thing as gender, that there is no need for a police force, and that the very existence of police somehow magically brings criminals into existence.

- On the right you have absolute dumb-dumbs who believe that Trump has been sending super soldiers armed with 5.56 miniguns to free captured children from underground pedophile strongholds hidden beneath pizza parlors, even though Trump and Epstein have probably sucked each other off atop a mountain of children with bloodied butt holes. These same dolts believe that tariffs are paid for by the exporter (China) as opposed to the importer (you), and that deregulating corporations will *not* turn you into a techno-feudal peasant slave. They also think that they are *all* headed to heaven *no matter what they do* because they have a "friend in Jesus."

One side dreams of creating a communist paradise even though all past attempts to create one have ended in some sort of hell on earth, while the other side dreams of some Christian fascist version of an Islamic Caliphate. Again, the average IQ in the United States is only 98 and so what we are experiencing in these final days are the consequences of living in a nation populated with literal dummies. So on one side you have the mentally ill, and on the other side you have the utterly stupid. How can this country ever be fixed if this is who is voting? It can't, and the rest of the world is just as bad if not worse.

As if nobody learned anything from World Ware II, now we are poised for World War III to begin. People will say that comparing Trump to Hitler is crazy talk, but have you noticed the number of celebrities and influencers openly preaching anti-semitism since he was elected for a second term? Kanye West is literally writing songs praising Hitler, Nick Fuentes is suddenly famous and "uncancelled," and Dan Bilzerian is being invited onto major television broadcasts with the likes of Piers Morgan to openly preach hatred of Israel.

I know all you idiots who spend too much time in places like "4chan" will say shit like, "Yeah because the world is finally waking up to the Jew problem." No stupid, these people are openly promoting this trash because some "hidden hand" *wants* them to promote it. Every powerful nation is always trying to take advantage of, or else gain advantage over, other powerful nations. Every powerful nation either has, or is currently engaging in, things like genocide. I am not saying these things are right or justifying them, just pointing out the obvious, and that whenever something becomes popular, no matter if it is anti-semitism or the latest pop-cultural icon, it is only because *something or someone* behind the scenes *wants* it to become popular, and what "they" want is *never* in your best interests so the alarm bells should be going off in your empty heads. But they *aren't*, and that is the problem.

No matter what problems Israel may present, it is ultimately not the problem. If you look beyond the usual suspects, guilty as they all may be, you will ultimately find the Satanic goal of converting this aspect of The Divine Father's creation into a clockwork. To make a mockery of it by dispensing with free will. I know most of you got the vaccine, but do not make the same mistake when they try and force you to take a chip inside of your body. I am sure you have all heard the song "Freewill" by Rush that was released in 1980?

Choose free will. It was *never* the problem. The problem has always been the choices you make with it. Just align yours with the will of The Divine Father and everything will be fine.

Back Poolside

I began this book talking about my poolside humiliation at the hands of some woman playing house with a 37 year old man-child. So I am sitting poolside today and that hot blonde is no longer with this man child (what a shock). Instead he is with some 40-something year old, fat, tattooed woman who has the same sexual market valuation he does. The pool is a tad crowded today, and he is in the water up to his armpits and she is standing on a poolside "shelf" which means only her calves are under the water. Thinking he is some "bad boy" player just because some hottie "played house" with him since the beginning of summer, while carnies completed repairs on the local cock carousel, he got the idea to grab this new girl and pull her into the water in front of everyone to look like some super alpha fun dude. But this 40-something year old woman was *way* stronger than him and he made three consecutive attempts, each time struggling with all of his might, and each time failing to pull her into the water. What... a... fucking... loser... This is exactly why you need to hit the gym. When you can't pull some woman into the water with you, you can't sink much lower. I am also pretty sure her pussy dried up instantly, and I just sat there smirking. Incidentally, I found out he drives a Jeep, so that is *one* thing he gets right.

THE FOUR ESSENTIAL BOOKS

So there are four books I want to introduce to you here:

The first book is *"The Manipulated Man"* by Esther Villar which has been banned and is no longer published. It was first published in 1971, the year in which I was born. Esther Villar herself was a very beautiful medical doctor who was a staunch anti-feminist and men's rights advocate. While it is hard to say if she really loved men or just pitied them, either way her feelings towards them motivated her to author this book which pulled back the curtain on how men are manipulated and abused by women the world over, while living under the illusion that they are in control and living in a patriarchy.

The second book is *"The Tyranny of Ambiguity"* by Simon G. Sheppard which is a documentary account of experiments the author did on the streets of Amsterdam, which led to the discovery of how, by the manipulation of sex, females influence society. The book also discusses the concept of neurosis and its impact on female sexuality, while pointing out the brutal reality that success with women requires that you become as neurotic as they are - the antithesis of what "being a real man" is actually all about. "The Tyranny of Ambiguity" is not an easy read due to the material being presented in a very academic manner, yet worth the effort.

The third book is *"Listen Little Man"* by the notorious Wilhelm Reich, who was a student of Sigmund Freud. Reich is most famous for inducing precipitation (making it rain) using "cloud busting" technology which inspired the song with the same name by the insanely talented Kate Bush, and for promoting esoteric medical theories involving the cure of cancer with an energy he called "orgone." It was the latter that landed him in Federal prison where he subsequently died (probably murdered).

However, Reich's real contributions involved his study of trauma, neurosis and their impact on sexuality and society as a whole - especially with regards to extreme political movements such as communism and fascism. He also created very physical therapeutic protocols for dealing with trauma and neurosis.

The fourth book is *"The Origins of War in Child Abuse"* by Lloyd DeMause. He also wrote companion books and kept up an academic journal for many years. "The Origins of War in Child Abuse" is probably one of the single most important books ever written, yet almost nobody has ever heard of it. The book explores the connection between childhood abuse and trauma, and violent and aggressive behavior in adulthood. Especially the phenomena of war and genocide. The book argues that war and violence are the *inevitable* result of childhood abuse, with adults re-enacting childhood trauma by substituting the parent or abusive figure with the "motherland." What is so disturbing about this book, is that it reveals the full extent of the world-wide, perpetual cycle of physical and sexual abuse of children at the hands of adults - both in the historical past, as well as in the present day. When you combine the horrifying reality of just how widespread child molestation and incest actually are, with the trauma of no-fault divorce after it's introduction in the 1970s, it is not shocking that society is in the current state that it is in.

www.ingramcontent.com/pod-product-compliance
Lightning Source LLC
Chambersburg PA
CBHW060852120626
46553CB00001B/52